DocBook Publishing

Joe "Zonker" Brockmeier
Kara Pritchard

A Division of Prima Publishing

 A Division of Prima Publishing

Prima Publishing and colophon are registered trademarks of Prima Communications, Inc. PRIMA TECH is trademark of Prima Communications, Inc., Roseville, California 95661.

Linux is a registered trademark of Linus Torvalds. The Linux penguin, Tux, is used with permission from Larry Ewing (lewing@isc.tamu.edu). Ewing created this image using The GIMP (http://www.gimp.org). Modifications to Tux were made by Jim Thompson.

Microsoft, Windows, Windows NT, Internet Explorer, and Notepad are trademarks or registered trademarks of Microsoft Corporation in the United States and/or other countries.

Apple, Mac and Macintosh are trademarks of Apple Computer, Inc. registered in the United States and other countries.

Netscape and Netscape Navigator are trademarks or registered trademarks of Netscape Communications Corporation in the United States and other countries.

Important: Prima Publishing cannot provide software support. Please contact the appropriate software manufacturer's technical support line or Web site for assistance.

Prima Publishing and the author have attempted throughout this book to distinguish proprietary trademarks from descriptive terms by following the capitalization style used by the manufacturer.

Information contained in this book has been obtained by Prima Publishing from sources believed to be reliable. However, because of the possibility of human or mechanical error by our sources, Prima Publishing, or others, the Publisher does not guarantee the accuracy, adequacy, or completeness of any information and is not responsible for any errors or omissions or the results obtained from use of such information. Readers should be particularly aware of the fact that the Internet is an ever-changing entity. Some facts may have changed since this book went to press.

ISBN: 0-7615-3331-1
Library of Congress Catalog Card Number: 00-10961
Printed in the United States of America

01 02 03 04 05 II 10 9 8 7 6 5 4 3 2 1

Publisher
Stacy L. Hiquet

Associate Marketing Manager
Heather Buzzingham

Managing Editor
Sandy Doell

Acquisitions Editor
Kim Spilker

Project Editor
Melody Layne

Technical Reviewer
Kara Pritchard

Copy Editor
Kate Talbot

Proofreader
Jeannie Smith

Interior Layout
Marian Hartsough

Cover Design
Prima Design Team

Indexer
Johnna Van Hoose Dinse

This book is dedicated
to all users and developers
of Free and Open Source software.

Acknowledgments

One of the perks of being the author of a book is that you get to publically acknowledge the people who have contributed to your success. There aren't many professions that allow you to do that, and I feel pretty lucky having the opportunity.

Naturally, I'd like to thank my family and friends. David, Brad, and Shawn, for being awesome little brothers. My friend Denise and her family, thanks for being a wonderful second family.

All of my friends in Denver and elsewhere, Jim, Bonnie, Suzanne, Jason, Barb, Chuck, Jeremy, Hannah, Jo, Emily, Julie, Adam, Lara, Bob...you all make life much more fun.

I'd also like to thank the folks at Prima, of course, for making this book possible. Kim and Melody, thanks for being the nicest editors in the world.

—Joe "Zonker" Brockmeier

First, I always like to extend special thanks to the community of Linux developers, supporters, and activists who are responsible for the opportunities that I have today. Without their work and dedication I would never have had the freedom to pursue my career and contribute to this community.

I would like to thank Zonker for asking me to work on this book with him, originally as an editor and then as a co-author. His expertise in DocBook has been quite a resource, and he has been great fun to work with.

In addition, I would like to thank the Prima staff I've worked with, Melody Layne and Kim Spilker, for giving me the opportunity to work with a new publisher. Their patience and pursuit for quality technical resources should be commended.

A personal thank you to my husband, Steven Pritchard, who is my unsung hero, the built-in technical editor for all my works. His support and encouragement keeps me going.

—Kara Pritchard

JOE "ZONKER" BROCKMEIER is a long-time user of Linux and other Free and Open Source software. Zonker is a contributing editor for Linux Magazine and UnixReview.com, and has had articles published in Sys Admin, Enterprise Linux Magazine, ComputerEdge, and IBM's DeveloperWorks.

KARA PRITCHARD is currently the Director of Exam Development for the Linux Professional Institute, working to develop the standard for Linux certification. As an independent consultant, Kara has been promoting the use of Linux in both corporate and educational facilities since late 1995. She published her first book, *RHCE Exam Cram*, in 1999 (2nd ed. 2000). Kara runs the Linux Users Groups resource project at http://www.linuxusersgroups.org/. You can contact her at kara@luci.org.

Contents at a Glance

Contents

Welcome to *DocBook Publishing*, a book for anyone who would like to learn about DocBook. You don't have to be a computer guru or technical whiz, and this book is user friendly and fun. We hope that you will enjoy reading it as much as we have enjoyed writing it.

About This Book

DocBook Publishing is a gentle guide to using DocBook to create nearly any type of documentation or publication. We decided to write a book about DocBook for two reasons. First, we are convinced that DocBook is an excellent solution for anyone who needs to produce publications that will be distributed in a variety of media. Unfortunately, DocBook is not as well known as it could be, outside of a very small group who mostly use it professionally. We will, at length, talk about the respective merits of DocBook versus other methods of production, but basically we're hooked on it, and we'd like to see more people hooked as well. We're hoping that this book will be a good resource to make the transition to DocBook easier and encourage people to consider DocBook over other, less elegant, solutions.

Second, we have found that very little user-friendly documentation is available for DocBook, and that's a shame. Without the information on how to use this wonderful set of tools, known collectively as DocBook, the majority of users who could benefit will pass it over instead. We're hoping that the book you're holding in your hands will provide all the information you need in order to be productive in DocBook and that the reading won't be too painful. We have tried to avoid over-jargonizing, and where jargon is absolutely unavoidable, we have provided explanations that make sense.

Why Use DocBook?

Why should you use DocBook? Well, maybe you shouldn't—that is, if you don't need to produce professional-quality documentation or if you want to continue learning the intricacies of word processors and stay on the upgrade treadmill forever. However, if you'd like to use a markup language that enables you to think about the writing instead of the formatting, read on.

DocBook has advantages over word processors and typesetting programs in that it is extremely portable and much more flexible than your average word processor.

Portability

You can produce raw SGML and XML DocBook documents in any text editor or word processor on any platform. It's not necessary to read a proprietary document format to exchange DocBook files—all you need is the ability to read and produce plain ASCII text. No computing platforms are incapable of doing that. In fact, you could (if you were insane enough to want to) produce a fully compliant DocBook document on a Palm Pilot.

With existing tools, you can export DocBook documents to RTF, PostScript, HTML, ASCII, PDF, DVI, and possibly other formats. There is really no limitation on the type of files you can create with DocBook. If, for example, Microsoft decided to support DocBook, it could use DocBook as a file format for Word or simply import DocBook files into Word. The specification is completely open and available to everyone, and it was designed with portability in mind.

Flexibility

When creating documents, you will find DocBook very flexible. Want to write a Web page? No problem. Want to author a book and send it to the printer without mussing about with a typesetting program? No problem. Want to create a Web page, PDF brochures, and a printed manual? No problem. Want to restore that '57 Chevy in the garage and increase your sex appeal? Okay, there are a few limits.

Later in the book we discuss ways you can change DocBook tools or stylesheets to get exactly the output you want. It's entirely possible to customize DocBook to fit your needs.

Who Should Read This Book

For whom did we write this book? Admittedly, not for everyone. Some folks don't need the power and flexibility of DocBook, and that's okay. Heck, some people— horror of horrors—don't even use a computer on a regular basis. However, DocBook is appropriate for a large number of users, many of whom have never heard of DocBook or believe it's too complicated to learn. DocBook is not much more difficult to learn than HTML, and it is much more flexible.

> DocBook will look familiar if you've worked with HTML at all. That's because HTML and DocBook are both subsets of SGML. If you've already dabbled with HTML successfully, have no fear. DocBook is just as easy.

NOTE

In a moment, we'll give a more in-depth summary of the groups who can benefit from DocBook. Suffice it to say that if you're currently producing any serious volume of written material on a computer, you'd likely benefit from DocBook. It doesn't have to be technical documentation, although DocBook is excellent at that. Any written material that is intended for publication in some form is a candidate for DocBook. User manuals, news stories, recipe books, poetry, prose, electronic brochures—DocBook handles a multitude of tasks very well. The nice thing is that you only have to learn the bits about DocBook that apply to you. You don't need to learn how, for instance, to create tables and figures in DocBook if you're going to publish a book of poetry with it. You don't need to fuss with making an index if you're just doing articles.

In a nutshell, DocBook lends itself to many types of documents that are typically prepared in word processors or typesetting programs. Unfortunately, these programs are limited in scope and designed to produce only one or two types of output. They also require the author to concentrate too much on the program, which distracts from the document itself.

Authors and Technical Writers

People who write professionally should take the time to look into DocBook. Technical writers, in particular, will benefit from the features of DocBook because it was originally designed for technical documentation. It allows authors to work with indexes, glossaries, tables, figures, and other components of documents by using a markup language that does not require attention to the actual physical presentation.

Moreover, the features that make DocBook attractive to technical writers also make DocBook ideal for writing tasks of all flavors.

Students and Instructors

Writing academic papers requires a great deal of formatting that takes away from concentrating on the writing itself. Each word processor has its own way of dealing with formatting, each slightly different.

We don't think that we're alone in thinking that worry about formatting detracts from writing. Footnotes, block quotes, italic, and other formatting necessities are something that have to be relearned in each word processor. With DocBook you can specify, for instance, that a section of a paper is a block quote, and it will format accordingly, without the distraction of learning a word processing program.

Chapter 2, "Writing a Technical Article," covers specifics of DocBook that will come in handy for those writing academic papers to be published in print or electronically.

Software Developers

DocBook is ideal for software developers who are working on documentation as they write software. Because DocBook does not require a word processor, developers who work in a text editor such as vi or Emacs can work on documentation simultaneously.

DocBook also provides markup elements specifically suited for documenting just about any type of software. Chapter 7, "Collaborative Work," walks you through using DocBook on collaborative projects, including how to use DocBook with CVS. If Vim is your favorite text editor, Chapter 8, "Using Vim," shows you how Vim syntax highlighting and other features make editing DocBook files easy. If Emacs is your editor of choice, Chapter 9, "Using Emacs" walks you through all the advanced Emacs features designed to simplify editing DocBook documents.

Who Should Not Read This Book

Okay, DocBook is not for everyone. It's true—some writing tasks don't require the power and flexibility of DocBook. You probably don't need DocBook to write a letter or make up a grocery list. If you don't do a lot of writing, you probably won't have to use a markup language to handle your formatting. Although we don't think that DocBook is particularly complicated, using DocBook to write a letter or do very simple documents is like using a shotgun to kill flies.

Make no mistake—learning DocBook will require an investment of time and effort. If you don't have to produce professional or academic-quality documents, you probably don't need DocBook.

Conventions

The following is a list of conventions that you will find in *DocBook Publishing*. On the CD-ROM you will find the DocBook template used to create this book, and you will also find sample code that you can compare with the book to see how we marked up the chapters.

Cautions generally tell you how to avoid problems.

CAUTION

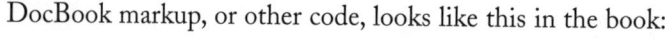

Buzzwords are terms that aren't used in everyday speech but are useful to know when dealing with DocBook.

DocBook markup, or other code, looks like this in the book:

```
<!DOCTYPE book PUBLIC "-//OASIS//DTD DocBook V3.1//EN" [
<!ENTITY introduction SYSTEM "introduction.sgm">
<!ENTITY chap1 SYSTEM "chap1.sgm">
]>
<book>
<bookinfo>
<date>2000-07-11</date>
<title>DocBook Publishing</title>
<subtitle><trademark class="registered">A Gentle Guide to DocBook</subtitle>
</bookinfo>
&introduction;
&chap1;
</book>
```

Notes provide additional helpful or interesting information.

Tips often suggest techniques and shortcuts to make your life easier.

What's Included

Because *DocBook Publishing* should be a complete resource, we've included some extra goodies. Also, to get additional information and news about DocBook, be sure to visit the Web site that accompanies this book (**http://www.ZonkerBooks.com**).

The CD-ROM includes all the necessary software and DTDs to use DocBook, so you don't have to hunt all over the Internet. Everything on the CD-ROM is current at the time of this writing, but it may be outdated by the time you read this book. You don't necessarily have to have the latest versions to produce documentation with DocBook, but you might want to stay current. Luckily, DocBook does not change frequently, or radically, so this text should remain current for quite some time.

In addition to the DTDs, Jade, and SGMLTools-lite, we have included templates for many types of documents on the CD-ROM. All the examples used in *DocBook Publishing* are included on the CD-ROM, as well as templates for MLA-style academic papers, indexes, books, articles, and Web-based manuals. No matter what you use DocBook for, one of the bare-bones templates included on the CD-ROM will give you a jump-start.

What Is DocBook?

So, what is this DocBook stuff anyway? Technically, DocBook is an SGML or XML Document Type Definition—*DTD*, for short (more on SGML and XML in a moment). However, *DocBook* is often used to refer to the parsing tools, the stylesheets, and other tools used to work with DocBook collectively. Generally speaking, when the term *DocBook* is used in this work, it refers to the entire collection of tools used to produce documentation in DocBook, not just the DTD and stylesheets.

History of DocBook

Obviously, DocBook did not magically appear. In one form or another, it has been around since 1991. DocBook began life as a DTD designed by O'Reilly and Associates and HaL Computer Systems to help convert UNIX documentation into an easily exchangeable format.

O'Reilly then passed DocBook to the Davenport Group, an organization created by O'Reilly and Associates to provide a forum for companies and organizations producing computer documentation. This lasted through the third version of DocBook. Eventually, the Davenport Group began to focus on XML, and DocBook development took a back burner.

DocBook found a home with OASIS in 1998.

OASIS

OASIS is the Organization for the Advancement of Structured Information Standards, a nonprofit, international consortium. It creates industry specifications based on public standards such as XML and SGML and, to a lesser extent, other standards related to structured information processing.

OASIS has a technical committee dedicated to overseeing DocBook development that was formed in July 1998. The OASIS DocBook Technical Committee maintains the SGML and XML versions of the DocBook DTD. The DocBook Technical Committee is also in the process of developing a DocBook XML Schema, but there is no official release at this time.

You can find OASIS at **http://www.oasis-open.org/**.

DocBook and Open Source

A number of Open Source projects are using DocBook, most notably, the Linux Documentation Project, which has switched from the LinuxDoc DTD to DocBook.

Because DocBook is an *open standard*—portable across platforms and designed to output HTML, PostScript, RTF, PDF, ASCII text, and several other file formats—it is ideal for projects that want printable documentation, online documents, and electronic documents that look exactly like printed documents.

SGML/XML

Buzzword

Metalanguage is a definition or description of language, a language used to talk about language. The rules of English grammar could be described as metalanguage, language that enables us to understand word usage in the English language. *Meta* is a prefix that, depending on context, refers either to change (as in *metamorphosis*) or, in information technology, to something more comprehensive (as in *metadata*).

You've probably heard the terms *SGML* and *XML* a few times but might be confused about what they are. *SGML* stands for *Standard Generalized Markup Language*, and *XML* is the *Extensible Markup Language*. To make things even murkier for the beginner, XML is often talked about as a separate technology, but in reality, XML is a subset of SGML.

What are SGML and XML? SGML is a metalanguage used to define rules for how a document can be described. SGML DTDs spell out exactly what allowable markup is and how it is to be used. For example, HTML is an SGML DTD. In HTML, the DTD is the full description of the HTML language, and it offers information about HTML markup. If you've ever used HTML, you know that the DTD tells a browser or other HTML rendering engine that `<b></b>` makes text bold, `<i></i>` makes text italic, and `<img></img>` describes the attributes of an image—including where the image can be found and possibly the height, width, and alternative text for the image. However, because the DTD does not describe a `<woohoo>` tag, browsers will probably ignore the tag or render it improperly.

XML, as mentioned before, is a subset of SGML. XML is an official recommendation from the W3C—the World Wide Web Consortium, the organization also responsible for HTML specifications. XML is actually a number of specifications for documentation that are designed to be SGML-compatible, human and machine readable, and Web friendly, making the creation of documents easy. That's a tall order, but the W3C has been successful at creating a recommendation that is being adopted even before the final specification has been approved.

XML is being used for a number of tasks. Microsoft is using XML to some extent in its Office file formats, many programs use XML configuration files, and quite a few companies are using XML to exchange data with one another for business-to-business transactions over the Internet. That's just a few of XML's other roles, aside from the XML DocBook DTD.

For more information on XML, check out Appendix C, "More DocBook Resources," for more XML resources.

Markup Languages

We've mentioned already that XML, HTML, and SGML are markup languages. What does that mean?

A *markup language* is a set of elements used to describe how data should be handled. For instance, as mentioned earlier in the chapter, in HTML the `<b></b>` tags tell a browser how to handle text that is enclosed within those tags: Make it bold. HTML is an SGML DTD that describes the use of all HTML tags. A well-formed HTML document fits completely within the definition of the HTML DTD, and no elements used in the document are misused or not present in the HTML DTD.

DocBook is also a markup language. We've explained what a markup language is but not necessarily what its benefits are. A markup language enables the author to specify what a piece of text is supposed to be—bold, italic, emphasized, code, a level-one header, and so on—without worrying about how that text is formatted. It allows for abstraction, basically, and removes the author from dealing with the formatting directly.

SGML

The SGML DTD for DocBook is the most widely used, and for quite some time the SGML was the only official DTD for DocBook.

Although standards organizations like to emphasize whether something is the official standard, in practice this often doesn't amount to much. HTML, for example, has a standard that is approved by the W3C. However, the actual practice is that Microsoft Internet Explorer, Netscape Navigator, and many other browsers support tags that are deprecated. They don't support tags that are part of the official standard and also support proprietary tags invented by their respective companies in their quest to rule the Web and make their browsers the dominant browser.

The rush to start adopting XML has not been hindered because it is not an official standard (at least, at the time of this writing—it could easily change before publication).

Although it would be a wonderful world if everyone could agree to follow the standards these organizations put out, that's unlikely to happen anytime soon.

The version of the SGML DTD used in this book is 4.1. If you get hold of documents written with earlier versions of DocBook, the DocBook.org Web site does archive earlier versions of the DTD—mostly for historical purposes. If you are using a Linux distribution that comes with DocBook DTDs and stylesheets already installed, check whether they're the latest version. If you are using something from the 3.x series, you will want to upgrade because there are incompatibilities between major versions of the DocBook DTD.

XML and the Future

If you are brand new to DocBook and SGML, we heartily recommend that you think about using the XML DTD instead of the SGML DTD. It isn't that the XML DTD is better; rather, it seems that more organizations are standardizing on XML technologies. Theoretically, other than minor differences, the XML and SGML versions are the same, so it is also possible to learn both, if necessary, without too many headaches.

The XML DTD version described in this book is 4.1.2. Although there are previous versions, 4.0 was the first official version of the XML DocBook DTD released by the DocBook Technical Committee of OASIS.

NOTE

> Quite frankly, when you start dealing with XML, SGML, and standards organizations, things become hideously complicated. Standards hinge on other standards; the documentation is jargon filled and agonizing to read. The whole purpose of this book is to help you approach DocBook in a complete but user-friendly manner that negates the need to slog through documentation that would put an insomniac to sleep.

Now that you have whetted your appetite to learn more about DocBook, it's time to move on to the real thing. We hope that you enjoy using DocBook and find this book an easy read. If you have questions, comments, or concerns, feel free to write to Zonker at jbrockmeier@earthlink.net. He can't promise that he'll respond to all inquiries, but he promises that he will read them all.

Chapter 1: Getting Started

Creating DocBook Documents

Understanding DocBook Markup

Now that all the introductory stuff is out of the way, it's time to get started with DocBook. The purpose of this chapter is to prepare you for writing DocBook documents. This chapter covers the major differences between SGML and XML DocBook, how to use the DocBook DTD, and how to read DocBook markup so that it doesn't look like a foreign language. We'll also talk briefly about stylesheets, which are used to give a DocBook document its "look and feel."

Unlike the majority of this book, the material in this chapter is mostly foundation for the hands-on type material later in the book. It might seem slow, so you might prefer to start with one of the other chapters and refer back to this chapter when you get stuck.

Creating DocBook Documents

Creating DocBook documents is simple. All you need in the way of tools is a text editor and perhaps an image or photo editing tool if you want to produce documents with images.

SGML or XML?

The first thing to do is choose the DTD or Schema you're going to use; the document declaration comes before anything else when you're writing a document. In some cases, this might already be chosen for you by a manager or editor. If you're the manager or editor, however, you will have to make an educated decision about which DTD is best for you, from a practical and financial standpoint.

If your company or project is largely concerned with print-only publications, then you may want to pick SGML because of the number of applications that are available for SGML like Adobe FrameMaker+SGML or WordPerfect. On the other hand, XML is probably better suited for Web-based publishing because it was developed primarily for electronic data exchange.

As of DocBook version 4.0, there are two official versions of the DocBook DTD: the SGML DTD and the XML DTD. The XML DTD has been around for a while, but the 4.0 version of the XML DTD was the first "official" release of an XML DTD. It's likely that there will soon be an "official" XML Schema for DocBook as well.

Chapter 11 covers XML Schemas in detail, though they aren't used in examples throughout the rest of the book. The reason for this is that the first experimental DocBook Schema was only recently introduced. The XML Schema is not yet in wide use. However, Chapter 11 was added because I felt that the topic should not be ignored completely and XML Schemas are likely to play an important role in DocBook development in the future.

The SGML DocBook DTD has been around longer (since 1991, in one form or another) and has more supporting tools and documentation. If you're going to be sharing documents with other organizations or companies that are using DocBook, the odds are that they're using the SGML DTD and tools that are already available. If that's the case, you will want to stay the course and use the SGML DTD, unless you're willing to convert existing documentation to XML. This can be more trouble than it's worth, unless you need features provided by XML.

On the other hand, if you're using DocBook for the first time and you're going to be setting a standard, XML is probably the way to go. XML is one of today's hot technologies, and it looks as though XML is capturing the hearts and minds of IT professionals in a way that SGML never did. Learning XML while learning DocBook could have some positive side effects later on because you will pick up much about XML that will apply to technologies beyond DocBook.

Delving into all the benefits of XML and SGML is beyond the scope of this humble little book about DocBook. However, XML and SGML are both fascinating topics you will probably want to examine in more depth after you've tackled DocBook. To help you on your quest for knowledge, some links to resources that will get you started can be found in Appendix D, "More DocBook Resources." Enjoy!

Finally, XML is designed from the ground up for use on the Web. Using XML opens up the possibility of using DocBook documents for more than just standard publishing.

Differences between SGML and XML DocBook

The SGML and XML DTDs are designed to be fully compatible. However, SGML allows for some shortcuts—better known as minimization—that are not allowed in XML. Because the goal of this book is to bring you up to speed with both SGML and XML DocBook, I won't demonstrate any of the minimizations in this book. No need to start bad habits!

Another difference between SGML and XML is case-sensitivity. SGML allows for uppercase, lowercase, and mixed-case elements and attributes. `<Sect1>`, `<SECT1>`, and `<sect1>` are all valid markup when working with SGML, but only lowercase elements and attributes are valid with the DocBook XML DTD. The reason for this is that XML is designed so that a well-formed XML document can be parsed without a DTD. Even though there is a DTD for XML DocBook, XML tools should be able to work with a DocBook XML document without having a DTD.

> The XML specification from the W3C does not require that elements be lowercase, but it does require that elements be used as they are defined in the DTD. The DocBook DTD defines all elements in lowercase for simplicity.

Keywords, on the other hand, must be uppercase to be considered valid with XML. If this seems confusing, don't worry. If you follow the conventions and examples in this book, you'll be fine. All the examples in the book have been designed to be XML and SGML DTD compatible. Remember, valid XML is also valid SGML, but the reverse is not true. Designing your documents to be compatible with both, even if you're using the SGML DTDs now, can save you headaches later.

When you have settled on using SGML or XML, you will start your documents with one of the declarations.

Buzzword

In a DocBook document, keywords are used to designate sections that should receive special handling. For instance, the CDATA keyword is used to indicate that markup within a certain section marked should not be processed.

Using the SGML DTD

To declare a document using the SGML DTD, use the following markup:

```
<!DOCTYPE root element PUBLIC "-//OASIS//DTD DocBook V4.1//EN>
```

I'll break this down into the basic components so that it's easier to understand.

DOCTYPE

The DOCTYPE declaration should be the first tag in every DocBook document. SGML requires this element so that any parsing application can identify the type of document it is working with and what DTD it is going to be using to validate the document.

The DOCTYPE tag is followed by attributes that further define the type of document, including the DTD and the root element of the document.

The Root Element

When you think of a root, what do you picture? What the designers of SGML want you to picture is a structure similar to a tree. The root element, like the roots of a tree, is the beginning of a structure. The root element is the foundation of the document. You can find all the valid root element types in Appendix B, "DocBook Element Reference."

Public and System Identifiers

To use a DTD, an application has to be able to find it. If a document has a public DTD, the application looks to a catalog file to resolve the name of the DTD to find the actual file, in this case:

```
-//OASIS// DocBook V4.1//EN
```

On my system this would resolve to

```
/usr/share/sgml/dtd/docbook/4.1/docbook.dtd
```

By declaring a system identifier, you bypass the need to lookup a catalog file and simply tell the application exactly where the file containing the DTD is. If I were using a system identifier instead of a public identifier, my document declaration would look like this:

```
<!DOCTYPE root element SYSTEM"/
usr/share/sgml/dtd/docbook/4.1/docbook.dtd">
```

If you prefer, you can use both a public and system identifier, but you must use at least one of them. Chapter 6, "Parsing DocBook," goes into more detail about the nitty-gritty details of using DTDs.

Using the XML DTD

Technically, as mentioned earlier, XML documents do not require a DTD. However, because you're working with a specific DTD (DocBook), you will

Buzzword

You might be wondering what it means to say that a document is being parsed. Originally, *parse* was a linguistic term for dividing words or phrases into their component parts and analyzing them. If you diagrammed sentences when studying grammar in elementary school, you were parsing the sentences.

The same is true in computerspeak. An application breaks down the document into its component parts for further processing. Netscape, for instance, has to parse an HTML document before it can display the document in human-readable form. Sometimes a parsing application also performs *validation*, which is to say that it also checks whether your document conforms to the DTD and is properly structured.

want to declare it. Unlike the SGML document declaration, you must also specifically call attention to the fact that your document is XML.

The declaration for an XML document is slightly longer than the SGML equivalent, as you can see in the code sample and Figure 1.1:

```
<?xml version="1.0"?>
<!DOCTYPE root element
PUBLIC "-//OASIS//DTD DocBook XML V4.1//EN"
"file:///usr/share/xml/docbook/4.1/docbookx.dtd">
```

Unlike SGML, XML requires a system identifier when you are specifying a DTD. A system identifier in XML should be a fully qualified uniform resource identifier (URI).

A *uniform resource identifier* (URI) is a method for locating content on the World Wide Web. The Internet Engineering Task Force came up with the specification to locate any type of resource on the Web. A URI provides the following information:

- The protocol used to locate the resource (HTTP, FTP, FILE, and so on).
- The name of the computer where the resource is located. (In the case of a file:///, it is assumed that the location is the local host instead of a remote computer.)
- The specific location of the file.

Buzzword

URIs are used for a lot more than just XML markup. If you're interested in learning more about URIs, check the Internet Engineering Task Force's (IETF) current RFC about URIs at **http://www.ietf.org/rfc/rfc2396.txt**, or read the W3C's overview at **http://www.w3.org/Addressing/**.

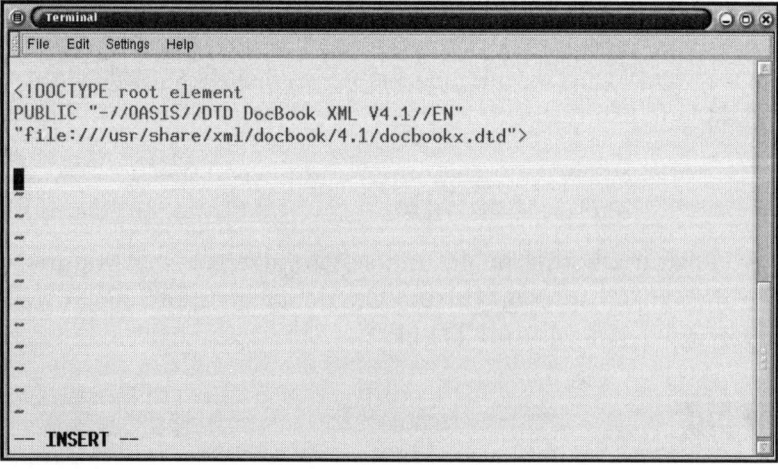

Figure 1.1 *An XML document declaration*

It is optional to declare a public identifier but generally a good idea to do so. All examples in this book include both, as well as all the XML DocBook templates located on the CD-ROM.

Understanding DocBook Markup

DocBook markup might look daunting at first, especially if you are new to markup languages. The next section of this chapter explains the "physical" aspects of DocBook markup so that you can easily read DocBook markup and learn to write it as well.

Document Division

Documents are often divided into distinct parts to better organize and present material. Sometimes they are even divided into separate physical parts for ease of distribution when the amount of material warrants separate volumes. DocBook makes provisions for both logical divisions and physical divisions. You will take a brief look at these types of divisions in this section and then learn about division of material in more detail in Chapter 4, "Preparing a Book with DocBook."

Logical Division

A logical division in DocBook is indicated with markup such as the Sect1 element, which indicates the beginning or end of a level 1 section; the Chapter element, which indicates the beginning or end of a chapter; or even the Set element, which is used to enclose a group of book elements. You can have all these elements present within one file, or you can separate them into different files, depending on how you prefer to work with material.

Physical Division

DocBook also deals with the physical division of documents by providing a means to include a number of files in the document declaration, rather than try to manage a huge file with an entire book or set of books. DocBook allows you to include another file by using a call to an external entity.

If you're anxious to learn all about how to deal with document divisions, check out Chapter 4, where you will find all the fun and exciting ways to work with book-sized documents.

What Are Entities Anyway

Now, when I talk about an entity in DocBook parlance, I'm not talking about those mysterious villains who make appearances in Star Trek episodes. An entity is a reference to a bit of information or data. An entity can be internal or external, and you can save an enormous amount of time by learning to use entities. Say that you're writing a document for the Enormously Huge Corporation of Software Stuff but don't want to type that name every time you refer to the company. Instead, at the beginning of your document, you declare the entity with the following line of code:

```
<!ENTITY huge "Enormously Huge Corporation of Software Stuff">
```

Now, to have the name of the company automagically inserted in your document, simply type **&huge;**, and it will be expanded into Enormously Huge Corporation of Software Stuff in the final output.

If you're writing a book, you can separate each chapter into separate files and call them from the book declaration like this:

```
<!DOCTYPE book PUBLIC "-//OASIS//DTD DocBook V4.1//EN" [
<!ENTITY intro SYSTEM "intro.sgml">
<!ENTITY docbookch1 SYSTEM DocBookCh1.sgml">
...
<!ENTITY appendixd SYSTEM AppendixD.sgml">
]>
<book>
&intro;
&docbookch1;
...
&appendixd;
</book>
```

This will include all the chapter files when the document is parsed and output, without your having to maintain one big file. Pretty neat, huh? Figure 1.2 shows what the DTD looks like with several entities included.

Elements

I have used the term *element* already, so perhaps it's time to step back and see exactly what it means to refer to an element in DocBook lingo.

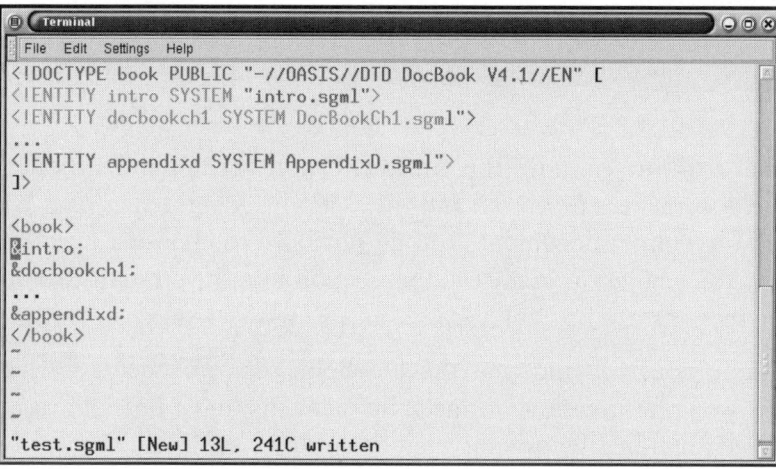

```
<!DOCTYPE book PUBLIC "-//OASIS//DTD DocBook V4.1//EN" [
<!ENTITY intro SYSTEM "intro.sgml">
<!ENTITY docbookch1 SYSTEM DocBookCh1.sgml">
...
<!ENTITY appendixd SYSTEM AppendixD.sgml">
]>

<book>
&intro;
&docbookch1;
...
&appendixd;
</book>
~
~
~
"test.sgml" [New] 13L, 241C written
```

Figure 1.2 *Calling multiple files from the document declaration*

An element describes a document, either a part of its structure or some of the text inside it. Elements are often referred to as *tags* when they're used in marking up a document. Again, if you're familiar with HTML, you will be comfortable with the concept of elements.

The content inside a set of tags sometimes needs more description than an element of markup by itself provides, so many elements also have *attributes*, which further describe the content within the markup.

Elements and their potential attributes are described in the DTD. You can't make up elements or their attributes on the fly; they must be described in the DTD to be valid.

Technically speaking, you can make up elements on the fly in XML documents, but not if they're using the DocBook DTD. XML is designed to allow authors to create well-formed documents that need no DTD. However, for the purposes of DocBook, you will always want to stick to the elements described in the DTD. Why? Because DocBook is designed to be portable and to allow others to share information. If you stray from the DTD, you will negate the benefits of working with DocBook in the first place.

NOTE

The content of attributes, however, is often open. One example would be the `<sect1>` element. It's perfectly valid to use the `<sect1>` element by itself, and it is also valid to further describe the `<sect1>` element by using the label attribute, like this:

```
<sect1 label="1.1">
```

Using the label attribute can give the document more meaningful structure later when the document is processed and the section is identified as part 1.1 of the printed (or online) document. You do not have to choose a numeric label, however. You can just as easily call that section John if you want to, and the next three sections can be Paul, George, and Ringo.

More than likely, you will find that the DocBook set of elements is rich enough that it won't be necessary to make up elements; most possible cases have already been handled by existing elements. However, if you absolutely have to add an element for one reason or another, it can be done. See Chapter 10, "Customizing DocBook," for more information on how to tailor DocBook to your specific needs.

> I don't recommend adding elements to DocBook. However, there is a simplified DocBook DTD that contains a subset of the DocBook elements for those authors who don't want the entire set of DocBook elements. I cover the simplified DTD in Chapter 10, "Customizing DocBook."

NOTE

Next you will see what an element looks like in a document and what each bit means.

Anatomy of Markup Elements

If you haven't spent much time with HTML or a computer language, DocBook markup might look scary at first. It is, after all, designed to compress a lot of information into a small space. Like any type of jargon, it is generally confusing to the uninitiated.

Each element is represented by a start tag and an end tag.

Here is an example of a normal element, with attributes:

```
<trademark class="registered">Linux</trademark>
```

The first part of the element, the start tag, begins with the < symbol and is closed with the > symbol. The first word after the < is the element itself, and anything after that is an attribute of that element. In this case, `class` is the attribute, and `registered` is the value of the attribute. Sometimes the value of an attribute is predefined; other times it is freeform. Appendix B explains each element, which attributes (if any) it takes, and their possible values.

The > character ends the start tag. After that is the content of the element, until the end tag, which begins with </ and signals the end of the element.

There is one type of element that only has one tag and that is the empty element. So-called empty elements are both a start and end tag unto themselves. An empty element is one that does not enclose any nonmarkup content, such as the `ImageData` element. The `ImageData` element provides all the information necessary as an attribute of the element and does not enclose other content.

If you're dealing with an empty element, it will contain all the information necessary within the beginning element. There are a few possible ways to express empty elements. When working with SGML, you can type an empty element like this:

```
<emptyelement attribute="empty"></emptyelement>
```

or like this:

```
<emptyelement attribute="empty"></>
```

With XML, an empty element is expressed like this:

```
<emptyelement attribute="empty"/>
```

This is one of the few ways that SGML and XML are not quite compatible in their markup.

The < and > characters are reserved for denoting elements in DocBook markup. That means that if you want to output a document with one of those characters, you must use the escape characters for them. If you want to use the right angle bracket, also called the greater-than symbol, you use the escape code >. The < escape code is used for the less-than symbol.

CAUTION

DocBook Comments

Because DocBook was created to be shared by multiple authors and editors and because DocBook markup can become complex, you have the ability to add comments in your markup that will not be processed by the parser. If you see a line that begins with the markup <!- and ends with the markup -> (see Figure 1.3), it is a comment.

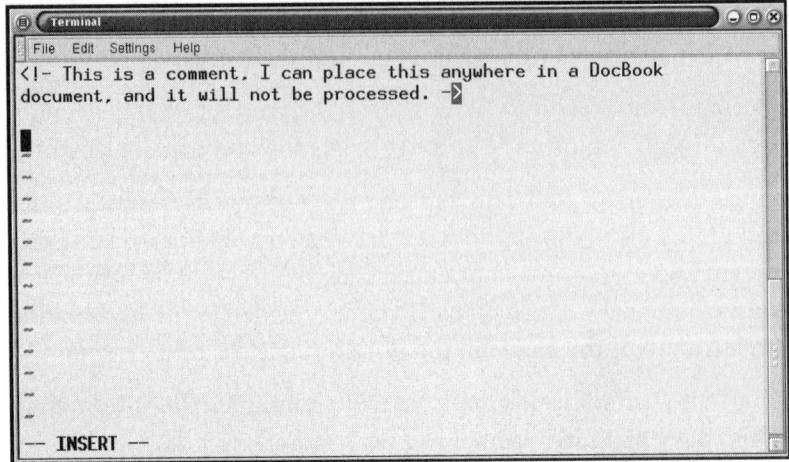

Figure 1.3 *A DocBook comment*

It's a good idea to use comments to communicate with other authors and editors on a project or to remind yourself exactly what the markup in a particularly complicated section does. You might be surprised how something that seems obvious becomes completely confusing in six months, when you've forgotten why you did it in a particular way.

I often use comments to leave notes for myself in documents, such as "Revise this when the next version comes out" or "Don't forget to add more detail in this section later." You will also find many comments in the templates on the CD-ROM that explain exactly what certain markup does and how you can modify it for your own nefarious purposes.

Stylesheets — What They Are and How to Use Them

The DTD describes all the elements that can be used in a markup language, their possible attributes, and so on. However, what a DTD does not do is to describe what the content of elements should look like when the document is published in one form or another.

The look and feel of a document is described by *stylesheets*. A stylesheet gives an application the necessary information to create a finished HTML, Post-Script, PDF, audio, braille, or other type of document (see Figure 1.4).

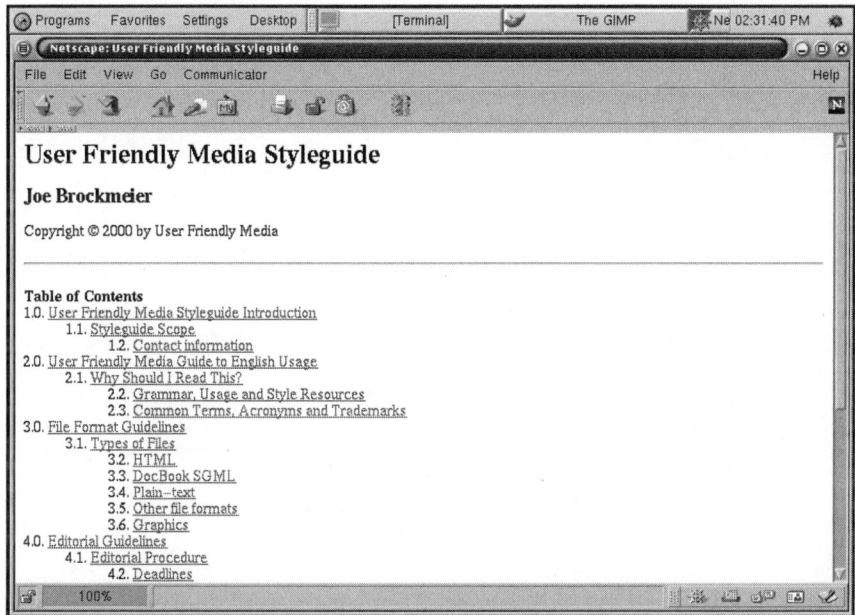

Figure 1.4 *A DocBook document converted to HTML as viewed in Netscape*

> Yes, that's right. DocBook can be used to create nearly any type of output a computer is capable of creating. If you have the right type of application, just about anything is possible. DocBook was designed to handle more than just print output. That's a feat even your average word processor or typesetting program can handle!

NOTE

Several stylesheets for DocBook are publicly and freely available. Most notably, Norman Walsh makes available stylesheets for use with the Jade and OpenJade engines. Jade and OpenJade are programs that take a DocBook document, parse it, take that data and compare it against the stylesheet, and then produce output of one type or another (see Figure 1.5).

Chapter 6 describes using stylesheets and the Jade and OpenJade engines in great detail. Chapter 10 covers customizing existing stylesheets and creating your own. Unlike customizing the DocBook DTD itself, customizing stylesheets is definitely encouraged and easy to do after you get the hang of it.

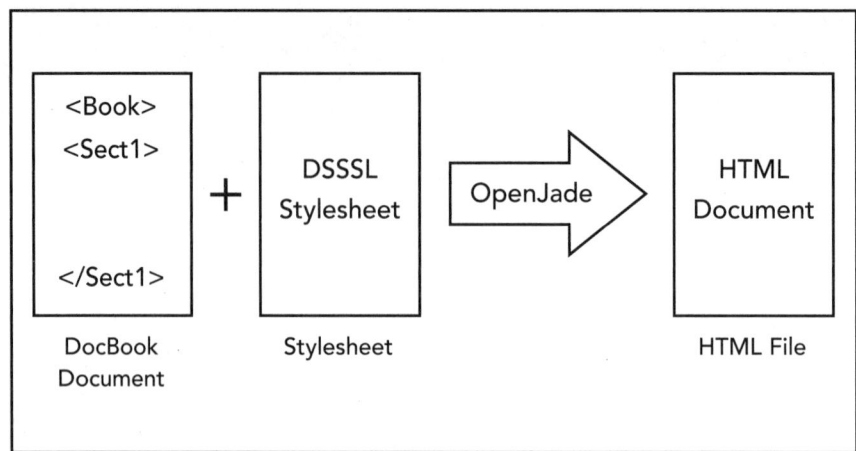

Figure 1.5 *From a DocBook file to publication*

Summary

This chapter explains the basics of DocBook in very general terms. In the rest of the book, I'll take these building blocks and show you how to create DocBook documents and create output from them. Although some of the concepts in this chapter might seem complex, if you work with DocBook for a short while, they will become much easier to grasp.

You will probably also find that you don't have to memorize most of the information here. Usually, you will need only a small percentage of the elements and features of DocBook to create useful documents. DocBook has a huge number of elements to cover a wide variety of needs, but each person might use only a small percentage of them.

Enough background. Let's get on with using DocBook!

Chapter 2: Writing a Technical Article

Article Elements

Standard Tags

Preparing for Publication

In Chapter 1, "Getting Started," I covered some basics of DocBook. Now I'll take you step by step through the process of creating a technical article with DocBook. Although DocBook is used primarily for technical documentation, there's no reason not to use it for any type of article, short story, college paper, or text. This chapter is your guide to creating your own article-type documents. With DocBook, you can create one master document that can be converted into a number of formats suitable for printing, posting online, or sharing electronically. One DocBook file can be converted into plain text, PDF, HTML, PostScript, DVI, or RTF.

For the purposes of this chapter, I do not concentrate on the type of editor used to create your DocBook document. Instead, I focus on the basics of writing a short article with DocBook. Because it would not be possible to demonstrate every tag you might use in a document, I try to focus on the most common tags. A comprehensive list of DocBook elements appears in Appendix B, "DocBook Element Reference."

Now It's time to start creating a DocBook article. I will assume that you are creating a stand-alone document without appendixes, indexes, or other additional files. For more complex documents, see Chapter 4, which covers larger projects.

Start by firing up your favorite text editor or word processor to create a new file. Differences between the SGML and XML DocBook standards are noted in the chapter as they occur.

Remember that although you can create DocBook files in word processors, you must be sure to save the files as plain text. If you save a DocBook file in Microsoft Word format, you will end up with a file that cannot be properly parsed. It's perfectly okay to use Microsoft Word to write the document if that's what you're comfortable with, but the file format has to be plain text. Editors such as vi, Emacs, or Windows Notepad save the files as plain text by default.

Article Elements

Articles aren't much different from other types of DocBook documents, but some elements are specific to articles. Now might be a good time to point out that if you're writing the article in SGML but plan on porting it to XML at some point in the future, you should keep all elements lowercase to maintain compatibility.

Declaring an Article

Call the file *Article.sgm* (or *Article.xml* if you're going to use XML) and begin by declaring the document type:

```
<!DOCTYPE article PUBLIC "-//OASIS//DTD DocBook V4.0//EN">
<article>
</article>
```

To declare an XML DocBook document, use

```
<?xml version="1.0"?>
<!DOCTYPE article PUBLIC "-//OASIS//DTD DocBook XML V4.0beta1//EN"
"http://www.oasis-open.org/docbook/xml/4.0/docbookx.dtd">
<article>
</article>
```

By declaring the document as an article, the parser knows what type of document it is working with. The declaration also states which version of the DocBook DTD is being used (see Figures 2.1 and 2.2). This is important because of the changes between each version of DocBook that might cause problems if the parser doesn't know what it's dealing with. The `<article></article>` elements begin and end the article.

Although DocBook elements might look similar to HTML tags, remember that DocBook parsers are much more demanding than your average Web browser. You can get away with not declaring an HTML document or even skipping some required tags, but DocBook is not quite so forgiving. Be careful to include all required elements and use them in their proper order.

TIP

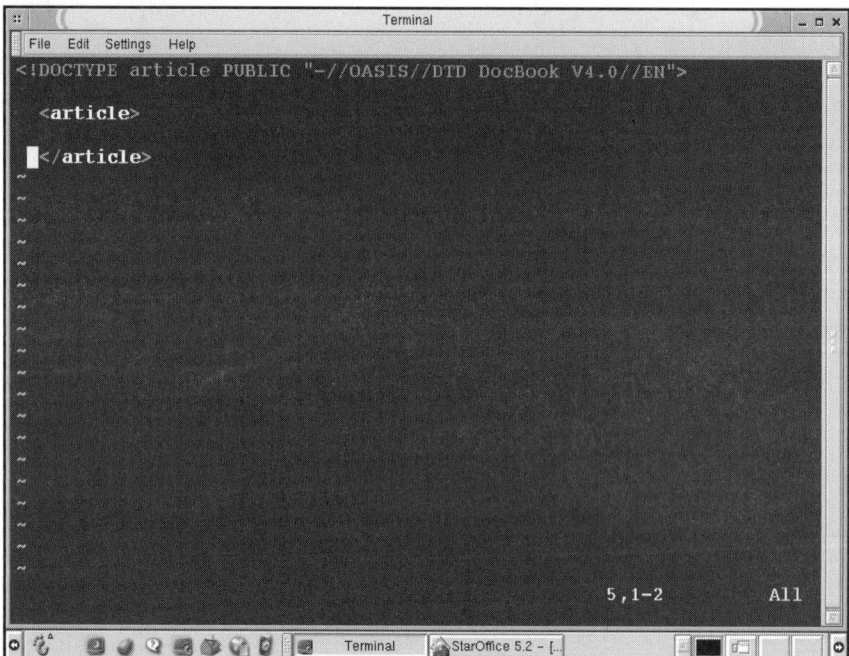

Figure 2.1 *DocBook SGML Declaration*

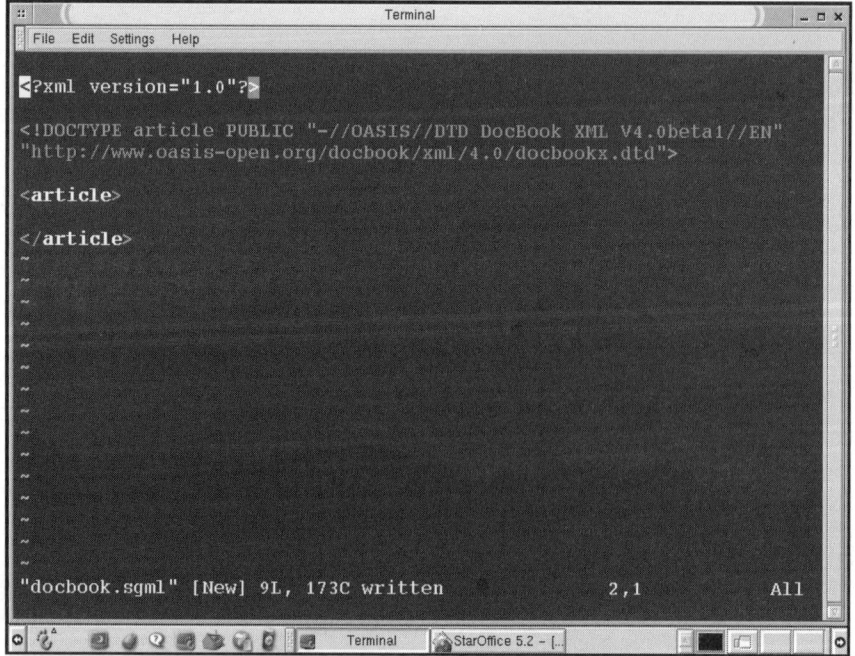

Figure 2.2 *DocBook XML Declaration*

Article Info

Now you can start putting some vital information into the article—such as the title, who wrote it, and other fun and interesting details.

```
<article>
<articleinfo>
<title>Really Awesome Article</title>
<author>
        <firstname>Joe</firstname>
        <othername>"Zonker"</othername>
        <surname>Brockmeier</surname>
</author>
</articleinfo>
</article>
```

This is straightforward. The Author element contains information about the author, and the Title element contains information about the title of the article. Everything contained within the Articleinfo element is information about the article document. No surprises there, I hope. One thing that is important to note, however, is the order of the elements. The Firstname and Surname elements must be within the Author element because the Author element is the parent element. The following, for example, would not be valid.

```
<article>
<author>
        <firstname>Joe</firstname>
        <othername>"Zonker"</othername>
</author>
        <surname>Brockmeier</surname>
</article>
```

If you get errors when parsing documents, be sure to check the syntax of the elements in your document. Often, you will find that the problem is as simple as a misplaced element.

So far, this isn't a terribly exciting article, so you should probably go about putting in a bit of content now. Here's what an extremely short DocBook article would look like.

```
<!DOCTYPE article PUBLIC "-//OASIS//DTD DocBook V4.0//EN">
<article>
<articleinfo>
```

```
<title>Really Awesome Article</title>
<author>
        <firstname>Joe</firstname>
        <othername>"Zonker"</othername>
        <surname>Brockmeier</surname>
</author>
</articleinfo>
<sect1>
<title>First Section Title</title>
<para>
This is a paragraph - it can be long or short, but it has to end with
another Para tag!
</para>
</sect1>
</article>
```

I've already covered the Articleinfo element and its children, so now look at the actual body of the article.

> If any terms in this chapter confuse you, be sure to check the DocBook glossary in Appendix A, "DocBook Glossary." Most of the jargon in the book is covered there.

The Sect1 element is required for the body of the article. Theoretically, you can have a document with only one Sect1 element, but more likely you will have several subsections to your article. The Sect1 element is one of three section elements available in the DocBook DTD. These elements are

- **Numbered Sections.** The Sect1–Sect5 elements that can be nested within one another and are explicitly numbered. This is the most commonly used section element.

- **Undeclared Sections.** The Section element might be used for sections that will be nested but not explicitly numbered. If your document might undergo revisions that will cause sections to be restructured, it would be best to use the Section element instead of explicitly numbered Sect1–Sect5 elements.

- **Simple Sections.** The SimpleSect element is used for sections of a document that will have no subsections.

Note that your document has only one section so far. If you were to add a Sect2 element, it would look like this.

```
<sect1>
<title>First Section Title</title>
<para>More fun and exciting text...</para>
        <sect2>
        <title>A Second Section Title</title>
        <para>Yet more text!</para>
        </sect2>
</sect1>
```

The Sect2 (or lower) elements must be nested within a Sect1 element. This is a parent-child relationship between elements—one element is dependent on the presence of the other. If the elements are arranged improperly, the document will not parse correctly.

The next element is the Para element. Para is easy to remember because it stands for *paragraph*. You will probably find that the majority of DocBook elements make sense, and you probably won't have to look up the most common elements after writing one or two documents with DocBook.

> If you want to save a little time and effort, be sure to check for templates in the CD-ROM that comes with this book. It contains templates for the most common types of DocBook documents to give you a jump-start on working with DocBook.

Finally, the Article element closes out the article document. That's a barebones, but compliant, DocBook article. Now I'll concentrate on other elements you will probably need in order to write a typical document.

Standard Tags

There are more DocBook elements than you can shake a stick at, but don't worry—I'll concentrate on the ones you're likely to need in the near future. Remember that authoring a document in DocBook is different from writing a document in a WYSIWYG word processor. The physical formatting of a document is taken care of by the tools you use to parse the DocBook files. You don't have to worry about using different-size fonts, bold or italic text, or

Buzzword

Automagically is a popular term in the Open Source and hacker community. To quote the Jargon File, it means "automatically, but in a way that, for some reason (typically because it is too complicated, or too ugly, or perhaps even too trivial), the speaker doesn't feel like explaining to you."

You can find other fun hacker expressions in the Jargon File, maintained by Eric S. Raymond, **http://www. tuxedo.org/~esr/ jargon/**

whatnot—all of that is taken care of "automagically" by the tools you choose to produce output from your DocBook document.

Typical Markup

The following sections will introduce you to some typical DocBook markup.

The Abstract Element

The `Abstract` element contains information about the article itself, usually a short paragraph or two about the contents of the article.

This example shows basic usage of the `Abstract` element. The `Title` element is optional.

```
<abstract>
<title>Basic Article Abstract</title>
<para>Summary of the article</para>
</abstract>
```

The Abbrev Element

To denote an abbreviation within a document, use the `Abbrev` element. (Appropriately enough, *abbreviation* is abbreviated. Ever wonder why *abbreviation* is such a long word?) This example shows the standard use of the `Abbrev` element.

```
<para>
You can find our new offices in Santa Clara, <abbrev>Calif.</abbrev>
</para>
```

The Acronym Element

The `Acronym` element is used to denote an acronym used in the text of a document, such as KDE, GNOME, or FBI. Depending on the stylesheet, the contents of the `Acronym` element might be displayed differently than regular text. The code example shows the standard use of the `Acronym` element.

```
<para>
No one likes it when the <acronym>IRS</acronym> or the
<acronym>FBI</acronym> shows up on the doorstep.
</para>
```

The Ackno Element

The `Ackno` element indicates an acknowledgment within the body of the article. The contents of the `Ackno` element may be set off from regular body text. Note that the `Ackno` element can *not* be nested within the `Para` element, only within the `Article` element as demonstrated in the example below.

```
<article>
<ackno>
<para>
Before I start the article, I would like to thank everyone who helped
make it possible. A big thanks to everyone at Prima and Linux Magazine.
</para>
</ackno>
</article>
</para>
```

The Attribution Element

As we all know, it is very important to give credit where credit is due. The `Attribution` element is used to indicate the source of a quotation set off as either a `BlockQuote` element or an `Epigraph` element. This element is particularly useful when writing academic papers, as a stylesheet can be designed to automatically format attributions in the proper citation format. This is a simple example of a `Attribution`.

```
<blockquote>
<attribution>John Lennon</attribution>
Life is what happens when you're busy making other plans.
</blockquote>
```

The `Attribution` element is unusual in that it cannot be contained within the `Para` element. It is used only within the `BlockQuote` or `Epigraph` elements, which do not have to be contained in a `Para` element.

The Author Element

As covered earlier in this chapter, the `Author` element contains information about the author of the article.

The AuthorBlurb Element

Usually, when an article is published, there is a short bio or other information about the author. The `AuthorBlurb` element contains this sort of information and can be located just about anywhere in the document. The example here shows it nested within the `Article` element because that seems the most logical spot to me.

```
<article>
<authorblurb>
<para>Joe "Zonker" Brockmeier is a world-famous author and frequently has
delusions of grandeur.</para>
</authorblurb>
...</article>
```

The BlockQuote Element

Often, in an article or technical paper it is necessary to set off a quotation as a block of text unto itself. The `BlockQuote` element is used to set off a quote and can be used outside the `Para` element. The `BlockQuote` element comes in particularly handy when you are writing articles for academic journals or scholarly papers. The example below is from one of my favorite authors, Mark Twain. I'm sure he would have loved DocBook if only it were available to him when he was writing. Figure 2.3 shows what a `BlockQuote` looks like when rendered into HTML.

```
<sect1>
<blockquote>
<attribution>Mark Twain</attribution>
There are gold men, and tin men, and copper men, and leaden men, and
steel men, and so on—and each has the limitations of his nature, his
heredities, his training, and his environment. You can build engines
out of each of these metals, and they will all perform, but you must
not require the weak ones to do equal work with the strong ones. In
each case, to get the best results, you must free the metal from its
obstructing prejudicial ones by education—smelting, refining, and so
forth.
</blockquote>
</sect1>
```

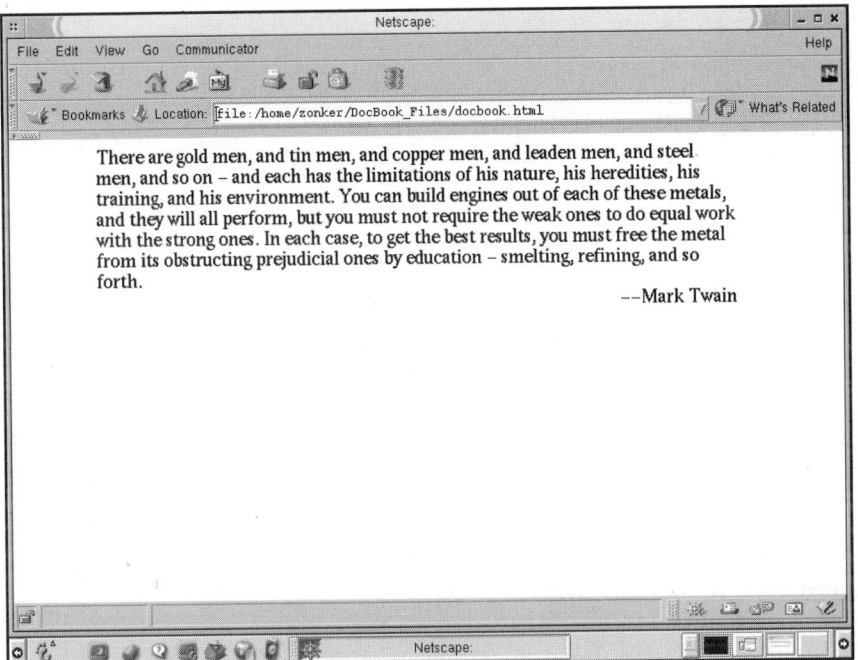

There are gold men, and tin men, and copper men, and leaden men, and steel men, and so on – and each has the limitations of his nature, his heredities, his training, and his environment. You can build engines out of each of these metals, and they will all perform, but you must not require the weak ones to do equal work with the strong ones. In each case, to get the best results, you must free the metal from its obstructing prejudicial ones by education – smelting, refining, and so forth.

--Mark Twain

Figure 2.3 *The BlockQuote element rendered in HTML*

The Caution Element

The `Caution` element is used to create a callout section with a caution to the reader of the article. Depending on the output medium, the `Caution` element may create a box set off from other text or perhaps add a yellow sign with an exclamation point to emphasize caution. The following example also includes a title for the `Caution` element. Although this isn't necessary, it is recommended.

```
<caution>
<title>Watch out for misplaced tags!</title>
<para>If you don't nest your elements properly, your document will not
parse properly and will cause you a great deal of frustration</para>
</caution>
```

The Copyright Element

The `Copyright` element should be used at the beginning of the article to indicate the copyright holder of the article itself. It does not refer to copyrights used in the text of the article. Those are covered by the Trademark element. The following example includes the copyright holder and the year of the copyright.

```
<!DOCTYPE article PUBLIC "-//OASIS//DTD DocBook V4.0//EN">
<copyright>
<year>2000</year>
<holder>Prima Publishing</holder>
</copyright>
<article> ...
```

NOTE

While this isn't directly related to DocBook, it might be worthwhile to mention that it is a good idea to affix a copyright notice to any work you produce. Copyright is granted when a work is produced, not when it is registered. Though it is a good idea to apply for copyright when you produce a significant work, it is not necessary to get the rights to the work.

The Email Element

The Email element is used to denote an e-mail address. Depending on the output medium, the text will either be formatted differently or, in the case of a hypertext document, create a link to the given e-mail address (see Figure 2.4). This example shows the Email element nested within the Para element, though there are a number of other elements that Email may be nested in as well.

```
<para>
You can reach me at <email>jbrockmeier@earthlink.net</email>
</para>
```

The Figure Element

The Figure element is one of the elements that enable you to include an image in your document. The Figure element automatically numbers itself when used, so each figure is numbered consecutively in the document without your explicitly having to number them. This is a very basic example of the Figure element; see Chapter 3 for more on using images with DocBook.

```
<figure>
<title>A very useful figure</title>
```

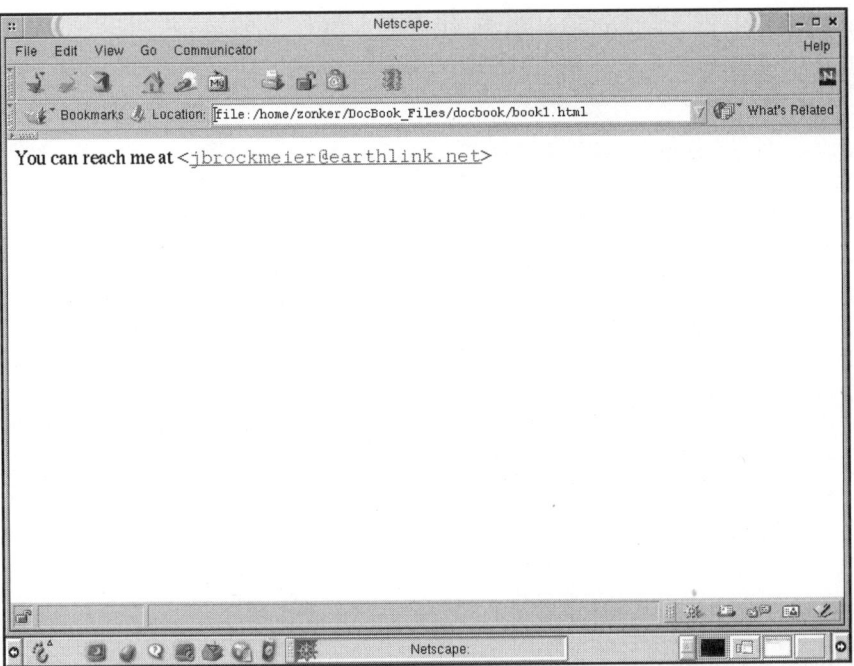

Figure 2.4 *Email element output in HTML*

```
<graphic fileref="images.d/figure2"></graphic>
</figure>
```

In this example, the figure is titled "A very useful figure," and the Graphic element specifies the name of the file to use for the figure—figure2 in the images.d directory.

> Including images in DocBook documents is a hefty topic all by itself. To get the full scoop on images, check out Chapter 3, "Using Images."

The Filename Element

When writing technical articles about computers, you will probably have to refer to the specific name of a file from time to time. Generally, text specified with the Filename element is in a different font or typeface in the final output document to distinguish it from the regular text. As shown in the next example, the Filename element may be used alone or with an optional Class attribute. The `Class` attribute has three possible values: `Directory`, `HeaderFile` and `SymLink`.

```
<para>
Now open the file <filename>passwd</filename> in the <filename
class="directory">etc/</filename> directory.
</para>
```

The `Filename` element enables you to further specify certain classes of filenames: `Directory`, `HeaderFile`, or `SymLink`.

The ItemizedList Element

The `ItemizedList` element contains a number of items designated by the `ListItem` element. The `ItemizedList` element generates a list of bulleted items instead of numbered items. See the `ListItem` element next for an example of its use.

The ListItem Element

The `ListItem` element is used in the `ItemizedList` and `OrderedList` elements. Unlike the `<li>` tag in HTML, the `ListItem` element requires that a `Para` element be nested inside it. Generally, the `ListItem` output is part of a bulleted or numbered list. In the following example, you also see that the `ListItem` element is not an empty element, unlike the `<li>` HTML tag.

```
<para>The world's best bands are</para>
<itemizedlist>
<listitem>
<para>The Beatles</para>
</listitem>
<listitem>
<para>The Who</para>
</listitem>
<listitem>
<para>Pink Floyd</para>
</listitem>
</itemizedlist>
<para>Note that Britney Spears is not on the list.</para>
```

Figure 2.5 shows what the markup looks like in the Vim editor, with syntax highlighting. More on Vim and using syntax highlighting can be found in Chapter 9.

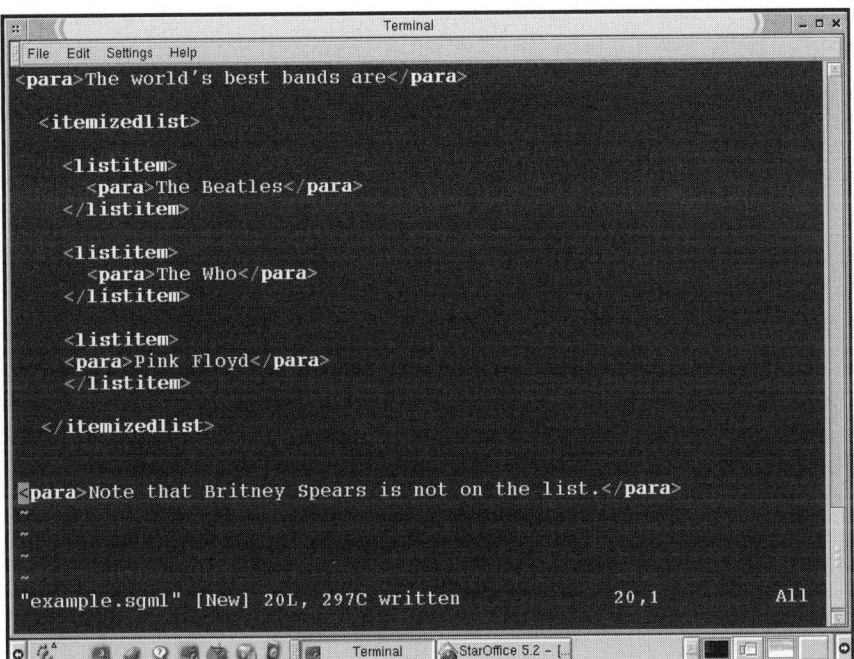

```
<para>The world's best bands are</para>

  <itemizedlist>

    <listitem>
       <para>The Beatles</para>
    </listitem>

    <listitem>
       <para>The Who</para>
    </listitem>

    <listitem>
    <para>Pink Floyd</para>
    </listitem>

  </itemizedlist>


<para>Note that Britney Spears is not on the list.</para>
~
~
~
"example.sgml" [New] 20L, 297C written          20,1          All
```

Figure 2.5 *ItemizedList markup in Vim*

The Note Element

The Note element is similar to the Caution element in that it sets off a note from the author in a block of text separate from the rest of the body text. The Note example also contains a Title element, which is optional.

```
<note>
<title>A Note from the Author</title>
<para>I hope you're enjoying the book so far...</para>
</note>
```

The OrderedList Element

The OrderedList element contains ItemizedList elements and produces a list of items that are explicitly numbered. The OrderedList element's Numeration attribute allows the author to specify Roman numerals, Arabic numerals, or alphabetical enumeration. The default enumeration is Arabic numerals. This example utilizes Roman numerals.

```
<orderedlist numeration="upperroman">
<listitem>
```

```
<para>First item</para>
</listitem>
<listitem>
<para>Second item</para>
</listitem>
<listitem>
<para>etc...</para>
</listitem>
</orderedlist>
```

> One of the wonderful things about DocBook is the way that the markup language enables you to concentrate on the text rather than worry about numbering a list of items or performing other tedious tasks.

The Quote Element

Unlike the BlockQuote element covered earlier in this chapter, the Quote element is meant for *inline quotes*—basically, quotes used within the Para elements, as opposed to longer quotes that are set off on their own as block quotes. It can also set off phrases in quotes. It would be possible to enter the character entities for quotation marks instead, but you would lose some flexibility by doing it that way, and the Quote element is easier to type as well. This is a simple example of a Quote element.

```
<para>
<quote>This is the best book on DocBook I've ever seen,</quote>
said the reviewer.
</para>
```

The Tip Element

The Tip element sets off a block of text from the main body of the text. This element is used to set off a tip from the author to call attention to the material contained within it. The Tip element is very similar to the Note, Caution, and Warning elements. It is up to the author to determine which elements to use under which circumstances. The next example is a simple demonstration of the Tip element. Note that the Para element is nested within the Tip element, and not the other way round.

```
<tip>
<para>
It's probably not a good idea to make a wookie angry.
</para>
</tip>
```

The Title Element

The `Title` element is not used to name the title of a book, film, or other media. Instead, the `Title` element is used in conjunction with other elements, such as the `Sect` elements and the `Caution`, `Warning`, and other callout elements. The `Title` element is used to designate a title for a particular section of a document. See one of the elements already mentioned for an example of the `Title` element in use.

The Trademark Element

The `Trademark` element is used in the body of a document to indicate a trademarked or copyrighted work. The `Trademark` element is not used to indicate the copyright of the article. To indicate copyright information for the article itself, use the `Copyright` element. Note that the `Trademark` element has an optional `Class` attribute, which is used in the example.

```
<para>
<trademark class="registered">Linux</trademark> is a registered trademark
of Linus Torvalds.
</para>
```

The Warning Element

The `Warning` element is another callout element. Use the `Warning` element to indicate dangerous tasks or procedures within your article. The following example contains some good advice that your Mom probably gave you as a kid.

```
<warning>
<title>Running with Scissors</title>
<para>It's a really bad idea to run with scissors, so don't do it!
</para>
</warning>
```

If you haven't found a tag you're looking for, feel free to check Appendix B, which is all about DocBook elements.

Preparing for Publication

When you've finished your article and checked it twice for syntax errors, you're just about ready to publish the document. Make sure that any and all of the images referred to in the text are available and in the proper format. For Web publishing, you must have the images in JPEG or GIF format; for PDF or PostScript, you must have the images in EPS format. See Chapter 3 for more on images.

Be sure that the document has the end Sect and Article tags so that it will parse correctly. It is easy to overlook simple things like that when doing a complex document.

The next step to publishing a DocBook document is parsing it and getting the appropriate output. If you're ready to roll, skip ahead to Chapter 6, "Parsing DocBook," to walk through getting output from your DocBook document.

Summary

In this chapter I've covered the basics of using DocBook markup to create an article. As you can see, creating a DocBook document isn't much harder than writing a document in a word processor. It is simply a matter of using the DocBook markup to create structure or to indicate special information. You don't need to worry about formatting while writing at all, really. Leave that up to the stylesheets. In the next chapters you'll look at more complex documents, using images, and getting usable output from a DocBook file.

Chapter 3: Using Images

e've all probably heard the saying "A picture is worth a thousand words." Strictly speaking, this isn't entirely true—I've never had an editor who was willing to accept two pictures in place of a 2,000 word article, for instance. However, it is true that images and figures are often helpful in documentation.

This chapter explains how you use DocBook markup to include images in your DocBook documents, how you create tables using DocBook markup, and how you prepare documents with images for multiple output formats. It also briefly looks at using MathML, a markup language for mathematical equations that can be used with DocBook XML, and gives a brief overview of using TeX and LaTeX for figures and equations with DocBook SGML.

It might also be a good time to note what DocBook isn't appropriate for. While DocBook is excellent for books, technical articles, creating online documentation, and many other tasks, it isn't a replacement for programs like QuarkXPress or Adobe Illustrator. You won't be able to do super-fancy tricks with text or do exotic things with graphics like you see in *Rolling Stone* or other graphics-intensive magazines. If you're working in that kind of environment, it still makes sense to have authors submit work in DocBook, but do the actual layout in the program of your choice.

NOTE

TeX, prounounced "tech," is a typesetting program written by legendary hacker Donald Knuth. *LaTeX*, pronounced "la-tech," is a collection of macros that are designed to make typesetting with TeX much easier, allowing the author to concentrate more on the document structure and content rather than on the presentation. (Sounds a little like DocBook, doesn't it?) Just because TeX and LaTeX are used specifically for typesetting doesn't mean that they're WYSIWYG programs or that they're easy to use. TeX markup makes DocBook markup look like a piece of cake.

Including images in your documentation is easy with DocBook and helps you convey your message with even more clarity, so let's get to work.

Types of Images

DocBook is not picky about the types of images you use. However, before you create image files, you must decide which types of formats you'd like to output. If you're aiming for Web publication, you work with files that can be viewed with a Web browser—JPEG, GIF, or PNG files. If you're planning to create PostScript files for printing, you work with Encapsulated PostScript files, also known as *EPS*. EPS files are also the preferred file format for creating PDF files.

> DocBook doesn't care about the types of images you specify because it doesn't worry about your output medium. That's a job for—no, not Superman (sorry, comics fans!)—whatever program you use to parse and render DocBook. Remember, you can use DocBook to create any type of output you can imagine—as long as you or someone else has written a program that can parse and render output in your preferred format. Theoretically, you could use sound files instead of images if you had a program that outputs audio. Does that sound silly? Not if you realize that the same DocBook markup that creates Web pages and prints documents can also be used to create braille output or even audio output for blind readers.

With the increased emphasis on multimedia Web content, I should point out that you're not limited to static image files. Chapter 5, "Making Online Documents," covers including multimedia files in your documents for use on the Web.

Preparing for Web Publication

Right now there are two dominant graphics formats on the Web, and another rapidly gaining popularity. The old-school formats are JPEG and GIF files. PNG is the up-and-coming format that's taking the Web by storm. (Okay, maybe not "by storm," but it sure sounds more dramatic that way.) JPEG is pronounced *jay-peg* and stands for *Joint Photographic Experts Group*, which is the group of folks who came up with the JPEG standard in the first place.

JPEG

JPEG images are smaller files produced by compressing the image data and leaving out some of the image information based on the known limitations of the human eye. This is called a *lossy* image format because it loses some of the image information in the process of compression. Basically, the algorithm tries to omit data that is harder to perceive as missing. One advantage to the JPEG standard is that you can decide how much to compress the image and, therefore, what type of quality you will get from the image. Although JPEGs are not suitable for publication, they are suitable for use on the Web.

> There's not quite room to go into JPEGs in great detail in this book, but the way they are created is interesting, at least, if you are a computer geek like me. If you want to find out more about JPEGs visit the JPEG-FAQ index at **http://www.faqs.org/faqs/jpeg-faq/**.
>
> You will learn everything you ever wanted to know about JPEGs but were afraid to ask.

Almost any photo-manipulation program can produce JPEGs of Web-ready quality. Adobe Photoshop, Adobe Illustrator, The GIMP, PaintShop Pro, and many others can produce an image suitable for using on the Web.

Usually, JPEGs are saved with the extension .jpg or .jpeg. For conformity's sake, all images in examples and document templates use three-letter extensions in lowercase format. When you are parsing and rendering DocBook documents, it's common to get errors because the case of the image name differs from the markup and the real filename. Chapter 7, "Collaborative Work," gives some tips for preventing that type of confusion when working with multiple authors on a document.

JPEGs are supported by just about any browser that supports images, so it shouldn't be worrisome if you're producing a site that will be viewed with older browsers.

GIF

The GIF format is the other common format on the Web. GIF is usually pronounced *jiff*, but many variations abound. GIF stands for *Graphical Interchange Format*.

The GIF format is a raster data type and tends to be slightly smaller and of lower quality than JPEG. The main advantages of the GIF format are that GIFs can have animated, as well as static, images and that GIF images allow transparency, whereas JPEGs do not. GIFs are also as widely accepted as JPEG images in browser compatibility. GIFs do not allow a full color palate, however; they are limited to 256 colors.

GIF files are a product of a patented algorithm, LZW compression. *LZW* stands for *Lempel, Ziv, and Welch*, the inventors of the compression. Unfortunately, Unisys, the holder of the patent for GIF files, has decided to take an unusual stance with regard to its patent. Unisys feels that it should receive licensing fees for its patent from commercial programs that output the GIF format and, also, from Web masters who use GIFs on their Web site.

Most of the Internet community is outraged not only because Unisys is asking for this fee but also because the price is $5,000 per license. I'm not aware of any sites being shut down for using GIFs, but I see no reason to tempt fate when other suitable image formats are available.

For more information about the LZW/GIF patent issue, visit Don Marti's Burn All GIFs Web site at **http://www.burnallgifs.org/** (see Figure 3.1).

Because of the controversial nature of GIFs, I do not use them in any examples in this book. I mention them simply because so many people already have GIF images, but I do not encourage their use in production until the patent expires or Unisys changes its policies.

Because of the patenting issues with GIFs, the PNG format was invented. I'll cover that one next. If you have some GIF images that you need to convert to PNG format, you can find suitable tools for the job on the Portable Network Graphics Web site at **http://www.libpng.org/pub/png/pngapcv.html**.

PNG

PNG, pronounced *ping*, stands for *Portable Network Graphics*, or *PNGs Not GIF*, depending on whom you ask. PNG development started partly because of Unisys's licensing policy but also because many people thought that there was room for improvement over GIFs.

Figure 3.1 *The Burn All GIFs Web site*

The only drawback to using PNG images is the question of software and browser support. PNGs are supported by the latest versions of Netscape Navigator and Internet Explorer, but older versions may not handle PNGs well or at all. Some features of PNGs (transparency, for example) may also be unavailable in certain browsers. If you are catering to Netscape or Internet Explorer versions 3 or earlier, it's probably best to stick with JPEGs. If you are certain that your audience is going to be users with newer browsers, use PNGs with confidence.

By the same token, if you're using early versions of Adobe Photoshop or other image-manipulating programs, you may not have support for saving graphics in the PNG format.

PNGs offer the best of both worlds: a non-lossy image format that has a small image size, offers transparency, and supports indexed-color, grayscale, and truecolor images (see Figure 3.2).

To test your browser, point it at this URL: **http://www.w3.org/Graphics/ PNG/inline-alpha.html**.

Now that you know what your options are, you will look at using DocBook markup to include images in documents.

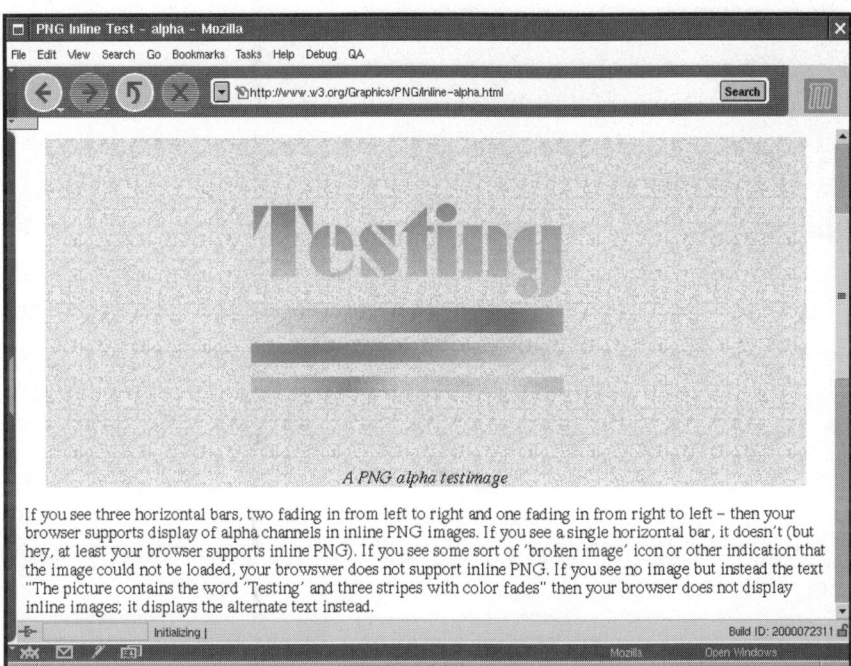

Figure 3.2 *An example of a PNG image in a fully compliant browser*

Marking Up Images for the Web

A number of different elements can be used in DocBook to include images, but many of them are now deprecated.

As DocBook is developed, the OASIS Technical Committee occasionally decides that something can be done better than it is currently being done or that new technologies indicate a need to do something differently. The committee makes changes in the DocBook DTD to reflect that.

However, the policy is to avoid making drastic changes in the DTD in a short period of time. An element that is to be eliminated will be supported, but its use discouraged. This keeps incompatibilities between major versions of DocBook at a minimum.

Although you still can use deprecated elements, such as when you get an older DocBook document from someone else, I avoid using them in this book to minimize confusion and avoid starting bad habits.

Buzzword

A *deprecated* element is one that is still valid but is being phased out in favor of a new element or is simply being eliminated.

NOTE

The three elements I use here to include a graphic in a document are `MediaObject`, `ImageObject`, and `ImageData`. Unlike HTML, it isn't sufficient to stick in an `Img` element and let it go at that. The `MediaObject` element isn't limited to graphics, and may also contain an `AudioObject` element and/or a `VideoObject` element.

The `MediaObject` element may also contain the `TextObject` element and its child element, the `Phrase` element, but not alone. The `TextObject` and `Phrase` combination have to be used in conjunction with the `ImageObject`, `AudioObject`, or `VideoObject` element. The `TextObject` should not be confused with the `Caption` element, which is used to produce a standard caption for display in addition to the image, not alternative text for display in place of the image.

Right now, you are concerned only with the use of the `ImageObject` element in conjunction with the `TextObject` and `Phrase` pair to produce output suitable for the Web.

In a typical Web page, you will see this markup to display an image with alternative text, in case the browser does not support images or they are turned off:

```
<img src="image.jpg" alt="This is an image">
```

This produces the output shown in Figure 3.3.

If viewed in a text-only browser, such as Lynx, you will see the output shown in Figure 3.4, instead.

To render this output in HTML, you must include all the necessary information in DocBook markup, as shown in Figure 3.5.

```
<mediaobject>
<imageobject>
<imagedata fileref="image.jpg">
</imageobject>
<textobject>
<phrase>
This is an image. If you could view images, you would see a nifty image!
</phrase>
</textobject>
</mediaobject>
```

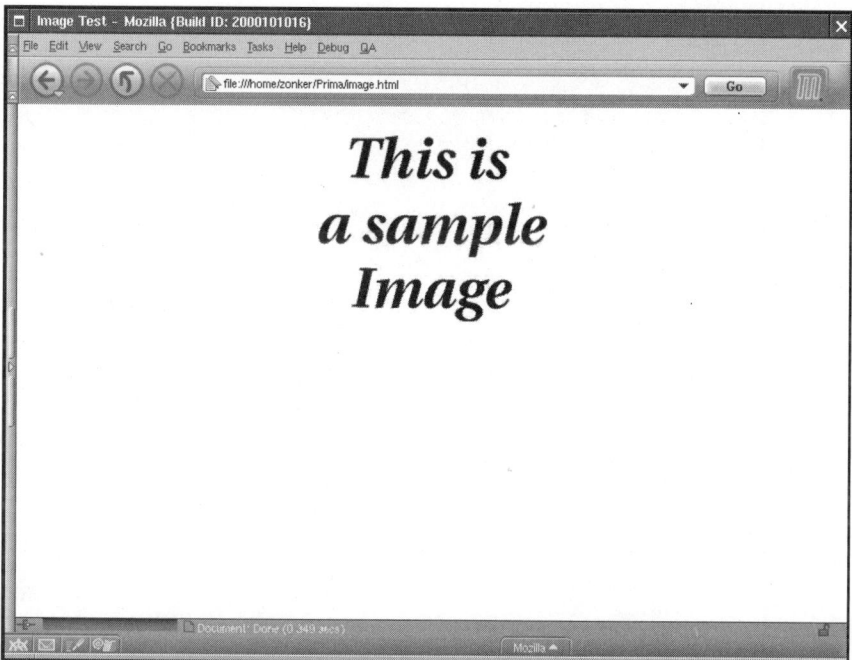

Figure 3.3 *An image with alternative text*

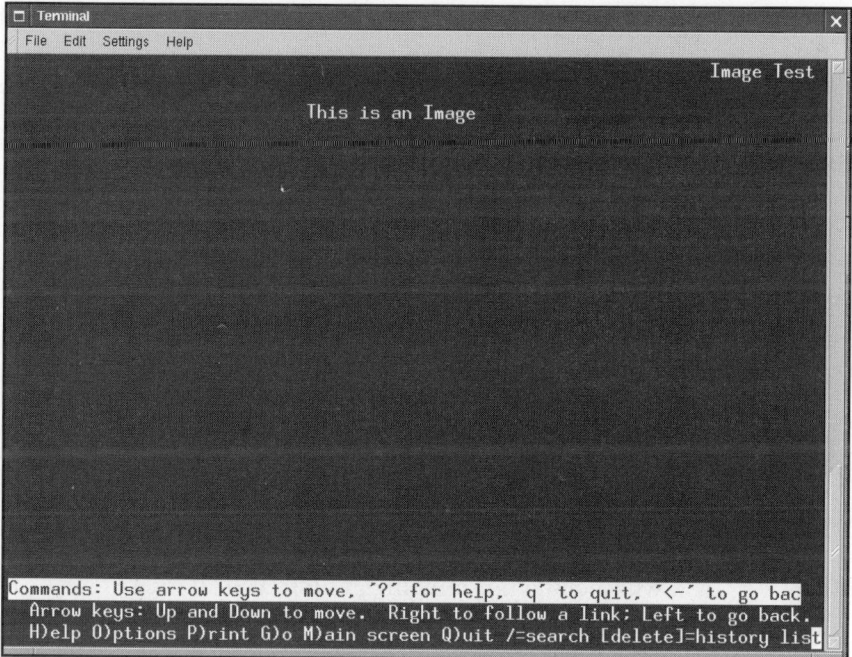

Figure 3.4 *Alternative text displayed in Lynx*

```
┌─ Terminal ──────────────────────────────────────────────────── X ─┐
│ File  Edit  Settings  Help                                         │
│ <mediaobject>                                                      │
│                                                                    │
│   <imageobject>                                                    │
│     <imagedata fileref="../images/image.jpg">                      │
│   </imageobject>                                                   │
│                                                                    │
│   <textobject>                                                     │
│                                                                    │
│     <phrase>This is an image. If you could view images, you would see a nifty │
│ image!</phrase>                                                    │
│                                                                    │
│   </textobject>                                                    │
│                                                                    │
│ </mediaobject>                                                     │
│ ─                                                                  │
│ ─                                                                  │
│ ─                                                                  │
│ ─                                                                  │
│ ─                                                                  │
│ ─                                                                  │
│ ─                                                                  │
│ ─                                                                  │
│ "scratch.sgml" 13L, 230C written                 13.1        All   │
└────────────────────────────────────────────────────────────────────┘
```

Figure 3.5 *DocBook markup to display images and alternative text*

Note that the ImageData element is an empty element, so in XML markup, you must include a trailing slash in the markup to indicate an empty element, like this:

```
<imagedata fileref="image.jpg"/>
```

> Remember that an *empty* element is an element that doesn't require a closing or end tag, not an element that contains no information. An empty element contains all its information as an attribute or requires no additional information.

Although it takes more markup to include an image in DocBook than in HTML, it's still not difficult. Remember, if you plan to render HTML documents, it's a good idea to go ahead and include the TextObject and Phrase elements. That way, you will include not only images but also alternative text for those who are using text (or speech) browsers or have images turned off. If you use DocBook to get multiple formats, don't worry—most programs that parse and render DocBook files into different formats know enough to ignore data they don't need. I'm sure that they all ignore extraneous data, but I'll stick with *most programs* in case one out there I haven't tried doesn't do this.

Creating PostScript and PDF Output

When preparing a DocBook document for print publication, the markup for including images is the same, but the images themselves are different.

Encapsulated PostScript

The Encapsulated PostScript (EPS) image format is used when exporting to PDF or PostScript files. The programs you use to produce output from Doc-Book documents, Jade or OpenJade, do not convert JPEG, PNG, or GIF images into EPS format for inclusion in PostScript or PDF files. If you want to export to one of those formats, you must provide an EPS file for graphics, as well as a JPEG, GIF, or PNG file for HTML output.

In Chapter 6, "Parsing DocBook," you will look in greater detail at the various tools for converting DocBook into different formats. Note that Jade and OpenJade do not try to include images in RTF and plain-text output.

EPS files are a graphic format based on PostScript. As you probably already know, PostScript is a language originally designed for printing. However, encapsulated PostScript files are not necessarily designed for printing on their own; they're actually graphic files in the PostScript language. EPS files can be ASCII or binary files, depending on the program that creates them. Occasionally, you will find programs that output EPS files that are not strictly EPS. Therefore, it's a good idea to get a test EPS file and try it with Jade or OpenJade before you go into a project depending on EPS files that do not work with your chosen rendering program.

The markup for including an EPS image is the same as the markup for including JPEGs or PNGs, except that you specify EPS filenames instead. There are a few ways to handle multiple output formats. One is to use markup like that shown in Figure 3.6.

```
<mediaobject>

<imageobject>
```

```
<imagedata fileref="../images/image.jpg">
</imageobject>
<textobject>
<phrase>This is an image</phrase>
</textobject>
<imageobject>
<imagedata fileref="../images/image.eps">
</imageobject>
<caption>
<para>
This is an EPS image
</para>
</caption>
</mediaobject>
```

By specifying both an EPS and a JPG file, your rendering program can skip the inappropriate file formats for the output it is trying to produce and use the correct file formats.

Another, easier, way is to specify the filename for the image without the extension to indicate the file type (see Figure 3.7). The tools used to parse and

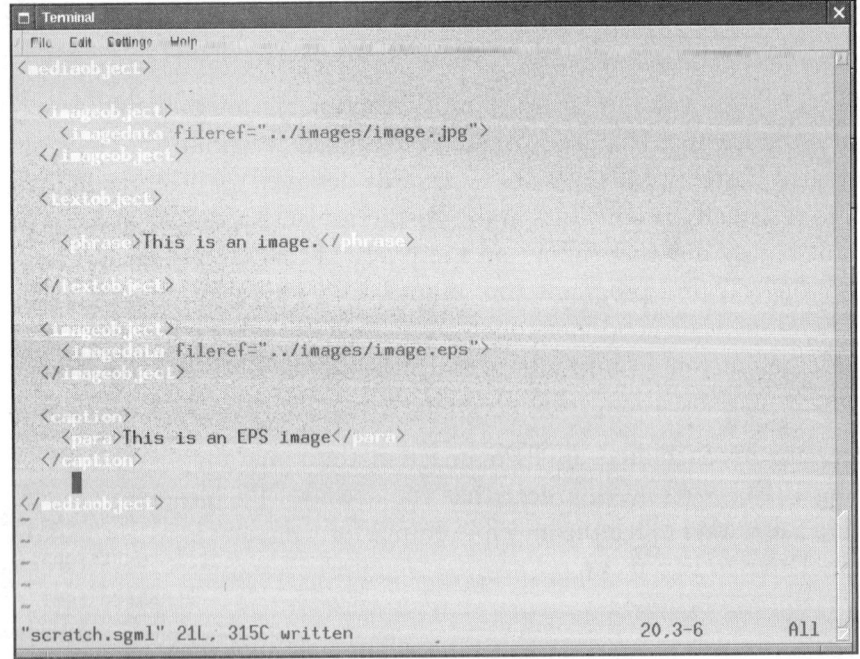

Figure 3.6 *DocBook markup for multiple output formats*

```
□  Terminal                                                    ×
 File   Edit   Settings   Help
<mediaobject>

  <imageobject>
    <imagedata fileref="../images/image">
  </imageobject>

  <textobject>

    <phrase>This is an image.</phrase>

  </textobject>

</mediaobject>

~
~
~
~
~
~
~
~
~
~
 '
~
"scratch.sgml" 13L, 172C written                13,1         All
```

Figure 3.7 *The easy way to include multiple image types*

render DocBook will automatically decide what type of file to look for, depending on the type of output you are trying to produce.

```
<mediaobject>
<imageobject>
<imagedata fileref="../images/image">
</imageobject>
<textobject>
<phrase>This is an image</phrase>
</textobject>
</mediaobject>
```

Helpful Tools

Although a good text editor is all that's necessary to create DocBook markup, you still need some extra tools to make any images that have to be included in the final documents.

This section covers some more popular Open Source tools available to create, manipulate, or acquire images for use with your documents. This isn't by any means an exhaustive list of available Open Source and Free Software programs. These are the tools I've found useful, and they cover the bases for working with images under Linux. Whether you're making your own images, taking pictures with a digital camera, or scanning in existing images with a scanner, these four programs should have you covered. If you're a graphics buff, you might want to visit Freshmeat (**http://www.freshmeat.net/**) and check out the wide selection of graphics programs available for Linux.

NOTE

You might have noticed that I distinguish between Free Software and Open Source software in the preceding paragraphs. That's because there is a difference, at least to the detail-oriented. Richard M. Stallman, head of the Free Software Foundation, objects to the use of the term *Open Source* when referring to software licensed under the General Public License. Although GPL'ed software does meet the definition of Open Source, not all Open Source software is truly free. To avoid lumping free software with non-free (by Stallman's definition) software, he prefers the term *Free Software*, even if it gives the wrong impression to some people. Remember, the *Free* in *Free Software* is not about price; it's about freedom. Although these types of rhetorical discussions make some people's heads swim, they're very important to others. If you'd like to learn more about Open Source and Free Software, visit the Free Software Foundation's Web site at **http://www.fsf.org/** and the Open Source Initiative's site at **http://www.opensource.org/**.

The GIMP

The GIMP is one of the most popular free software tools around. *GIMP* stands for the *GNU Image Manipulation Program*, which is exactly what it is. It's licensed under the GPL and available for most Linux and UNIX-type platforms. Also, ports are being developed for OS/2 and the Win32 platform.

The GIMP started as an Adobe Photoshop clone, so if you're familiar with Photoshop, it shouldn't take long to get the hang of the GIMP. They're not exactly alike; each has different features and tools, but if you've used Photoshop, switching to the GIMP will be easy. (The reverse is also true, I suppose.) As an added bonus, the GIMP opens a huge number of file formats, including Paint Shop Pro and Photoshop files. If you're collaborating with an artist using Photoshop or Paint Shop Pro, you might be able to swap images in the native PSD format.

The GIMP may not handle files saved with the very latest revision of Photoshop or Paint Shop Pro or any program with a proprietary image format. Generally, developers have to reverse-engineer the file formats, which takes time, and each new release of a commercial program usually brings new additions, extensions, or changes to the file format, which require further tweaking. Therefore, the version of the GIMP you're using might not have been fully tweaked. Before you begin a huge project, run a few test images with a variety of features, colors, and layers of a similar size and color depth to the files you expect to create during production. This will save you enormous headaches down the road.

CAUTION

If you're using Linux, odds are that you already have installed The GIMP. If you open an xterm, type GIMP, and press Enter, you should see The GIMP starting up (see Figure 3.8). Note that you want to type GIMP and not GIMP because Linux or any UNIX-type OS is case-sensitive.

The GIMP can create EPS files, JPEGs, GIFs, PostScript files, and TIFFs, to name a few of the file formats it can save. (More than likely, by the time you read this, it will read and save two or three more filetypes.)

Figure 3.8 *The GIMP version 1.1.26*

To download the latest version of The GIMP, visit The GIMP Web site at **http://www.gimp.org/** (see Figure 3.9). You can find a wealth of information about the GIMP, its plugins and extensions, and documentation on its use.

gPhoto

One of the neatest inventions in the past 10 years, in my opinion, is the digital camera. Unfortunately, although many digital cameras come with software for the MacOS and Windows, they usually don't come with software for Linux or other operating systems. Fortunately, gPhoto (see Figure 3.10) comes to the rescue with support for (at the time of this writing) more than 105 camera models on the following operating systems:

- Linux
- FreeBSD
- HPUX
- NetBSD
- OpenBSD

Figure 3.9 *The GIMP Web site*

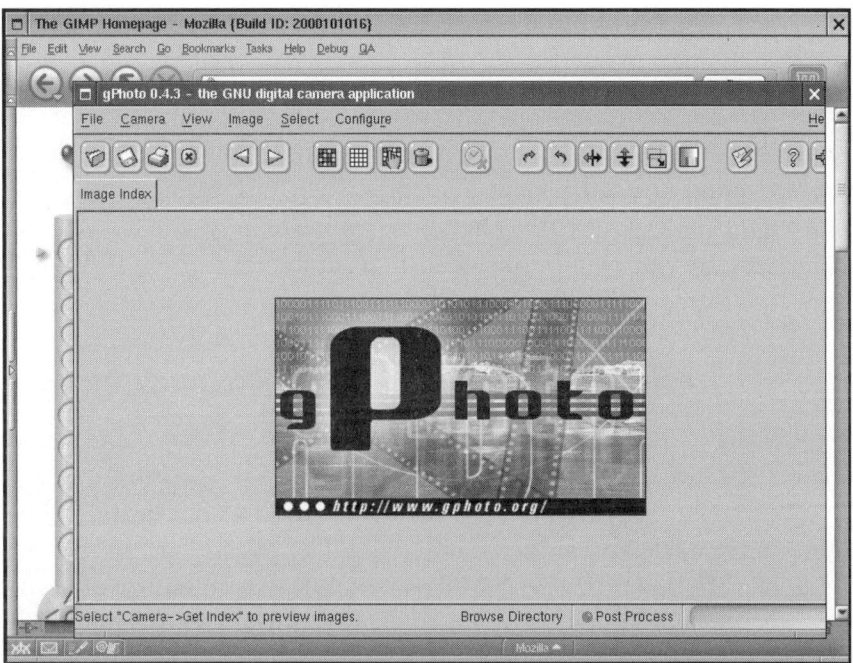

Figure 3.10 *gPhoto in action*

The gPhoto application allows easy management of images stored on a digital camera, simple photo manipulation, color balancing, and scaling. You can use gPhoto to manage your images for your DocBook documentation or your personal Web page or just to keep track of vacation photos.

Because gPhoto is licensed under the GPL, most recent versions of Linux come with gPhoto. To check for the latest version, updates, and information, visit the gPhoto home page at **http://www.gphoto.net/**. You can also find gPhoto on the CD-ROM that comes with this book.

Dia

No technical article or book is complete without diagrams, flowcharts, or other illustrations that guide the reader visually. Dia can create flowcharts, network diagrams, UML models, database diagrams, circuit diagrams, and several other visual representations that make your documents come alive. Dia can save in several useful formats, including the Encapsulated PostScript and Portable Network Graphics formats, which makes Dia a great part of a DocBook publication setup.

Dia is included with most Linux distributions, but for the latest version, check the Dia home page (see Figure 3.11). The current version of Dia (as of this writing) is on the CD-ROM included with this book.

Dia is currently on version .85, so a bit of development is yet to be done. However, I've found Dia to be stable and easy to use for creating simple diagrams (see Figure 3.12). Currently, Dia has no online help system to speak of, but it is hoped that help will be included in a future version soon. A FAQ available on the Dia Web site may be of help.

XSane

Finally, rounding out the quartet of tools is XSane. Despite the sound of the name, it's not a psychological test for authors. It's a front end for SANE, or Scanner Access Made Easy. SANE is an API (Application Programming Interface) that provides a standard method of accessing nearly any type of scanner or similar device. SANE supports a large number of scanners. You can find the entire list at **http://panda.mostang.com/sane/sane-backends.html**.

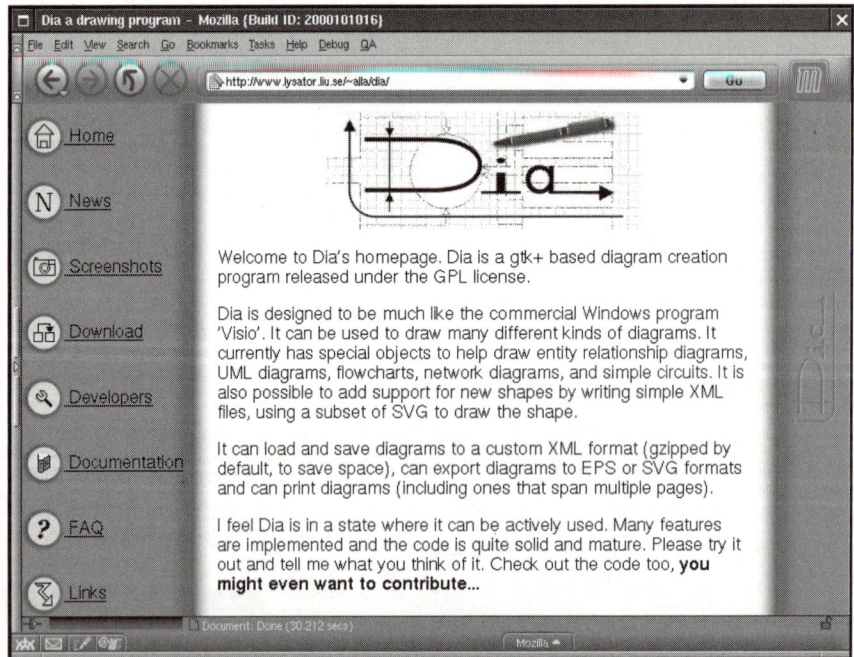

Figure 3.11 *The Dia home page, at http://www.lysator.liu.se/~alla/dia/*

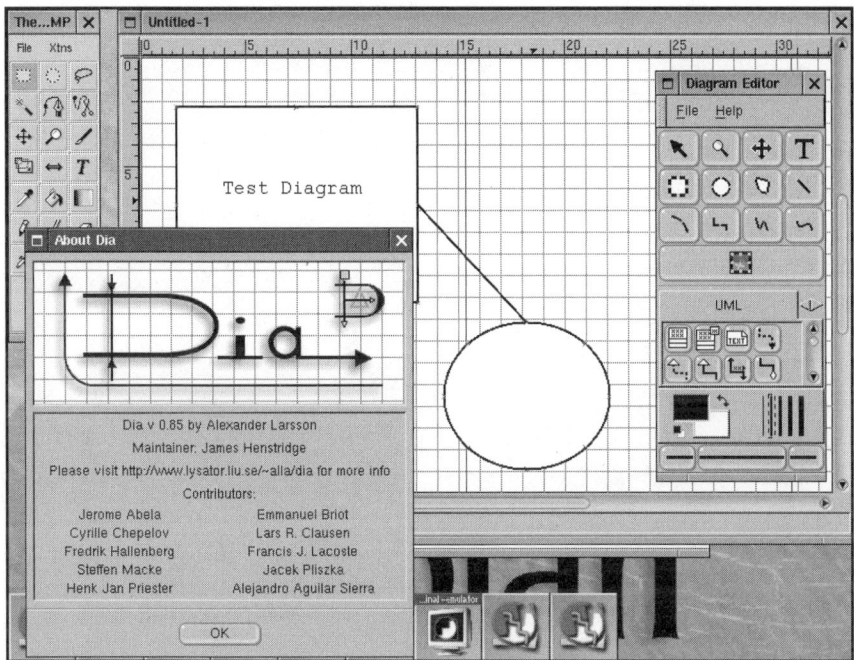

Figure 3.12 *Dia in action*

If you know that you will be using a scanner for your projects, you should consult this list before you purchase anything. SANE, unlike most scanner software, is also designed to allow networked access to scanners. Any machine on a network (instead of only the computer hooked directly to the scanner) can connect to a supported scanner via the network.

XSane is a GUI front end that enables you to utilize the features of SANE from a friendly interface. To brush up on all the options XSane offers, visit the XSane Web page at **http://www.wolfsburg.de/~rauch/sane/sane-xsane.html** (see Figure 3.13).

XSane allows you to save acquired images in several formats, including JPG, PNG, and PostScript. To use PostScript images with Jade or OpenJade, you can convert them to EPS with The GIMP or another graphics program. XSane supports a variety of color depths and resolutions, although the features of your scanner determine exactly what color depth and resolution you will be able to get.

Both XSane and SANE are available under the terms of the GPL and are included on the CD-ROM that accompanies this book. Check the XSane Web site for updates and further information about XSane.

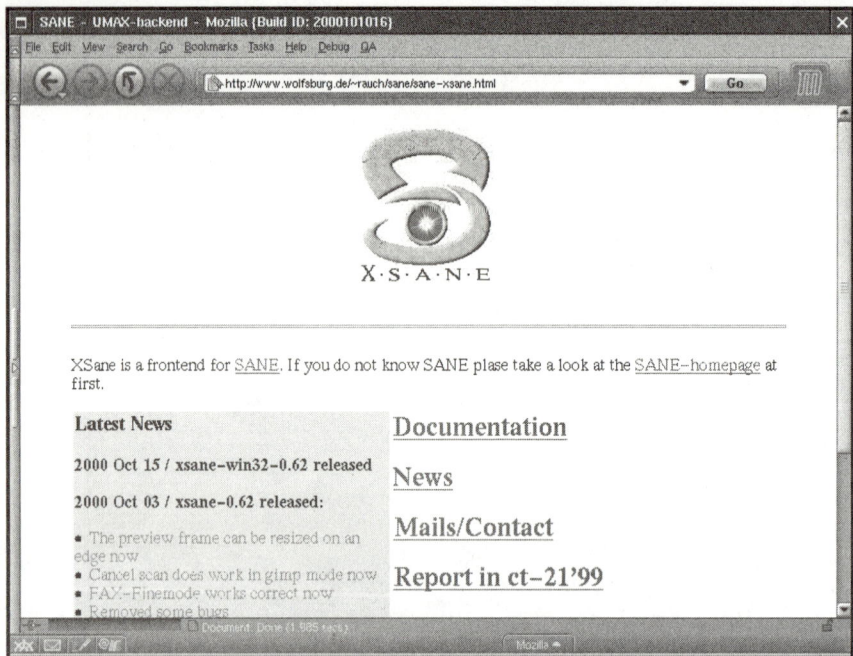

Figure 3.13 *The XSane home page*

I hope that this brief overview of some of the graphics applications available under Linux has piqued your interest and that if you have a need for software to work with graphics, you will try these applications. Again, an enormous amount of Free and Open Source software is out there. It's always worth checking to see whether you can find the application you're looking for among the available Free and Open Source software. I think that you will be very pleased with the quality of the available software.

Marking Up Tables and Figures

Tables and illustrative figures are very important to technical documentation. The reason I've separated tables and figures from the rest of the graphic elements is because they can be created with DocBook markup instead of a separate program. DocBook is good, but it can't produce an 8×10 colored picture, with circles and arrows on the back of each one. It can, however, create tables and some figures, using a little help from TeX/LaTeX or MathML in the case of XML DocBook.

Making Tables

If you've created tables in HTML, you know that they can become complicated when you're making a table that's more than one or two rows. Unfortunately, DocBook markup is slightly more complicated than the HTML markup to create tables, and there are more options. Don't worry, I'll cover them all and try to make it as simple as possible.

> I should mention, you can cheat when including a table or figure. Just because you can create a table or figure with DocBook markup doesn't mean that you have to. If your output formats are limited to print output and Web output, you can get away with including the table or figure as a graphic. However, the advantage to making tables with DocBook markup is that you will be able to output to other formats that can't handle included graphics, such as plain-text format.

Table Markup

DocBook markup has a couple types of elements to create tables. There are the aptly named `Table` element and the popular `InformalTable` element. The `Table` and `InformalTable` elements are virtually the same, except that the `Table` element has a title, and the `InformalTable` does not. No title, therefore informal—get it? Actually, other than listing a title with a table in the text, there is a good reason for making a distinction between formal and informal tables. If tables include a title, then an index or listing of all tables can be automatically generated when rendering DocBook output. Nifty, isn't it?

> You can create a table-like structure using the `SimpleList` element because it allows you to specify vertical or horizontal columns. However, this is a kludge and should not be used in place of a true table, if that's what you need. Remember, the idea behind DocBook markup is not to concern you with the look of the document but with the structure. If, indeed, you have a simple list, use that element. If your information is really a table, use that instead. The `SimpleList` element is covered in more detail in Appendix B, "DocBook Element Reference."

Now you will look at a small table to see how to create a table in your document.

```
<table>
<title>Example Table</title>
<tgroup cols="2">
<thead>
<row>
<entry>Column 1</entry>
<entry>Column 2</entry>
</row>
</thead>
<tbody>
<row>
<entry>This is a cell in the table</entry>
<entry>So is this!</entry>
</row>
<row>
<entry>Column 1 Row 2</entry>
<entry>Column 2 Row 2: This is easy!</entry>
</row>
</tbody>
</tgroup>
</table>
```

As you can see, the markup to create a table in DocBook, shown in Figure 3.14, is more complicated than the markup in HTML, shown in Figure 3.15. However, it's all easy to remember after you've made a few tables.

The Table or InformalTable element begins a table. The tgroup element holds the actual content elements of the Table or InformalTable element. The tgroup and Table and InformalTable elements are not optional.

The thead, tbody, and tfoot elements indicate a heading, body, or footer section of the table, respectively. The thead and tfoot elements are not required in a table, but the tbody element is.

The row element holds the rows in a table, whereas the entry element actually holds the information content in the rows.

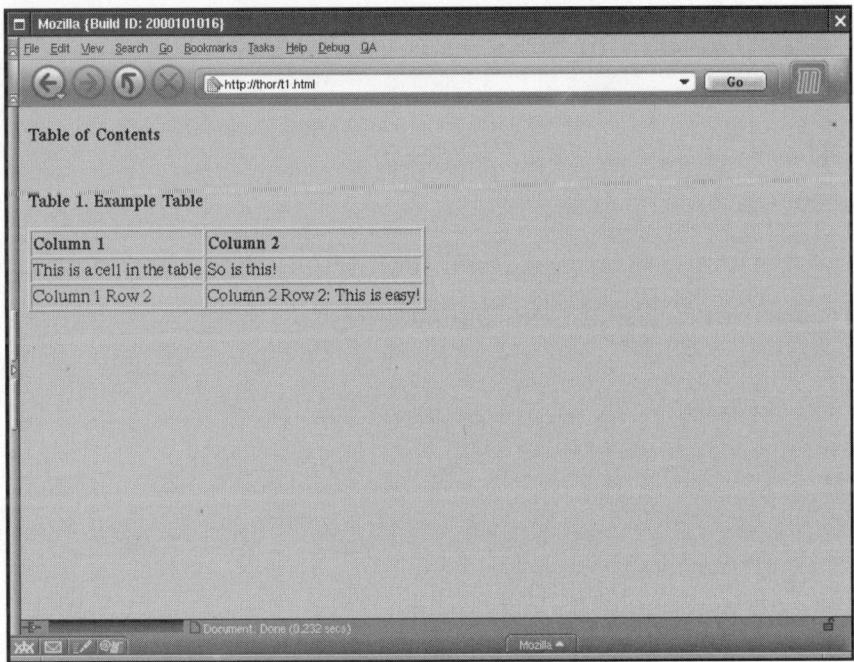

```
!DOCTYPE article PUBLIC "-//OASIS//DTD DocBook V3.1//EN">
<article>
<sect1>
<table>
<title>Example Table</title>
<tgroup cols="2">
<thead>
<row>
<entry>Column 1</entry>
<entry>Column 2</entry>
</row>
</thead>
<tbody>
<row>
<entry>This is a cell in the table</entry>
<entry>So is this!</entry>
</row>
<row>
<entry>Column 1 Row 2</entry>
<entry>Column 2 Row 2: This is easy!</entry>
</row>
<row>
<entry>Column 1 Row 3</entry>
</row>
</tbody>
</tgroup>
"test.sgml" 30L, 481C                          1,1        Top
```

Figure 3.14 *Basic table markup*

Figure 3.15 *Output from the markup in Figure 3.15 rendered in HTML*

You might have noticed that some of the names of the table elements aren't consistent with the names of most DocBook elements. Specifically, they aren't referred to with an initial uppercase letter the way that Doc-Book elements are. This is keeping consistent with the way that the elements are described in the CALS specification. Remember, the DocBook Technical Committee didn't come up with all of the table elements; they use a different specification that was already in popular usage.

The same markup applies to an `InformalTable` element, but it does not have a title.

It is possible to include a subtable within a table by using the `Entrytbl` element. The `Entrytbl` element has a required attribute, the `Column` attribute, called `Cols`. The next example shows a table with a subtable.

```
<!DOCTYPE article PUBLIC "-//OASIS//DTD DocBook V3.1//EN">
<article>
<table frame=all><title>Sample Table</title>
<tgroup cols=2 align=left colsep=1 rowsep=1>
<tbody>
<row>
<entry>Column 1</entry>
<entry>Column 2</entry>
</row>
<row>
  <entrytbl cols=1>
    <tbody>
      <row>
        <entry>This is a sub-table</entry>
      </row>
    </tbody>
  </entrytbl>
</tgroup>
</table>
</article>
```

The `Table` and `InformalTable` elements are different from most DocBook markup because they allow for so much specification of exactly how the table should look—which is not what structured markup is all about. It's important to remember that not all output formats support all specifications. If you output to plain-text format, for example, it will be very limited in the ways it can display table information beyond the bare basics. This is also true, to a lesser extent, of HTML and RTF. The PostScript and PDF formats should be able to realize any formatting options fully. If the look of the table is very important, it might be best to include an image of the table rather than rely on markup.

> For more information on the CALS Table Model, you can check the documentation found on the OASIS Web site at this URL:
>
> **http://www.oasis-open.org/html/a502.htm**

Making and Including Figures and Equations

There are a few ways you can go about including figures and equations in DocBook documents. I've already talked about including standard images created in programs like Adobe Photoshop and The GIMP. In the next section you will look at making figures and equations with markup.

Using LaTeX for Figures and Equations

Because LaTeX is such a complicated markup language, I'm going to cheat here. Rather than try to give you a full tutorial on LaTeX, which is well beyond the scope of this book, I'll share a nifty Open Source tool with you that you can use to generate LaTeX.

LyX is a program that allows you to create LaTeX markup, DVI output, and even PostScript output. Even better, LyX has great features for working with mathematic equations.

As you can see in Figure 3.16, LyX comes loaded for bear to create equations.

How do you use these wonderful toys with DocBook? One way is to use LyX to create a PostScript file for inclusion with your document. However, as mentioned before, you must have an Encapsulated PostScript file to include as an image, not a plain PostScript file. If you generate a PostScript file, you must use something like The GIMP or Adobe Photoshop to convert the PostScript file to EPS. This might seem like a lot of steps, but it does guarantee that your equation will look exactly as you want it to. You will also have the advantage of being able to convert PostScript files to other image formats for output to HTML or other formats.

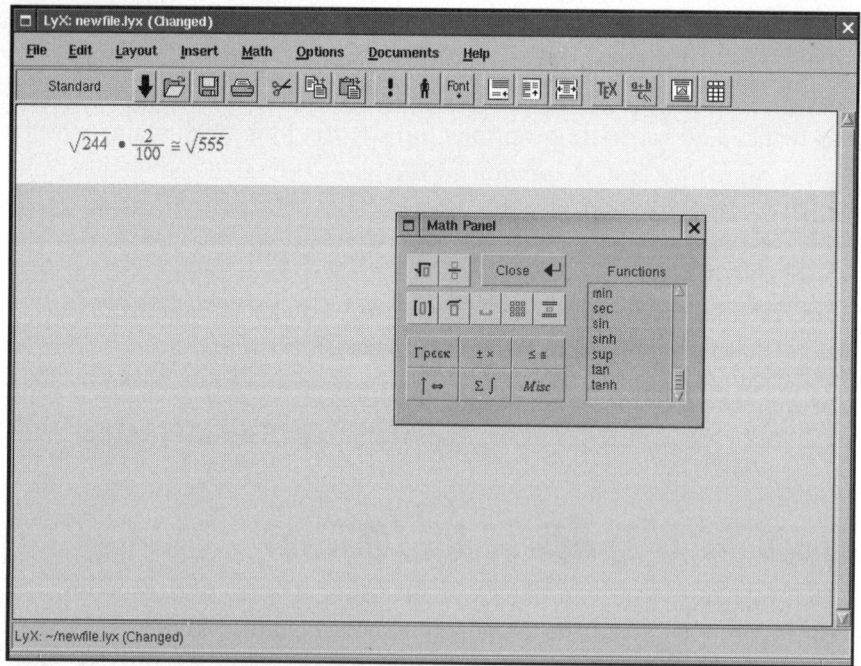

Figure 3.16 *The LyX Math Panel*

The other method is to create LaTeX output from LyX and create a LaTeX version of your DocBook document, cutting and pasting the figure into the document before processing the LaTeX file for final output. You will look at this procedure in more detail in Chapter 6, "Parsing DocBook." Finally, if you're using the DocBook XML DTD, you can export LaTeX to MathML using LaTeX2HTML, WebEQ, and WebTeX. This is complicated, but it can be done. An excellent tutorial, as well as all the necessary software, is located at **http://www.geom.umn.edu/~ross/webtex/webtex/**.

Using MathML for Mathematical Equations

If you're using the XML DTD, you have the option of including MathML equations in your DocBook document. MathML is a markup language for mathematical and scientific content. Mainly, MathML is designed for sharing equations via the Web; it is not as concerned with print and other forms of output. However, with the appropriate use of stylesheets, there's no reason that MathML can't produce excellent print output as well.

To include MathML markup in your document, use the following declaration:

```
<!DOCTYPE book PUBLIC "-//OASIS//DTD DocBook MathML Module V1.0beta3//EN"
  "http://www.oasis-open.org/docbook/xml/mathml/1.0beta2/dbmathml.dtd">
```

You must also install the MathML DTD for Jade or OpenJade to be able to process MathML markup.

MathML allows for two types of markup: presentational and semantic. Presentational tags explicitly spell out how the equation should look. Semantic tags, on the other hand, specify the structure and leave it to stylesheets to create the presentation.

Here is an example of semantic markup, taken from the W3C's page on MathML:

```
<apply>
        <plus/>
        <apply>
            <power/>
            <ci>x</ci>
            <cn>2</cn>
        </apply>
        <apply>
            <times/>
            <cn>4</cn>
            <ci>x</ci>
        </apply>
        <cn>4</cn>
    </apply>
```

The presentational markup for the same output looks like this:

```
<mrow>
    <mrow>
            <msup> <mi>x</mi> <mn>2</mn> </msup> <mo>+</mo>
                <mrow>
                    <mn>4</mn>
                    <mo>&invisibletimes;</mo>
                    <mi>x</mi>
                </mrow>
        <mo>+</mo>
        <mn>4</mn>
    </mrow>
    <mo>=</mo>
    <mn>0</mn>
</mrow>
```

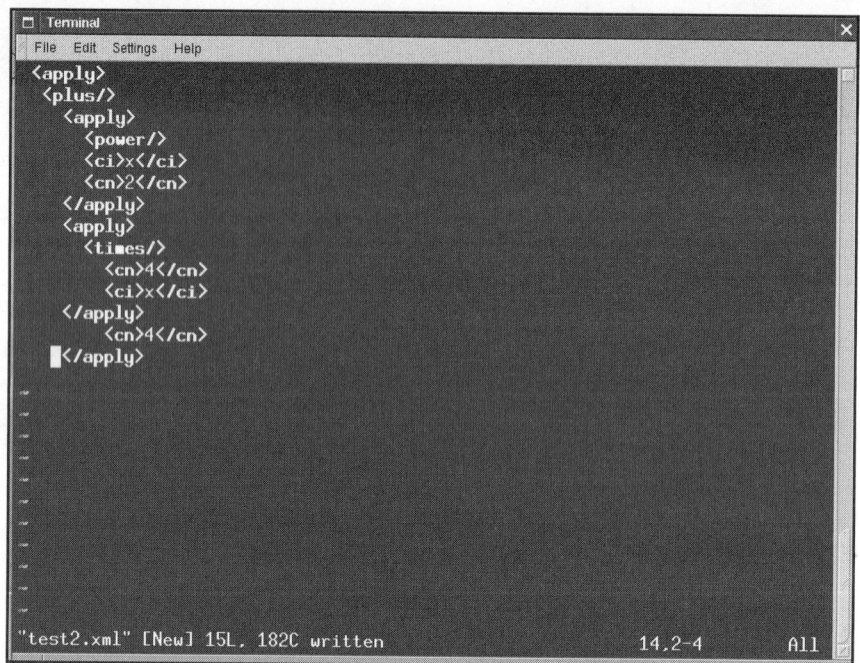

Figure 3.17 *MathML markup in Vim*

Figure 3.17 shows the MathML markup in Vim.

Fully covering MathML markup is beyond the scope of this book, but you can find a tutorial and the entire specification on the W3C's site at **http://www.w3.org/TR/2001/REC-MathML2/**.

Summary

Including images, figures, tables, and equations makes your documents come alive for those who are more visually oriented. Be sure to plan your strategy for including images before starting a large project. DocBook is fairly flexible in what you can do graphically, so be sure that you take full advantage of its capabilities.

Chapter 4: Preparing a Book with DocBook

Planning for a Book

Declaring a Book

Book Structure Elements

This chapter walks through creating a book with DocBook. Specifically, you will look at the most common appropriate elements used within a DocBook Book element. If you're preparing a book with DocBook, you will find examples of all necessary structural elements for a book within this chapter, as well as examples of elements commonly used in a book, thrown in for good measure.

A Book is a document type within DocBook. Each DocBook document must start with a document type element; common elements include Book, Article, Set, and Chapter. When a document is declared to be a Book, the Book element is the top-level, or *root*, element. A Book often has several Part elements that contain a Preface, a Dedication, Chapters, an Index, and other components. Nearly every DocBook element is valid within the Book element, with the exception of the Set element.

> When I say that nearly all elements are valid within the Book element, I mean that they fit somewhere in the hierarchy below the Book element. They might not be valid directly under the Book element, but they are valid nested within an element that is valid within the Book element. For example, the Sect1 element cannot be used directly beneath the Book element, but it might be used under the Chapter element, which is valid under the Book element.

A DocBook Book element can be used regardless of the medium in which you eventually intend to distribute the book. Although we traditionally think of a book as being a collection of dead-tree pages bound within a cover, a DocBook Book can also be output and distributed as HTML, PDF, or even plain text. This can be particularly useful if you are distributing software, for instance. Many software manuals, frankly, go unread.

Although it would be a very bad idea not to include documentation with a piece of software, why spend the money on printing a manual with your software when you can include documentation in electronic format? The users are going to be at the computer when they need the documentation anyway. Why not include a format that is searchable and easier to browse on the computer?

Note that it's probably a bad idea to eschew the printed documentation if it relates to setting up the computer in the first place. This also allows for easier distribution of your software. If everything is in electronic format, you can distribute your software via download, avoiding altogether the costs of printing, software media, and boxes.

> Of course, including only electronic documentation does preclude your users' reading your documents on long car trips or in the bathroom, but think of all the trees you will be saving!

NOTE

Planning for a Book

Writing a book requires much planning—at least, that's what my editors tell me. It sounds like a logical theory, so I'm willing to go with it. Before you start writing, you will want to do some planning. If you're writing a technical book, you will probably want to commit to a proposed table of contents and write to that.

DocBook, because it is highly concerned with structure, is helpful in these prewriting sessions. Write your outline using DocBook structure elements such as the `Part`, `Chapter`, and `Sect1` through `Sect5` elements. When you have roughly laid out your book down to the `Sect5` level, perhaps even with a few `Para` elements sketched in, you're ready to start writing. DocBook can be a very handy tool even before you start serious writing. DocBook is designed to make authors think about structure, so use it to its fullest.

If you can't map out a book to that level of detail, you probably need to do more research and planning before sitting down to write. As an editor, you can require an author to lay out his or her book to that level of detail before giving the go-ahead to start writing.

Dealing with Multiple Files

Although it's possible to have all the contents of a Book in one file, it's certainly more convenient to separate the `Chapter` elements into different files. This is much more manageable, particularly if one author is not writing all the chapters. When you look at the first example of a document declaration for a book, notice that each of the book's chapters is its own file.

Also, if your book will contain images, it's a good idea to plan for them at the beginning of the project. You don't have to decide exactly what images you're going to include, but it helps to know what procedure you're going to use and what formats you'll work in. Decide which types of output you will want to create, and save your images in the appropriate formats. Also, for management purposes, save images in separate directories by chapter or section, and come up with a naming scheme that can be used to organize the images by chapter and number. Figure 4.1 shows files from a work in progress.

If you haven't read it yet, Chapter 3, "Using Images," deals with images in greater detail.

> When you create images, save them first in a format that can easily be converted to other formats without loss of picture quality—such as EPS or PhotoShop's PSD format. You might only be doing an online document now, but at some later date you might want to create a print version. If all you have are JPG files, you're not going to have the quality necessary to create attractive images in print.

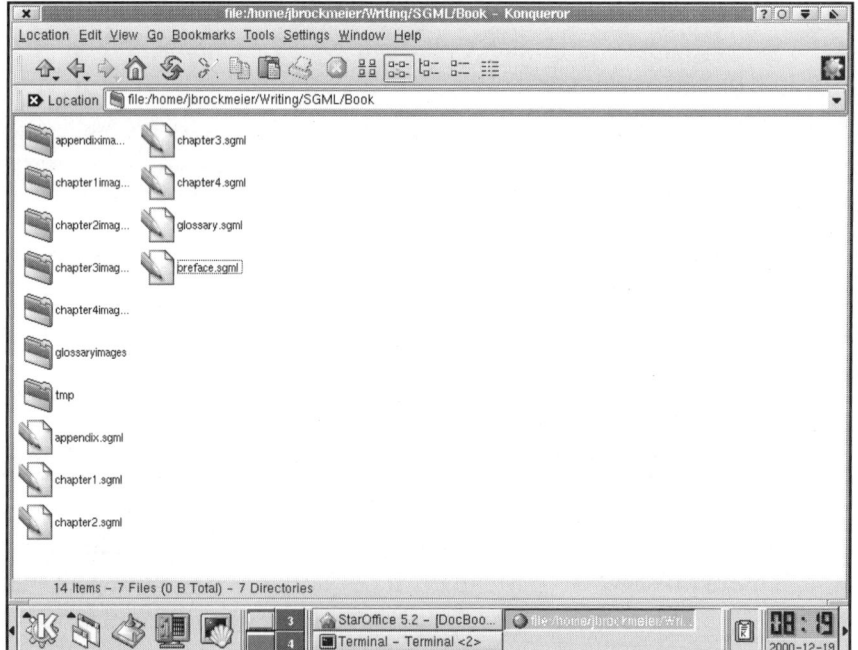

Figure 4.1 *Organizing images and files by chapter*

Finally, if more than one person is working on a book simultaneously, it's a good idea to implement a centralized version-control system. A system that allows people to check out and check in materials while maintaining the original files will allow multiple people to work on the same files while keeping the originals for later reference. You might find that you want to undo some changes made by an editor or another author. Having the old versions of the files makes this much easier. You can learn more about version control systems and the Free Software CVS program in Chapter 7, "Collaborative Work."

> There are many version control systems, but CVS is one of the most popular versions available. It also has the virtue of being Free Software and having several GUI front ends to make life simpler for those who aren't fond of the command line.

NOTE

Declaring a Book

In DocBook, the first step in producing a book or any DocBook document is to declare your document type. I cover document types extensively in Chapter 1, "Getting Started," so if you're not comfortable with document declarations, you might want to return to Chapter 1 and review a bit. This is a simple declaration for a book with a preface, four chapters, an index, a glossary, an appendix, and a bibliography (see Figure 4.2). You will name this file book.sgml, or book.xml if you're working with XML.

```
<!DOCTYPE book PUBLIC "-//OASIS//DTD DocBook V4.1//EN" [
<!ENTITY preface SYSTEM "preface.sgml">
<!ENTITY chapter1 SYSTEM "chapter1.sgml">
<!ENTITY chapter2 SYSTEM "chapter2.sgml">
<!ENTITY chapter3 SYSTEM "chapter3.sgml">
<!ENTITY chapter4 SYSTEM "chapter4.sgml">
<!ENTITY index SYSTEM "index.sgml">
<!ENTITY glossary SYSTEM "glossary.sgml">
<!ENTITY appendix SYSTEM "appendix.sgml">
<!ENTITY bibliography SYSTEM "bibliography.sgml">
]>
<book>
&preface;
&chapter1;
```

```
&chapter2;

&chapter3;

&chapter4;

&index;

&glossary;

&appendix;

&bibliography;

</book>
```

That is a valid declaration for an SGML DocBook Book. Note that it doesn't contain any text within the book itself.

To break it down, the first line is the document declaration itself. Here, you're telling any application that is going to parse the file, which type of document this is, and what to expect. The following lines, enclosed in brackets and beginning with <!ENTITY, are declaring entities for the parser. These are not DocBook entities; they're entities that refer to files on your system. This allows you to refer to the entities under the Book element by enclosing

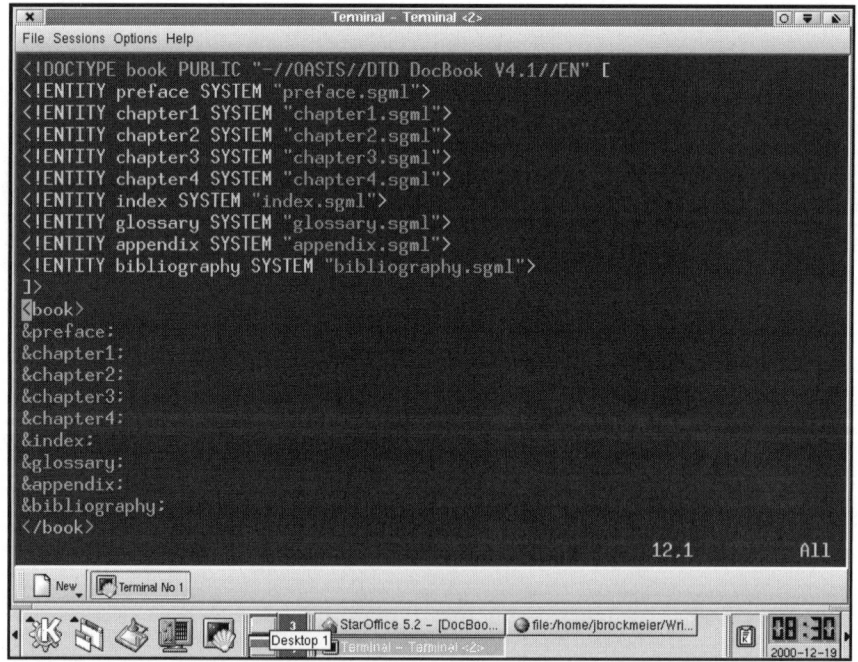

Figure 4.2 *The Book declaration in Vim*

the declared entities with an ampersand (&) and a semicolon (;). Rather than include the entire text of the book in one file, you split it into a number of files, which you declare as entities and then call from the main book.sgml file. For instance, instead of including the text of the preface, you simply include a reference to the preface. When the document is parsed, the parser will read the line &preface; as "include the system document preface.sgml and parse it."

The XML declaration is nearly the same. Figure 4.3 shows how the declaration looks for the XML document.

```
<?xml version="1.0"?>
<!DOCTYPE book PUBLIC "-//OASIS//DTD DocBook XML V4.1//EN"
"file:///usr/share/xml/docbook/4.1/docbookx.dtd" [
<!ENTITY preface SYSTEM "preface.xml">
<!ENTITY chapter1 SYSTEM "chapter1.xml">
<!ENTITY chapter2 SYSTEM "chapter2.xml">
<!ENTITY chapter3 SYSTEM "chapter3.xml">
<!ENTITY chapter4 SYSTEM "chapter4.xml">
<!ENTITY index SYSTEM "index.xml">
<!ENTITY glossary SYSTEM "glossary.xml">
<!ENTITY appendix SYSTEM "appendix.xml">
<!ENTITY bibliography SYSTEM "bibliography.xml">
]>
<book>
&preface;
&chapter1;
&chapter2;
&chapter3;
&chapter4;
&index;
&glossary;
&appendix;
&bibliography;
</book>
```

That's all there is to the declaration for a document with the Book document type. The Book element and the entities called from within the Book element in the example are not part of the declaration itself but are included to help illustrate what a DocBook book will look like.

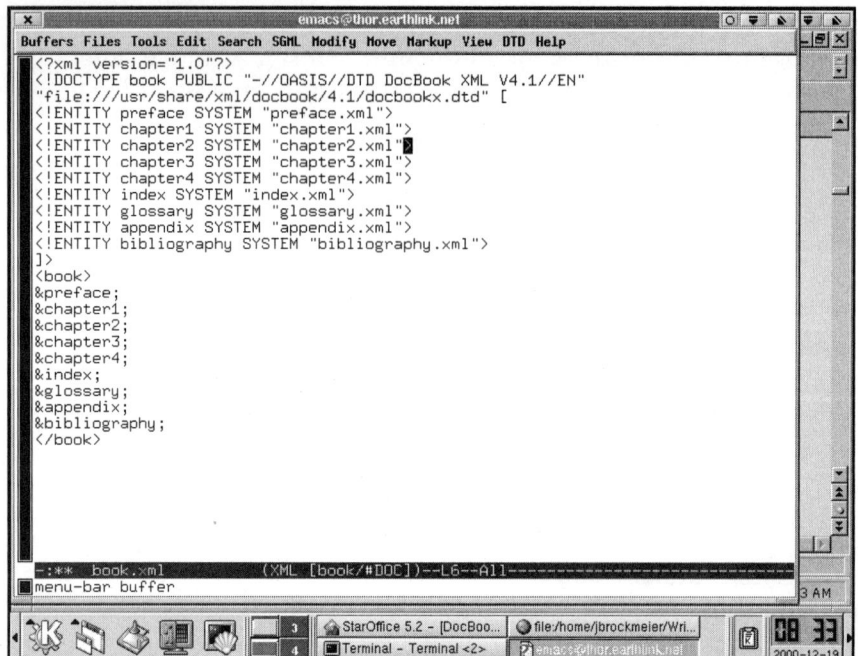

Figure 4.3 *The XML declaration in Emacs*

The BookInfo Element

There is some other information you will probably want to include about the book, things such as the title of the book, the name of the author or authors, the copyright holder, and other meta information about the book itself. To do that, you start with the BookInfo element.

You will look at two examples of the BookInfo element, a simple one and a more complex example that illustrates the range of information you can include within the BookInfo element.

The first example is for a book with only one author and includes a copyright holder and the year of the copyright (see Figure 4.4):

```
<book>

<bookinfo>

<title>DocBook Publishing</title>

<author>

<firstname>Joe</firstname>
```

```
<surname>Brockmeier</surname>
<othername>"Zonker"</othername>
</author>
<copyright>
<year>2001</year>
<holder>Prima Publishing</holder>
</copyright>
</bookinfo>
</book>
```

The BookInfo element is valid only within the Book element itself. You cannot use the BookInfo element within any other element. None of the information included in the BookInfo element is required; you do not have to have an author, copyright holder, or year. The BookInfo element can contain as little or as much information as you see fit to include.

For a more complicated example, you will create a BookInfo entry for a book with multiple authors and an editor and include edition information, the ISBN, and the part number of the book.

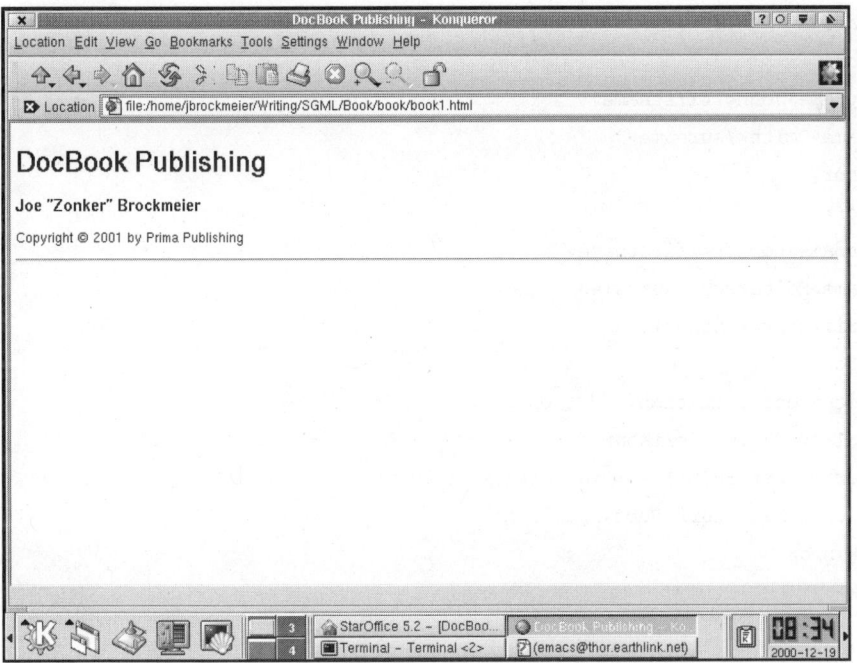

Figure 4.4 *BookInfo information rendered in HTML*

Why would you want to include the part number information about a book? For those who are making use of DocBook XML, this sort of information can be used to streamline your production systems. If the inventory information is included in the document used to produce the book, specialized stylesheets can be made to help generate catalogs, online ordering information, and much more. This has the potential to save a company some money for data entry and other manual labor.

Remember, you can find these examples, and templates, on the CD-ROM included with this book.

```
<book>
<bookinfo>
<title>The Great American Novel</title>
<authorgroup>
<author>
<firstname>Joe</firstname>
<surname>Brockmeier</surname>
<othername>"Zonker"</othername>
</author>
<author>
<firstname>John</firstname>
<surname>Smith</surname>
</author>
<editor>
<firstname>Robert</firstname>
<surname>Editorguy</surname>
<honorific>Dr.</honorific>
</editor>
<edition>Second Edition</edition>
<isbn>1-57423-103-7</isbn>
<invpartnumber>2000-12-1</invpartnumber>
<publisher>Neatstuff Pubs</publisher>
</bookinfo>
</book>
```

As you see from this example, you can include quite a bit of information about your book using the `BookInfo` element and its children. I would encourage you to include as much as possible from the beginning; you never know when it will come in handy to have the information available in your document.

You might be surprised to note that there is no `Lastname` element. Instead, DocBook uses the `Surname` element because it is more useful. In some cultures the surname, or family name, is not placed last.

The `OtherName` element can be used for middle names, nicknames, or whatever. You should probably consult authors before bestowing a nickname on them, or at least make sure that they don't know where you live. If you or one of the authors or editors has an honorific title, you can include it using the `Honorific` element. Because this is a free-form element, you can include any title you want. Usually, the element is used for people with *Dr.* in front of their names, *Professor*, or any other honorary title. *Lovemonkey* would be a valid title, although not recommended.

The `ISBN` element is the element for including the International Standard Book Number. Almost all books published have an ISBN, which makes ordering books much simpler than trying to track down a book by title or author. There might be 200 books by John Q. Smith titled *I Hate My Parents for Giving Me This Name*, but each has a unique ISBN. If you're not going to be selling or distributing your book, you probably won't need an ISBN.

> You will make grammarians and picky people happy by not referring to ISBNs as *ISBN numbers. ISBN number* is redundant because the phrase that makes up the acronym includes the word *number*. If you use ISBN in your document, be sure to enclose it in the `Acronym` element.

NOTE

The `InvPartNumber` element is used to include a part number for the book. Bits of information such as the ISBN or part number are not always displayed when the document is rendered. Some stylesheets ignore that information for printed output because it is mainly for administrative purposes.

For other valid elements within the `BookInfo` element, please see Appendix B, "DocBook Element Reference."

Making the Book's Dedication

Almost all books contain a dedication to someone. Perhaps the author wants to thank his or her eighth-grade English teacher, mom, or current spouse. (If you have a spouse, I would highly recommend including him or her in the book's dedication. It's much cheaper than a divorce lawyer.) The Dedication element is the proper wrapper for a book's dedication.

The following is an example of a basic book dedication (see Figure 4.5). Note that the text of the dedication is contained in a Para element and that the only valid parent element for the Dedication element is the Book element. This means that the Dedication element cannot be nested within any other element.

```
<book>
<bookinfo>
<author>
                <firstname>Joe</firstname>
                <othername>"Zonker"</othername>
                <surname>Brockmeier</surname>
</author>
<copyright>
                <holder>Prima Publishing</holder>
                <year>2001</year>
</copyright>
<dedication>
<para>
This book is dedicated to my dog.
</para>
</dedication>
...
</book>
```

The Preface Element

Another component found in most books is the preface. Just like the first 20 minutes at work, no one jumps directly into a book without piddling around a bit. The preface gives the author an opportunity to explain to the reader the goals of the book and what to expect on the pages that follow. It also gives college students something to skim the morning before the semester final

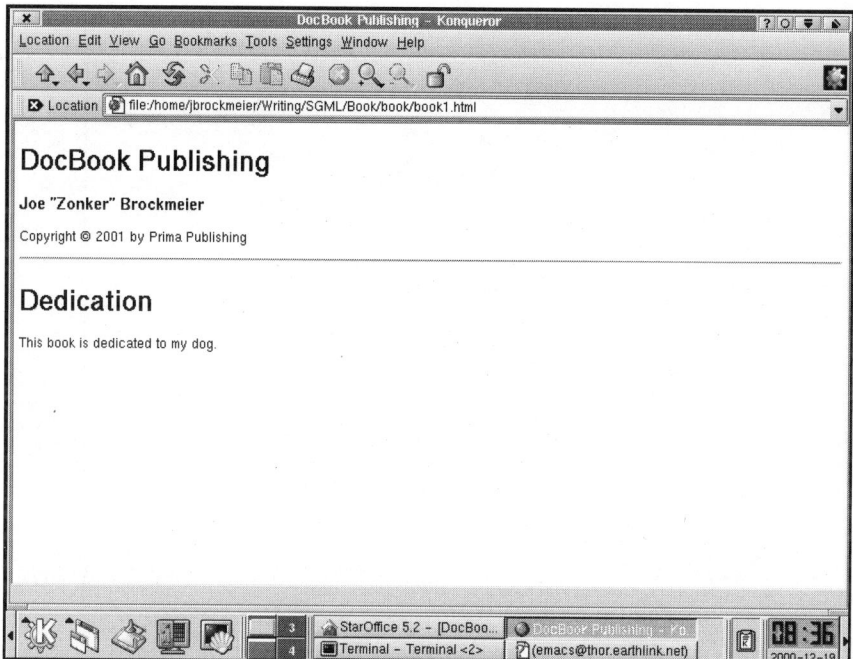

Figure 4.5 *A book dedication output to HTML*

when they haven't read the textbook, so be kind and include at least a brief synopsis of the text.

The `Preface` element is used for any introductory matter in a DocBook book. This may include a preface, an introduction, chapter introductions, a forward written by someone else, epilogues, and other such material. Depending on your stylesheets, the preface may or may not be formatted differently than a regular chapter.

The `Preface` element may be contained within the `Book` or `Part` elements but not within any other elements. See Appendix B for all the possible child elements for the `Preface` element. I will cover the `Part` element in more detail next.

The following example contains a very brief forward to a book, a title for the forward, and the name of the forward's author (see Figure 4.6):

```
<book>
<preface>
<title>Read with Caution</title>
```

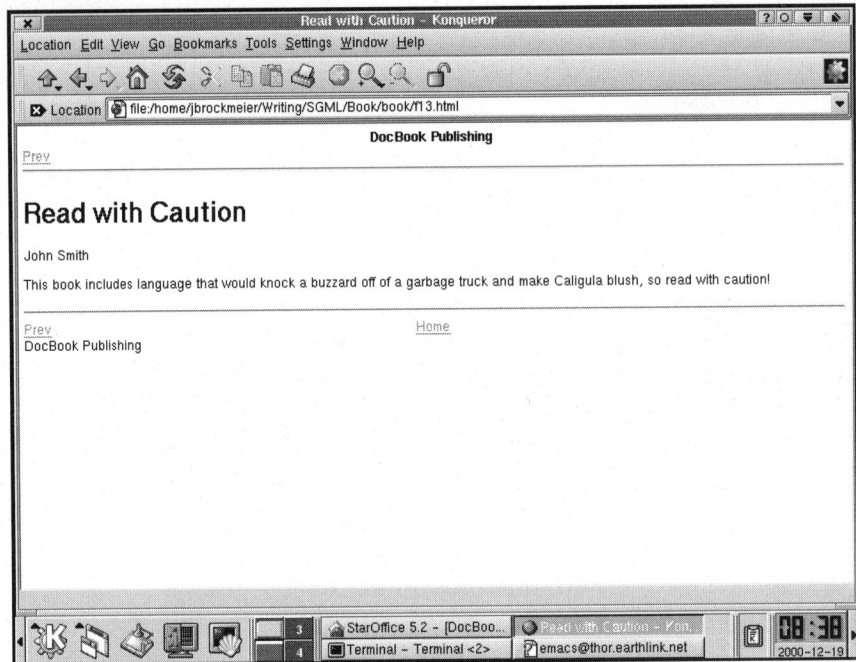

Figure 4.6 *The Preface output in HTML*

```
<author>
<firstname>John</firstname>
<surname>Smith</surname>
</author>
<para>
This book includes language that would knock a buzzard off of a garbage
truck and make Caligula blush, so read with caution!
</para>
</preface>
</book>
```

Working with the Part Element

Sometimes it is useful to organize the chapters of a book by parts. For example, if you were writing a book about the American Revolution, you might have several chapters about specific events leading up to the American Revolution, followed by chapters about battles of the Revolution and other noteworthy events that took place during the Revolution. Finally, you'd probably have several more chapters that cover the aftermath of the American Revolution.

To make the book easier to follow, you could organize the chapters into distinctive parts composed of chapters with related topics, or you could organize the book chronologically. Also, you could just divide it into even parts of three chapters each.

The Part element can contain most other elements, with the exception of the Set element or the Book element. The Part element can only be nested directly under the Book element. (It can be nested under the Set element but only within the Book element. You won't find a part of a book as part of a set.)

The Part element is simple to use. In this example, shown in Figure 4.7, the Part element contains the chapter files declared as entities in the first example:

```
<!DOCTYPE book PUBLIC "-//OASIS//DTD DocBook V4.1//EN" [
<!ENTITY preface SYSTEM "preface.sgml">
<!ENTITY chapter1 SYSTEM "chapter1.sgml">
<!ENTITY chapter2 SYSTEM "chapter2.sgml">
<!ENTITY chapter3 SYSTEM "chapter3.sgml">
<!ENTITY chapter4 SYSTEM "chapter4.sgml">
<!ENTITY index SYSTEM "index.sgml">
<!ENTITY glossary SYSTEM "glossary.sgml">
<!ENTITY appendix SYSTEM "appendix.sgml">
<!ENTITY bibliography SYSTEM "bibliography.sgml">
]>
<book>
<part label="Part I: Introduction and Forward">
&preface;
</part>
<part label="Part II: Chapters">
&chapter1;
&chapter2;
&chapter3;
&chapter4;
</part>
<part label="Part III: Index and Appendices">
&index;
&glossary;
&appendix;
&bibliography;
</part>
</book>
```

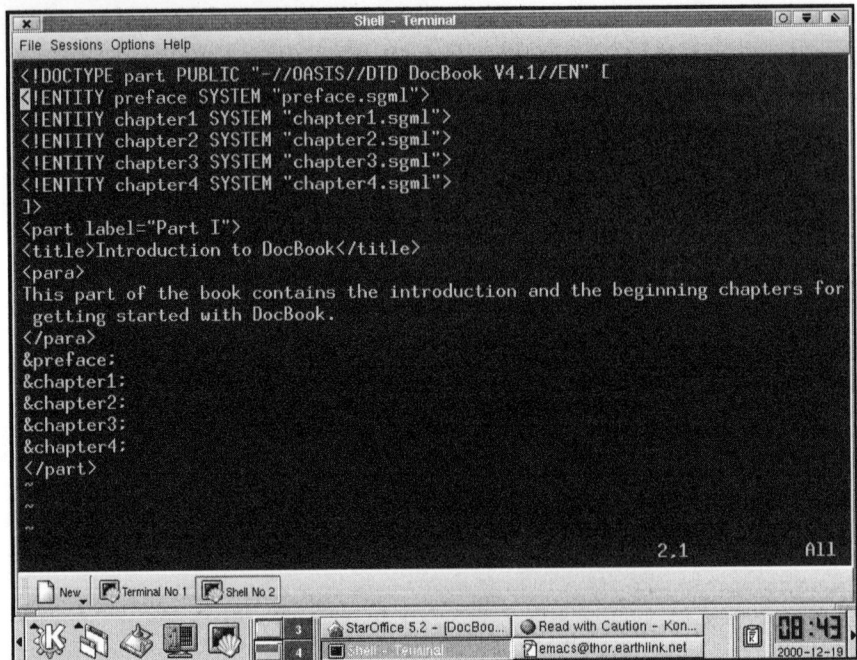

Figure 4.7 *The Part markup in Vim*

If you were working with a particularly large book with several parts containing many chapters, you could separate the Part elements into their own files the same way you did with the Book element. For example, you could have a Part element containing a preface and four chapters, like this:

```
<!DOCTYPE part PUBLIC "-//OASIS//DTD DocBook V4.1//EN" [
<!ENTITY preface SYSTEM "preface.sgml">
<!ENTITY chapter1 SYSTEM "chapter1.sgml">
<!ENTITY chapter2 SYSTEM "chapter2.sgml">
<!ENTITY chapter3 SYSTEM "chapter3.sgml">
<!ENTITY chapter4 SYSTEM "chapter4.sgml">
]>
<part label="Part I">
<title>Introduction to DocBook</title>
<para>
This part of the book contains the introduction and the beginning chapters for getting started with DocBook.
```

```
</para>
&preface;
&chapter1;
&chapter2;
&chapter3;
&chapter4;
</part>
```

If you were to break up the book like this, you would have a Book document that would look something like the following:

```
<!DOCTYPE book PUBLIC "-//OASIS//DTD DocBook V4.1//EN" [
<!ENTITY part1 SYSTEM "part1.sgml">
<!ENTITY part2 SYSTEM "part2.sgml">
<!ENTITY part3 SYSTEM "part3.sgml">
<!ENTITY part4 SYSTEM "part4.sgml">
]>
<book>
&part1;
&part2;
&part3;
&part4;
</book>
```

You may or may not want to divide your book into separate parts, depending on the complexity of the book and the number of chapters involved. Remember, it's not necessary to use the Part element for a Book to be valid. It's mainly for the benefit of the reader in terms of structure to have a book broken down into parts, and possibly more convenient for the author and editors.

Declaring and Working with Chapters

The next element I'll cover is the Chapter element. Chapters are straightforward. Because I covered making chapters their own files, I will explain declaring a Chapter document type and show an example of a short chapter. Note that there is no length requirement for a chapter. It can be one page long, one hundred pages, or a thousand. However, it might be in the best interest of the readers (and your sanity) to keep each chapter short and sweet. Anything longer than fifty pages can probably be divided into smaller, more easily digested chunks.

NOTE

My personal rule of thumb is that if you can't read a chapter all the way through in the time it takes to listen to "Sgt. Pepper's Lonely Heart's Club Band," it's too long. I'm referring to the Beatles' classic album, not the horrible abomination wrought upon the world by the Bee Gees in the late 70s. Some things just never should have been done, and most of them occurred in the 70s.

Here's a sample Chapter declaration. The name of the sample chapter file will be chapter1.sgml, or chapter1.xml if you're working with DocBook XML.

```
<!DOCTYPE chapter SYSTEM "chapter1.sgml" PUBLIC "-//OASIS//
DTD DocBook V3.1//EN">
<chapter>
...
</chapter>
```

To declare an XML chapter, use the following declaration. Note that it is much the same as the SGML declaration but includes the XML statement first and has both a public and system identifier. If you've forgotten the difference between a public and system identifier, you might want to skim Chapter 1 again or check the glossary.

```
<?xml version="1.0"?>
<!DOCTYPE chapter PUBLIC "-//OASIS//DTD DocBook XML V4.1//EN"
"file:///usr/share/xml/docbook/4.1/docbookx.dtd">
<chapter>
...
</chapter>
```

A Chapter element does not contain any text itself. Actual content is contained within Para elements, which are usually nested within one of the Sect1 through Sect5 elements (I'll cover these shortly).

The ChapterInfo Element

You might want to include some meta information about the chapter, such as who wrote it, keywords describing the content of the chapter, or maybe an abstract. The ChapterInfo element replaces the much overworked DocInfo element from DocBook version 3.x. If you're converting an older document from DocBook 3.x to 4.x, you replace any instance of the DocInfo element describing a chapter with the ChapterInfo element.

Book Structure Elements

I'll be talking a lot about elements that aren't so much concerned with the content of a DocBook document as the structure. I've already touched on a few of them; the `Chapter` element and the `Book` element are structural in nature. However, the `Sect` elements that I'll be covering in a bit are solely concerned with the structure of the documents.

Working with Navigational Elements

Why think about structure, other than the reasons already mentioned in this chapter? Well, DocBook documents derive their formatting from stylesheets, which format each element of a document according to its structure or content. For example, the `Title` element contained within a `Sect1` element is probably going to be formatted differently than a `Title` element contained within the `Sect2` or `Sect5` elements.

These elements become navigational elements when the document is rendered for publication. In a printed book, the titles are in the table of contents as section headers; in HTML the elements become navigational elements quite literally. You can click on them and jump straight to the section they describe. It's important to pay close attention to structure so that at this point readers can navigate your document easily and find the information for which they're looking.

Working with Sections

I have already mentioned quite a few times that DocBook is very concerned with the structure of a document. Nowhere is this more evident than in the number of elements dedicated to the hierarchy of sections in a document. DocBook has seven, yes, seven elements that are concerned with sections of a document. Five of these elements have been briefly touched on already, the `Sect1` through `Sect5` elements. DocBook also has a `SimpleSect` element and a `Section` element that do not have specific levels.

This is a list of all the section elements, including the informational elements:

- `Sect1`
- `Sect1Info`
- `Sect2`
- `Sect2Info`

- Sect3
- Sect3Info
- Sect4
- Sect4Info
- Sect5
- Sect5Info
- SimpleSect
- Section
- BridgeHead

The Sect1Info through Sect5Info elements contain meta information about the section in which they are located. For instance, if you want to include meta information about part of a DocBook document that is contained within a Sect1 element, you use the Sect1Info element. The Sect1Info element cannot be used in any of the other sections and replaces the DocInfo element in older DocBook documents. It might also bear mentioning that the Sect1Info element contains meta information only about the Sect1 in which it is contained, not all Sect1 elements throughout a document.

The SimpleSect element is a section element that contains no subsections, although it may be a subsection of another Sect element. For instance, the following example would be valid:

```
<sect1>
<title>Example Section</title>
<para>
This is an example of a Sect1 element containing a SimpleSect element.
</para>
<simplesect>
<title>SimpleSect Title</title>
<para>
The SimpleSect element may contain a Title element and a Para element,
but it may not contain another Sect element.
</para>
</simplesect>
</sect1>
```

However, if another section element was nested within the SimpleSect element, it would not be valid. For a full list of valid child elements for the SimpleSect element, consult Appendix B.

A chapter or another document may contain multiple sect1 elements, which may also contain multiple sect2 elements, which may contain sect3 elements, and so on. However, DocBook is strict about maintaining the hierarchy of sect elements. You may not skip sect elements. For example, it is not valid to nest a sect3 element in a sect1 element directly. The following is a valid example of the hierarchy of sect elements, including the simplesect element and section element (see Figure 4.8):

```
<chapter>
<section>
<para>
You can include a Section element in a Chapter element but not within any
of the Sect1 through Sect5 elements or the SimpleSect element.
</para>
<sect1>
<para>
This is a Sect1 element.
</para>
<sect2>
<para>
This is a Sect2 element.
</para>
<simplesect>
<para>
This is a SimpleSect element, which can be placed under any of the Sect
elements, but not the Section element. Note that you have to close the
SimpleSect element before the next element.
<para>
</simplesect>
<sect3>
<para>
This is a Sect3 element.
</para>
</sect3>
<sect3>
<para>
This is another Sect3 element, which also contains a Sect4 and Sect5 ele-
ment. Note that we do not close this element until after the Sect4 and
Sect5 elements are closed, but don't forget to close the Para element.
</para>
```

```
<sect4>
<para>
This is a Sect4 element.
</para>
<sect5>
<para>
This is a Sect5 element, the low element on the totem pole.
</para>
</sect5>
</sect4>
</sect3>
</sect2>
</sect1>
</chapter>
```

When working with Sect elements, you have to be very careful to nest them properly. This means that the closing tags should appear in reverse order, from Sect5 (if you have one) to Sect1.

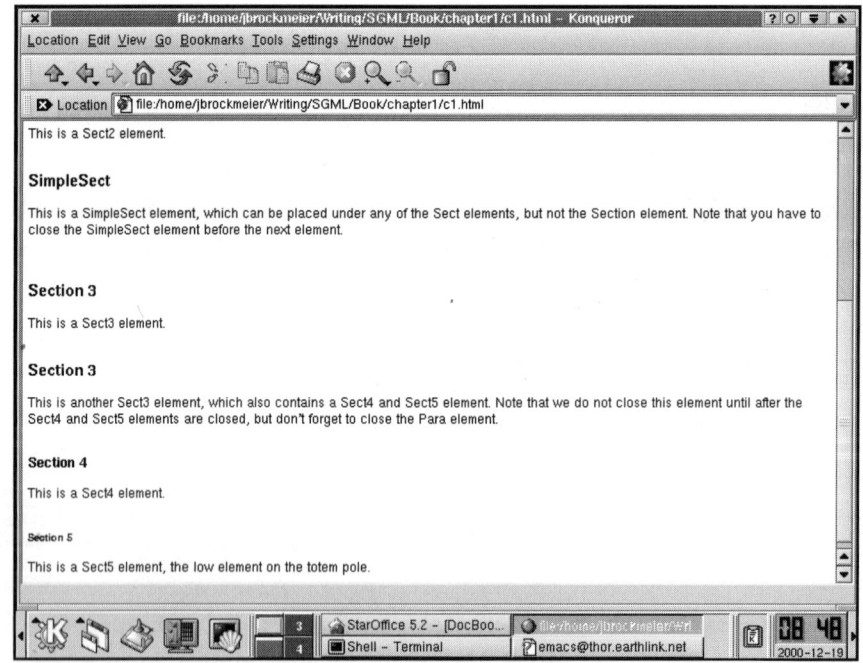

Figure 4.8 *A plethora of sections output to HTML*

If you have a chapter with many Sect elements, it's very easy to forget to close one or neglect to nest them properly unless you're using an editor with syntax highlighting, such as Vim or Emacs. For more on Emacs and Vim, see Chapter 8, "Using Emacs," and Chapter 9, "Using Vim."

Reference Pages

With some books, you might want to include reference pages in the appendixes or maybe even in the chapters themselves. The Reference element was originally designed to handle UNIX-type manpages but has evolved somewhat. Figure 4.9 shows what a manpage looks like, in case you haven't seen one before.

Buzzword

Manpage is short for *manual page*, basically an online help file that existed in UNIX long before anyone thought of including online help with PC operating systems.

A Reference element can occur only within a Book or Part element, much like a Chapter element. Actually, you can view the Reference element as a specialized type of Chapter element. Here's a simple Reference element with its child elements; the output is shown in Figure 4.10:

```
<!DOCTYPE reference book PUBLIC "-//OASIS//DTD DocBook V4.1//EN">
<reference>
<title>A Short DocBook Reference</title>
<refentry>
<title>Book Element</title>
<refsect1>
<para>
The DocBook Book element is an element that encloses all of the elements
or components that make up a book.
</para>
</refsect1>
</refentry>
<refentry>
<title>Chapter Element</title>
<refsect1>
<para>
The DocBook Chapter element contains the elements or components that make
up a chapter.
</para>
</refsect1>
</refentry>
</reference>
```

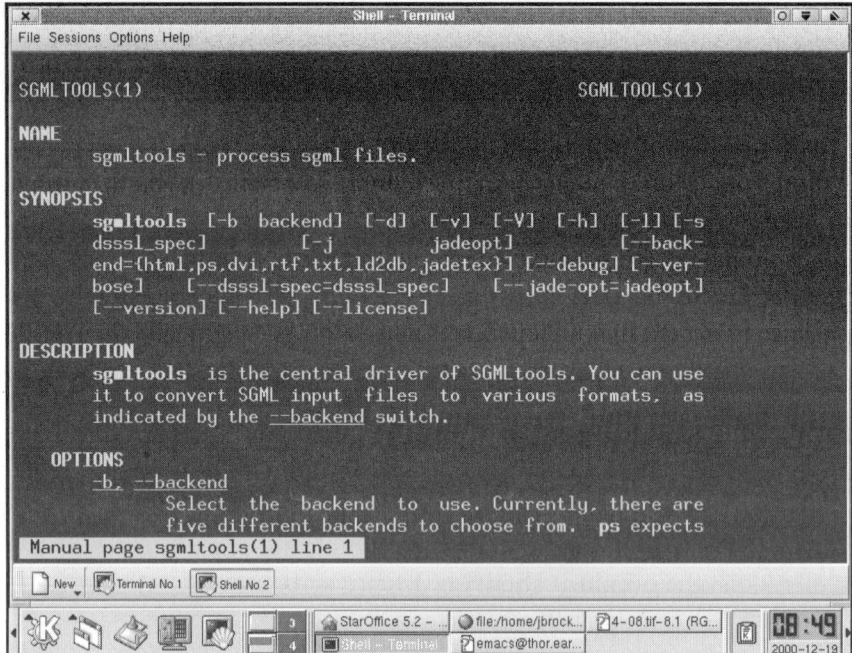

Figure 4.9 *A man page viewed in an xterm*

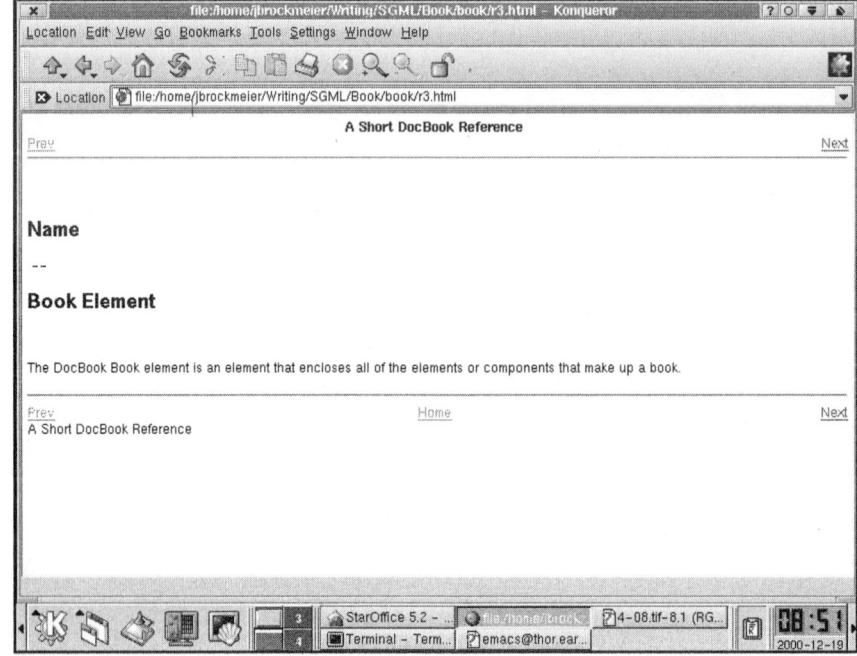

Figure 4.10 *Reference output*

The `Reference` element contains the `RefEntry` and `RefSect1` elements, which contain the actual contents of the reference. The `RefSect1` element is confusing because its name implies that other `RefSect` elements exist. However, that is not the case; `RefSect1` is the only reference section level. I'm not sure why the DocBook committee chose to name it in that manner.

If you are creating a technical reference or something similar, you will find the `Reference` element and its children to be quite useful.

Creating an Index

Indexing a document is a big deal. In the publishing industry there are folks who make a living doing nothing but indexing documents. It's an actual science, or as some would have it, an art.

Even the book that you hold in your hands now was professionally indexed. Although DocBook contains many tools that help automate the process of producing and publishing a book, nothing compares to the ability of a real live human being to make editorial decisions. The bean counters might have wished to automate one more job, but DocBook parsers just aren't savvy enough to do a good job of indexing a book thoroughly and intelligently.

NOTE

You can include an `Index` element in a `Chapter`, an `Article`, or under several other elements. However, if you're developing an index for an entire book, it might be best to develop it as its own document and include it as shown in the first example in this chapter.

The following example shows a simple index with two entries, to give the feel of the markup for the `Index` element. The index is developed as its own document in this example, even though you would probably include a two-entry index within another document normally.

```
<!DOCTYPE index PUBLIC "-//OASIS//DTD DocBook V4.1//EN">
<index>
<indexinfo>
<editor>
<firstname>P.K.</firstname>
<surname>Une</surname>
</editor>
```

```
<title>Sample Index</title>
<indexentry>
<primaryie>Index 100-101, 201</primaryie>
<secondaryie>elements, 200</secondaryie>
<secondaryie>keywords, 203</secondaryie>
<seealso>DocBook Elements</seealso>
</indexentry>
<indexentry>
<primaryie>IndexEntry 102, 200</primaryie>
<secondaryie>elements, 200</secondaryie>
</indexentry>
</index>
```

This probably looks intimidating at first. Many elements are bouncing around here, so I will break it down a bit at a time.

All the index information is contained within the `Index` element itself. The next element is the `IndexInfo` element, which is similar to the other info elements available in DocBook 4.x.

NOTE

Before DocBook 4.x, the `DocInfo` element was the catchall element for meta information about a component of a DocBook document. In version 4.x, `DocInfo` has been replaced with more specific elements that provide meta information about specific components of a DocBook document. The new elements include `AppendixInfo`, `ArticleInfo`, `Bibliography-Info`, `ChapterInfo`, and so on. See Appendix B for the full list of new elements. If you are converting a DocBook 3.x document to 4.x, you must replace `DocInfo` elements with more specific elements.

The `IndexInfo` element is optional, but it is probably a good idea to include all the information you have available, for the benefit of the reader and to give credit to the indexer as well. I used the `Editor` element for the name of a fictitious indexer. Unfortunately, DocBook does not have an indexer element at this time.

The next element is the `Title` element, which you've used quite a few times in other contexts, so it should be familiar. The syntax for the `Title` element is the same here as in the other examples covered so far. It's probably a good idea to include a simple title with your index, at least *Index* or something similar.

The actual information for each entry in the index is contained in the appropriately named `IndexEntry` element. The first index reference is contained within the `PrimaryIE` element. Usually, there is only one `PrimaryIE` element in each `IndexEntry` element, but it is possible to include more than one. The `SecondaryIE` element contains information about less relevant entries in the text concerning the `IndexEntry`. As you can see, it's also possible to have multiple instances of that element within an `IndexEntry` element.

Each `PrimaryIE`, `SecondaryIE`, and `TertiaryIE` contains the terms and page numbers for that `IndexEntry`. Figure 4.11 is an example of an index generated by SGMLtools in HTML.

However, marking up text by hand probably seems like very difficult work. The good news is that it's possible to automate generating an index in DocBook if you use the proper markup when creating your document, and if your parser and rendering programs support doing so.

The elements used to generate an index automatically are different from the elements used to do so by hand. If you want to generate the index from markup placed in the text rather than create an index from scratch, you use the `IndexTerm` element.

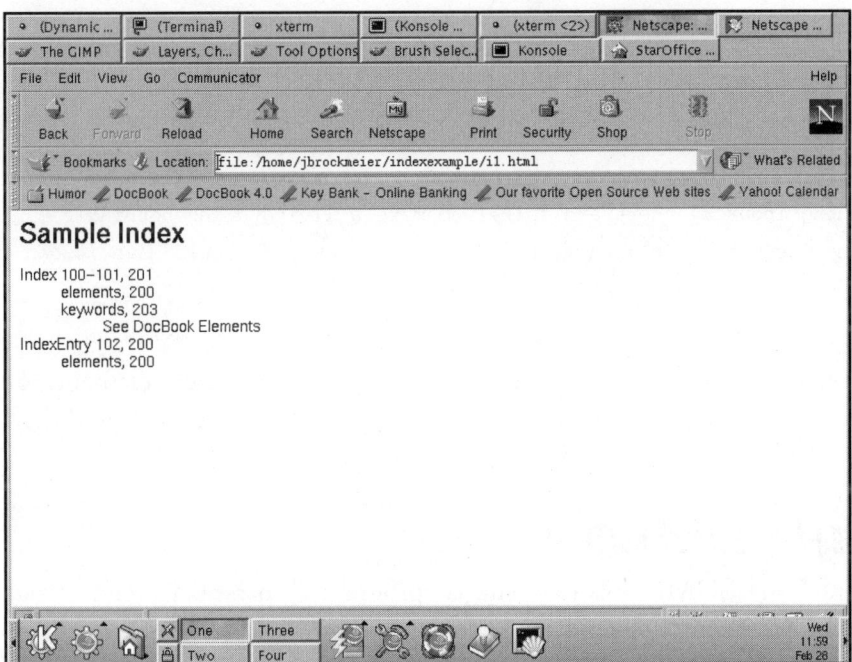

Figure 4.11 *The index rendered in HTML*

The simplest way of using the `IndexTerm` element is to place it in the section of text you'd like indexed. However, the `IndexTerm` doesn't quite work as you might expect. Instead of your simply enclosing a term used in the text with the `IndexTerm` element, the `IndexTerm` element is text that is *not* processed and rendered with the rest of the text. That is to say that the output of your document will not contain the `IndexTerm` information.

Instead, you add the `IndexTerm` markup to existing text. This example shows how to add an `IndexTerm` entry in a paragraph about DocBook.

> Even though this method of indexing is easier, you will probably want to have a professional indexer go through the text and do the indexing, or you should at least buy a book on indexing and read through it to get more background on indexing.

```
<sect2>
<title>Indexes in DocBook</title>
<para>
<indexterm><primary>Indexing</primary><secondary>Index Element</sec-
ondary></indexterm>
Indexing a document is a big deal. In the
<indexterm>
<primary>Indexing</primary>
<secondary>Publishing</secondary>
</indexterm>
publishing industry there are folks who make a living doing nothing but
indexing documents. It's an actual science, or as some would have it, an
art.</para>
</sect2>
```

The `IndexTerm` allows for `Primary`, `Secondary`, and `Tertiary` elements, as well as the `See` and `SeeAlso` elements. For more on these elements and their use, see Appendix B.

Creating the Table of Contents

If you're using SGMLtools or a similar program to parse and render your DocBook document, you're in for a pleasant surprise—a table of contents is generated automatically when you render your document. This means no plowing through the document trying to figure out which page each section begins on and then writing a table of contents that will change if many revisions are made. Nope, it's generated on-the-fly each time you process the document to create output.

However, I'll include a brief example of a table of contents so that you can see the work you're avoiding. The elements used to create this table of contents are ToC, ToCPart, ToCchap, and ToCentry. Although this is helpful to understand, I've always found the table of contents generated on-the-fly to be good enough, as long as you include the Title element for each Sect and Chapter and similar elements.

```
<toc>
<tocpart>
<tocchap>
<tocentry pagenum="1">How to make a ToC</tocentry>
<tocentry pagenum="2">How to avoid making a ToC</tocentry>
</tochap>
</tocpart>
</toc>
```

Creating a Glossary

If you use many unfamiliar terms or jargon in your book, you should include a glossary to which readers can refer. Any technical reference worth its salt (and many other types of books) includes a glossary. The Glossary element can be contained within a Chapter element (or any of the Sect1 through Sect5 elements), the Book element, and several others. If you have several entries for a glossary, you might want to set it off in its own file, similar to the examples for the Chapter elements in this chapter.

Glossaries with more than a few entries should probably make use of the GlossDiv element, which allows the glossary to be divided into manageable divisions. Generally, I would recommend divvying up your glossary alphabetically, unless there is a more logical way to divide it.

The following example shows a DocBook glossary with two logical divisions and a few sample entries. Of course, a real glossary would be much heftier than this, but this should be sufficient to give you an idea of what the markup looks like for the Glossary element and its children. Figure 4.12 shows the glossary rendered in HTML.

```
<!DOCTYPE glossary PUBLIC "-//OASIS//DTD DocBook V4.1//EN">
<glossary>
```

```
<glossaryinfo>
<editor>
<firstname>Joe</firstname>
<othername>"Zonker"</othername>
<surname>Brockmeier</surname>
</editor>
</glossaryinfo>
<title>Really Neat Sample Glossary</title>
<para>You can include an introduction to the glossary if you like.</para>
<glossdiv>
<title>A</title>
<glossentry>
<glossterm>Abstract</glossterm>
<glossdef>
<para>The Abstract element contains information about an article, book,
or other work. An abstract is a brief summary or description of the con-
tents of a work.</para>
</glossdef>
</glossentry>
</glossdiv>
<glossdiv>
<title>B</title>
<glossentry>
<glossterm>Book</glossterm>
<glossdef>
<para>The Book element contains all the components of a DocBook
book.</para>
</glossdef>
</glossentry>
</glossdiv>
</glossary>
```

The Glossary element contains the GlossDiv, GlossEntry, GlossTerm, and GlossDef elements. Again, using the GlossDiv element is optional, depending on whether your document is large enough to be divided. The GlossEntry element starts a new entry in your glossary; the GlossTerm element contains the term being defined in this glossary entry. The GlossDef element contains the actual definition of the GlossTerm. Be sure to nest the elements properly, as shown in the preceding example, or your parser will produce a number of errors.

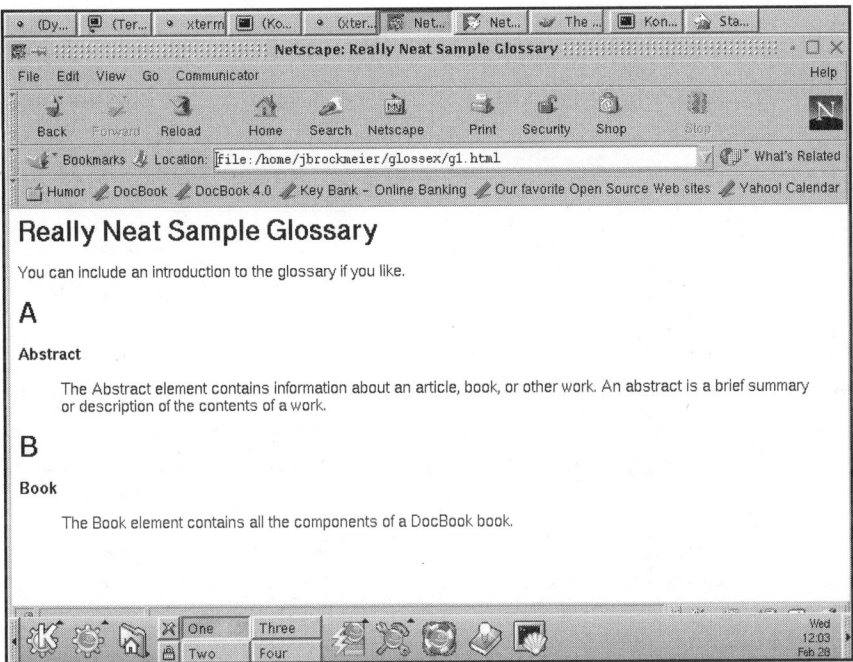

Figure 4.12 *A glossary in HTML*

The `GlossInfo` element is also optional. As with other info elements, you can include a wide range of information using the `GlossInfo` element.

Creating an Appendix

Appendixes often appear in technical and reference works and include information from the text of the book but in a distilled and more concise form.

As with this book, most of the information found in the appendixes is in the text of the book itself, although some is not. However, it can be very inconvenient having to thumb through the book's examples to find out how the `Book` element is used and the appropriate syntax. Therefore, there's an appendix dealing with all the DocBook elements. It is easy to browse and more complete than would be readable in the body of the book. How boring, for example, to have a full and complete reference of all possible permutations of the `Book` element in the text of the book, but how much more useful when collated and included as a reference in an appendix.

A DocBook book need not include an appendix to be valid, but it is useful for the reader with certain types of books. There is also no limit on or minimum of appendixes in a DocBook book. As the following example shows, the `Appendix` element is used in much the same way as the `Chapter` element. The only valid parent elements for an appendix are the `Article`, `Book`, and `Part` elements. An appendix may not be included in a chapter, for example.

```
<!DOCTYPE appendix PUBLIC "-//OASIS//DTD DocBook V4.1//EN">
<appendix>
<title>This is an Appendix.</title>
<para>Not too difficult, is it?</para>
</appendix>
```

Not much to that at all, is there. As of DocBook version 4.x, the `Appendix` element may also contain an `AppendixInfo` element if you want to include meta information about the appendix. Also, just as with the `Chapter` element, you can include a number of other elements within an appendix, including a `Sidebar`, a `Table`, an `ItemizedList`, and many others. See Appendix B for the full list of potential child elements.

NOTE

You should familiarize yourself with the appropriate child elements for each other element. Sometimes it jogs your memory to include further information about something you have forgotten. For instance, the `Sidebar` element is valid within the `Appendix` element, which might remind you to include a sidebar about something in the appendix you have forgotten or have structured differently.

Creating a Bibliography

The last major element I'm going to talk about in this chapter is the `Bibliography` element. A bibliography, if you're not familiar with one, includes information about books used for reference in writing an article or book or perhaps about books that are suggested reading.

If you've ever written college term papers, you're probably painfully familiar with bibliographies. The nice thing about the `Bibliography` element and its children is that if your stylesheet is set up to output in the proper formats, it is much easier to generate a bibliography in MLA or APA formats than in a traditional word processor. All you have to do is fill in the proper elements, and the processing program should do the rest. I'll talk more about stylesheets in Chapter 10, "Customizing DocBook."

> *MLA* stands for the *Modern Language Association*, and *APA* stands for the *American Psychological Association*. If you've never had to format a paper in one of these formats, you're quite a lucky person.

A sample bibliography would look like this:

```
<!DOCTYPE bibliography PUBLIC "-//OASIS//DTD DocBook V4.1//EN">
<bibliography>
<biblioentry>
<author>
<firstname>Theodore</firstname>
<surname>Giesel</surname>
<othername>Dr. Seuss</othername>
</author>
<title>The Lorax Strikes Back: The Unpublished Tales of Dr. Seuss</title>
<publisher>
<publishername>Random House</publishername>
</publisher>
<copyright>
<year>2001</year>
<holder>Random House</holder>
</biblioentry>
</bibliography>
```

It's all straightforward. All the elements included in the Bibliography element are elements you've already encountered in other elements and other uses. If you are going to try to output an MLA or APA format bibliography, you must also include the Address and City elements under the Publisher element. Obviously, if the book has multiple authors and editors, you can add the proper markup for those as well.

Summary

In this chapter you've looked extensively at elements used in making a DocBook book. A DocBook book can be simple and include very few elements, or it can be a complex affair with multiple files, glossaries, appendixes, reference pages, prefaces, and many other sorts of components. The larger and more complex the project the more you can make use of DocBook's unique features to make the process easier. Although writing a book is never easy (at least I've never heard it described as being easy), it can be less difficult if you use the tools at hand.

If you want to delve further into any of the elements in this chapter, look them up in Appendix B. You will find any information you want on any element.

Very few of the elements used in this chapter are complex. The Index elements can be hairy, but for the most part, the elements used in DocBook are simple on their own. When you have a larger document, it becomes complicated because of the size of the project but not necessarily because a DocBook document or its elements are inherently complex.

In the next chapter, you will look at making DocBook documents ready to be published online, including DocBook books.

Chapter 5: Making Online Documents

Creating Online Documentation

Converting to HTML

If you plan to output HTML from DocBook, you will want to read this chapter. Here are tips and tricks for making the most of DocBook for online documents and articles. You will also learn how to clean up the automatically generated HTML with Tidy.

Creating Online Documentation

Creating documents for display online is not much different from creating documents for print where DocBook is concerned. Remember, DocBook is designed to enable the author to create a structured document that is portable and can be rendered into many formats.

However, you can do some things to make the output even better. For example, including URLs, e-mail addresses, and using the XRef tag will make your online documents more navigable and more useful.

Including Links with DocBook

One of the wonderful things about hypertext is your ability to link to other sections of a document or to other documents or sites in your text. The old days of cumbersome footnotes and references are gone. Rather than use a footnote with a pointer to a section in the back of the book that leads you to a page in another book (which you may or may not have), you can simply link to the resource, and the reader can zap straight to it.

Having said that, I will show how you can include links in your documents and make the most of DocBook's capabilities.

The elements you will be working with are

- Anchor
- CiteTitle
- Link
- OLink
- ULink
- XRef

To start, let's say that you want to do something very basic—include a link in your document to a Web site. This is almost as easy in DocBook markup as it is in HTML markup.

> You could also consider Email a link, but I will deal with that case separately.

To include a basic link to another site in your document, you use the ULink and CiteTitle elements. The ULink element contains the URI or URL. The CiteTitle element is not specifically concerned with links but with any cited title of a work—such as a book, poem, song, white paper, or Web site.

In this example, you're including a link to the official DocBook Web site. Remember, it's a good idea to include this information even if you don't plan to render your document in HTML. The information will be available if you decide to do it later, without your having to go back and re-edit the entire document, and the link will appear in the printed document as well—at least, as long as you're using the default stylesheets.

```
<para>
<ulink url="http://www.oasis-open.org/docbook/">
<citetitle>The Official DocBook Website</citetitle>
</ulink>
</para>
```

The ULink element does need to be nested within the Para element or one of its other parent elements. For a complete list of parent elements for the Ulink element, see Appendix B, "DocBook Element Reference."

The URL attribute is required to generate a working hyperlink when the document is rendered into HTML.

> Although you're mostly concerned with HTML in this chapter, because it is the dominant medium for the Web at the time of this writing, it is possible that in the future other types of output will take full advantage of hyperlinks as well. For instance, more than likely there will be stylesheets to output XHTML in the near future as more browsers support XHTML. Remember, DocBook can be used to generate just about anything, depending on the stylesheets used to generate output.

Buzzword

What, exactly, are a URL and a URI? You have probably heard the terms before and understand that they have something to do with hyperlinks on Web pages. URLs and URIs are nearly the same thing. *URL* is short for *uniform resource locator; URI* is short for *uniform resource indicator.* URLs are a subset of URIs designed to locate Web pages or other resources on the Internet by protocol, host name, and filename. You can find out more about both URIs and URLs on the Internet Engineering Task Force home page at **http://www.ietf. org/**. URIs are RFC number 1630; URLs are RFC number 1738.

Figure 5.1 shows what the ULink looks like after being rendered into HTML using the default stylesheets. However, the information is not lost in print publications. Figure 5.2 shows the same DocBook markup output to PostScript.

Obviously, you can't click on a link in a paper document and go to a Web site. However, the URL for the site is neatly printed next to the title of the site so that it can be manually entered if the reader wishes.

The ULink element can also be used for linking to files on an FTP server or to an Archie or Gopher server—it could also be used for protocols that don't even exist yet.

To give another example, maybe your document should link to an FTP server to retrieve extra documentation (see Figure 5.3). The syntax is much the same:

```
<para>
You can find supplemental documentation at this FTP site:
<ulink url="ftp://ftp.yourserver.net/documents/extra.sgml">
<citetitle>ftp://ftp.yourserver.net/documents/extra.sgml</citetitle>
</ulink>
</para>
```

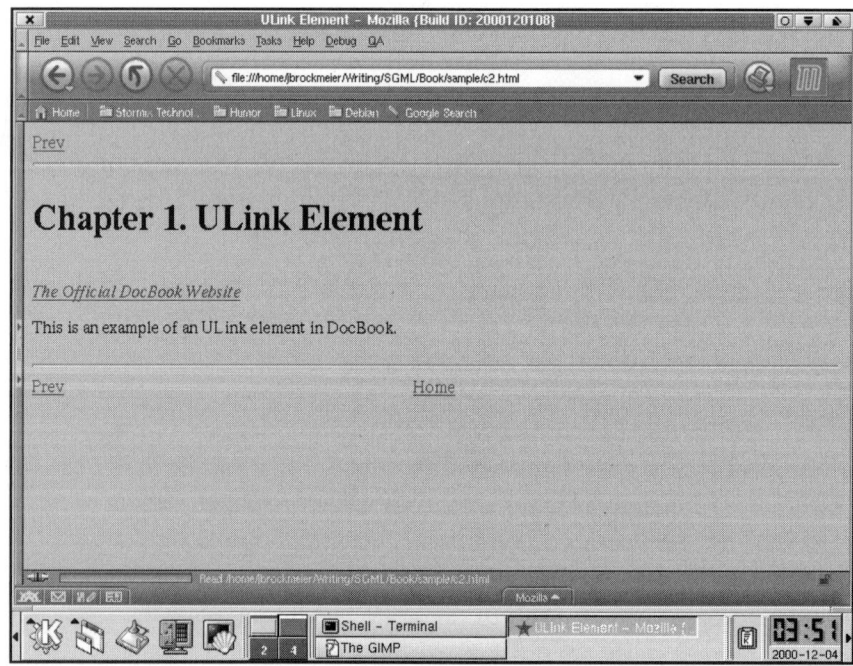

Figure 5.1 *A link from DocBook in HTML*

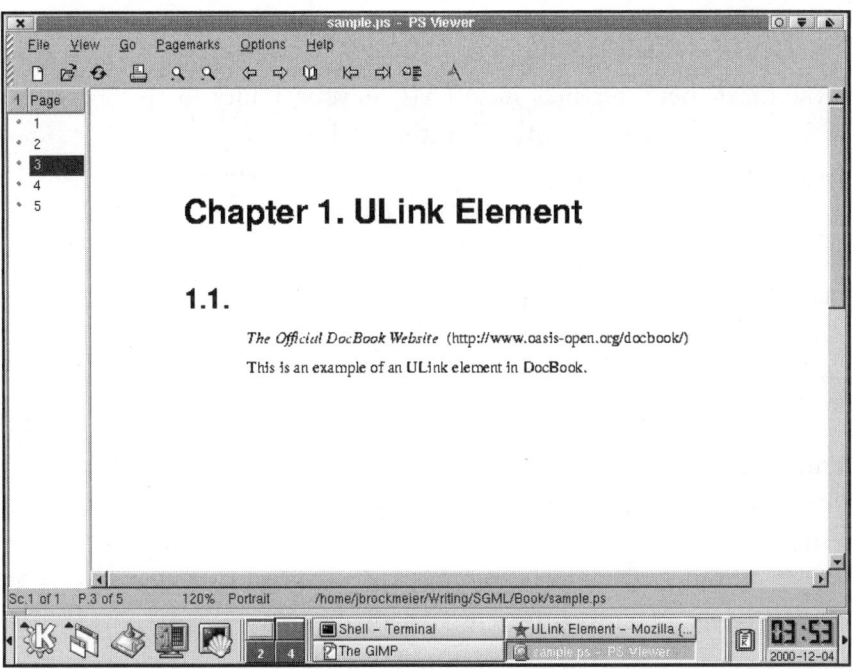

Figure 5.2 *PostScript output*

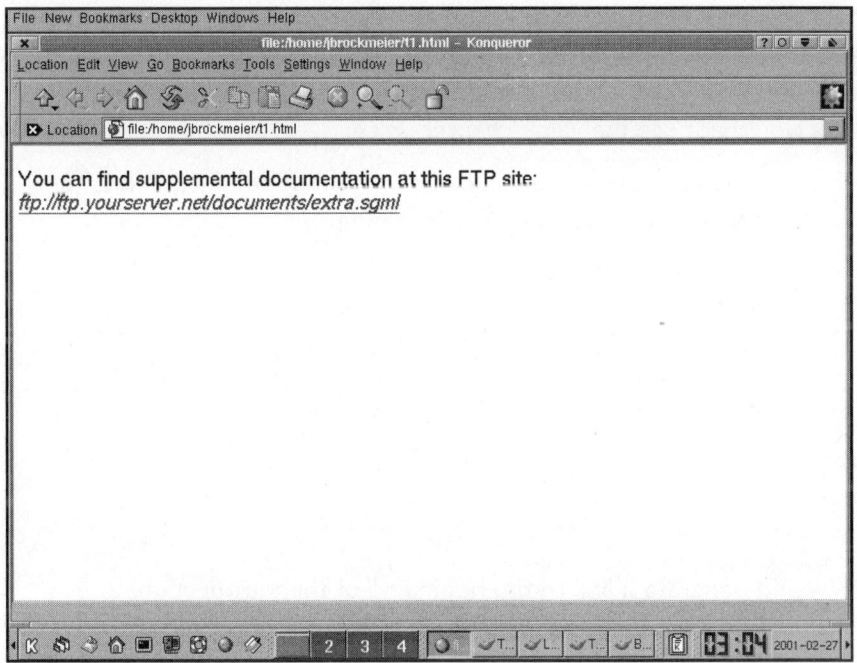

Figure 5.3 *Linking to an FTP server*

Linking within a Document

One of the most useful features in HTML is your ability to create relative links within a document to other portions of the document. DocBook markup also enables you to create links within your document to other portions of your document, but they're not as straightforward as the system used in HTML markup.

In HTML you can simply use an anchor element for both the link and the target. The XRef attribute for the Anchor element generates the link, and the Name attribute provides a target for the link. In DocBook markup, you can use several elements to generate internal links.

The elements used for links within a document are Anchor, Link, and XRef. XRef is capable of doing more than just generating a link to other text, however. With the XRef element, you can also pull text from other DocBook elements, such as the Title attribute from the Chapter element. The XRef element uses the ID attribute from other elements.

The Anchor element is used to provide a reference point for the XRef element when another element with an ID attribute to link to does not exist.

Remember, when using an ID attribute, it must be unique within the document. For instance, you can use *chapter2* and *chapter3* as values for the ID attribute for two consecutive chapters, preferably Chapters 2 and 3, but you would not use the value *chapter* twice.

Although the ID attribute must be unique, there can be multiple pointers to one ID—for example, if you have this markup:

```
<chapter id="introduction">
<title>Introduction</title>
</chapter>
```

You can have this markup at the end of every other chapter:

```
<para>
<xref linkend="introduction">
</para>
```

which would generate a link to the beginning of the Introduction.

How XRef Works

XRef pulls the information needed from the ID attribute and the Title element, or if the element does not contain a child element, it uses the XRefLabel attribute. If an element does not support the Title child element or the XRefLabel attribute, you must use the separate Anchor element, which can be located virtually anywhere within a document, as long as it is nested within one of its parent elements.

Is your head swimming from all the jargon? Are child and parent elements and attributes confusing you? If you skipped the Introduction, now might be a good time to backtrack and skim through it. You can also check out Appendix A, "DocBook Glossary," if you are just a little fuzzy on the terms.

If you do feel confused, don't think that you're alone: DocBook wasn't created with user-friendliness in mind. The concepts behind DocBook aren't impossible to get a handle on, but it might help to take a breather occasionally and absorb what you've covered.

DocBook markup is literally another language, admittedly a limited one based on English but still a foreign tongue. Everyone knows that it takes patience and time to pick up a foreign language; the same goes for Doc-Book. The downside to DocBook, compared with real languages, is that there's nowhere you can go to immerse yourself in the spoken language, and there's no native cuisine for DocBook either—unless you count native geek foods such as pizza, Chinese takeout, and any caffeinated beverage.

NOTE

To use XRef to link to a section within your document, you do something like the following:

```
<sect1 id="xref">
      <title>Using XRef</title>
...
</sect1>
<xref linkend="xref">
```

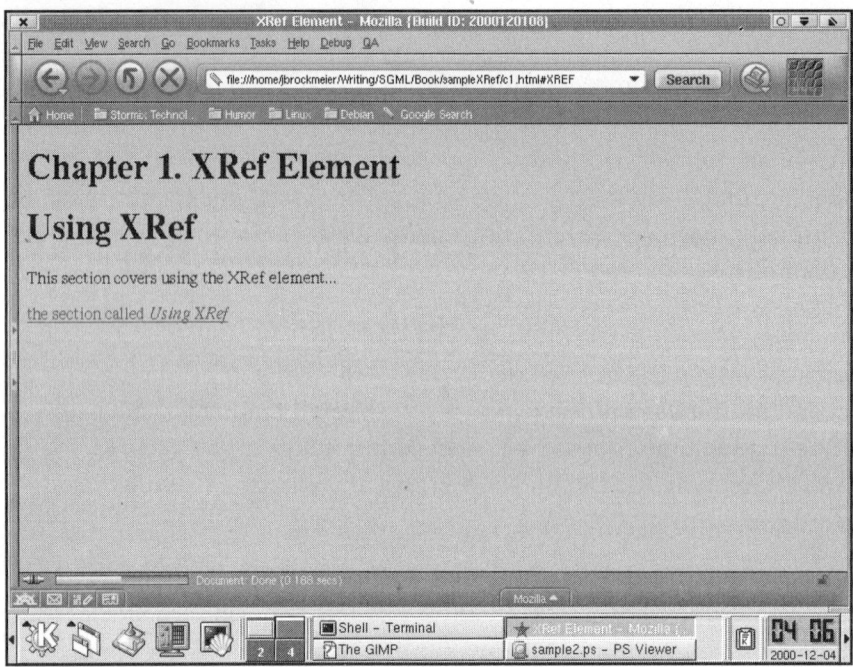

Figure 5.4 *An XRef link*

The LinkEnd attribute value xref that is called by the XRef element will correspond to the ID attribute value xref when the document is parsed. If you are creating an HTML document, you will get output like that shown in Figure 5.4.

Note that the XRef element is an empty element. If you were using the Doc-Book XML DTD, you would use this markup for the XRef element instead:

```
<xref linkend="xref"/>
```

The only difference in the markup is the closing / character. However, it will cause errors if the / character is missing.

If you're rendering your document in PostScript, RTF, or other print formats, your markup will look like that shown in Figure 5.5.

Using the Anchor Element

Note that unlike a link in HTML, you do not have to supply the descriptive text for the link—the text is derived from the Title element instead. If you're using the Anchor element, you supply the descriptive text for the link with the XRefLabel attribute.

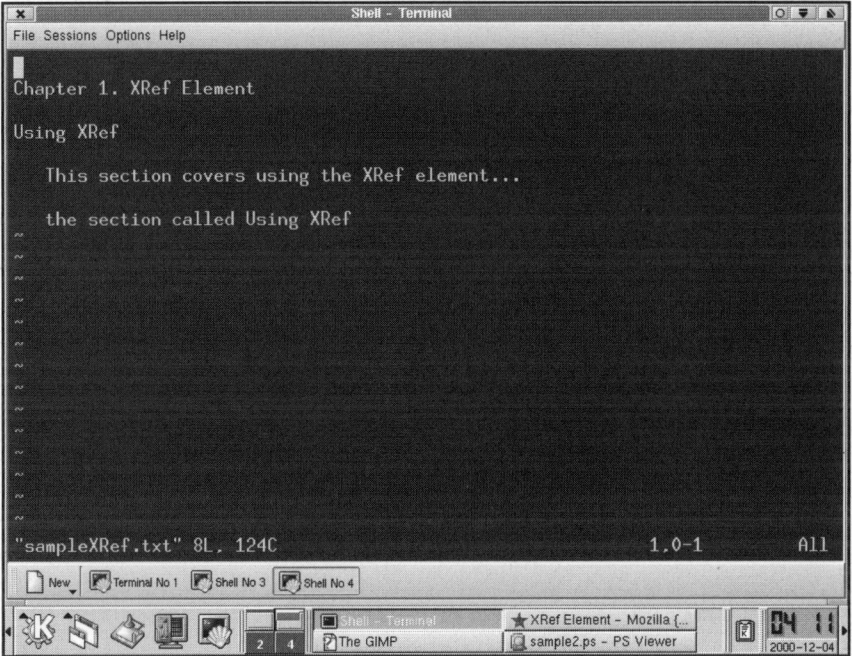

Figure 5.5 XRef *output in static text*

> Note that the Anchor element in DocBook markup (<anchor>) and the Anchor element in HTML (<a>) are completely different and do not use the same syntax. Although they have the same purpose, generating hyperlinks and references, they do not bear much other relation.

To use the Anchor element, use the following syntax:

```
<para>
This is an example of the <anchor id="xref.example" xreflabel="XRef
Example"> XRef and Anchor elements.
</para>
```

The Anchor element is also an empty element. If used with the XML DTD, you must be sure to close the element with the / character, like this:

```
<anchor id="xref.example" xreflabel="XRef Example"/>
```

You might have noticed another trick I introduced with the ID attribute in the example. Earlier, you started a Sect1 element with the ID attribute value xref, which you can't use again in the document because if you do, it will cause parsing problems.

However, because you're probably writing an entire section about the XRef element, you want to use ID values that relate to the topic they describe—just as you would use descriptive variable names when programming, you want to use descriptive names in your ID attribute values.

Because I couldn't reuse xref, I used xref.example, which is perfectly valid because it is also unique within the document. If you're writing an entire section on a particular topic, I would suggest using a simple descriptor like xref for the ID value of the top-level of the document hierarchy and then using derivatives of that value for the rest of the section. This helps as your documents become more and more complex, if you use values that are easy to remember and flow logically. I would not recommend simply using chapter or section numbers or any type of numbering scheme. If you become dependent on a numbering scheme, you will find yourself redoing a lot of markup when you add an extra section or otherwise revise the document. Remember that the ID attribute's values are not seen within the finished documents, so you can be relatively verbose and descriptive with your ID values.

Using the Link Element

The Link element behaves more like the Anchor element from HTML markup than the other linking elements used in DocBook. The Link element is used in a similar fashion to the XRef element, but it is not an empty element. This can be useful if you want to link to something with a Title element but do not want to use that title for the link text.

The syntax of the Link element is as follows:

```
<sect2 id="link">
<title>Using Link Elements</title>
<para>
Some Web sites, <link linkend="website">like this one</link>, are examples
of excellent Web design.
</para>
</sect2>
<sect2 id="website">
<title>Themes.org</title>
<para>
```

```
<ulink
url="http://www.themes.org/"><citetitle>Themes.org</citetitle></ulink> is
one of my favorite sites. You should visit there soon!
</para>
</sect2>
```

The `Link` element sends the user to the beginning of the section with the `ID` value of `website`. As with the `XRef` element, you can also use the `Anchor` element in conjunction with the `Link` element. If you wanted to link directly to the content of the `ULink` element, you could give the `ULink` element an `ID` attribute value and link to that, like this:

```
<sect2 id="link">
<title>Using Link Elements</title>
<para>
Some Web sites, <link linkend="website.direct">like this one</link>, are
examples of excellent Web design.
</para>
</sect2>
<sect2 id="website">
<title>Themes.org</title>
<para>
<ulink url="http://www.themes.org/"
id="website.direct"><citetitle>Themes.org</citetitle></ulink> is one of my
favorite sites. You should visit there soon!
</para>
</sect2>
```

Note that the only change necessary is to give the `ULink` element its own `ID` attribute value of `website.direct` and change the `Link` element's `LinkEnd` attribute value to match it. A `Link` can have only one `LinkEnd` value, however. If you want to provide multiple targets, you must insert multiple `Link` elements or `XRef` elements.

Using OLink

I saved the best, or at least the most confusing, for last. The `OLink` element is for very special cases and probably not for typical documents.

The `OLink` element is used to link to a target indirectly. That is, the `OLink` element does not contain a direct link to a part of the document or a URL.

Instead, the OLink element contains LinkMode, LocalInfo, and TargetDocEnt attributes that help it return a value. The OLink element need not always point to the same target within the document or URL. The OLink element is designed to be used with dynamic content.

The LinkMode attribute points to the ModeSpec element, which is declared in the DTD of the document. The ModeSpec element describes an application to resolve Olinks, such as a search query against a database or other dynamic values.

The LocalInfo attribute provides information to the method used by the ModeSpec element. For example, if the ModeSpec element was a SQL query against a MySQL database, the LocalInfo attribute could supply the names of the tables or fields to search, or it could contain keywords to search. The ModeSpec element could be an interface to searching Google or any of the Web-based search engines, or it could query your parts database or pass a value to a PHP script.

The TargetDocEnt attribute value contains information used to resolve the OLink.

The OLink element is beyond the scope of this chapter; it is a rarely used element, though useful in integrating DocBook with other applications. For more information on the OLink element, see Appendix B.

E-Mail

After you've completed your masterpiece and sent it into the world, you can include your e-mail address and receive the adoration and thanks from your readers via e-mail. (If you're really lonely, you can include your phone number using the Phone element, but that's another chapter.)

Seriously, though, you will usually want to include your e-mail address to get feedback on your document, updates, or error corrections. Also, you might want to include someone else's e-mail address if you're writing an article or document that contains information about others.

Whatever the reason, it's probably going to come up at some point. Including the e-mail address is easy. Just use the following syntax:

```
<para>
To send the author compliments, comments, and declarations of love and
adoration, use the following email address:
```

```
<email>jbrockmeier@earthlink.net</email>. If you have complaints or criti-
cism, I'd love to get them. Please send those to
<email>bill@microsoft.com</email>. Thanks!
</para>
```

Yup, it's that easy! I bet you were starting to think that all DocBook markup is hard, so I saved the easy one for last. Depending on the output format, the link will either be a hypertext link that opens your mail client in Netscape Communicator or Internet Explorer, or it will generate a plain-text e-mail address formatted in monospace font.

Figure 5.6 shows what you get in HTML. If you render the same markup into PostScript or RTF format, the output will look like that shown in Figure 5.7.

You could conceivably use the ULink element to generate a hyperlink with the *mailto:* syntax used by browsers to send an e-mail, but it wouldn't be as smooth, and the output in plain text would contain extraneous information.

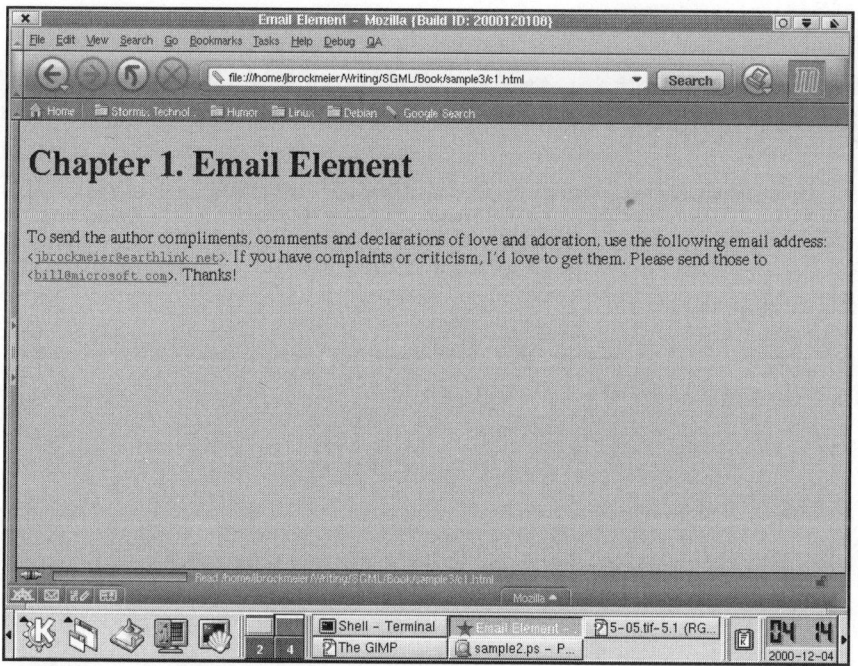

Figure 5.6 *Rendering an HTML document with an e-mail address*

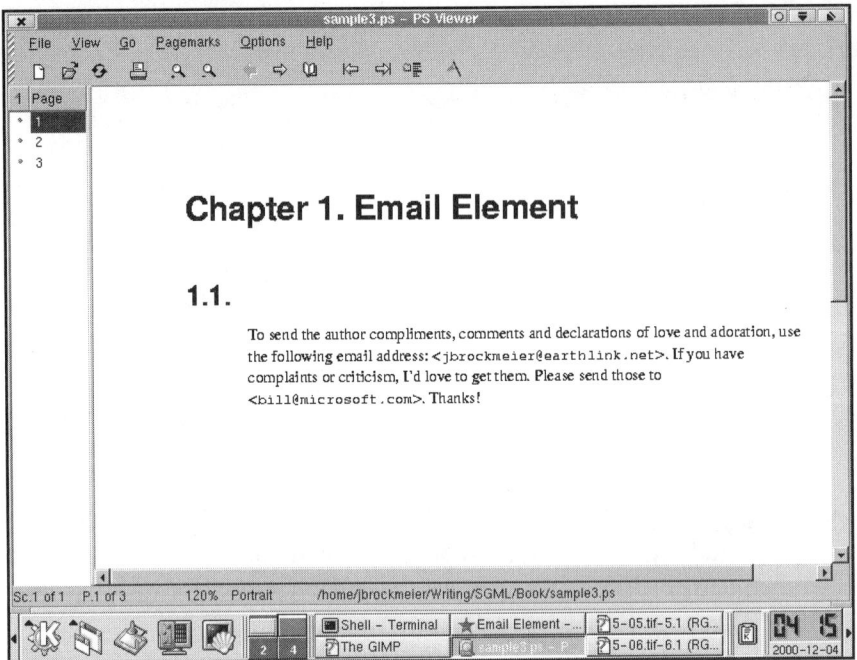

Figure 5.7 *PostScript output*

Converting to HTML

Converting your document to HTML is more thoroughly covered in Chapter 6, "Parsing DocBook." However, I'll run through the steps quickly here because I want to share with you some finishing touches that pertain to HTML.

If you're using SGMLtools or SGMLtools-lite to output HTML from a DocBook document, use the following syntax:

```
sgmltools -b html document.sgml
```

or for XML documents, use

```
sgmltools -b html document.xml
```

If no problems, or at least no serious problems, occur with the markup in your document, you will have one or more files generated by SGMLTools.

> If you have a document with multiple chapters and such, SGMLtools will generate one main page with an index of links to the various chapters and links for navigation at the top and bottom of each page.

As you can see from Figure 5.8, the standard HTML output from SGML-Tools is clean, a little plain but serviceable. You're not looking for flashy pages anyway because you're probably more concerned with the substance and structure of the document than presentation.

The HTML output by SGMLTools is perfectly valid, at least, according to any Web browser I've ever used to view it. However, the code generated by SGMLTools is a bit on the homely side, to say the least. Figure 5.9 shows an example of the output from SGMLtools. As you can see, it's rough. It also relies heavily on formatting tags such as the Font element and other elements now deprecated by the World Wide Web Consortium (W3C).

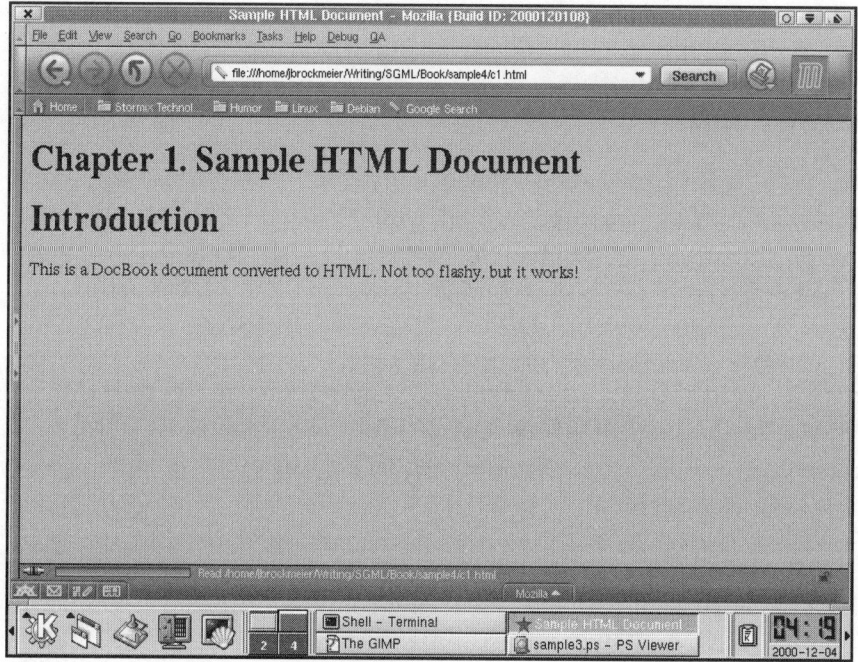

Figure 5.8 *DocBook output to HTML*

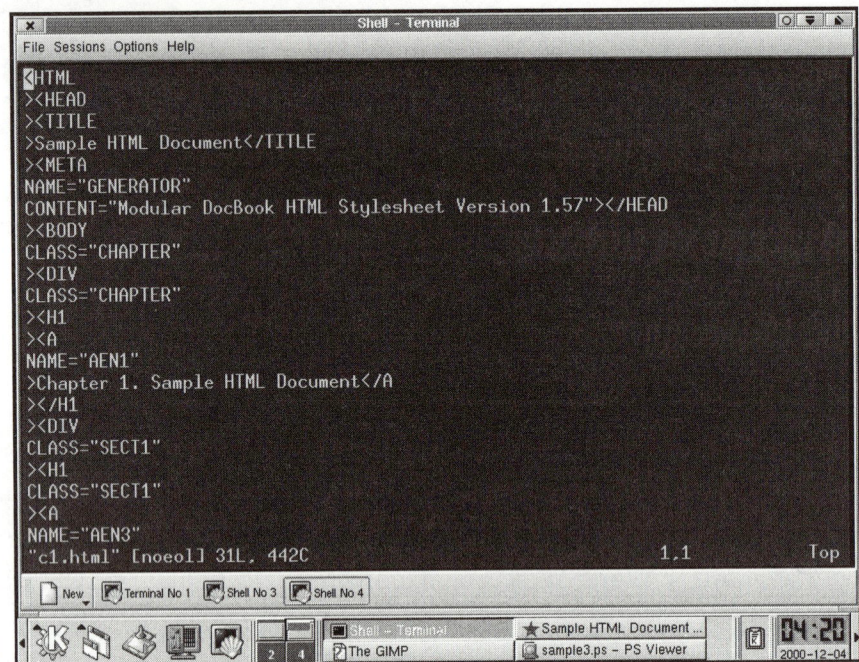

Figure 5.9 *Code generated by SGMLTools*

Using HTML Tidy

HTML Tidy is an application provided by the W3C that, well, tidies HTML. HTML Tidy was not written with DocBook HTML output in mind but works amazingly well with it. Actually, HTML Tidy was developed to fix small errors in HTML syntax and to make HTML files easier to read.

> If you're a word processor user who likes to output documents to HTML, run HTML Tidy on them. It will do wonders for the output. Most HTML rendered by word processors is indescribably ugly, even if it renders properly in a Web browser.

HTML Tidy is available for just about any computing platform known to man. Tidy supports Windows (all flavors), the MacOS, Linux, UNIX, BeOS, Solaris, and many more. If you're using it to produce DocBook, odds are that HTML Tidy will run on it. Even better, the price is right—there's no license fee for HTML Tidy. It's provided to help make the World (Wide Web) a better place.

You can download the appropriate version of HTML Tidy from this site, **http://www.w3.org/People/Raggett/tidy/**. Just look for the appropriate file for your operating system. If you're using Linux, Windows, or the MacOS, there are versions on the book's CD-ROM for you. You can also download source code, if you're so inclined.

Now that you have HTML Tidy, I will give an example of how to use it. To use Tidy from the command line, use the following command to run Tidy on the index.html file and write any errors to a file:

```
tidy -f errs.txt -m index.html
```

Unless there are terrible errors in your file, Tidy will run and update the index.html file. Tidy will clean up the syntax, reduce extraneous white space, and add cascading stylesheets to help get rid of deprecated elements.

In Figure 5.10, you can see your file before HTML Tidy. Figure 5.11 shows your file after running HTML Tidy.

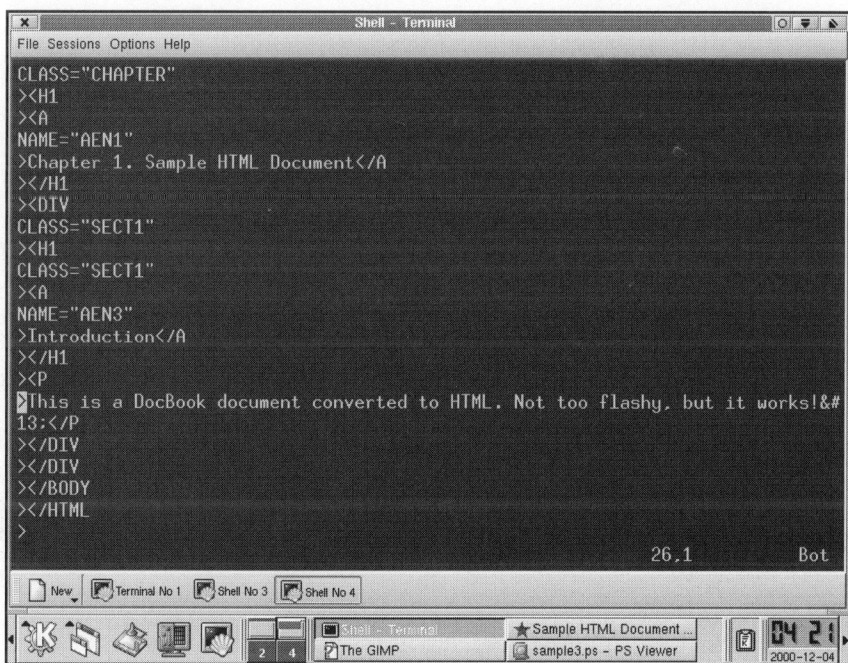

Figure 5.10 *An ugly HTML file*

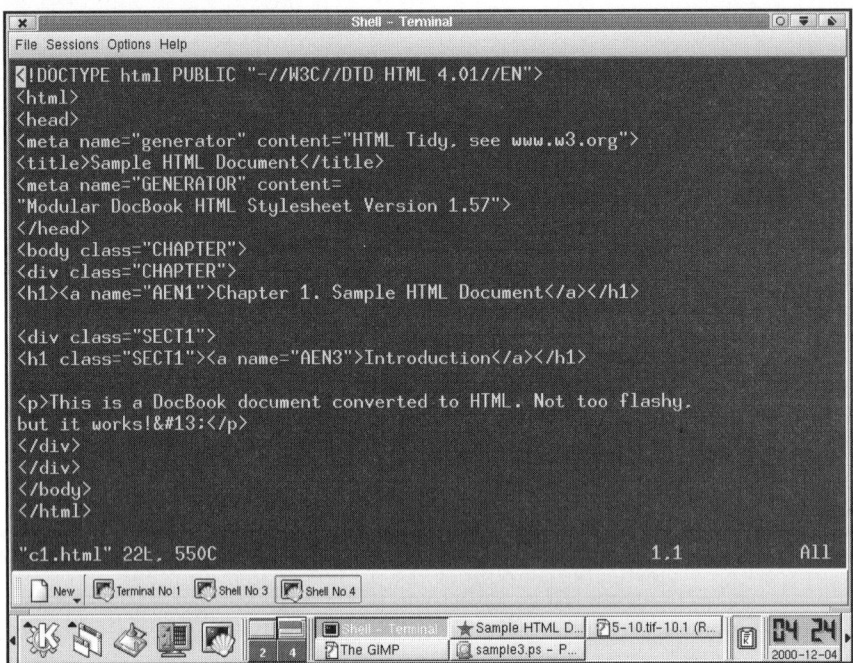

```
!DOCTYPE html PUBLIC "-//W3C//DTD HTML 4.01//EN">
<html>
<head>
<meta name="generator" content="HTML Tidy, see www.w3.org">
<title>Sample HTML Document</title>
<meta name="GENERATOR" content=
"Modular DocBook HTML Stylesheet Version 1.57">
</head>
<body class="CHAPTER">
<div class="CHAPTER">
<h1><a name="AEN1">Chapter 1. Sample HTML Document</a></h1>

<div class="SECT1">
<h1 class="SECT1"><a name="AEN3">Introduction</a></h1>

<p>This is a DocBook document converted to HTML. Not too flashy,
but it works!&#13;</p>
</div>
</div>
</body>
</html>
```

Figure 5.11 *A pretty HTML file*

If you want to clean up the file more and add some tabbed indenting, you can use the following command:

```
tidy -m index.html -i -clean
```

This takes the index.html file, indents it to make it more easily readable, and modifies it in place—in other words, the file is written out to index.html. I also prefer to throw the -o option in there, which strips optional end tags such as the paragraph end tag. Figure 5.12 shows output from HTML Tidy, indented to make the code easier to read.

HTML Tidy is not required, but it certainly makes your HTML output much cleaner.

Integrating Images

Chapter 3, "Using Images," covers in great depth how to include images in your document, so I won't revisit old territory. However, it bears repeating that the only image types consistent with outputting HTML are GIF, JPEG,

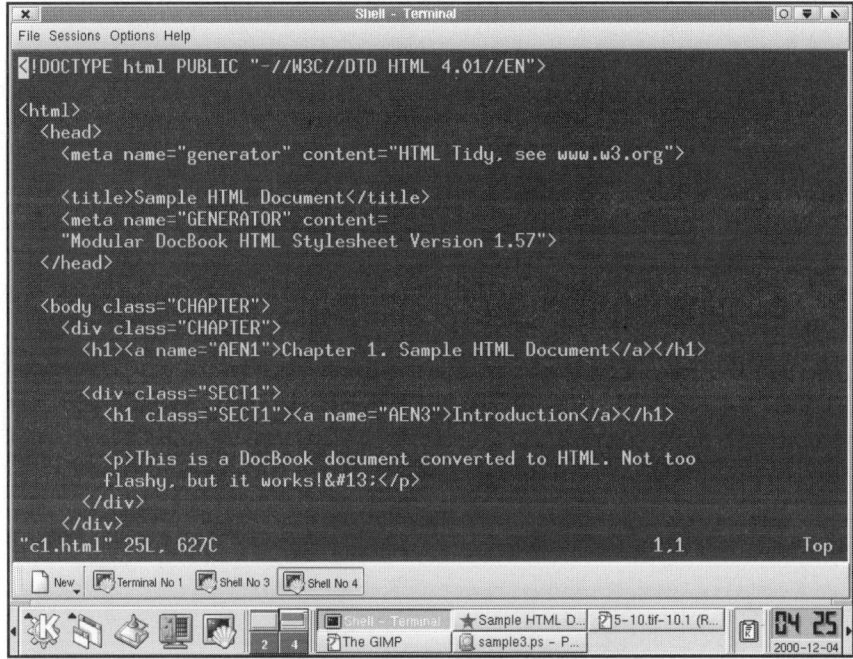

Figure 5.12 *Indented HTML output from HTML Tidy*

and PNG images. If you are anticipating an audience that is using the latest browser, I recommend PNGs. If, however, you're expecting an audience that is still using older browsers (3.x or lower), you might want to stick with JPEGs. Be sure to check out Chapter 6 for the whole story.

Testing Output

Testing your output is easy. Fire up your favorite Web browser, and open up the files produced by SGMLTools. However, I can't stress enough the importance of testing your output thoroughly. No matter how careful you've been, there's a good chance that a broken link exists somewhere in your document, and you don't want to annoy your audience with broken links.

You should also make sure that you can view your document in Lynx and that the images are represented by Alt tags so that any audience that is using Lynx or is vision-impaired can enjoy the document as well.

Test all links at least once from the Web browser of your choice. If you're very picky, you can test them in multiple browsers to see how they appear.

Summary

This chapter covers the aspects of writing DocBook for output to HTML. In particular, the chapter focuses on linking between various parts of the document and resources located on the Web.

Even if you don't plan to output to HTML for online use now, I very much encourage you to write your documents as if you are going to. Although it might take longer, it will save you a great deal of time later. If you try to go back and "webalize" your documents after the fact, you won't remember everything you wrote (not as well), and the links to resources in the document will be lost.

It doesn't hurt a document being output to PostScript to have the extra elements necessary for HTML output, but it is a big pain to convert the document later.

Chapter 6: Parsing DocBook

ow you've gone through a few chapters, and you have actual DocBook
documents from which you want to produce output.

> If you haven't created any documents yet, you might want to go back
> through the first several chapters and create one. If you are just going to
> be parsing documents sent to you by other authors, feel free to grab one
> of the DocBook templates off the CD-ROM included with this book.

In this chapter you will look at how to configure a Linux or UNIX-type system and produce output from your documents. We will also touch on some Windows-based solutions, but the main processing tool in this chapter, SGMLtools, is not available on Windows.

Before you can process DocBook and render it into new formats, you must acquire the DTD, stylesheets, and assorted modules if they're not already installed on your system.

Getting the Current DTD

The first step is to get the DocBook DTD and the stylesheets. The best place to get these is from the official DocBook site at **http://www.oasis-open.org/docbook/**.

You can find both the current SGML and XML DTDs, as well as older versions that are archived on the site for historical reasons. You can download all of the necessary files individually, or in a Zip archive.

SGML

The SGML DTD is found at **http://www.oasis-open.org/docbook/sgml/index.html** (see Figure 6.1).

If you are curious about what older (and simpler) versions of the DocBook DTD looked like, download the DocBook DTD version 1.0. While I don't recommend using the 1.0 DTD, it's very educational to open it up and take a

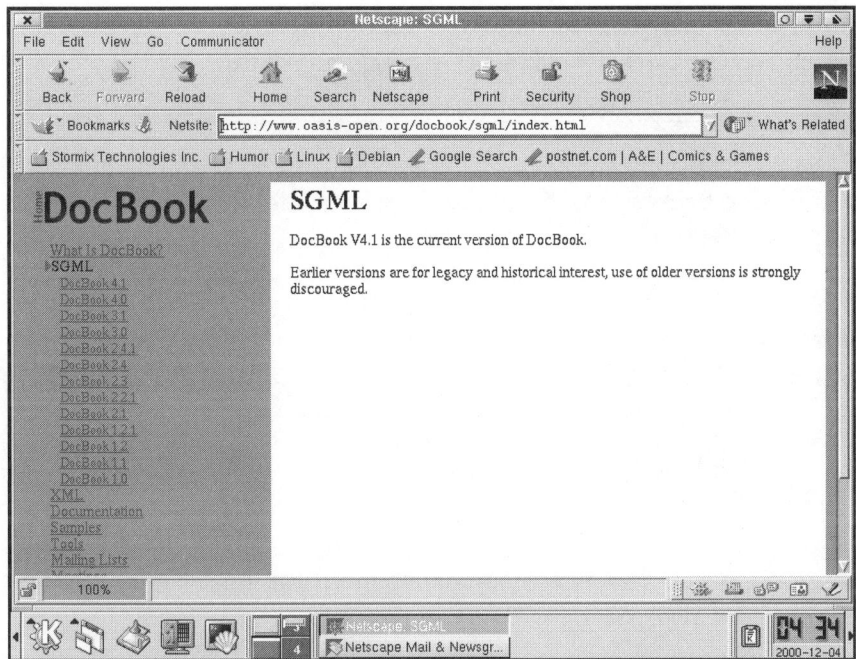

Figure 6.1 *The official DocBook SGML page*

look at what's going on in a DTD. It's certainly much easier to browse through than the current collection of files that make up the DocBook DTD. You will notice that the original DocBook DTD was only one file that clocked in at 683 lines. The latest version, 4.1, is 14 files that add up to approximately 10,630 lines! DocBook has certainly grown since 1992. Aren't you glad you didn't have to write your own DTD?

XML

The Official DocBook site also has all the necessary files for using DocBook XML.

> At the time of this writing, the OASIS DocBook site is being recon-
> structed from some sort of crash. I've tested all the URLs in the book,
> and they are live at the time of this writing. However, some links on the
> site are still broken. It is hoped that they will be fixed soon, but if not,
> you can check the other DocBook site, at **http://www.docbook.org/**.

In addition to the XML DTD and stylesheets, there are also DTDs and examples on the site for EBNF, HTML forms, and MathML.

> EBNF is an extension to the XML DocBook DTD used to create diagrams in the extended Backus-Naur form (*EBNF*). It is new to versions 4.1.2 and later of the XML DTD.

If you do not require EBNF, HTML forms, or MathML, you need not download those files unless you receive documents with that sort of markup in them.

When you use the DocBook XML DTD, you must also have the XML ISO Entity sets, which are distributed separately on the DocBook site at **http://www.docbook.org/xml/4.1.2/ent/** (see Figure 6.2). The DocBook Technical Committee does not create or maintain the ISO Entity sets but provides them out of necessity.

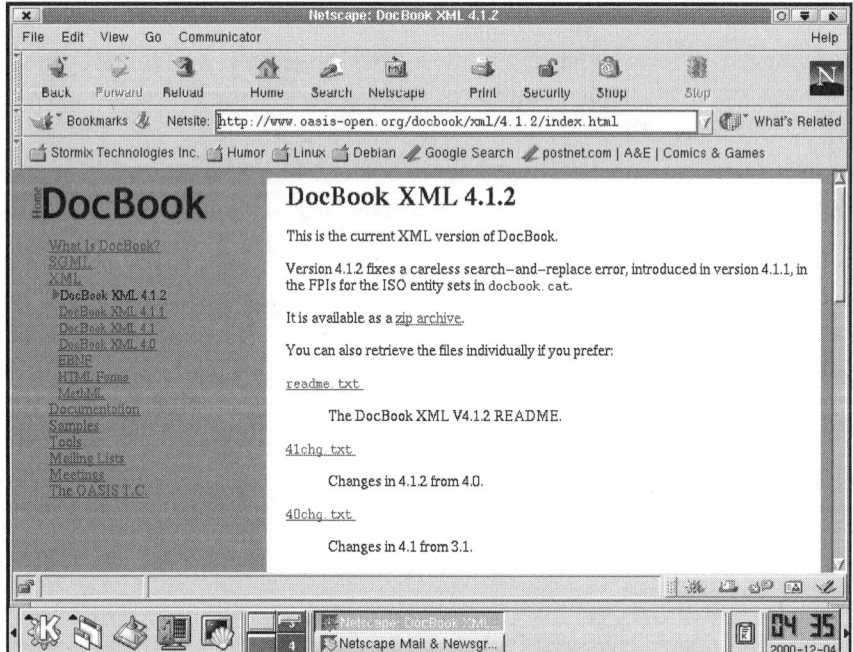

Figure 6.2 *The DocBook XML DTD page*

If, for some reason, you already have a set of DTDs, but you're not sure whether you have the XML or SGML DTDs, check the filenames. Most DocBook XML filenames have an *x* in them to identify them as XML. For instance, the main DocBook SGML DTD filename is docbook.dtd; the XML DTD is named docbookx.dtd.

Note that none of the DocBook files indicate which version number of Doc-Book they are. If you have more than one version of the DTDs floating around, be sure to put them in separate folders.

Installing the DTDs and Stylesheets

When you have the files containing the DocBook DTD and stylesheets, you put them into their own directory. If you downloaded them from the Doc-Book site, copy the ZIP file into a directory. Then unzip it with WinZip if you're on Windows or with unzip if you're on Linux or a UNIX-type operating system.

It doesn't matter where you put the DocBook directory and files. Some popular locations on UNIX-type operating systems are under the /usr/local, /usr/local/share, and /usr/share directories. On my system, they're located in /usr/share/sgml/docbook/.

Because the world is a fast-moving place, I'm including notes on how to install the DocBook DTD here. It's quite likely that between the time this book is written and the time it is published, a new version of the Doc-Book DTDs will become available. However, to make life simple, I've included the DocBook DTDs in three package formats for easy installation on Linux systems. You can find packages on the CD-ROM in tgz format, the Red Hat Package Manager format, and the Debian package format. One of these should work on your system. I'll also try to keep updated install packages on my site, at **http://www.ZonkerBooks.net/**.

Hopefully, you won't need these instructions. However, it's good to have them. Check the README files in the directories for installation instructions for the Linux packages.

NOTE

For Windows users, you might want to place them under C:\docbook\sgml\ or C:\docbook\xml\, depending on which version you're using.

You must also set up the ISO Entity sets for either SGML or XML. If you're using a Linux or UNIX-type system, the SGML ISO Entity sets are likely set up already. If not, you can find them on the CD-ROM. As mentioned earlier, the XML ISO Entity sets are available on the DocBook site, as well as on the CD-ROM for this book.

The Easy Way Out

One of the things my Dad taught me was to look for the easiest way to do something and get the right result. Whether that means finding the easiest way to cut a piece of lumber or do something on the computer, I took that bit of advice to heart.

If you're in an office or company with a large number of users who are going to be creating DocBook documents and rendering output from them, installing DocBook and all the appropriate tools on each computer may not be the answer.

If you happen to have an older computer laying around, a Pentium or Pentium II computer with a 3 or 4 GB hard drive, at least 64 MB of RAM, and an Ethernet card, you can turn it into a DocBook processing monster.

Any Linux distribution is sufficient, but I'd recommend Debian GNU/Linux for this task—and here's why: Debian has a wonderful package management tool called the Advanced Package Tool (APT). It makes installing any program that's been packaged for Debian a snap, especially DocBook's DTD and all of the requisite tools to create DocBook documents, including PSGML.

You'll find plenty of installation and usage information for Debian at **http://www.debian.org/doc/**.

Once you have Debian installed, you probably have SGMLtools and the DocBook DTDs installed already. If not, it's easy to do.

You should have a file called sources.list in the */etc/apt/* directory. Log in as root and edit that file to contain a line like this:

```
deb ftp://ftp.us.debian.org/debian stable main contrib non-free
```

This line should be appropriate for anyone in the United States. It tells the apt-get program where to check for packages—in this case, the FTP server **ftp.us.debian.org**—and to check the stable distribution of Debian for requested packages. If you're located elsewhere, you might want to visit the Debian Project's Web site and find a closer FTP mirror.

To install DocBook, SGMLtools, and other necessary files for working with DocBook, log in to a xterm or console as root and type

```
apt-get update
```

As long as your computer is hooked up to the Network, it will then connect with the server, and get the current list of packages. Then type

```
apt-get install task-sgml
```

This will fetch all of the necessary packages and install them for you. Once this is done, all you need to do is create user accounts for each person who is creating DocBook documents and let them have FTP or SSH access to the computer with all of the DocBook tools installed. This will allow your users to create DocBook documents in any text editor on any operating system; all they need is access to the DocBook system.

Making and Installing a Catalog File

As mentioned in Chapter 1, "Getting Started," you need catalog files to translate the Public Declarations to actual files on your system. This is necessary so that the parsing and rendering software can find the DTD and stylesheets. Without access to those files, tools such as Jade (discussed later in the chapter) are stumped—they have no idea whether your file is valid SGML or XML and how to process it if it is.

Although this might seem strange—having to install stylesheets and DTDs to process documents in DocBook—remember that most tools that process DocBook are also capable of processing other SGML or XML documents. Parsing programs like Jade and OpenJade were designed to take a DTD—any valid DTD—and stylesheets and produce output. They weren't designed exclusively with DocBook in mind. Front ends such as SGMLtools make using Jade and OpenJade easier, but they only pass more complicated commands to Jade or OpenJade. They still depend on accurate catalog files.

NOTE

Although it is possible to specify DTDs and stylesheets on the command line when using DocBook processing tools, it's not exactly an optimal situation. You end up typing some long commands, and if you're processing many documents, it gets old quick. After all, you're probably not learning DocBook for just one quick project or document.

Buzzword

Win32 is a way of saying the versions of Windows that make use of its Win32 API. This includes Windows 95, 98, NT, Millennium, and 2000.

Jade — James' DSSSL Engine

Jade, short for *James' DSSSL Engine*, is a collection of tools that implement the DSSSL-style language. Jade is required by SGMLtools-Lite and other programs to parse DocBook files.

Jade is available on both UNIX-type operating systems and Win32 systems, but there are no ports for the MacOS that I'm aware of. However, if you are in a mixed environment of Windows, Linux, and Macs, you can use SSH or Telnet to do your work on a Linux machine from your Mac.

Installing Jade on UNIX-Type Systems

Jade might already be installed on your system if you're running Linux or one of the *BSDs. If not, grab the source from the Jade Web site at **http://www.jclark.com/jade/** or off the CD-ROM for this book.

You will get Jade in a tar-gzip file. Copy that file to the /tmp directory and uncompress it as shown in the code example and Figure 6.3.

```
cp jade-1.2.1.tar.gz
tar -zxvf jade-1.2.1.tar.gz
cd jade-1.2.1/
./configure
make
make install
```

If you prefer to install binaries, you can find RPMs and Debian Packages on the CD-ROM as well. Instructions for installation of the RPMs and Debs are located on the CD-ROM with each.

Installing Jade on Win32

Installing Jade on Windows systems is quite easy. Simply download the binaries from the Jade Web site, or copy them from the CD-ROM. The files are

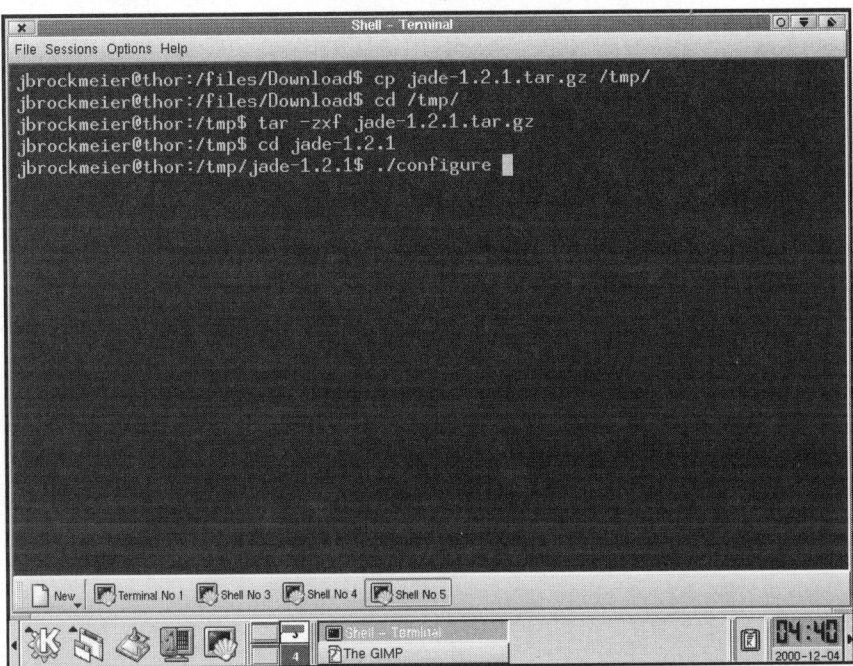

Figure 6.3 *Uncompressing and compiling Jade*

in a Zip format, so you create a Jade directory under the Program Files directory and unzip the files in that directory.

Using Jade

Generally, you don't use Jade by itself. Instead, Jade is called from other programs. However, you can use Jade to produce a few types of output directly from the command line.

To produce an RTF file with Jade from the command line, as shown in Figure 6.4, try this:

```
jade inputfile.sgml -t rtf -o outputfile.rtf
```

If Jade is installed properly, and your document is relatively free of errors, you should have an RTF file from the DocBook file.

To create a TeX file from your DocBook document, as shown in Figure 6.5, use the following:

```
jade inputfile.sgml -t tex -o outputfile.tex
```

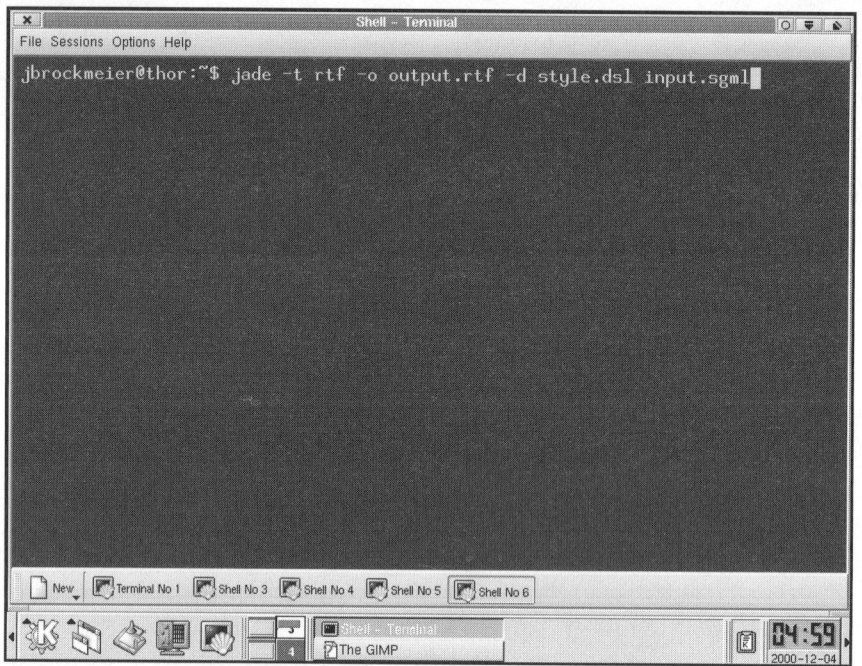

Figure 6.4 *Making RTF files with Jade*

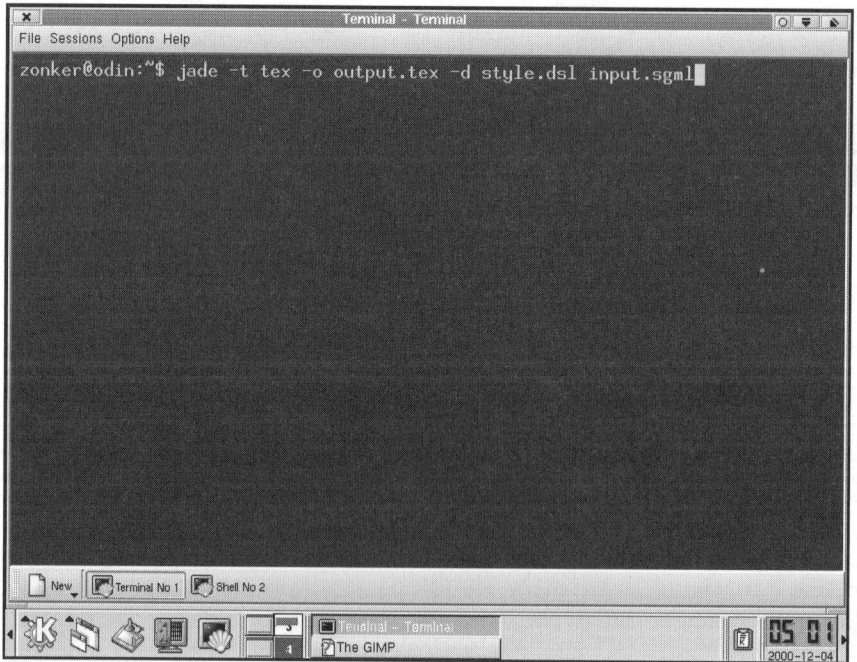

Figure 6.5 *Making TeX with Jade*

As you might have guessed, the -t argument tells Jade the type of output to create, and the *-o* argument tells Jade the name of the output file.

OpenJade

OpenJade is an extension of Jade created by the DSSSL community. Open-Jade is based on the original Jade by James Clark and operates in the same way. Again, OpenJade is not generally used by itself; you normally call it from one of the front ends.

Installing OpenJade

To install OpenJade, obtain the source code for UNIX-type systems or the binaries for Windows systems from the OpenJade Web site, or copy the files from the CD-ROM. I've also included prebuilt binaries in RPM form and Debian Package form so that you don't need to worry about compiling OpenJade. You can find OpenJade source and binaries at: **http://openjade. sourceforge.net/**

To install from RPM, use the following command:

```
rpm -i openjade-1.3.rpm
```

This should install OpenJade with no problems. The filename might be slightly different, depending on which distribution you are using.

Using OpenJade

OpenJade takes the same command-line arguments as Jade. For example, to output an RTF file with OpenJade, use the following command:

```
openjade inputfile.sgml -t rtf -o outputfile.rtf
```

Again, more than likely you won't want to use OpenJade by itself. Simply having OpenJade installed and working properly allows front ends such as SGMLtools to simplify producing output from OpenJade.

Using SGMLtools-Lite and SGMLtools

SGMLtools and SGMLtools-Lite are front ends for rendering output from DocBook files. The SGMLtools project was first, but it is no longer main-tained. However, the SGMLtools-Lite project is a continuation of the

SGMLtools project, albeit not quite as complete. Whereas the SGMLtools project included just about everything you need to process DocBook files, the SGMLtools-Lite project does not include packages such as Jade or OpenJade and the DocBook DTDs.

The reason I've included the SGMLtools software with the book, and in this chapter, is because a large number of Linux distributions still ship with SGMLtools and the SGMLtools software still works perfectly well. In fact, SGMLtools-Lite still has a few bugs and hasn't been updated too often, so if you happen to have working installations of the original SGMLtools, I'd recommend sticking with that. There are actually very few differences between SGMLtools and SGMLtools-Lite in terms of use, although installation is different.

SGMLtools and SGMLtools-Lite are only tested to run on Linux and UNIX-type OSes. You may be able to run them on Windows with some modification or by using a program like CygWin, but I haven't tried it. As mentioned earlier in the chapter, it might be worth turning an older computer into a dedicated DocBook box if you're going to be doing a lot of work with DocBook.

Installing SGMLtools-Lite

The SGMLtools-Lite home page is located at **http://sourceforge.net/ projects/sgmltools-lite/**.

There you can find the latest versions of SGMLtools-Lite, if there have been updates. You may want to find distribution specific packages, however, as they should have been tested against the distribution you'd be using.

One of the headaches I experienced when installing SGMLtools-Lite was a missing and/or misconfigured catalog file. To make life easier for you, I've included a working catalog file for each distribution on the CD-ROM. You should also add the following to your .bashrc to make sure that the proper location of the catalog file is in your environment:

```
SGML_CATALOG_FILES=/usr/share/sgml/catalog
```

Copy the catalog file for your distribution to the /usr/share/sgml/ directory. You might need to log in as root before you can create a file in that directory. You must also run this command to set the environment variable properly until you log out and back in:

```
export SGML_CATALOG_FILES=/usr/share/sgml/catalog
```

That sets the proper environment variable. Note that if you run the command in an xterm, the environment variable does not extend to other xterms or terminals.

Parsing Documents with SGMLtools and SGMLtools-Lite

After you install SGMLtools or SGMLtools-Lite, parsing documents with them is easy. For the purpose of these examples, assume that you have a file named book.sgml that you want to export to different file formats.

The syntax for both SGMLtools and SGMLtools-Lite is the same, and these commands should work with both, barring incompatibilities in future versions of SGMLtools-Lite.

Rendering PostScript with SGMLtools-Lite

To convert your document to PostScript, run the following command:

```
sgmltools -b ps book.sgml
```

Provided that no serious errors exist in the file, you will get a PostScript file suitable for printing. If you have a special stylesheet you'd like to apply, use this syntax:

```
sgmltools -b ps -d stylesheet.dsl book.sgml
```

This tells sgmltools to use a different stylesheet than the default stylesheets. The -b option is for *backend*; it tells SGMLtools what format to output.

As you can see in Figure 6.6, the PostScript version of this document is very professional-looking, even with just the default stylesheets. Note that you get page numbers and an index generated automagically instead of your having to do it manually.

Rendering DVI with SGMLtools-Lite

SGMLtools can also render output in the DVI, or *device-independent*, format usually generated from LaTeX or TeX. The benefit to doing this is that there are tools that can convert from DVI to formats such as PDF.

To get a DVI file from a DocBook document, as shown in Figure 6.7, use the following syntax:

```
sgmltools -b dvi book.sgml
```

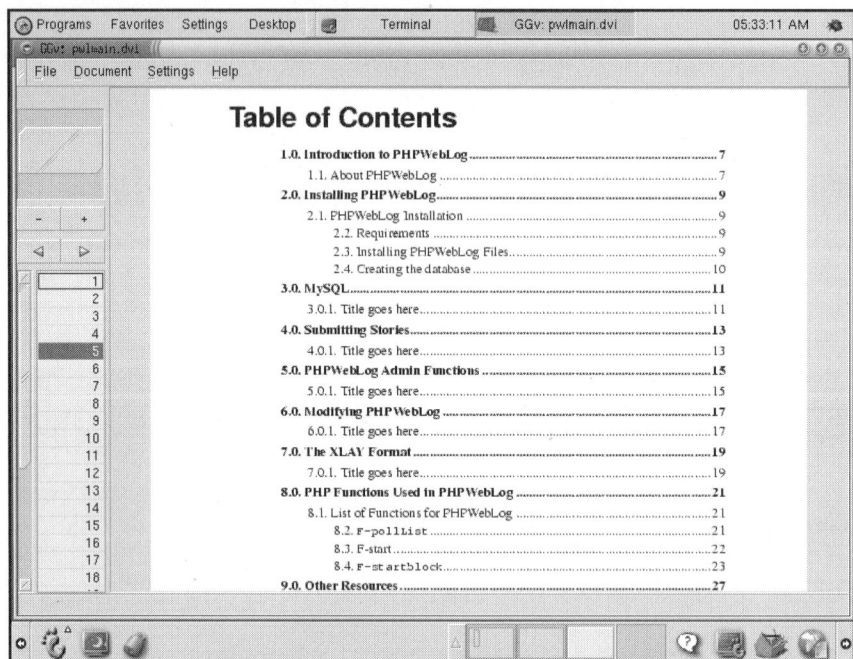

Figure 6.6 *A DocBook file converted to PostScript*

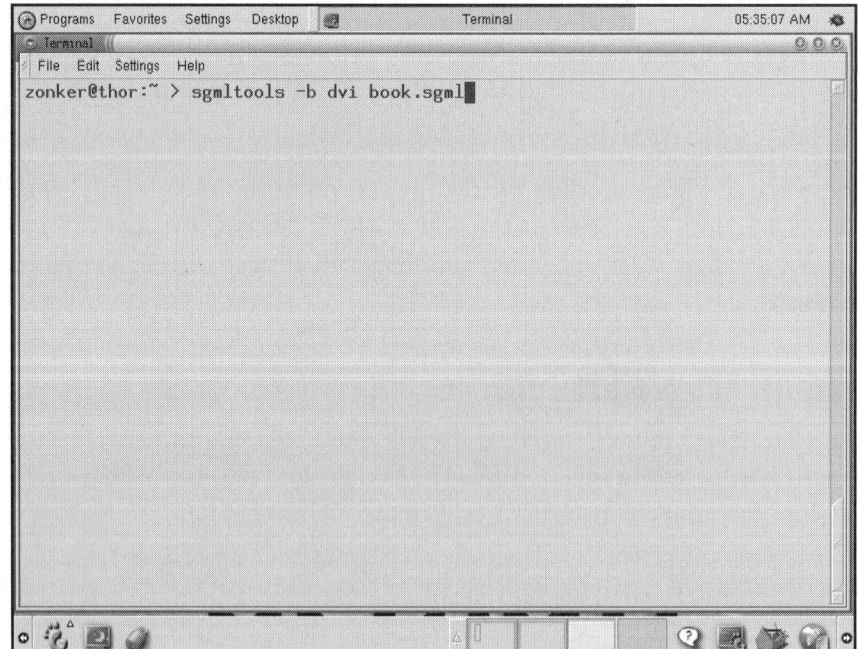

Figure 6.7 *Converting to DVI*

Rendering HTML with SGMLtools-Lite

To create Web pages from your DocBook documents, you use the HTML back end. Note that the HTML output, although valid, is ugly. In Chapter 5, "Creating Online Documents," are examples of using Tidy to clean up Doc-Book output and convert some of the physical formatting tags to cascading stylesheets.

To render HTML, use the following command:

```
sgmltools -b html book.sgml
```

This creates a directory named book/ with the HTML file or files in it. The number of files output depends on the sections you have in your document. Figure 6.8 shows HTML output from using SGMLtools.

Again, you have an index and navigation generated on-the-fly without your having to go through the drudgery of doing it by hand. When you create a document only once and never modify it, you don't see the benefits as much, but if you work with a document for a while (a living document, that is), the benefits of using DocBook rather than hand-coding HTML become very

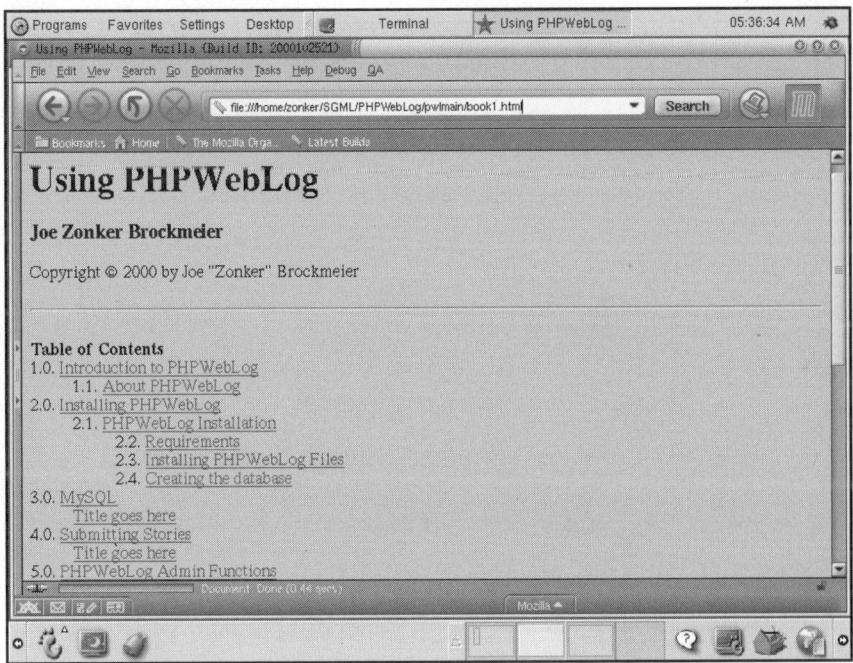

Figure 6.8 *HTML output from DocBook*

apparent. Even if you don't use DocBook to create any other type of output, the benefits from creating HTML alone are worth it. When you output PostScript or other formats, you maximize the benefits.

Text

Where would we be without plain-text files? This is the one format you can count on to be compatible with just about any platform.

To generate plain text from your DocBook document, you use the text back-end as shown in Figure 6.9.

```
sgmltools -b txt book.sgml
```

SGMLtools creates one ASCII text file from your document. This should be viewable on nearly any platform.

RTF

If you want to create a file for use with Microsoft Word, you use the Rich Text Format backend. Although this isn't a Word document, per se, it is compatible

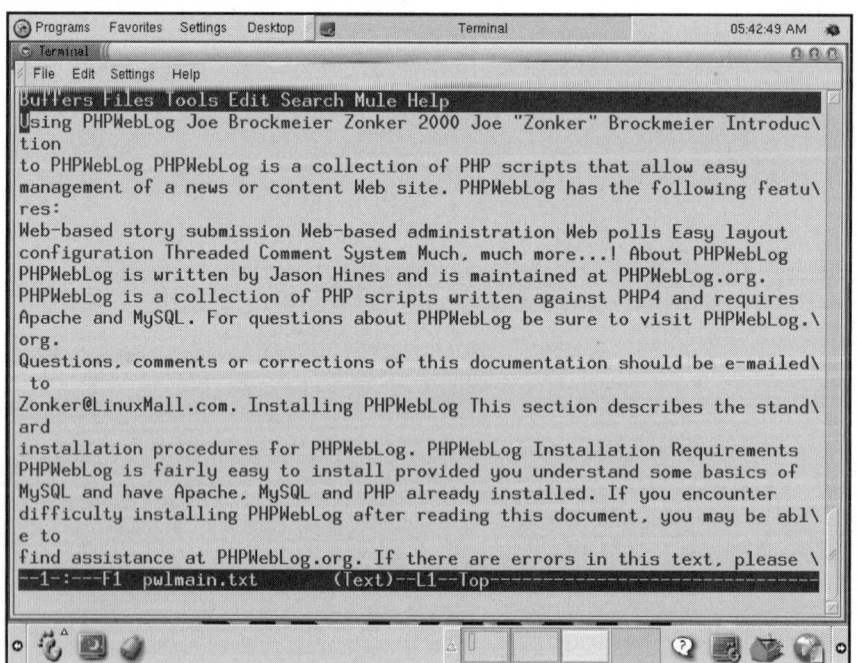

Figure 6.9 *The same file output to plain text*

with Word, and you can use DocBook to create a file and then pass it on to editors or management types in Word format so that they don't have to figure out another program.

To create RTF output, use the following command, also shown in Figure 6.10.

```
sgmltools -b rtf book.sgml
```

Converting LinuxDoc to DocBook

If you've inherited some LinuxDoc files to maintain, you might want to convert them to DocBook to make it easier on yourself and anyone else who will be working with them. It's always simpler to work with one standard format than two or more. Luckily, SGMLtools supports converting from LinuxDoc to DocBook.

To convert a LinuxDoc file to DocBook, use the same syntax as before, as shown in the Figure 6.11.

```
sgmltools -b ld2db oldbook.sgml
```

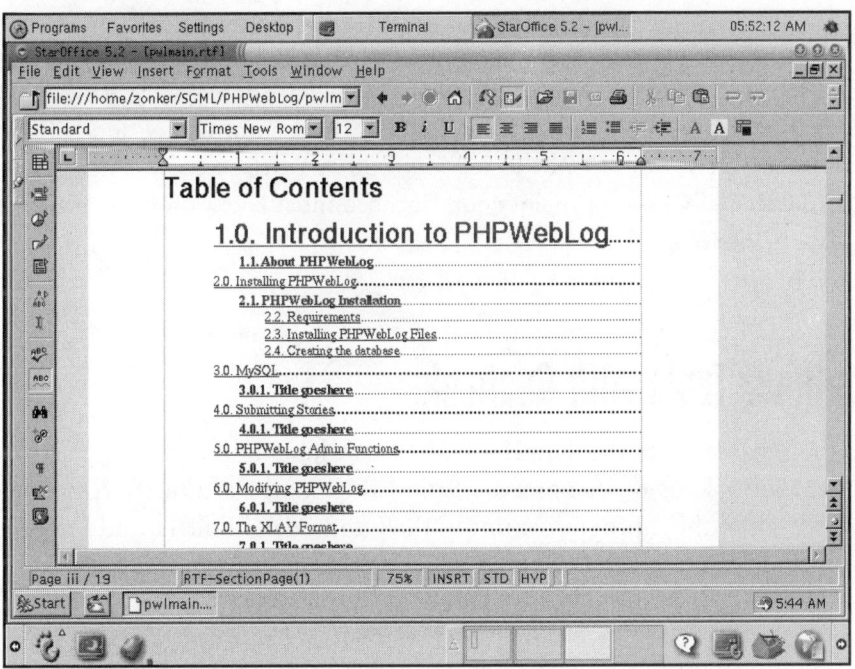

Figure 6.10 *RTF output in StarOffice*

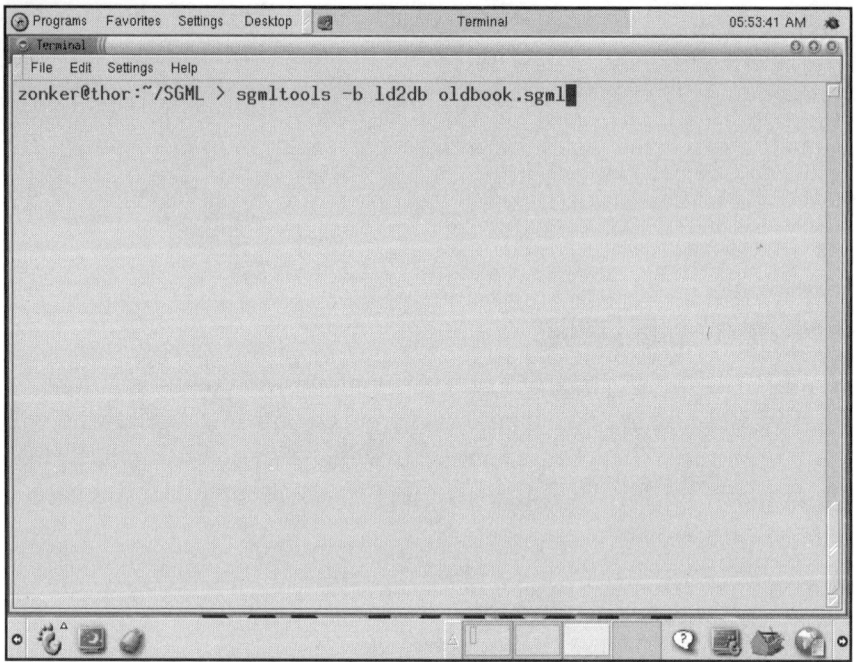

Figure 6.11 *Converting LinuxDoc to DocBook SGML*

The LinuxDoc DTD was designed for projects such as the Linux Documentation Project. Unless you work with folks in the Linux community, it's unlikely that you will come across this format. There's nothing wrong with the LinuxDoc DTD, but it is not as full-featured as DocBook and is no longer being developed or maintained because most Linux projects are now using DocBook.

Using Other Tools with DocBook

Other tools work with the DocBook DTD. Adobe FrameMaker+SGML supports DocBook, as do Arbortext's Epic Editor and SoftQuad's XmetaL. However, each of these programs runs in the hundreds of dollars, and I'm not able to include the software with this book. I want to give you tools that you can use to get up and running with DocBook right away.

If you're interested in keeping up with available tools for DocBook, visit my site, **http://www.ZonkerBooks.net**, for updates on available tools. If Open Source tools are available for DocBook, I'll be sure to list them on my site and make copies available for downloading or provide links to the project sites.

Summary

This chapter covers working with the tools used to create output from Doc-Book documents, from installion of the DocBook DTDs and stylesheets to some of the Open Source software available for processing DocBook files.

After finishing this chapter, you should be able to use SGMLtools or SGML-tools-Lite to produce usable output for printing and to display online and electronic distribution, as well as standard files that can be used by Microsoft Word or other popular word processors. The next chapter covers collaborative work with DocBook and how to manage files between authors and editors.

Writing a book or technical manual is often a collaborative process. For instance, on many books you have multiple people involved including authors, project editors, technical editors, technical reviewers, and copy editors. Needless to say, all these kindly souls have different ideas of what should be, or shouldn't be, in the text. This can create some serious confusion, if not outright chaos.

To manage such a project, you must implement some method to the madness. Overall, in a situation such as the one we're discussing here, a professional book development project, the project editor will track changes, comments, and suggestions between all participating individuals and implement the most appropriate ones in the final product. Other projects, however, such as corporate internal documentation, Open Source development documentation, or even educational material development, may not have such luxuries as editors available. To make these other projects manageable, and the professional editors more efficient, a method of document tracking should be used. This goal can be accomplished by implementing revision control. In this chapter, we will discuss various options for revision control, such as the GNU Revision Control System (RCS) and the Concurrent Versions System (CVS).

You Still Need Backups

Now is as good a time as any to point out that, despite the fact that both RCS and CVS make backup copies of files, it's best practice to regularly make a backup of your files on some kind of removable media, such as a Zip disk, tape drive, or even to a writeable CD-ROM. With this practice in place, even if your hard drive goes to the great junkyard in the sky, your data in a CVS repository is *still* housed and your colleagues won't feel the need to strangle you for having to rewrite all of your work because your cat dumped the goldfish bowl onto your computer.

In all seriousness, even if your CVS repository is on a remote server with a talented system administrator taking conscientious care of backups, it's a good idea to have a backup system for files on your local machine. Even one day of work is a lot to lose.

What Is Revision Control?

During the development process, software gets a revision number. Every time a change is made, such as new features or bug fixes, the program gets a new revision number. Sometimes you'll find this revision number in commercial software as the release version of the software, whereas other times you'll find the revision number in the release number or even service pack number. Revision numbers are typically more obvious in the case of Open Source development because there are frequent updates between major releases, which each have their own revision number.

Revision control is the practice of maintaining older versions of the code base to allow developers to "roll back" to earlier versions of the code base if changes introduce new and worse bugs, or just to allow for maintenance of an older version of the code base while a new version is started.

Revision control software automates the process, making it easier for developers (both software and documentation) to keep track of which revision is most current and which changes have been made between versions. If you're wondering what all this talk of programming versions and bug fixes has to do with managing a documentation project with DocBook, the overall process and benefits are the same. If you consider that a project editor or main author of a documentation project can allow all contributors to work on the same text simultaneously, each contributor will have his own release version, and if the editor or main author doesn't approve of the new release, the older version can be used. Through comment features the editors can track who is changing what, when, and manage who has permission to change what.

Going to the Library

In simple terms, you can compare version control systems to a library system. Like a library, content, whether it's text documentation or programming code, is checked out for viewing (and editing) and checked in to allow the librarian to keep track of the content and take care of it for other library card holders to use. With DocBook, Bob (library card holder) can start writing his program or document and save it to a file (library book). He can then *check in* the first revision of the code to a repository (librarian). When he's ready to start work again, he can *check out* the code from the system. Depending on the version control system he is using, RCS or CVS, Bob's file may be locked so other library card holders are unable to change the content until Bob checks the code back in.

Getting a Lock on It

If you are using the RCS version control system, your checked out file is locked (unless you only check out to read, and not edit, the file). Locking the file prevents others from checking in a revision of the file while you have it out. The practical upshot of locking the file means that when one person has the file and is making changes, no one else can contribute changes for that version until it is unlocked. The latest copy of the file can be checked out for someone else to compile or read, but that person can't commit changes to it.

This might sound like a pain, but for simple projects, or projects with only a couple contributors, file-locking may be easier for whomever is managing the project. If you consider a scenario with just one writer and editor working on a project, the writer can start a draft and check it in to the RCS. If done properly, the editor can check out the file and make changes, comments, revisions, or whatnot to the copy. While this is going on, the file is locked so that the author can't check out the file and make any revisions or changes until the editor has checked the revision back in and vice versa.

This assures that both parties are working, if you will excuse the expression, on the same page. It would be a nightmare scenario if the editor spent the better part of his or her weekend making changes and edits and on Monday the author posted a completely different draft.

This scenario can be prevented with a little more work and a complex program such as CVS. CVS manages changes. If two or more people try to commit changes that conflict with one another, CVS notifies the user of the offending change. This allows the contributor or editor to manually view and change the text without overwriting someone else's work. For larger projects with more contributors, file locking can become time consuming, not allowing various contributors to work at the same time; therefore a non-locking system, such as CVS, is more practical.

Using Revision Control Programs

For the general purpose of this book, we assume that everyone involved is using a Linux system or, at least, has access to one. This doesn't mean that you have to be using Linux to write and edit your files, just that the revision control systems, RCS and CVS, reside on Linux or UNIX based servers.

If you are working with another OS on your desktop, such as Microsoft Windows or MacOS, but still have access to a Linux- (or UNIX-) based server running CVS, you can either **ftp** or **scp** files to the Linux server, or you can use a local CVS client. Free GPL'ed graphical CVS clients can be found for Microsoft Windows or Macintosh at **http://www.wincvs.org/**.

Although not strictly DocBook-related, it's still worth mentioning that using unencrypted methods to move files about is a Very Bad Idea as a general rule. FTP is a very insecure method of transport these days. If you do need to use FTP instead of SSH and SCP, use logins and passwords that are exclusive to FTP.

For instance, if your system login is *bobsmith*, you don't want to use that for FTP. Instead, set up (or have your system administrator set up) an account such as *book* or *editor* for FTPing files back and forth. The permissions for the FTP account should be such that they are allowed to do only FTP. If someone does snoop the FTP password, he or she cannot, without further effort, log in to a shell on the system.

You should always remember that revision control is a great substitute for e-mailing code or copy back and forth, but it is no substitute for good communication. For best practice purposes, when planning a revision control system, set up a regular communication schedule to discuss any major project between your contributors.

Another item to consider if you choose to implement a version control system is the content you have to manage. RCS and CVS were both developed to deal specifically with text files. If your project includes graphical figures, you will have to design or implement a different system to manage them. CVS can also handle binary files allowing you to manage multiple revisions with the only limitation being you cannot use **diff** against the files.

Revision Control for Group Projects

As we've already discussed, the benefits of version control systems are aimed at large projects, typically with multiple contributors. Whether you opt for the simple, direct solution of RCS, allowing you to very simply manage the project files, or a more complex solution with CVS, allowing you to have multiple people working from multiple branches of code all simultaneously, in the long run you will have more efficiently completed your project.

Revision Control for Loners

If you're going to do a project by yourself, you might want to use revision control anyway. I've found that even for small articles or projects, it's nice to be able to roll back a version or two when I've deleted a paragraph or 10 paragraphs that I later decide to include in the piece. It's much simpler to use a version control system, after you become used to it, than to keep a dozen files in a directory, labeled *article1.sgml*, *article1.sgml.old*, *article1.sgml.bak*, and so forth.

The GNU Revision Control System (RCS)

The GNU Revision Control System is usually part of a default Linux installation. Odds are, if you have a Linux system, you have it installed already. To find out, type **rcs -V** at a shell prompt. You should see something like RCS version 5.7. RCS 5.7 is the latest version of RCS available at the time of this writing. If you don't have RCS or want to get a newer version, visit the RCS Web site at **http://www.cs.purdue.edu/homes/trinkle/RCS/**. The official GNU page for RCS is at **http://www.gnu.org/software/rcs/rcs.html** (see Figure 7.1).

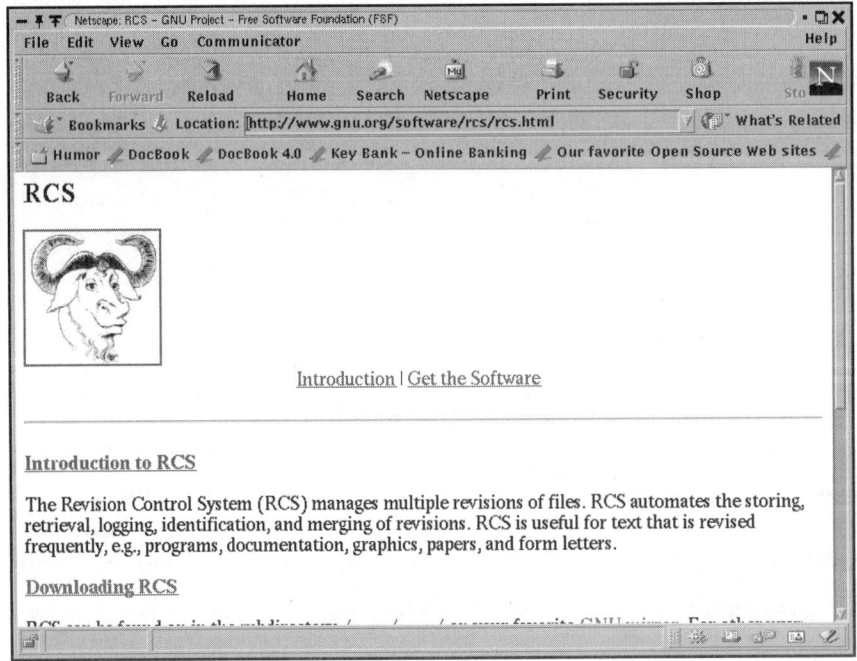

Figure 7.1 *The GNU Revision Control System Web site*

Installing RCS

RCS is easy to install. Download the tarfile from the RCS home page and unpack it in an appropriate directory by **cd**'ing to the directory and running the following commands:

```
gzip -cd rcs-*.tar.gz |tar -xvf -
```

That will create a directory rcs-X.XX (where X.XX is the version number). Next **cd** into that directory and run **./configure**. If you are not root on the system, you might want to run **./configure —prefix=$HOME** to build the software to install in your own home directory. Next run **make** followed by **make install**. If you are not installing to your home directory and you are not root, you will have to **su** before the **make** step.

> If you prefer packaged versions of applications, there are both RPM and Debian packages available for your distribution to download, if you don't have your CDs. For RPM versions, visit **http://www.rpmfind.net/** and search for RCS. You will receive a list of RPMs for source, binaries, development, and other platforms (Alpha, Sparc, etc.). You can search for Debian packages at **http://www.debian.org/distrib/packages**. With the packaged versions, you can install by using the appropriate package manager options.

Basic RCS

RCS is easy to use, especially the basic commands. To start with, **cd** to the directory you're going to be working in. Usually, I like to maintain a directory for each project I'm working on, under a /Writing directory.

> I try to keep one top-level directory, such as /Writing or something equally obvious, so that I know what to tar and gzip when I'm making a backup.

After you **cp** to the proper directory, you create an RCS directory for RCS to use to store revisions.

Run **mkdir RCS**, and RCS will use that directory to store any revisions you save in that directory. You must create an RCS directory in any directory containing files that are going to be managed with RCS.

Checking In a File

Now that you have created a directory, go ahead and check in your first file.

To create the first revision of a file, run **rcs -i testfile.txt**. You should see RCS output as in Figure 7.2.

You are asked to enter a description. Type in a brief description of the file, and press Enter. Then you get the prompt again, so type a period to tell RCS that you're finished with the comment.

Congratulations! You've created the first version of your file.

Creating a Revision

Now you want to create the first revision of the file. To do that, you use the check-in command for RCS, **ci**. (Isn't it nice the way UNIX-style commands are short and easy to type?)

Make a test file with a few lines of text in your favorite editor, and save it to the same directory under the name **testfile.txt**. When you're ready to save the

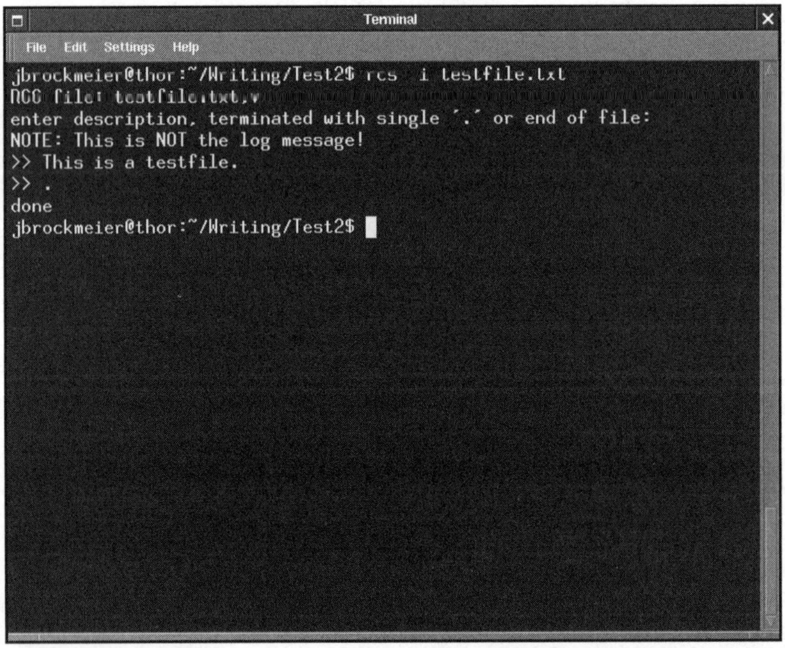

Figure 7.2 *RCS output*

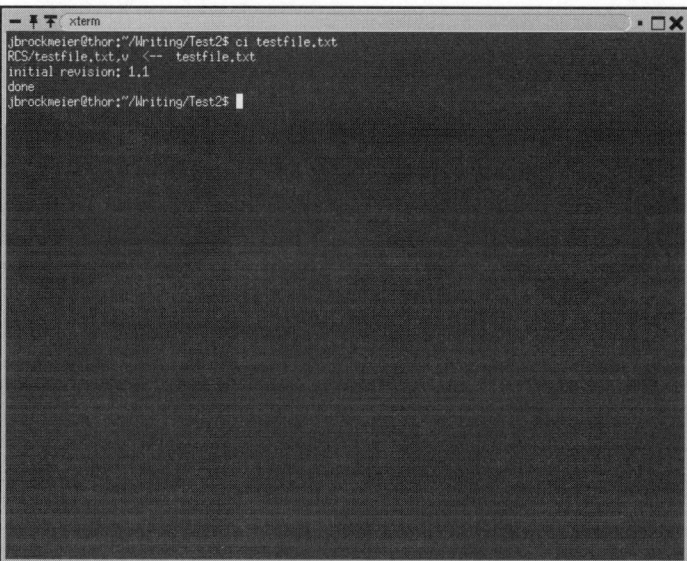

Figure 7.3 *Creating a revision with RCS*

first revision, type in **ci testfile.txt**. You will see RCS output as in Figure 7.3, if everything went smoothly:

Notice that the testfile.txt file is no longer in the directory. RCS deletes files when they are merged back into revision control. When you check out the file, RCS re-creates the latest version of the file for you, or the version you request.

> If you do not want RCS to delete your working copy of the file
> you've just checked in, instead of simply using **ci testfile.txt**, use **ci -l testfile.txt**.
>
> **NOTE**

Checking Out a File

If you want to edit the testfile.txt file, you must check it out of RCS to be able to work with it. To do that, you use the **co** command.

In addition to checking the file out of RCS, you lock it so that no new revisions can be committed until you've checked in your latest revision. At the shell prompt, type in **co -l** *filename.txt*. Provided that everything is correct, RCS will give you positive feedback, as shown in Figure 7.4.

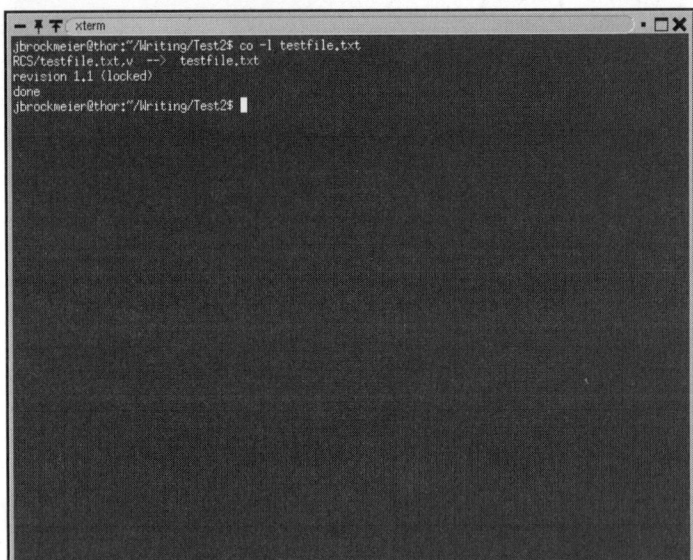

```
jbrockmeier@thor:~/Writing/Test2$ co -l testfile.txt
RCS/testfile.txt,v  -->  testfile.txt
revision 1.1 (locked)
done
jbrockmeier@thor:~/Writing/Test2$
```

Figure 7.4 *Checking out a revision*

The **co** command tells RCS that you want to check out a file, and the *-l* switch tells it to lock the file in the process. If you check out a file without locking it, RCS will complain when you try to check it back in. If you're checking out a file only to read the file, it's okay to do so without locking. That way, if others do try to check out the file, they can do so without a problem. If the file is locked, they cannot check it out for editing.

The reason the file is locked is, as we discussed previously in this chapter, to prevent anyone else from committing revisions while you (or they) are editing the file.

Rolling Back

If you have committed a few versions of your file and have decided that two versions ago it was perfect, no problem. You can still check out the old version and work with it. For example, if you're at version 1.8 now and you want to work with the 1.5 version, you use the *-r* switch with the **co** command to check out the older version of the file.

To check out version 1.5, type in **co -r1.5 *filename.txt***. Now you have the 1.5 version checked out for reading purposes. To check it out for editing pur-

```
- ¥ ₮ xterm                                               · □ X
jbrockmeier@thor:~/Writing/Test2$ co -r1.5 testfile.txt
RCS/testfile.txt,v  -->  testfile.txt
revision 1.5
done
jbrockmeier@thor:~/Writing/Test2$ co -l -r1.5 testfile.txt
RCS/testfile.txt,v  -->  testfile.txt
revision 1.5 (locked)
done
jbrockmeier@thor:~/Writing/Test2$ ▌
```

Figure 7.5 *Rolling back to an older version*

poses, use the *-l* switch to lock the file as well. Figure 7.5 shows the difference in RCS output when you lock a file using **co**.

> If you check out an older version of a file before you check in the newest,
> and they're in the same directory, you can end up overwriting the newest
> revision with the older one. RCS overwrites and deletes files without ask-
> ing, which is okay if you're using it properly. However, if you're not care-
> ful, you can lose work.

NOTE

Keyword Substitution

RCS can also work a little magic for you when you check out a file and give
you some information automatically. All you have to do is insert a keyword
into the text file, and RCS expands the keyword to contain the information
the keyword asks for.

For instance, if you'd like to know the date and time of each revision, include
the $Date$ keyword. The keywords for RCS are surrounded by the $ charac-
ter in front and back to prevent any confusion. If RCS sees the word *date* or

Date by itself, RCS will ignore it but will substitute revision notes in place of the keyword when it is expressed like this, $Date$. The following is an example of using the $Date$ keyword.

```
$Date$
<!DOCTYPE chapter PUBLIC "-//OASIS//DTD DocBook V3.1//EN">
<chapter label="7">
<title>[ct] Collaborative Work with DocBook (25)</title>
```

RCS supports keywords for the date and time, the user name of the person who last revised the document, the filename, the log entry that's typed in when the file is checked in, and several other options. For a full list of keywords, see the **co** manpage for all the possible keywords. Figure 7.6 shows the output of the $Date$ keyword when retrieved from RCS.

> Because Jade doesn't know anything about RCS keywords, if you parse a document that uses keywords with Jade, it produces errors when it sees something like $Date: 2001/01/22 12:48:56 $ in the header of a Doc-Book document. This doesn't affect the output, however, so it's nothing to worry about. I usually include keywords before the DocBook declaration so that any expanded text doesn't make its way into document output.

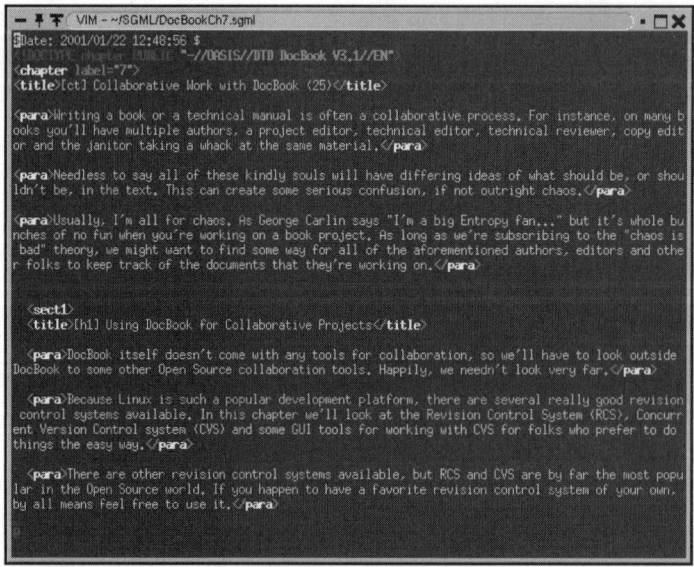

Figure 7.6 *Expanded RCS keywords*

Setting Revision Numbers Manually

RCS usually sets the revision numbers for a file automatically. However, at times you might want to set the revision number of a file manually, for instance, when you're working on a project as a technical editor and have access to the author's RCS.

There's no point in editing a file the author has not yet finished, even if he's checked in the latest revision. One way to make sure that this doesn't happen is to edit only files that have reached a certain revision number, such as 1.0 or something like that. By default, RCS sets revisions automatically, and they might not be in sync with your numbering scheme. To fix that, check in the file like this:

```
ci -r1.0 filename.sgml
```

This way, you can specify the revision number, beginning at the revision with which you want to start.

Numbering Conventions

RCS lets you give a file a revision number lower than 1.0 but does not accept a revision number like 1.01. Instead, it increments that number to 1.1. If you want to have a revision lower than 1.1 but higher than 1.0, use a numbering convention like 1.0.1. Also, RCS does not allow you to check in a revision of a file that's lower than the current version. If 1.0 is already checked in, you can't check in a revision 0.9, even if you specify it manually.

The Concurrent Versions System (CVS)

The Concurrent Versions System builds on the GNU Revision Control System to manage a collection of directories (branches) that contain file revisions, instead of just one directory like RCS.

With CVS, users maintain their own private copies of the files they work with while the CVS repository holds all the files, directories, and control files.

What Is CVS?

CVS is designed for distributed software projects of larger scope than RCS handles. One of the differences between CVS and RCS is that CVS does *not* expect file locking by default and several users may work on, and make changes to, the same file. CVS coordinates the changes in the files when a user commits a file back to the CVS repository. CVS merges the changes automatically unless there is an obvious conflict, in which case CVS reports it to the user to fix.

The Client/Server Model

The other major difference, and it's a biggie, between RCS and CVS is that CVS operates on a client and server model and is designed to work across network connections rather than just on the local machine. This makes life much easier for people who are all working in separate locations, at least in terms of committing and retrieving the latest versions of files. Don't think, however, that you are unable to use CVS on a single machine with multiple users. Your server and your clients may be located physically on the same hardware.

Installing CVS

If CVS is not already installed on your system, you can grab the source or binaries from the CVShome.org Web site at **http://www.cvshome.org/**. To find out whether CVS is already on your system, type **cvs --version** and you will see output such as that shown in Figure 7.7 if CVS is already installed.

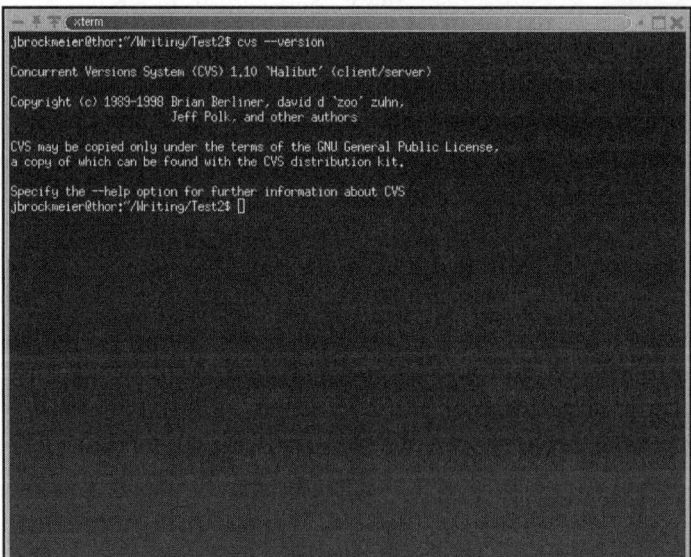

Figure 7.7 *CVS version information*

CVS, like RCS, is easy to install from source. Download the tarfile from the CVS home page and unpack it in an appropriate directory by cd'ing to the directory and running the following commands

```
gzip -cd cvs-*.tar.gz |tar xvf -
```

That will create a directory cvs-*X.XX* (where *X.XX* is the version number). Next **cd** into that directory and run **./configure**. If you are not root on the system, you might want to run **./configure --prefix=$HOME** to build the software to install in your own home directory. Next run **make** followed by **make install**. If you are not installing to your home directory and you are not root, you will have to **su** before the **make** step.

You will find several prepackaged RPMs and Debian files to install CVS, but you can download source or binaries for Linux. To obtain a prepackaged version of CVS, you can install from your distribution CD or download from multiple websites. For RPM packages, search for CVS at **http://www.rpmfind.net/**. For Debian packages, you can search for CVS at **http://www.debian.org/distrib/packages**. You can then install the packages with your appropriate package manager.

Basic CVS

CVS is more complicated than RCS but not difficult. All CVS commands follow this format:

```
cvs [cvs-option] command [cvs-command option] filename
```

This is probably different from commands you normally use, because it combines two commands in one. You start every CVS command with **cvs** and then any CVS options; next, the operation you'd like to perform, followed by any options that operation takes; and finally, the filename with which you're working. A real CVS command looks like the following:

```
cvs commit filename
```

This command simply tells CVS to commit a file into the CVS repository and to make it a new revision even if no changes occurred since the last one. In addition to full command-line names, such as *commit*, CVS offers abbreviated equivalents. For instance, cvs ci *filename* is the equivalent to cvs commit *filename*.

Creating a CVS Repository

Before you do anything with CVS, you have to create a repository for your files. Because you're setting up a repository for multiple users, you should set up the directory somewhere other than in your home directory. For example, you could dedicate an entire drive to your CVS repository and set up your repository as its own mountpoint in /mnt/cvsroot. The CVS root directory has to be readable and writeable to anyone accessing it, because they might need to create a lock file. Be careful that the CVS root directory is the only writeable directory.

Before you run the command to make the CVS repository, you must create the directory. For example, if you are going to make the directory /mnt/cvsroot the CVS repository, you must create it first. If you're planning to allow multiple users on the system to have access to the CVS repository, you must set up appropriate groups and ownership permissions to allow proper read/write access to your directories. First create a new group on your system (our example is using the group named *cvs*). Then, to set up the repository, run the following commands:

```
cd /mnt
mkdir cvsroot
chgrp cvs -R cvsroot
chmod g+w -R cvsroot
```

Now that you have the directory you're going to use, run the CVS init command to set up the directory as a repository, like this:

```
cvs -d /mnt/cvsroot init
```

Now the directory should be set up, and a CVSROOT directory should be created under the /mnt/cvsroot directory with all the necessary control files.

The examples in the following sections specify the CVSROOT directory by using **cvs -d /mnt/cvsroot** with each command. If you prefer, you can set the shell environment variable for CVSROOT so you do not have to specify **-d /mnt/cvsroot** in each command as the following examples show. To set your environment variable, run **export CVSROOT=/mnt/cvsroot**, or, if you're a C shell user, **setenv CVSROOT /mnt/cvsroot**. To check that you've properly set your environment variable, run **echo $CVSROOT**. If your CVSROOT variable is properly configured, you'll see the output as shown in Figure 7.8.

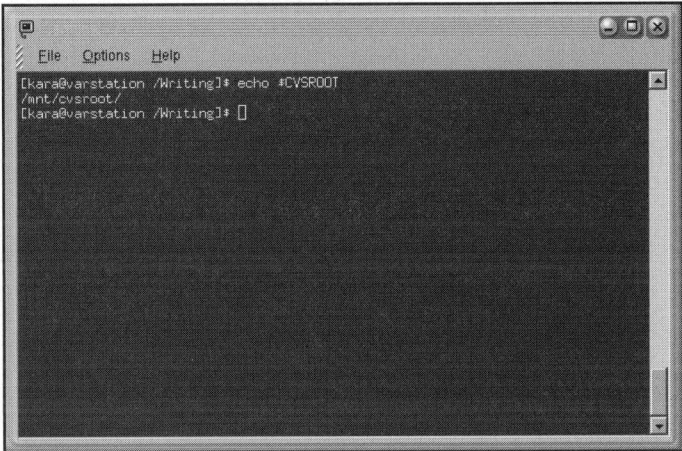

Figure 7.8 *Checking your environment variables*

Checking Files In

Now that you have created the CVS repository, you will probably want to check some files into it. CVS works differently than RCS in this regard. With CVS, you have the option of checking in (or out) entire filesystems (directory structures) or simply individual files.

Change directories to the directory that contains the files you want to commit to the CVS repository. For the sake of this example, you will say that the directory is the /Writing directory in your Home directory.

```
cd Writing
```

Now that you're in the directory, make sure that all the files you want to import are in the directory. Now you import the files from this directory into CVS.

```
cvs -d /mnt/cvsroot import -m "New Example Files" sample Kara A2
```

It probably looks like quite a bit going on there, so break it down into its component parts. Remember that you're really running two commands here—one that starts CVS and one that is the actual CVS command you want to use.

The -*d* flag tells CVS which directory to use as the CVS root, and the following directory (*/mnt/cvsroot*) is the directory for this example. If you don't want to type this all the time, you can set your CVSROOT environment variable to whichever directory is appropriate and save yourself a few keystrokes each time. If you're using only one directory, it's probably a good idea. If you have more than one project going at a time, it's probably just going to cause problems.

The next bit is the command you're actually running, **import**. This is telling CVS that you'd like to import the files in the directory under the module name *sample*. This means that the checked in files will be in /mnt/cvsroot/ sample/, the vendortag for this module is *Kara*, and the release is *A2*. The *-m* flag is telling CVS to write *New Example Files* as the log for this import to the repository. If you leave off the *-m*, CVS will prompt you for a log entry when you execute the command.

Provided that there are no syntax errors, you are rewarded with a message like that shown in Figure 7.9 if the import is successful.

Checking Files Out

To check a project out of the CVS repository, you use the **checkout** command, appropriately enough, which may also be simplified to **co**. There are two ways to check out an entire project. One is to check out by path name relative to the cvsroot, or you can check out by the module name.

You want to be careful where you run the **checkout** command. Whichever directory you're in is where it dumps the files from the project module, so you

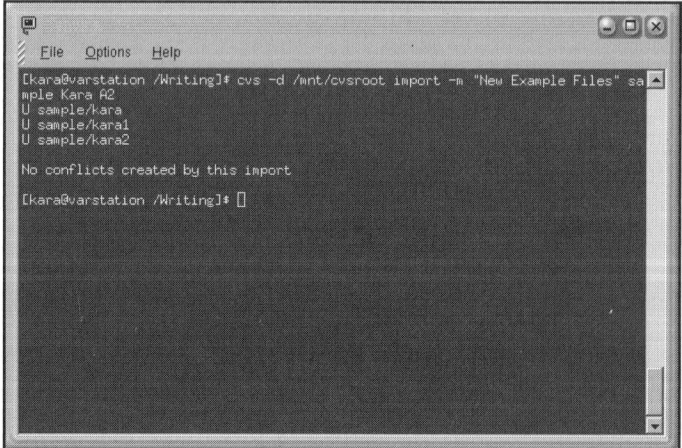

Figure 7.9 *Importing into CVS*

don't want to run the command in your home directory. Switch to a directory where you will work on the files, and then run the **checkout** command.

```
cd /Writing
cvs -d /mnt/cvsroot/ checkout sample
```

Again, there's quite a bit going on here with the checkout line. The first part, *cvs*, just starts CVS with the -d option specifying the cvsroot directory. Finally, the **checkout** *sample* section of the **checkout** command tells CVS to check out the module *sample*. If successful, you will have several files placed in the current directory that you can now work with.

Using CVS GUI Clients

For people who prefer not to memorize all the text-based commands for CVS, there are multiple graphical CVS clients available. Some available clients are Java-based, allowing the client to be run on multiple OS platforms. Setting up a Java environment is beyond the scope of this book, so we won't cover that here. One popular GUI client for multiple platforms is TkCVS.

Making CVS Simple with TkCVS

This section describes TkCVS, a GUI CVS client written in Tcl/Tk. The reason we chose this GUI client from other available clients is mostly that it's simple to set up and it's multiplatform. TkCVS runs on Linux and other UNIX-type OSes with Tcl/Tk 8.1 or higher, as well as Windows 9x or NT.

TkCVS does require Tcl/Tk version 8.1 or higher. Most Linux distributions come with this already. If you're running a relatively recent version of Linux, you should already have this installed.

Installing TkCVS

Installing TkCVS is particularly easy. You can download the latest version for either Linux or Microsoft Windows from the TkCVS Web site at **http://www.twobarleycorns.net/tkcvs.html**. You can also find the Linux version on the CD-ROM included with this book. The most recent version of TkCVS is 6.4.

When you download TkCVS, you will have a file named /tkcvs-6.4.tar.gz for your Linux system, or something similar if the version has changed. For your Microsoft Windows system, Zip files are available on the TkCVS Web site.

> This section discusses installation and examples only for the 6.4 version for Linux. If you are installing to another OS platform, or if TkCVS has been upgraded since this book was published, your software might include changes or installation steps that differ from the examples in this book. Make sure to read the INSTALL notes or README with your downloaded files to check for discrepancies.

Copy the file to an appropriate directory and decompress it. If you're installing TkCVS for use on the entire system, you must **su** to root before running the install script. See the steps that follow.

```
gzip -cd tkcvs-6.4.tar.gz | tar -xvf -
cd tkcvs-6.4/
su
./doinstall.tcl
```

If everything is working correctly, you should see the TkCVS Installer dialog box as displayed in Figure 7.10.

The installation defaults should be fine, so go ahead and press the Install button.

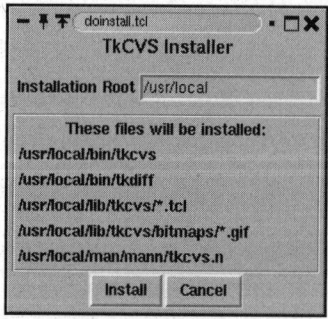

Figure 7.10 *The TkCVS Installer dialog box*

Using TkCVS

To start TkCVS, run the **tkcvs** command. TkCVS first checks to see what the CVSROOT environment variable is; if it's not set, you will get an error message. Be sure to set the environment variable before running TkCVS. To set the CVSROOT environment variable, run the following command.

```
export CVSROOT="/mnt/cvsroot/"
```

or if you are using C shell:

```
setenv CVSROOT /mnt/cvsroot
```

When TkCVS starts up, it opens as a file manager (see Figure 7.11). You can open and view text files with it and change directories just like any standard GUI file manager.

Getting to Know TkCVS

TkCVS is easy to understand. The menus at the top of the TkCVS tool bar control file operations, CVS reports, TkCVS options, and movement history.

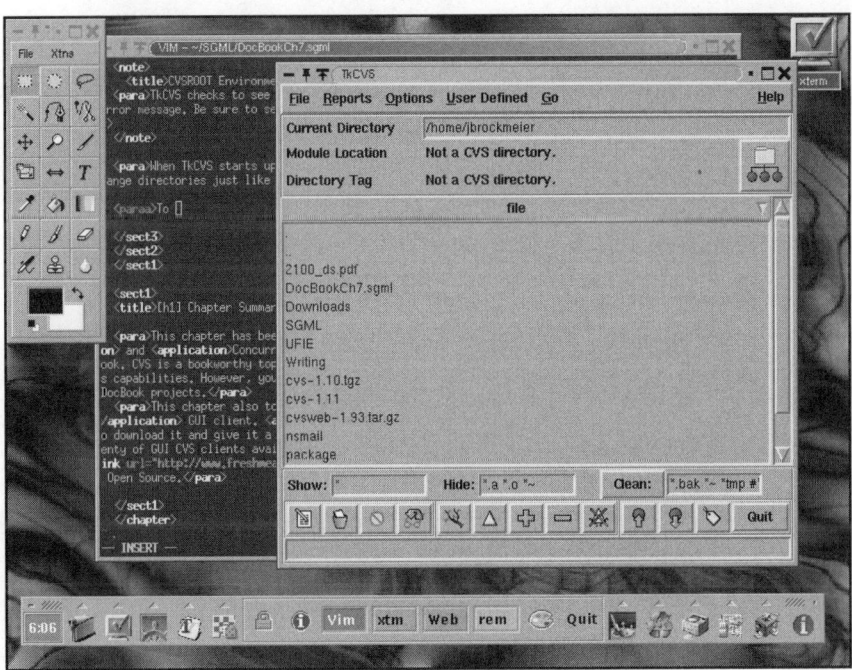

Figure 7.11 *TkCVS*

There's also a decent help menu with instructions on how to use the various features of TkCVS.

What the buttons at the bottom of the TkCVS window do is not obvious, but if you hover your mouse over one of them for a second, it gives you a description of the button (see Figure 7.12).

Committing Files with TkCVS

To commit files with TkCVS, browse to the directory you want to commit into CVS. Click the large button to the right of the application; it is the picture of a folder with several red dots underneath it (see Figure 7.13).

Checking Out Files with TkCVS

To check out files from the CVS repository, select the Options menu, and you will have a list of options from which to choose (see Figure 7.14).

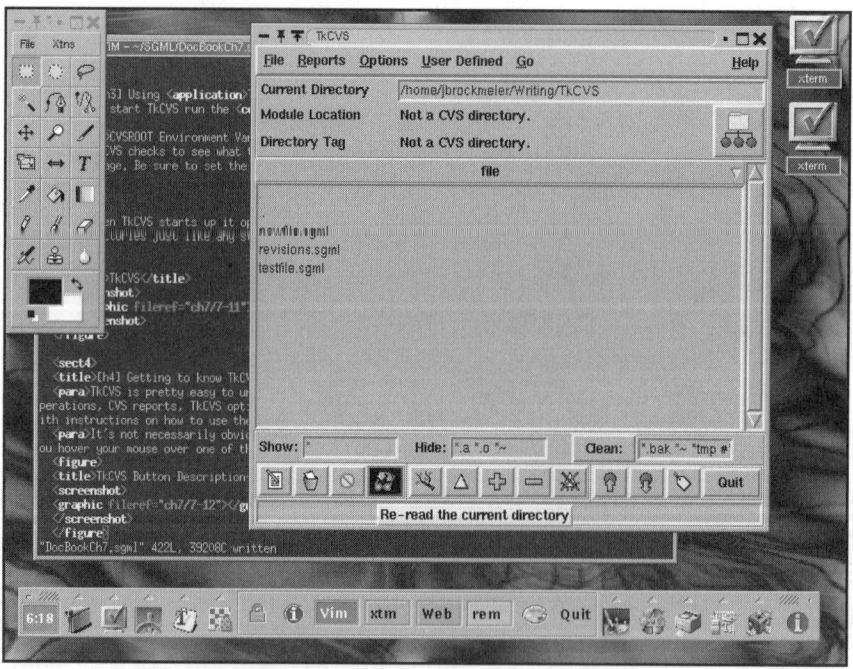

Figure 7.12 *A TkCVS button description*

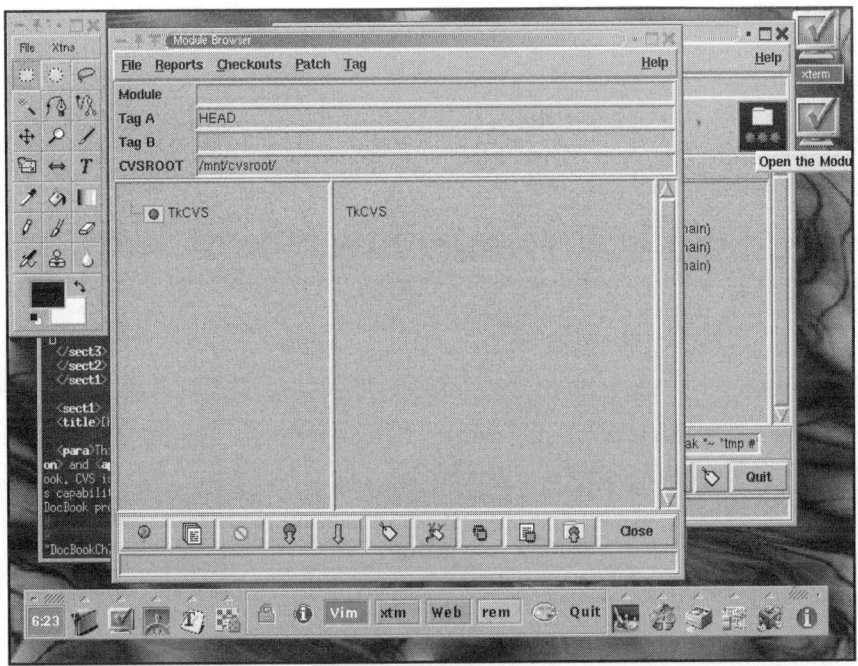

Figure 7.13 *The TkCVS commit browser*

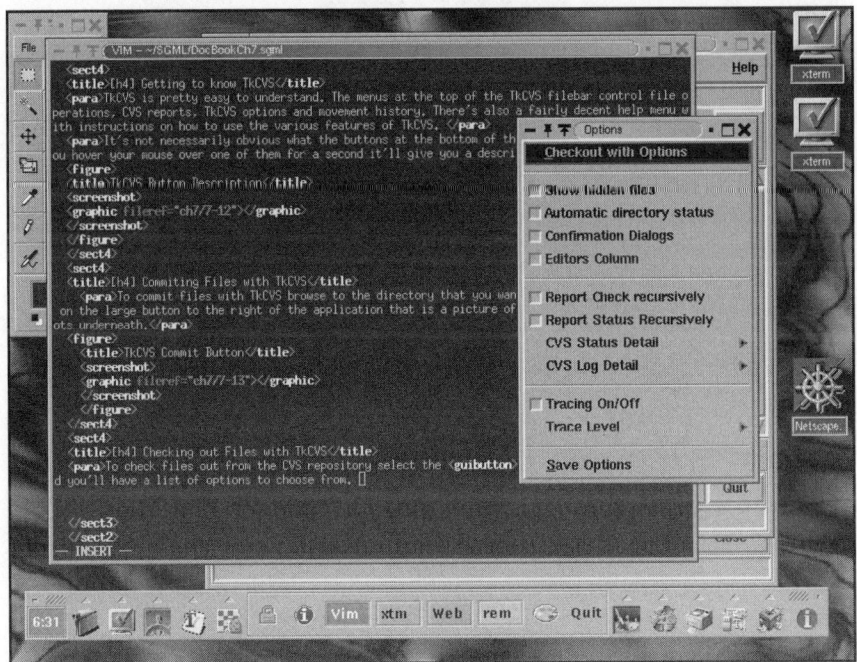

Figure 7.14 *The TkCVS Checkout with Options menu*

Viewing Revision Logs

A really neat feature of TkCVS is your ability to view the revision log of a file or directory. With command-line CVS, you can get the same information, but TkCVS makes it much easier to read by making it graphical. It's like a family tree for file revision, very handy.

To view a revision log, select a file in the left pane of TkCVS, and then click the button that looks like a tree branch at the bottom of the TkCVS window, shown in Figure 7.15.

More about TkCVS

TkCVS does much more than the basics you need for using it with DocBook. If you want to find out more about TkCVS for use as a developer, try the online help that comes with TkCVS, or visit the TkCVS Web site at **http://www.twobarleycorns.net/tkcvs.html**.

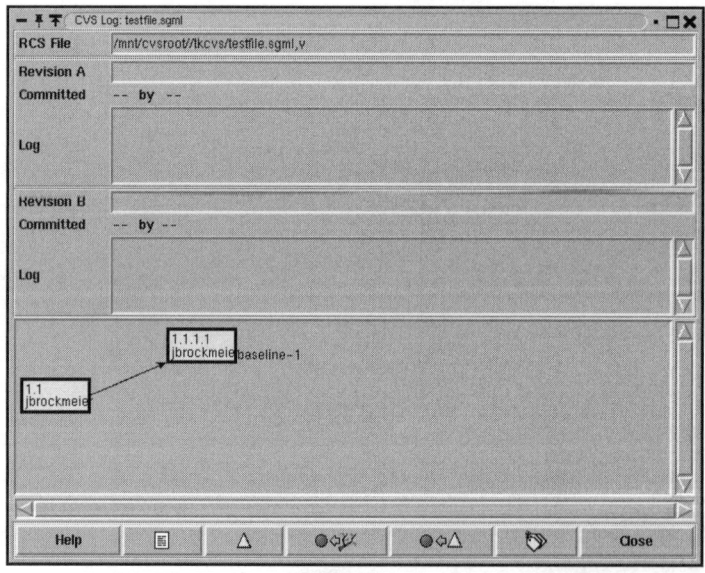

Figure 7.15 *Viewing revision logs*

Other GUI Clients for CVS

As we discussed earlier in this chapter, while we focus our examples and instructions on the clients for Linux, there are other Open Source clients available for Linux and for other operating systems. To experiment with other clients, visit the Web sites listed below. Please note that with the speed of development, this list is nowhere near complete, or may have outdated links by the time you read this book.

- **Cervisia.** KDE Client for Linux—**http://cervisia.sourceforge.net**
- **gCVS.** HP-UX, Linux, MacOS, Windows—**http://www.arachne. org/software/gcvs/**
- **jCVS.** Java—**http://www.jcvs.org/**
- **LinCVS.** Linux—**http://www.lincvs.org/**
- **MacCVS Pro.** MacOS—**http://www.maccvs.org/**
- **NetBeans.** Java—**http://www.netbeans.org/**

Summary

This chapter provides an overview of the GNU Revision Control System and Concurrent Versions System for revision control with DocBook. Both RCS and CVS are book-worthy topics of their own, and this chapter only touches the surface of their capabilities. However, you have enough information to utilize either RCS or CVS for collaborative DocBook projects.

This chapter also touches on managing and interacting with CVS using the TkCVS GUI client. TkCVS is freely available, and I encourage you to download it and give it a try. If TkCVS isn't for you, plenty of GUI CVS clients not listed above are also available for Linux and other platforms in various stages of development. Check Freshmeat at **http://www.freshmeat.net/** for other CVS clients that are Open Source.

Chapter 8: Using Emacs

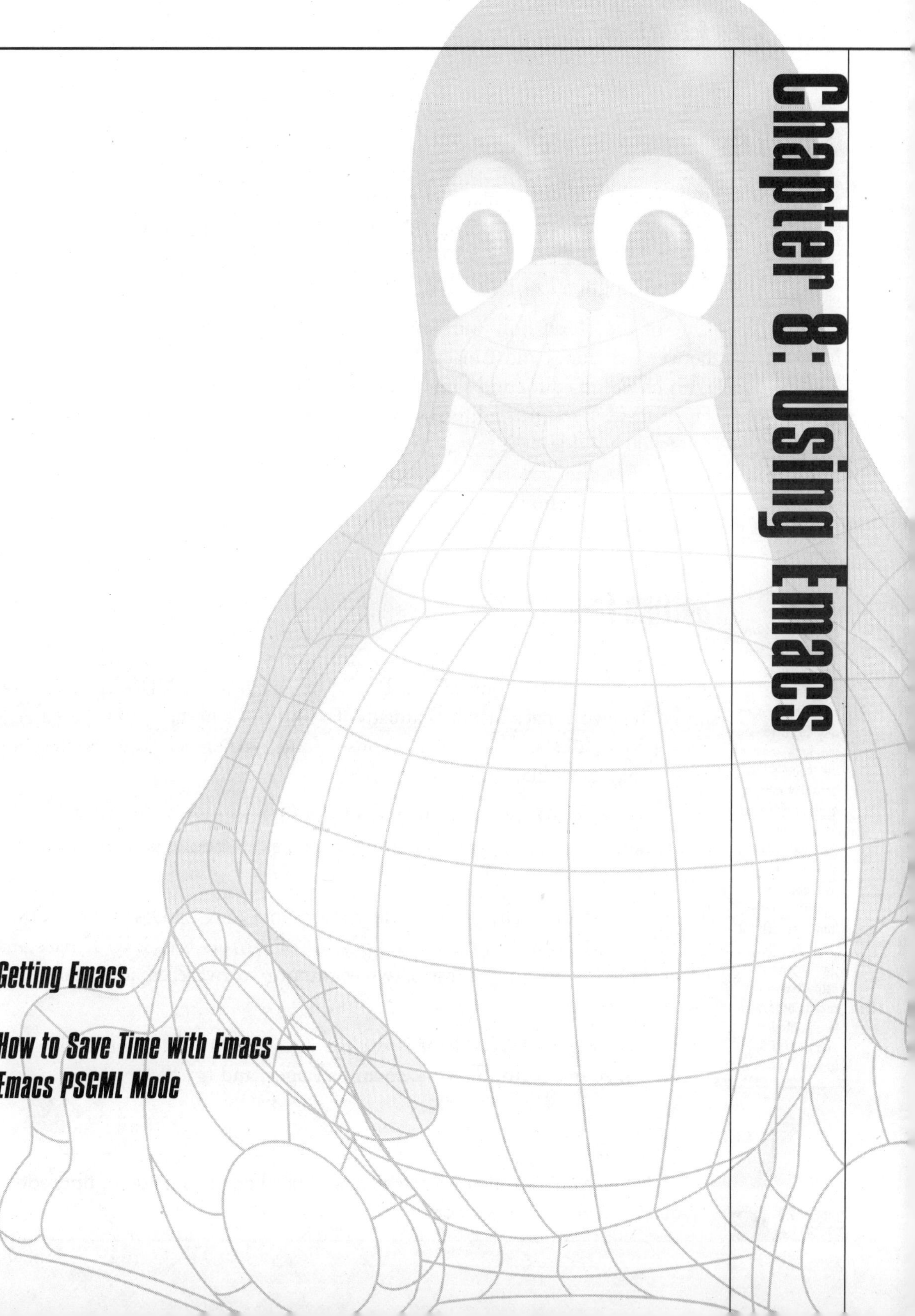

Getting Emacs

How to Save Time with Emacs — Emacs PSGML Mode

A *macro*, in computer lingo, is a set of saved instructions that can be recalled with a single command or keystroke. Originally, Emacs wasn't a true program unto itself, but a set of macros for the text editor *TECO (Tape Editor and Corrector)* on the *ITS (Incompatible Timesharing System)* operating system on the PDP-10 computer. Emacs' first iteration came into existence in 1976, quite a while ago for a computer program. The history behind Emacs is quite interesting but, sadly, outside the scope of this book. For more on the history behind Emacs, visit the Emacs FAQ at **http://www. geekgirl.com/ emacs/faq/index. html**, or check out the Emacs entry in the Jargon File at **http://www. tuxedo.org/~esr/ jargon/html/ entry/EMACS. html**.

One of the most popular text editors for creating documents with DocBook is *Emacs*, short for *Editing Macros*. Originally created by Richard Stallman at M.I.T., Emacs is a set of macros that eventually evolved into a full-fledged program known as *GNU Emacs*.

One of the oldest holy wars in the Linux/UNIX community is the schism between vi clones and Emacs. Proponents of each editor tend to be loyal to their choice of editor and somewhat derogatory of the other. It's really a matter of taste. Each text editor has features and properties that some love and others do not. I leave it to you to decide, and I recommend that if you've never used either one, you try both and see which one suits your working habits best. For those who prefer vi clones, the next chapter discusses the use of Vim to edit DocBook documents.

Getting Emacs

The first step, of course, is to install Emacs on your system. If you're running a Linux distribution, one of the BSDs, or any other UNIX-type OS, you probably have Emacs installed already. To find out whether you have Emacs, just open an xterm, or log in to a console and type **emacs**. You should get a screen that looks like Figure 8.1.

If you don't have Emacs installed, read on. I'll cover the installation process for Linux and UNIX-type operating systems, Windows systems, and the MacOS.

To get source or binaries for GNU Emacs on Linux or UNIX-type OSes, visit the GNU Emacs home page for a list of mirrors for GNU Emacs and other GNU software, at **http://www.gnu.org/software/emacs/emacs.html** (see Figure 8.2).

You can also find GNU Emacs on the CD-ROM that comes with this book—in source form, RPM, Debian packages, and tgz files.

NOTE

The Linux install instructions are also helpful when you decide to upgrade your GNU Emacs installation.

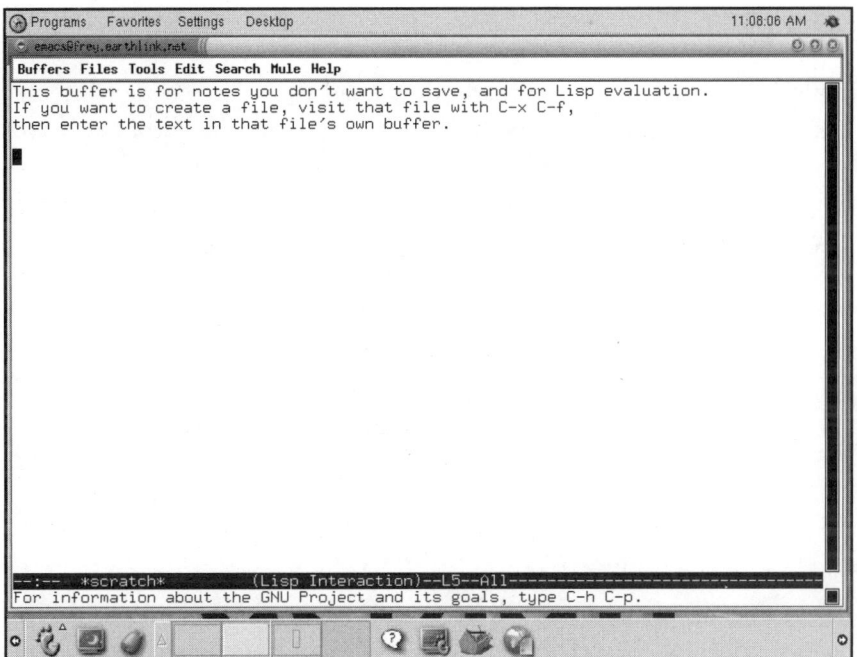

Figure 8.1 *GNU Emacs comes to life.*

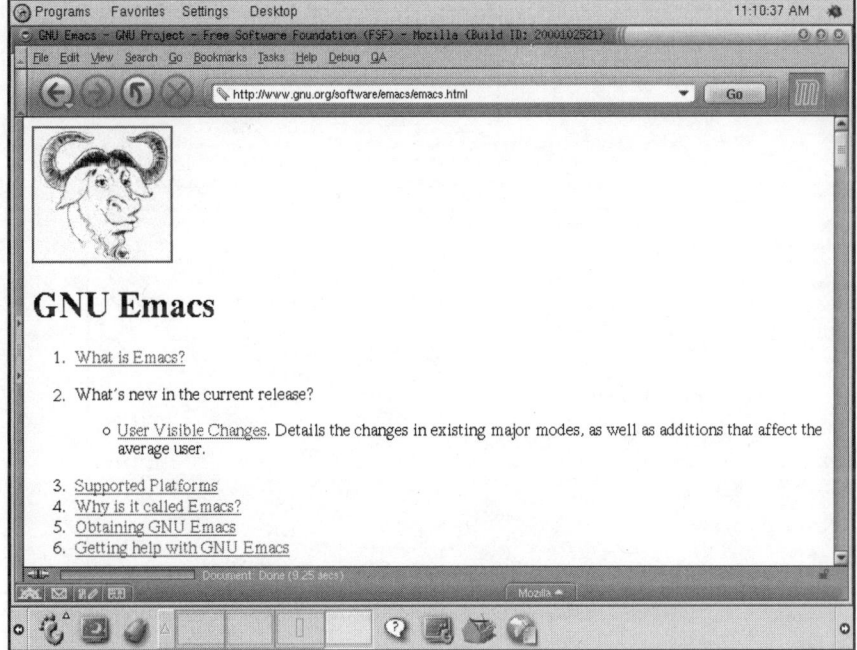

Figure 8.2 *The GNU Emacs home page*

Linux and UNIX

To compile GNU Emacs from scratch, download the source code from the GNU site, or grab it from the CD-ROM. You must log in as root—if you don't have the root password for your computer, see your system administrator. (And while you're at it, ask your sys admin why he or she didn't install Emacs!) Copy the tarball into your /tmp directory, and log in as root:

```
su
cd /tmp/
tar -zxvf emacs-20.7.tar.gz
cd emacs-20.7/
./configure
make
make install
```

You should see messages like those shown in Figure 8.3 while Emacs is compiling. Note that the name of the directory in this example is dependent on the version number. If the version number of Emacs has changed, the name of the archive and directory will change as well.

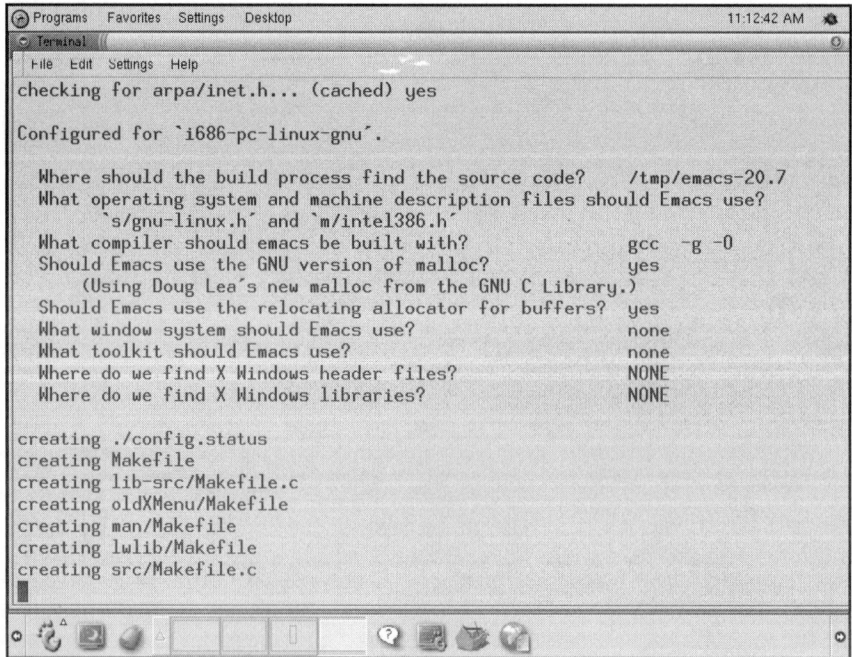

Figure 8.3 *Compiling Emacs*

Emacs on Win32

To get Emacs for Windows 9x or NT, you can find precompiled binary versions on the CD-ROM or check for later versions at **ftp://ftp.gnu.org/gnu/windows/emacs/latest/**.

You will find several files in this directory; the one to grab is the full, precompiled version of Emacs. It will be named something like emacs-20.7-fullbin-i386.zip, but the 20.7 part will change as version numbers change. The Web page specifically says that these Emacs versions run on Windows NT, 95, and 98, but no word on whether Emacs runs on Windows 2000 or Windows Millennium Edition (Windows ME). If you are running 2000 or ME, give this a shot—it's unlikely that your computer will burst into flames.

Unzip the file with WinZip or whatever program you prefer for unzipping Zip files.

In case you're wondering how to read that insidiously long filename, *emacs* is the name of the file, *20.7* is the version number, *fullbin* is short for *full binary* (meaning the entire program in executable form), *i386* is shorthand for machines with Intel processors in the x86 family, and finally, *zip* indicates that it is a Zip file.

There are no spaces in the filename because spaces aren't valid filename characters in UNIX-type operating systems. That's a good thing to remember if you're swapping DocBook files with folks on Linux or other UNIX-type OSes.

Figure 8.4 shows the GNU Emacs on Windows FAQ at **http://www.gnu.org/software/emacs/windows/ntemacs.html**.

To run Emacs under Windows (see Figure 8.5), just double-click on the emacs.exe file.

MacOS

Finally, if you're running the MacOS, you don't have to be left out in the cold. There's a port of Emacs for the MacOS as well. I've included the MacOS port on the CD-ROM, and you can find new versions at **http://mac-emacs.sourceforge.net/index.html** (see Figure 8.6).

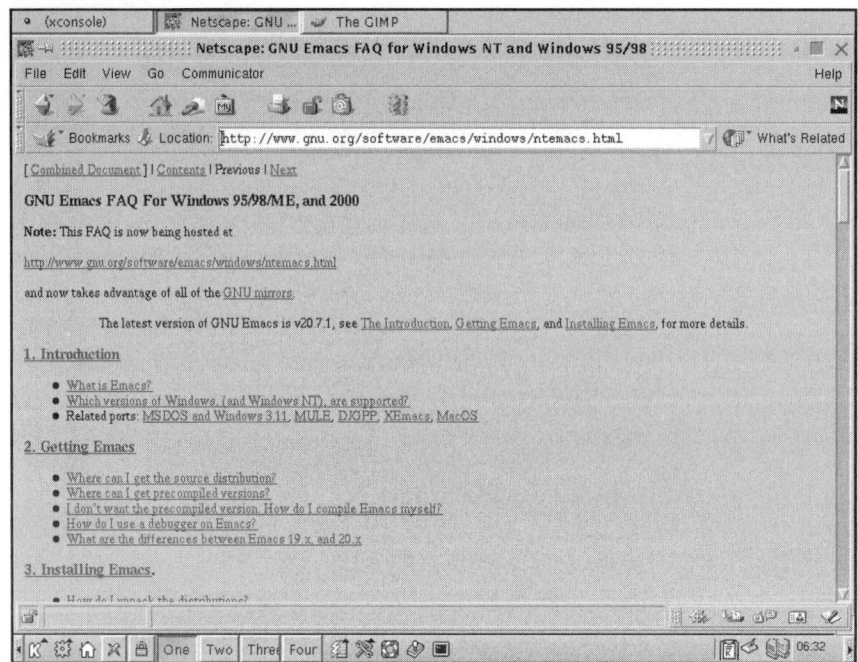

Figure 8.4 *The GNU Emacs on Windows NT and Windows 95/98 home page*

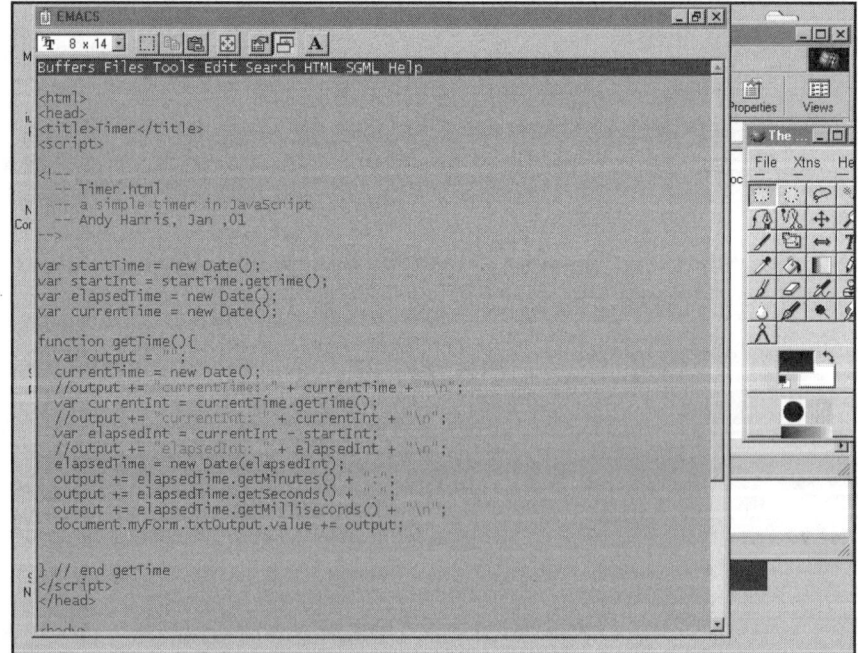

Figure 8.5 *Emacs running on Windows*

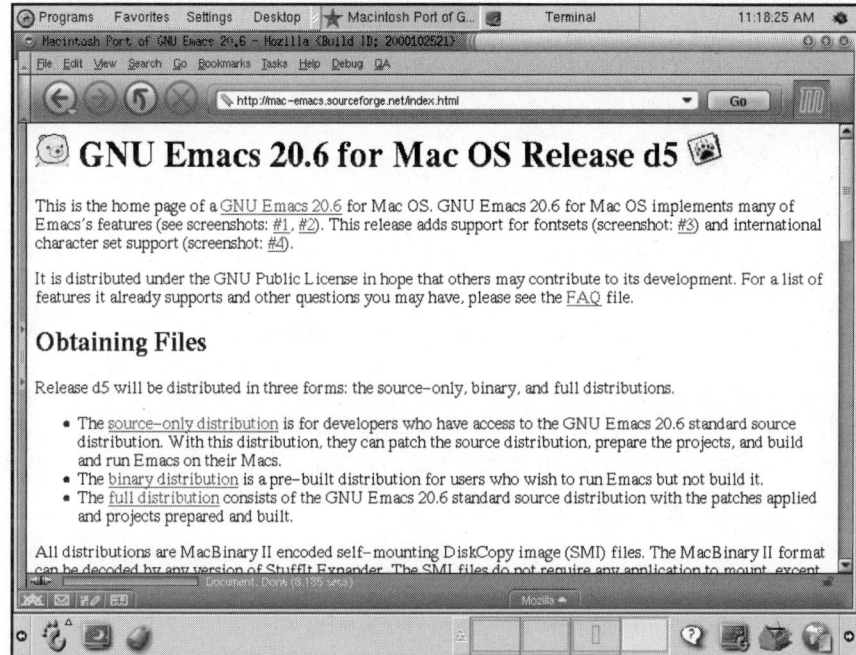

Figure 8.6 *The GNU Emacs for MacOS home page*

You can also sign up for a mailing list for users of Emacs for the MacOS and for a list for developers if you want to hack away at Emacs.

To use Emacs for the MacOS, you need MacOS 8.1 or later.

Now that you have installed GNU Emacs on the operating system of your choice, you can start using it.

Basic Emacs Guide

Before jumping into editing DocBook files with Emacs, take a moment for an introduction to Emacs basics. There's quite a bit to Emacs, so I cannot cover all the functionality available in Emacs. It would take an entire book to do that, maybe two (it has a lot of functions!). However, you will learn all the basics of text editing so that you can work comfortably with DocBook.

Key Conventions

There are two ways to do things in Emacs, via menus or hot-key combinations. In this section, you will concentrate on the hot-key combinations because they're the most common way of getting things done in Emacs. The following is a quick reference to the key conventions used in this chapter:

- **C.** The Control key
- **M.** The Meta key, usually the Alt key on your keyboard
- **ESC.** The Escape key
- **DEL.** The Delete key, often mapped to your Backspace key, as well as the Delete key in Emacs
- **C-** or **M-.** The Control or Meta key and another key

Often Emacs commands consist of two hot-key combinations. For instance, the combination **C-x C-c** (read as Control-x Control-c) exits Emacs. Note that the meta key is usually mapped to the Alt key or the Windows key on some newer keyboards.

To start Emacs, either type **emacs** in a terminal window, or double-click on the Emacs icon—depending on which operating system you're using. For the most part, the instructions in this chapter refer to the Linux version of Emacs. However, because Emacs uses the same key bindings across platforms, it shouldn't be a problem.

If you're using Emacs on the MacOS or Windows, Emacs simply runs in its own program window like any other program. In Linux, you can run Emacs at the console or in X. If you run Emacs in X, you can choose to start Emacs within a terminal window or as a separate window with menus with mouse support.

> When you start Emacs, you will note that it mentions a scratch *buffer* and refers to each file that is open as a *buffer*. Like Vim, Emacs considers each open file to be in a buffer—a space in memory until it is saved to disk—which is more accurate than your thinking that you are working on the file itself. When Emacs opens a file, it is making a copy in memory that you can safely tinker with, and no changes are made until you tell Emacs to save the file. At that point, the differences between the buffer you're working in and the file saved on disk are reconciled, and the file is written to disk—either over the existing file or as a new file.

To start Emacs at a console, type **emacs**. Within X, you can start Emacs by typing **emacs** in an xterm, and a special Emacs window like that shown in Figure 8.7 will appear.

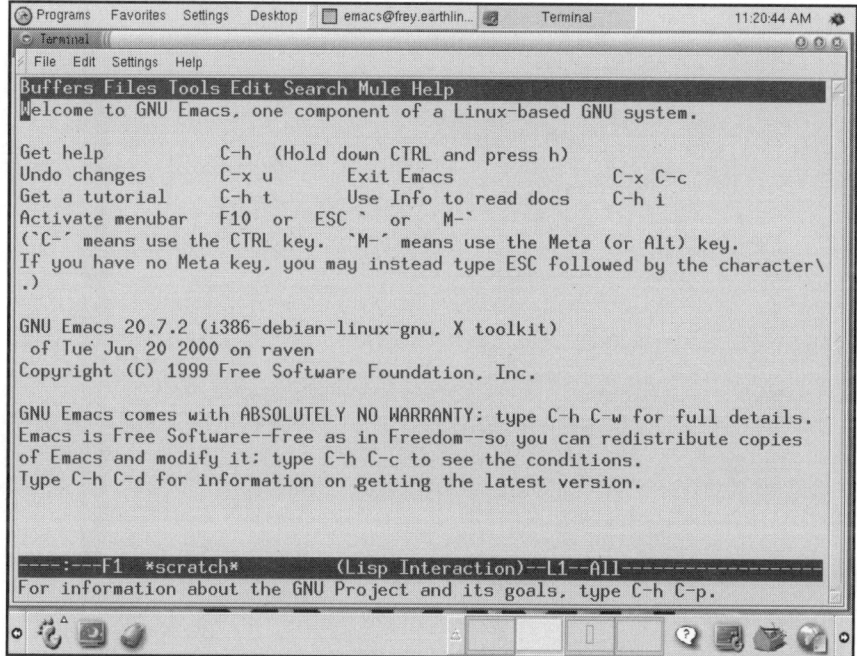

Figure 8.7 *Emacs in its own window*

If you'd prefer Emacs as it looks at the console, without the mouse support, type **emacs -nw** in an xterm.

Now that you're in Emacs, you are presented with the Emacs welcome screen. Next, you will practice getting around in Emacs by creating a new file.

To create a new file in Emacs, type **C-x C-f**. At the bottom of your Emacs screen, you will see text that says Find file: ~/, which means that Emacs wants to open a file in your home directory. However, because you want to start a new file, you type the name of the file with which you want to work (see Figure 8.8).

Although Emacs is a multiplatform program, it takes heavy influence from the UNIX environment. The ~ character, or tilde, is shorthand in UNIX for the user's home directory. For instance, if you want to indicate the path to a file in your home directory, you type **~/path/to/file.txt** instead of **/home/zonker/path/to/file.txt**, and the shell interprets the ~ character to mean the home directory.

NOTE

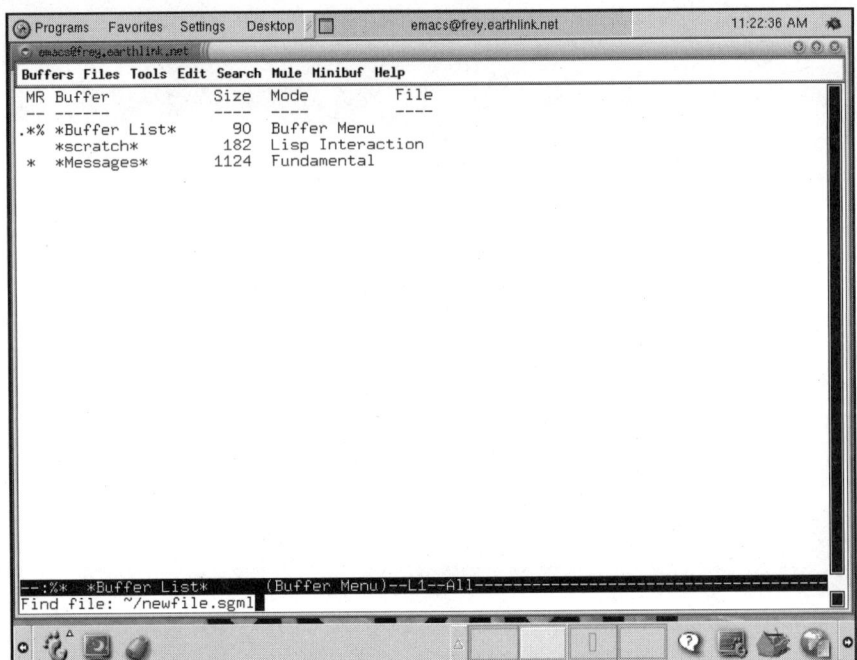

Figure 8.8 *Creating a new file with Emacs*

Now that you have a new file to play with, you can start working. First, though, let me explain how to bail out of a mistyped command. Emacs has many commands, and they can be confusing. Sometimes you might type the wrong command, or you might just have 10 thumbs like me. When you type **C-x C-f** (open or create file) instead of **C-x C-s** (save file), you must press Escape three times to bail out—that's **ESC ESC ESC**—and Emacs will return to normal operation.

Type a few lines in Emacs so that you have something to play with. Try the traditional "The quick brown fox jumped over the lazy dog" (see Figure 8.9).

Moving around in Emacs

Now that you're at the end of the sentence, move backwards a bit. You can move around in Emacs the traditional way—with the arrow keys at a console or with the mouse in a GUI environment—or you can get around even faster. Table 8.1 presents Emacs movement key bindings.

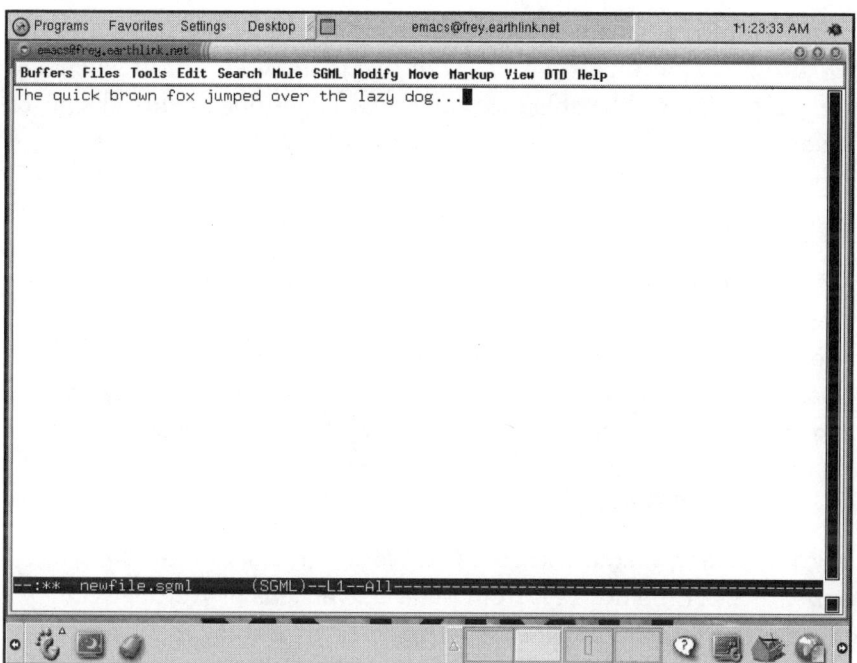

Figure 8.9 *Getting used to Emacs*

Table 8.1 Emacs Movement Key Bindings

Movement Commands	Action
C-v or the Page Up key	Forward one page
ESC-v or the Page Down key	Back one page
ESC < or the Home key	Beginning of the file
ESC > or the End key	End of the file
C-f	Forward one character
C-b	Back one character
C-p	Preceding line
C-n	Next line
C-a	Beginning of the line
C-e	End of the line
ESC-f	Forward one word
ESC-b	Back one word

Try moving around in Emacs using the hot-key combinations instead of the mouse or arrow keys. It might take a day or two to get used to, but when you do, it's very easy. You will be able to zoom around your documents like never before. Note that you need to use the Shift key as well to get the > and < characters.

Why, oh why, are there so many darned hot keys in Emacs and vi, you might ask yourself. Well, there's a very good reason. Both Emacs and vi were designed in days when mice were practically unheard of and most work was done on terminals by programmers, not average humans like you and me. Remember, the guys who invented Emacs and vi were from the old school, still using punch cards to enter data into computers. Hot keys were practically heaven compared to those.

Actually, Emacs and vi aren't so odd. Old WordPerfect users can probably remember most of the hot keys from MS-DOS versions of WordPerfect. In fact, nearly all modern applications respect F7 as the key to initialize spell check. (There are probably others, but spell check is the one I remember most.) Even today, in the world of ultra-slick word processors such as Microsoft Word and desktop publishing programs such as QuarkXPress, hot keys abound. You don't need to learn the hot keys to use Word, that's true. If you care to, though, you can use Word or QuarkXPress seldom ever touching the mouse, depending on what you're doing.

The bottom line for writing is that even though memorizing the hot keys might seem like a huge hurdle at first, you will see your productivity soar.

Searching and Replacing in Emacs

To move around even faster, try using the search functions of Emacs to move around the file. If you're in a lengthy document, even moving one page at a time can be slow. However, if you know that you're looking for the sentence with *wubba wubba wubba* in it, you can use the search function to cut to the chase and jump straight there. Table 8.2 shows a list of the Emacs search key bindings.

Table 8.2 Emacs Search key bindings

Search Commands	Action
C-s	Search forward.
C-r	Search backward.
C-s C-s	Repeat last forward search.
C-s C-r	Repeat last search backwards.
ESC %	Search and replace.
RETURN	End search.

In search and replace operations, Emacs asks for the string to search for and the replacement text, if any (see Figure 8.10).

By default, Emacs asks before replacing text. To approve the change, type **y** or press the Space key. If you don't want to replace the text, type **n** or press the Delete key. When you're done searching and replacing, type **RETURN** and you will return to the normal editing mode.

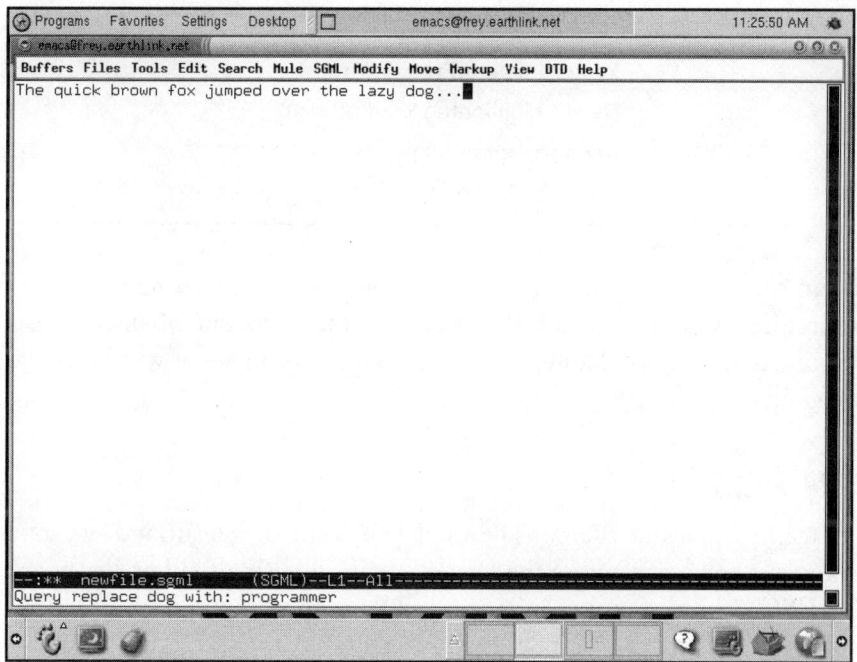

Figure 8.10 *Search and replace with Emacs*

Cutting and Pasting in Emacs

The cut and paste functions in Emacs are straightforward. Type **C-d** to delete the character the cursor is currently on and **DEL** to delete backwards. To make life easy, or at least easier, Table 8.3 shows the key bindings for cutting and pasting in Emacs.

> Depending on your key mapping, the Backspace key and Delete key may or may not do the same thing. You might have to get used to using the Delete key instead of the Backspace key, depending on how Emacs reads your key map. This is a throwback to keyboards with only a Delete key.

Table 8.3 Cutting and Pasting

Command	Action
C-d	Delete current character.
DEL	Delete preceding character.
ESC DEL	Delete the preceding word.
ESC d	Delete the next word.
C-y	Restore deleted text (paste).
C-w	Delete highlighted/marked text.
C-k	Delete to end of line.
C-x u	Undo the last edit.

As you can see, Emacs has a plethora of options for manipulating and moving text around. It might take a little while to get used to, but when you have the hang of Emacs, you probably won't want to work in a regular word processor ever again.

Accessing Menus

If you're using Emacs at the console or if you want to get around without using the mouse, you can access the Emacs menus by using the hot-key combination **ESC `**, which opens a split window with the menu choices (see Figure 8.11).

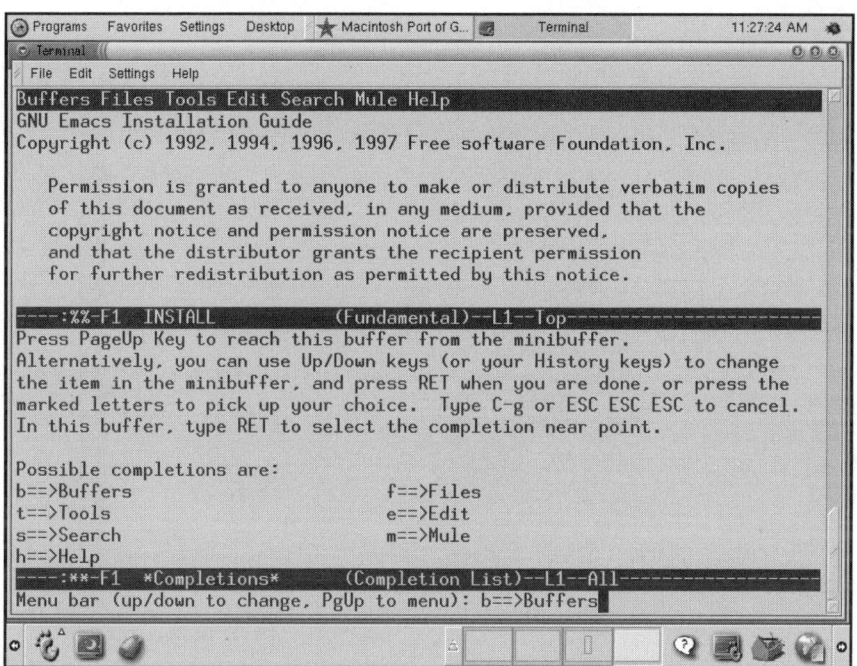

Figure 8.11 *Emacs displaying menus*

Help!

If you want to find out more about Emacs, try Emacs' online help function. To get a tutorial, type **C-h t** and Emacs will take you into its tutorial mode. To get information about a specific key combination, type **C-h k**, which will then give you a prompt to type the key combination about which you need more information. Figure 8.12 shows Emacs' help function in action.

You can also access the Help menu from the keyboard, although, oddly, some of the choices under the Help menu aren't related to help at all, such as the Options submenu.

How to Save Time with Emacs — Emacs PSGML Mode

Emacs, being the lovable customizable behemoth that it is, allows for various editing modes. One of the major modes for Emacs is the PSGML mode, which is for editing SGML documents.

Buzzword

Emacs has two types of modes, *major* and *minor*. Emacs may be in only one major mode in a buffer at a time and may have one or more minor modes in each buffer at a time. Basically, the major modes correspond to the type of documents Emacs is editing. There are major modes for TeX and LaTeX files, C and C++ programs, FORTRAN, and many other programming languages. By default, Emacs is in Fundamental mode, which is basically a generic mode suited for plain editing. Minor modes are things like whether Emacs turns on word wrap or autosaving of files.

Figure 8.12 *Emacs describing a hot key*

If you have not already installed PSGML, you can get the binaries or source from the CD-ROM or the latest source from the PSGML Web page at **http://www.lysator.liu.se/projects/about_psgml.html.**

PSGML works with more than just DocBook; the latest version should work with any valid SGML or XML DTD.

To install PSGML, you must put the files in a directory in Emacs' load path. On my system, I have an Emacs directory under my home directory and a psgml directory under that, so it looks like /home/zonker/Emacs/psgml/, with all PSGML *.el and *.elc files located in the psgml/ directory. You also need an .emacs file in your home directory, with the following lines:

```
(autoload 'sgml-mode "psgml" "Major mode to edit SGML files." t)
(autoload 'xml-mode "psgml" "Major mode to edit XML files." t)
```

As an example of a complete .emacs file, you can use mine for a reference (see Figure 8.13).

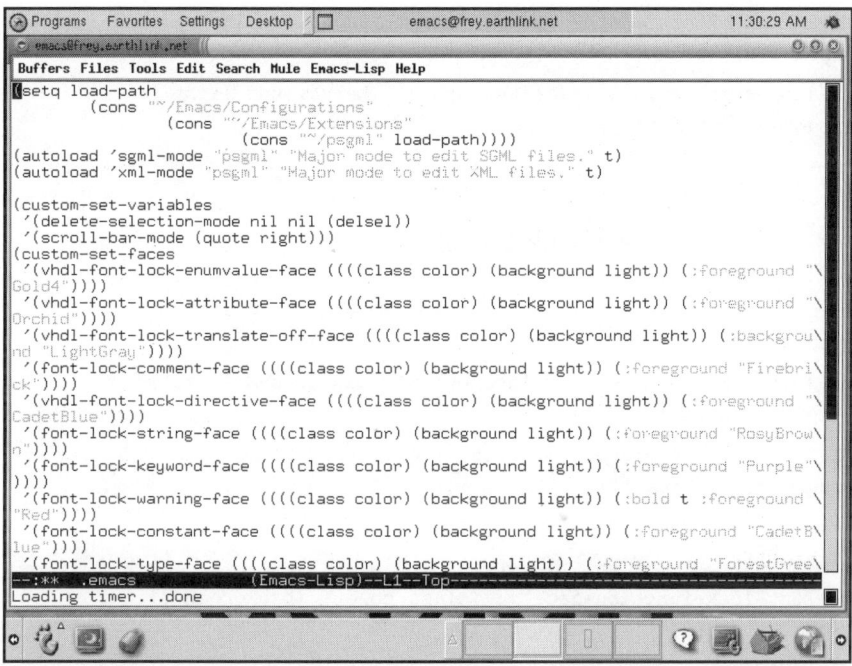

Figure 8.13 *My .emacs file*

```
(setq load-path
        (cons "~/Emacs/Configurations"
                (cons "~/Emacs/Extensions"
                        (cons "~/psgml" load-path))))
(autoload 'sgml-mode "psgml" "Major mode to edit SGML files." t)
(autoload 'xml-mode "psgml" "Major mode to edit XML files." t)

(custom-set-variables
  '(delete-selection-mode nil nil (delsel))
  '(scroll-bar-mode (quote right)))
(custom-set-faces
'(vhdl-font-lock-enumvalue-face ((((class color) (background light))
(:foreground "Gold4"))))
  '(vhdl-font-lock-attribute-face ((((class color) (background light))
(:foreground "Orchid"))))
```

```
 '(vhdl-font-lock-translate-off-face ((((class color) (background light))
(:background "LightGray")))))

 '(font-lock-comment-face ((((class color) (background light))
(:foreground "Firebrick")))))

 '(vhdl-font-lock-directive-face ((((class color) (background light))
(:foreground "CadetBlue")))))

 '(font-lock-string-face ((((class color) (background light))
(:foreground "RosyBrown")))))

 '(font-lock-keyword-face ((((class color) (background light))
(:foreground "Purple")))))

 '(font-lock-warning-face ((((class color) (background light))
(:bold t :foreground "Red")))))

 '(font-lock-constant-face ((((class color) (background light))
(:foreground "CadetBlue")))))

 '(font-lock-type-face ((((class color) (background light)) (:foreground
"ForestGreen")))))

 '(vhdl-font-lock-function-face ((((class color) (background light))
(:foreground "Orchid4")))))

 '(vhdl-font-lock-reserved-words-face ((((class color) (background
light)) (:bold t :foreground "Orange")))))

 '(font-lock-variable-name-face ((((class color) (background light))
(:foreground "DarkGoldenrod")))))

 '(vhdl-font-lock-prompt-face ((((class color) (background light))
(:bold t :foreground "Red")))))

 '(font-lock-function-name-face ((((class color) (background light))
(:foreground "Blue")))))

 '(font-lock-builtin-face ((((class color) (background light))
(:foreground "Orchid"))))))
```

Only the first few lines are concerned with loading the PSGML mode. The remainder are concerned with syntax highlighting. As .emacs files go, this is probably a short one.

> The .emacs file is in the Lisp programming language. Emacs runs a Lisp interpreter, which enables it to do all the wonderful things it does so well. Lisp is a programming language invented in the 1950s at M.I.T., originally known as the *List Processing Language*. However, the acronym is often explained as *Lots of Irritating Superfluous Parentheses* for reasons that should be obvious from the .emacs file example.

Editing DocBook in Emacs

To move from the Fundamental mode to the PSGML mode in Emacs, type **M-x sgml-mode**. If all the files are in the right places, you should now be in PSGML mode (see Figure 8.14).

The PSGML mode offers some advantages for marking up DocBook documents. You will note that when you enter the PSGML mode, you have additional menus to work with that are specifically concerned with SGML.

Using the menus in PSGML mode, you can insert elements and attributes, hide the markup to look only at the text, and even validate the document and look for errors.

The SGML Menu

The SGML menu in PSGML mode allows you to list valid tags by context, validate the current document, and toggle the warning log to see the kind of errors in your document (see Figure 8.15). Many functions available in the

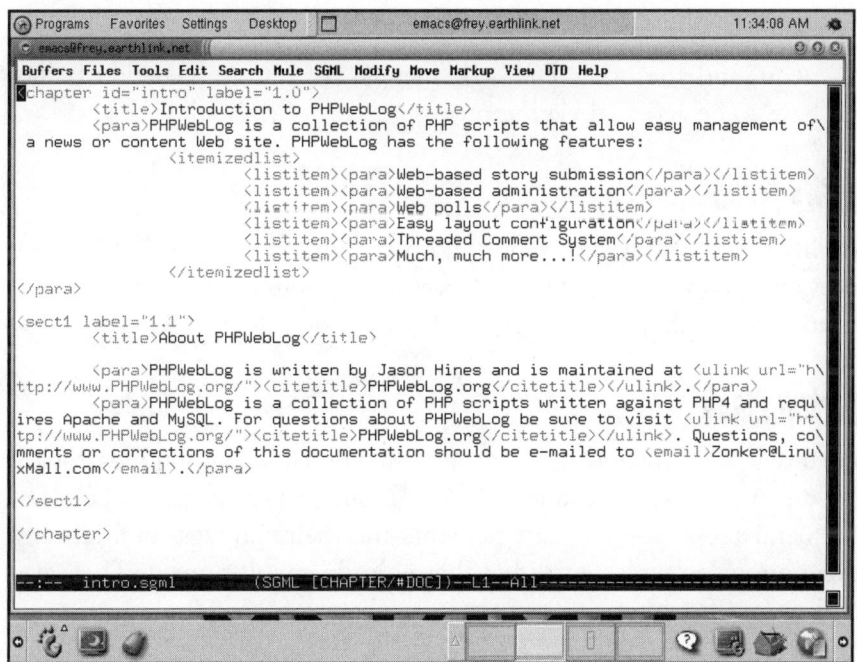

Figure 8.14 *Emacs in PSGML mode*

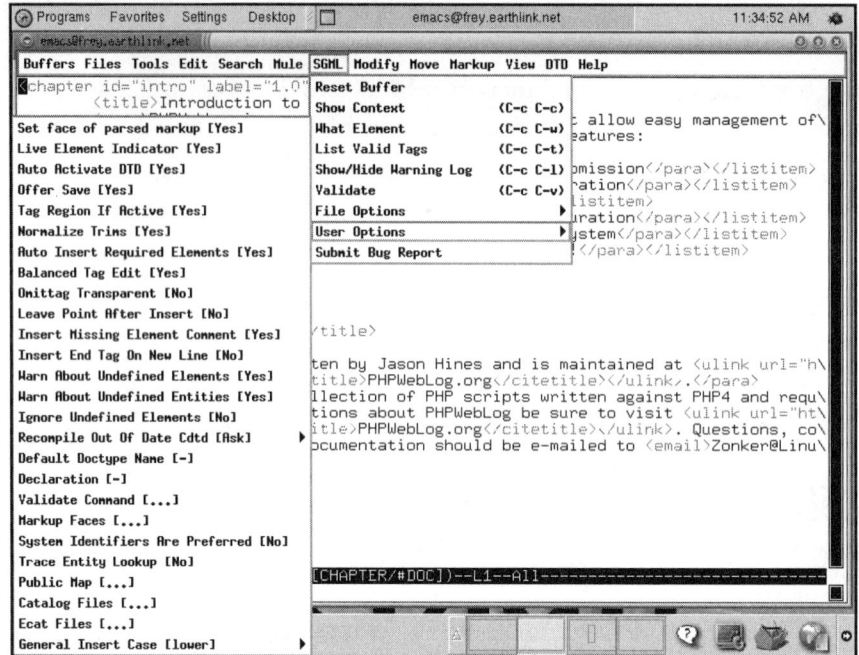

Figure 8.15 *The SGML menu in Emacs PSGML mode*

SGML menu, and the other PSGML menus, are not associated with hot keys but have to be accessed via the menus.

The Modify Menu

The Modify menu in PSGML mode allows the user to expand elements and references and to make character references and various other changes to elements and their attributes (see Figure 8.17).

The Markup Menu

The menu that will probably be of most use to you while editing DocBook is the Markup menu available under PSGML mode (see Figure 8.17). The Markup menu allows you to insert elements and their end tags automatically, depending on which tags are valid at that point in the document. This saves a lot of time and trouble when you get in the habit of using it.

To end the current element, use the command **C-c /**, which should be easy to remember because all end tags use the / character.

The Markup menu also gives users the ability to insert attributes in their tags.

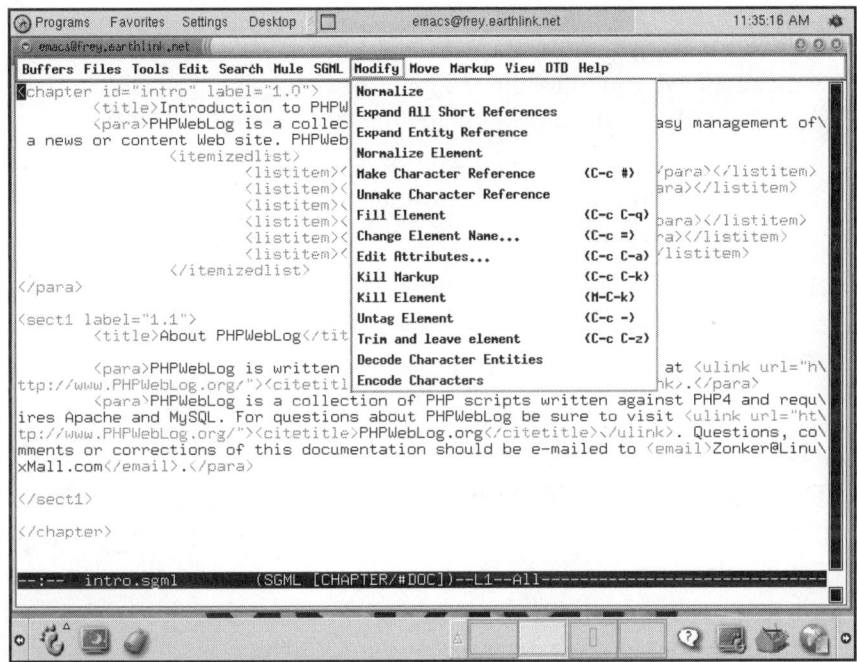

Figure 8.16 *The Modify menu in Emacs PSGML mode*

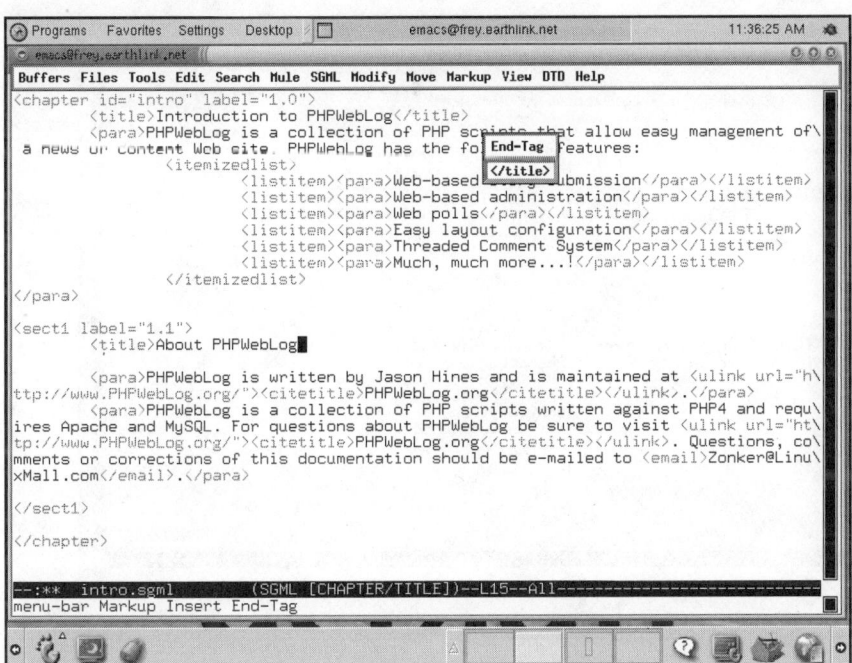

Figure 8.17 *Inserting an end tag in PSGML mode*

The View Menu

The View menu allows you to toggle the types of views you have of your document. Sometimes all the elements and attributes get in the way of the actual writing, so you want just to read the plain text. No problem! The View menu allows you to hide or show all tags and attributes while you're working so that you can work more efficiently.

Figure 8.18 is the before, and Figure 8.19 is the after. Notice how much easier it is to read the document in Figure 8.19—and all the information is still there. Emacs is just hiding it for the time being.

The DTD Menu

The DTD menu gives you all kinds of information on the current DTD and elements within the DTD (see Figure 8.20). You can use the DTD menu to list all valid elements for a DTD, the valid attributes and the elements with which they correspond, and the content that can appear in elements—including the other elements that can occur within them.

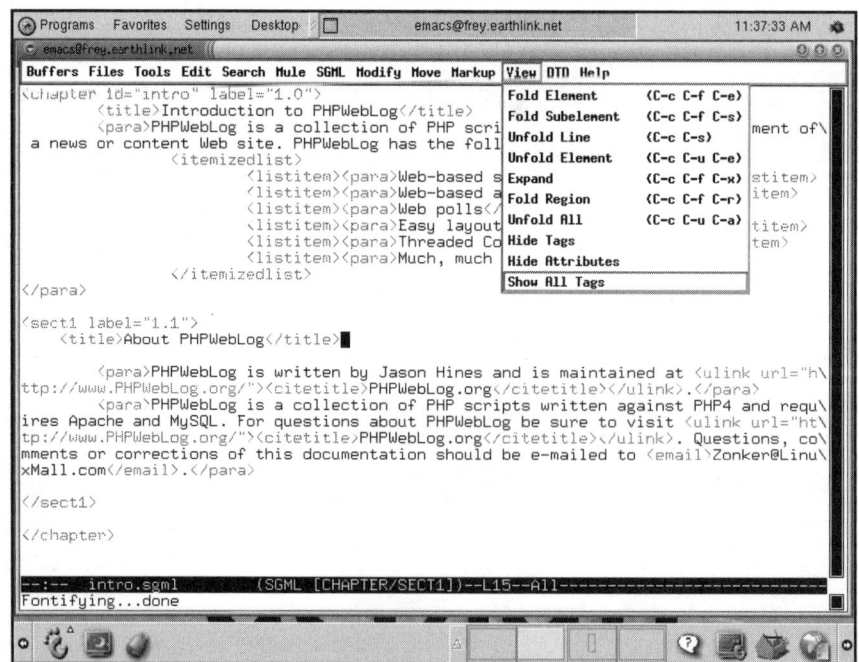

Figure 8.18 *The DocBook document with all elements visible*

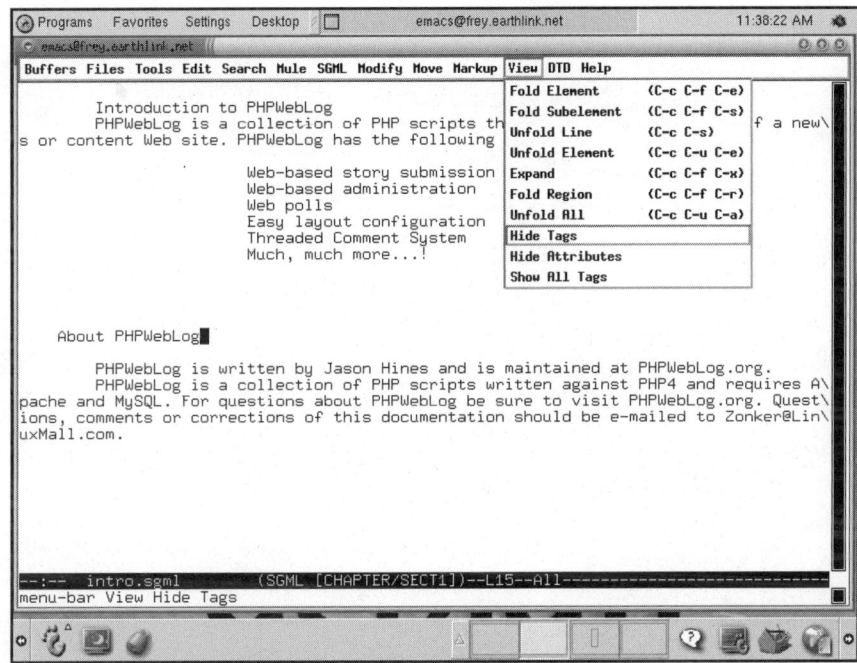

Figure 8.19 *The same document with elements hidden*

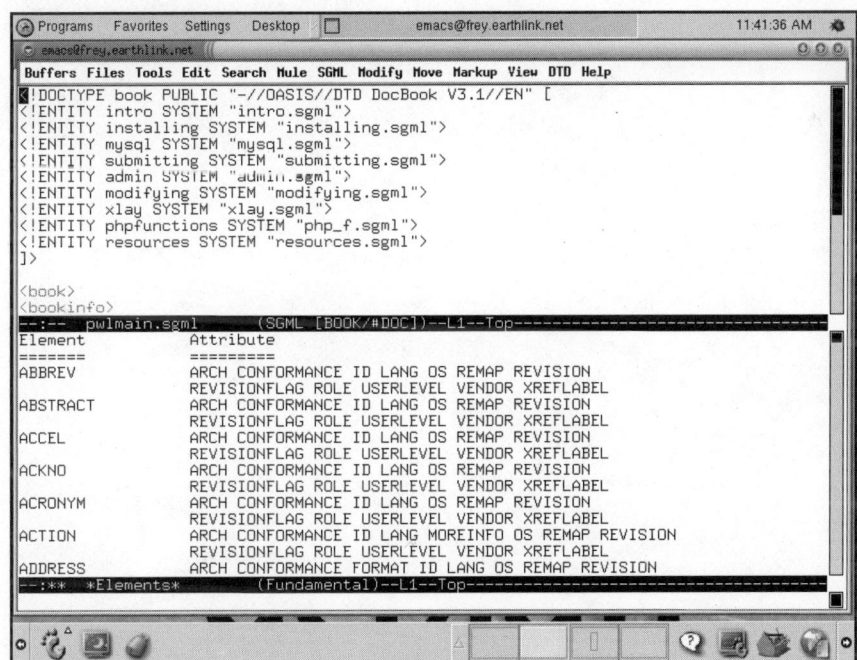

Figure 8.20 *A listing of valid elements from the DTD menu*

Summary

This chapter is a brief summary of Emacs and the PSGML major mode for editing SGML and XML documents in Emacs. Unfortunately, there's not room for an exhaustive look at Emacs, but this chapter presents enough information to get you started with Emacs and help you wade in comfortably. Emacs is not an editor to be taken lightly—Steven Hawking would probably need a couple of days to digest all the functions available in Emacs. However, when you get to know Emacs, you can become extremely proficient in it and very productive. Many programmers and writers—including Neal Stephenson, the author of *Snow Crash* and *Cryptonomicon*—prefer Emacs.

Chapter 9: Using Vim

Getting Vim

Using Vim SGML and DocBook Syntax

Vim, short for *Vi IMproved*, is one of the most popular text editors for Linux-type and Free UNIX–type operating systems. Vim is a vi clone, but is not quite identical. Vim has added features that are not available in the original vi. This chapter will show you how to work with DocBook in Vim and covers some of the basics of Vim in case you haven't used a vi-like editor before. It is not a comprehensive guide to the Vim text editor, but an overview to get you up and running with DocBook in Vim.

> Not only is vi a text editor, but it's also capable of editing binary files—if that's the sort of thing you're into. Also, vi has the distinction of being a part of the POSIX 1003.2 specification for shell utilities. Most vi clones conform, more or less, to this standard.

The original vi text editor was available on BSD, written by Bill Joy, and enjoyed unquestioned superiority until Emacs came onto the scene in or around 1984 (very Orwellian). The original vi did not have anywhere near the enormous number of features that Vim and other vi clones have. If you are a UNIX guru who has actually used another version of vi, you will find that Vim is mostly compatible with vi but includes many more features.

It also bears mentioning that the original vi is not actually available for Linux or most of the platforms that Vim supports.

> Vim is not the only vi clone available. There are a multitude of vi clones that approximate the functionality of the original vi, with additional functionality. However, Vim is probably the most popular vi clone, and the syntax-highlighting features of Vim make it ideal for editing DocBook documents. However, if you want to explore other vi clones, Appendix D, "More DocBook Resources," can point you towards a few other vi clones that you can try out.

As a matter of fact, Vim is my preferred text editor. It took a little while to get used to, but Vim's features make it ideal for writing prose or code. I should be fair and mention that Vim is not the only text editor with special features for working with DocBook. Emacs has the PSGML mode, which is ideally suited for working with DocBook. In fact, many people feel that Emacs and PSGML are the ideal combination for working with DocBook. It is also worth mentioning that Emacs has many more features than Vim for working with DocBook. However, with the additional features come additional complexity, that may not be worth the effort if you have another text editor that you're already comfortable with. Chapter 8, "Using Emacs," covers all the ins and outs of working with DocBook in Emacs.

Some of the advanced features of Vim include

- Color syntax highlighting
- Multi level undo
- Multiple windows. Edit two or more files in Vim at a time.
- Online help
- Word completion
- Command-line history
- Advanced search and replace features

Another advantage of Vim is that it is available for just about every computing platform known to humankind. Vim runs on Linux, FreeBSD, OpenBSD, NetBSD, Solaris, Windows NT and 9x, the Amiga, MacOS, and BeOS, just to name a few. If you happen to use Linux at home and Windows at work, you can still enjoy the benefits of Vim in both environments.

> I haven't actually tried this because I don't do any development work on Microsoft platforms, but apparently Vim can be integrated with Microsoft Developer Studio through OLE. For Windows developers who have developed on *NIX operating systems in the past, this should be very useful.

NOTE

Getting Vim

If you don't have Vim on your computer yet, you will have to visit the Vim home page to get the necessary files to run Vim. Most of you probably already have Vim installed on your system.

Linux/UNIX

Almost every Linux and *BSD distribution includes Vim in the standard installs. However, if you don't have Vim, or you have a really outdated version of Vim, you can get a copy of the latest version from **http://www.vim.org/download.html** (see Figure 9.1).

To find precompiled binaries of Vim, visit the Vim binaries page at **http://www.vim.org/binaries.html**.

To compile Vim from source, you will need to download three files from one of the FTP sites. First are the standard source files that are used to compile a binary, next are the runtime files that are used by Vim, and the last is a collection of extra files that are used by Vim. So you will have

- **vim-*x.xx*-src.tar.gz.** Source
- **vim-*x.xx*-rt.tar.gz.** Runtime
- **vim-*x.xx*-extra.tar.gz.** Extra

Where *x.xx* is the version number, be sure to download the latest version.

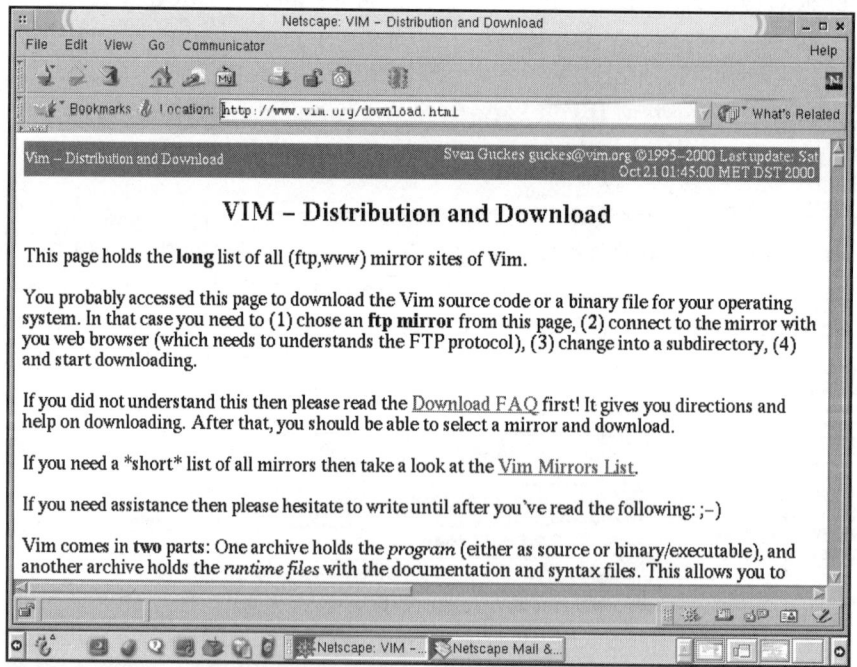

Figure 9.1 *The Vim download page*

After you have all the necessary files, move them to the /tmp directory (or wherever you like to work with source files), and unzip and untar the files. Follow these steps:

1. Execute the following command to become root:

   ```
   su -
   ```

2. Then unzip and untar the files:

   ```
   tar -zxvf vim-x.xx.src.tar.gz
   tar -zxvf vim-x.xx.tr.tar.gz
   tar -zxvf vim-x.xx.extra.tar.gz
   ```

3. After you have exploded the packages, you need to change directories to the new directory with the Vim source and other necessary files.

   ```
   cd vim-x.xx
   ```

4. After you have entered the new directory, configure and "make" the source files.

   ```
   ./configure
   make
   make install
   ```

> The above instructions should run on any Linux distribution, as well as just about any UNIX variant. However, I do not have access to all the various flavors of Linux, *BSD, and UNIX to actually try compiling Vim on them. If you run into issues, be sure to check the Vim Web site for more information. Also, I'd appreciate an e-mail regarding your experiences on various other flavors of UNIX, to include in future versions of this book.

After you've got Vim installed, simply type **vim** to start using Vim.

Windows and DOS

Vim also comes in Windows and MS-DOS versions. You can find Vim for Windows or MS-DOS on mirror sites in the /packages/vim/pc directory.

To install Vim for Windows, you will need to grab the runtime files, as well as a precompiled binary for the appropriate system.

Unfortunately, Vim versions for Windows tend to lag behind the versions for UNIX and Linux systems. At the time of this writing, Vim 5.7 is available for Linux, and 5.4 is the latest available version for Windows/DOS. Likely, this is because the majority of Vim users are on the Linux- and UNIX- type systems.

MacOS

Vim users on the MacOS need only to grab the appropriate *.sit file for their Mac. Currently, there are PPC and 68K versions of Vim 5.6 available.

You can find Vim for the MacOS at **http://www3.sympatico.ca/dany. stamant/vim/** (see Figure 9.2).

The Mac version of Vim is pretty much current, and it operates the same way as Vim on other platforms. Figure 9.3 shows Vim running on the MacOS. However, some of the functionality that Vim has on UNIX-type platforms

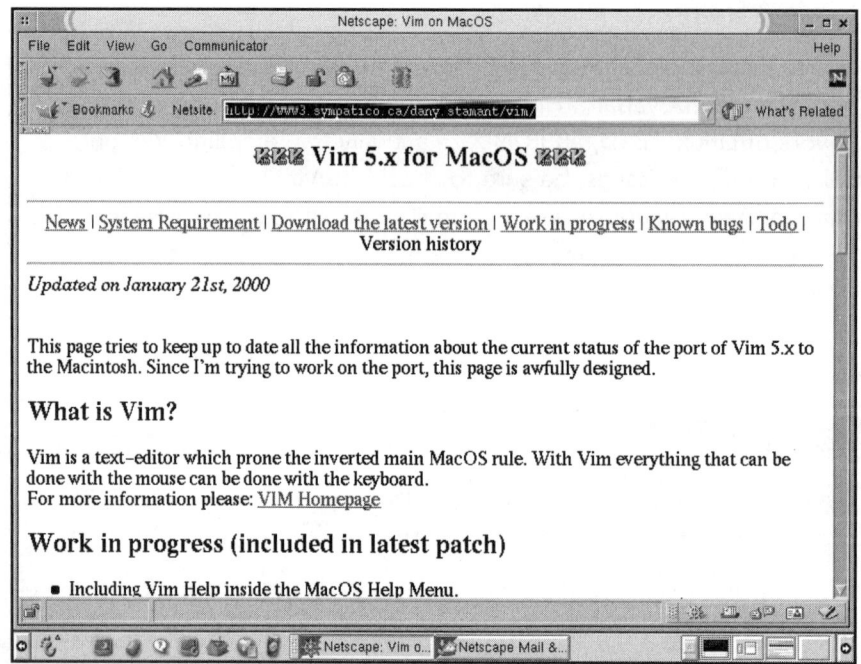

Figure 9.2 *The MacVim home page*

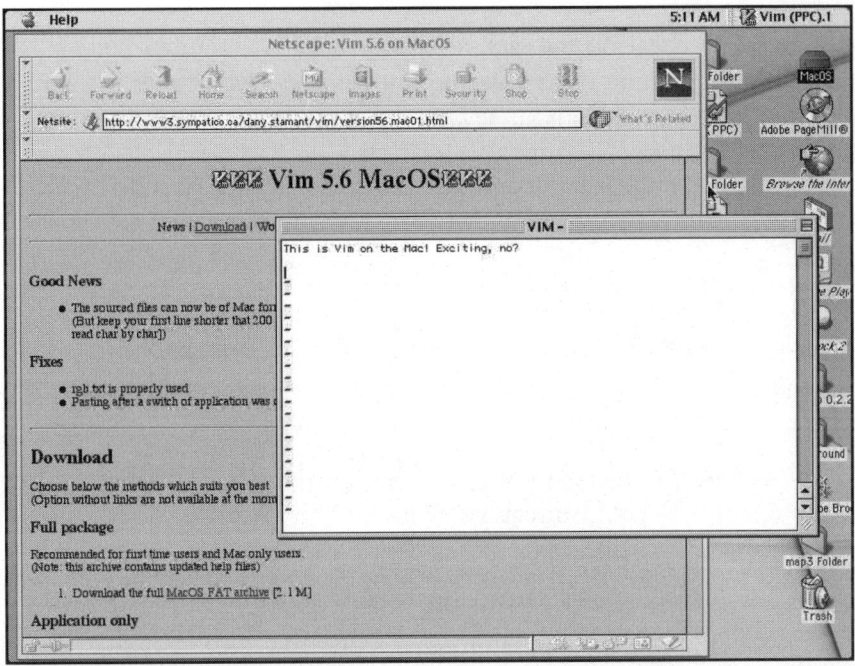

Figure 9.3 *Vim on the MacOS*

may be missing because you're not able to call the external UNIX programs from Vim. However, in terms of keybindings and such, MacVim is pretty much the same.

Using Vim SGML and DocBook Syntax

Now that you have a running version of Vim, it's time to get the syntax files for DocBook.

> If you do a great deal of programming or coding of HTML, you will probably be able to find a Vim syntax file that suits your needs. There are syntax files for HTML, C, Python, Perl, SGML, and many other languages available.

You can find Vim syntax files at **http://www.vim.org/lang.html** or by simply looking on the CD-ROM included with this book.

It might be worth checking the Vim.org Web site to see whether there are newer versions of the syntax files on the Vim.org Web site, as the existing DocBook syntax file is somewhat outdated. (It is written for DocBook 3.0/LinuxDoc.).

Installing Syntax Files

If you're lucky, your system administrator has been kind enough to install your syntax files and everything for you. If you are your own system administrator, however, you may need to install the syntax files on your own.

Copy the docbook.vim and sgml.vim files to the default /syntax directory. On my system, the /syntax directory is located in /usr/share/vim/vim56/syntax/—but this might differ depending on your distribution.

After you've copied the syntax files to the syntax directory, you will want to edit the .vimrc file to get Vim to automagically use the docbook.vim.

In your home directory, start Vim with the following command:

```
vim .vimrc
```

You'll want to add the following lines to your .vimrc file:

```
set syntax=on
let color = "true"
"
if has("syntax")
    if color == "true"
        " This will switch colors ON
        so ${VIMRUNTIME}/syntax/syntax.vim
    else
        " this switches colors OFF
        syntax off
        set t_Co=0
    endif
endif
```

After you've added these lines to your .vimrc file, you should be able to restart Vim, and whenever you edit DocBook files ending with .sgml or .xml, you'll have color highlighting.

Basic Vim

Learning Vim will take a bit of practice, but after you've got the hang of it a while you will find that you can be quite productive. This section isn't DocBook specific; it's only included only for the convenience of those who haven't gotten the hang of Vim yet.

Modal Editors

Vim, like vi, is what is known as a *modal editor*. While using Vim, you are either in the command mode or the insert mode, but unlike most text editors, you can't use both modes at the same time. Vim is designed to enable the user to keep his or her hands on the home keys of the keyboard while using the editor. This design enables users to improve their typing speed greatly because their hands don't have to leave the home keys, and thus, a user spends less time trying to use odd keys, such as function keys or meta keys. Users can delete, cut, paste, search, navigate, and more, by using the standard keys. This requires that the program differentiate between when the user is in an insert or append mode and when the user is in a command mode.

Buzzword

When you edit text in Vim, whether you're creating a new file or editing an existing file, the text is stored in a *buffer*—basically, a space in memory—until you write the changes to a file or discard them. If you start Vim without opening a file to edit, it creates an empty buffer in which you can begin working. Vim also stores existing files in a buffer, rather than working directly on them, and commits changes to the file after the write command is given. The practical upshot of this is that you can edit a file and save it under a different name to avoid making changes to the original.

> Actually, some would say that Vim has three modes: insert mode, command mode, and ex mode—or as the "Getting Started Guide" from the Linux Documentation Project calls it, the *last line mode* (ex commands are entered on the bottom of the screen). Many commands in vi are actually associated with the ex editor. Vim combines ex and vi into one handy text editor, so why complicate matters? However, if it ever comes up in a game of Trivial Pursuit, you will be prepared.

Starting Vim

To begin, putter around in Vim a little bit to get the hang of it. Type **vim** (**vi** should work, too) at the shell prompt, either at the console or in an xterm or its equivalent. Figure 9.4 shows Vim starting up. After you enter Vim with an empty buffer, you can type **i** to begin inserting text. You are now in Vim's insert mode. To leave the insert mode and return to command mode, press the Esc key.

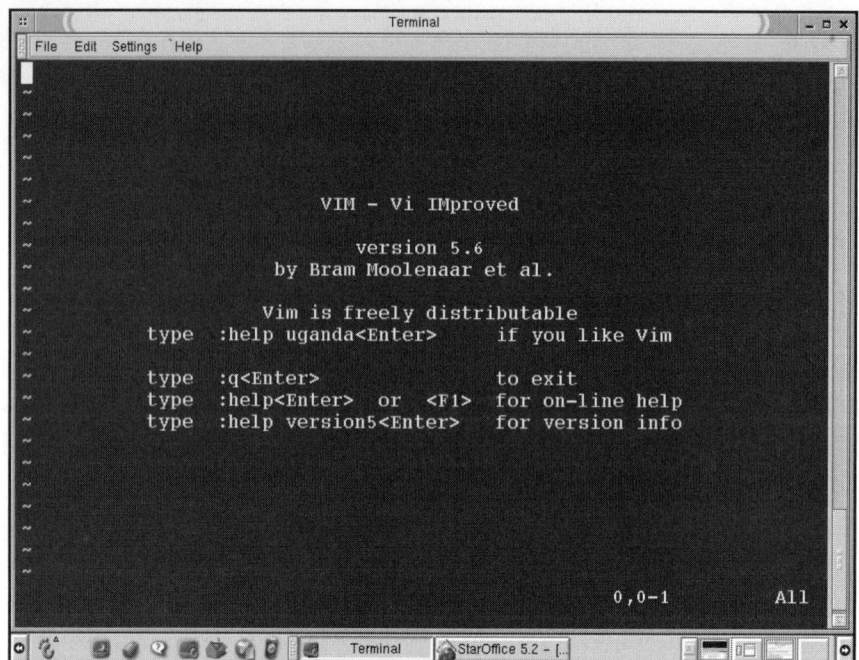

Figure 9.4 *Starting Vim*

Now that you're in Vim, try experiment by doing a little editing to get the hang of it.

1. If you're not in insert mode already, type **i** to enter vi's insert mode. There is no visual indication that you have changed modes, unless you've set Vim to the No Compatible mode in your vimrc, or by typing **:nc**. The i that you've typed doesn't appear unless you type it a second time.

2. When in the insert mode, type in a little text so that you have something to experiment with (see Figure 9.5).

3. Now that you have some text to play around with, press the Esc key to reenter command mode. Note that it no longer says --INSERT-- at the bottom of the screen (see Figure 9.6). It's not much, but that's how you know that you're in command mode.

4. Practice moving around a little bit. You can usually move around using the arrow keys, but sometimes if you're using Vim on a remote machine, the arrow keys are not recognized properly. Because Vim was

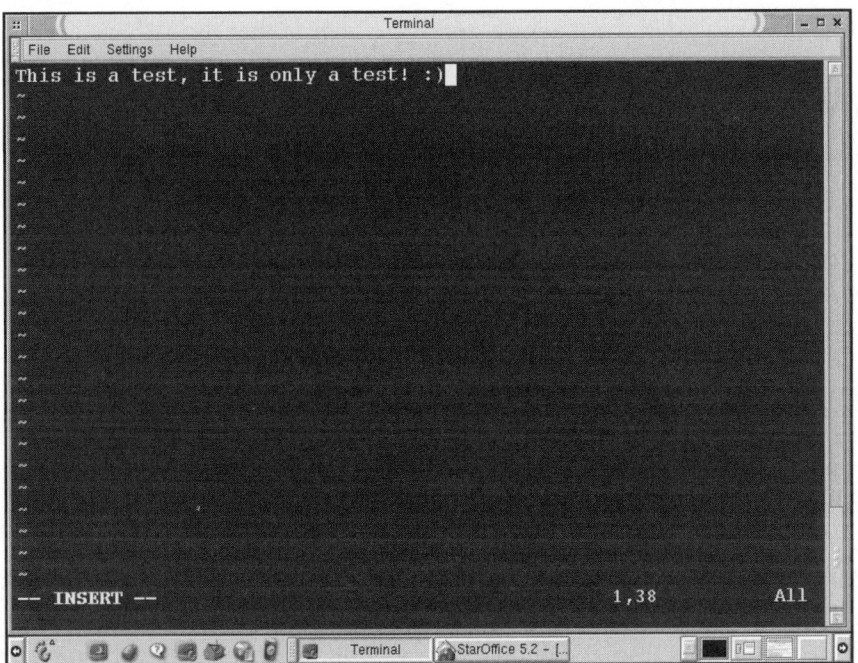

Figure 9.5 *Vim in insert mode*

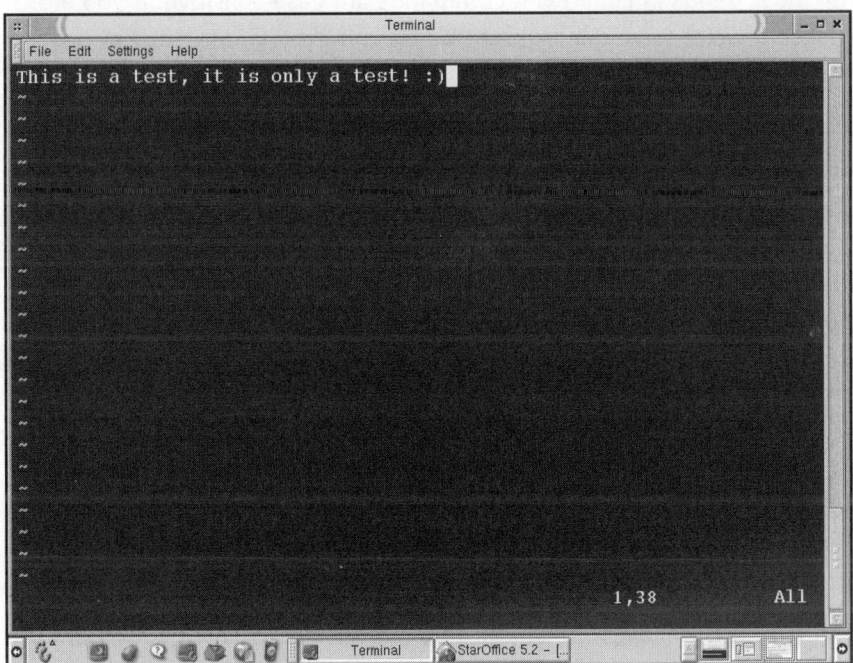

Figure 9.6 *Vim in command mode*

originally designed for machines with keyboards that didn't have arrow keys, use the following keys for navigating in vi:

- h   Left one character
- j   Down one line
- k   Up one line
- l   Right one character
- w   Forward one word
- b   Backward one word

Try moving forward and backward a little bit. If you've played some of the text-based games that come with Linux, or some other popular games on other platforms, you may are already be familiar with moving by using the h,j,k, and l keys. Typing **6h** moves you left six characters, and typing **3j** moves you down three lines. vi does not break lines by default, because it is designed to edit code, as well as typical text. Thus, a line can be much longer than the width of the screen on which it is displayed. Vim automatically wraps text while it is being typed, but it does not insert line breaks by default.

NOTE

As with most things in Linux, Vim commands are case-sensitive. If you are experiencing weird behavior, it might be because the Caps Lock key has accidentally been toggled. This happens more often than I might like to admit.

5. Because you're only dealing with only one sentence, moving one word at a time is probably sufficient. However, Vim is designed to edit large files, as well as small. The only practical limit to file size is memory in the machine. The following keys and key combinations are shortcuts for moving quickly through a file:

- o   Moves the cursor to the beginning of a line
- $ Moves the cursor to the end of a line
- g   Moves the cursor to the end of the file
- gg   Moves the cursor to the beginning of a file
- :*number*   Moves the cursor to a specific line number
- *number*%   Moves the cursor to a certain percentage of the file

6. After you've moved around a little bit, try editing the text a little. The following keys delete, cut, paste, and otherwise massage text. Remember, you have to press the Esc key to return to command mode.

- i   Insert mode.
- a   Append mode. Insertion begins next to the cursor, rather than where the cursor is placed.
- x   Deletes the character that the cursor is currently on.
- *n*x   Deletes *n* characters.
- dd   Deletes the entire line that the cursor is on.
- *n*dd   Deletes *n* characters.
- das   Deletes a sentence, not the entire line.
- dw   Deletes a word.
- cw   Changes a word. This deletes the word that the cursor is currently on and places you in insert mode so that you can replace the word.
- Y   Yanks a line. This copies the current line so that it can be pasted later.
- *n*Y   Yanks a number of lines.
- p   Pastes text below the current line.
- P   Pastes text above the current line.
- J   Joins two lines of text.
- .   Repeats last command.
- u   Undoes last command.

7. After a little editing, you're ready for the next step, which is actually to save the buffer that you're working on to a file. To write a new file, or to save to an existing file, use the last line mode of Vim. Entering last line mode is similar to command mode. Press the Esc key if you're not already in command mode, and then type a colon (:) to enter the last line mode. The commands for saving files work only in the last line mode:

- :w *filename*   Writes to a new file.
- :w!*filename*   Overwrites an existing file.
- :wq *filename*   Writes to a file and then quits vi.
- :wq   Writes to a file and quits vi, if a filename is already assigned.
- :q!   Quits without saving.
- :q   Quits.

Buzzword

Here's another little piece of Linux trivia that may might come in handy some-day. The excla-mation point (!) character is often referred to as *bang* when read-ing a command out loud. For instance, if you were instructing someone how to quit vi, you'd say, "Type colon, q, and bang, and press Enter."

That covers most of the basic capabilities of vi. It might take a few days of playing around with the keystrokes to navigate and do basic operations within vi, but after you become acquainted with it, you will find that you can get around quite quickly and be very productive in vi.

Using Vim's Online Help

One good thing to remember is that if you're getting stuck while using Vim, and you don't want to dig out a big book, try Vim's online help feature.

To get into the help feature, simply press F1, or get into last line mode and type **help**.

After you're in help, you can navigate normally, or if you find a topic that's "between bars," like this:

```
|set-option|
```

position the cursor on that text, and press Ctrl+] to jump to that help topic.

Opening Files with Vim

Opening a file with Vim is pretty straightforward. Typing **Vim** *filename* either opens an existing file or creates a file if there was not a file by that name previously.

You can also start at a specific part of a file by using one of the following methods. Typing **Vim +102** *filename* opens the named file and places the cursor at the beginning of line 102. You can also search the file for the first instance of a given term by using **Vim +/term** *filename*. This uses Vim's search capability to place the cursor at the first instance of the search keyword.

Advanced Vim

This chapter mostly has covered very basic functions within Vim. The advanced functions of Vim can be, and have been, the subject of entire books. Because DocBook is our focus, I won't attempt to cover all the features of Vim here. However, in the following sections are I will discuss a few features that shouldn't be overlooked.

Searching Text with Vim

To search through a file for instances of a string of text, you must be in Vim's last line mode. Instead of using the colon, however, you use either the forward slash (/) or question mark (?) to search through the text. Here are some of the commands you can use to search text with Vim.

- */text*. vi searches forward through the file or buffer for *text*.
- *?text*. vi searches backward through the file or buffer for *text*.
- **n**. vi searches forward for the next occurrence of the previous search term.
- **N**. vi searches backward for the next occurrence of the previous search term.

Searching and Replacing with Vim

If you've just written a manual for your company's hot new product, and management decides to change the name, don't fret. You can use Vim's search and replace functions to scour the file for the old name and replace it with the new one. No problem. However, there are no functions within Vim that will give the management folks a clue. Sorry, it's just a text editor.

Vim allows for advanced search and replace and other simple text editing functions. To use search and replace with Vim, enter the last line mode by typing a colon. Then enter the search term, and replacement text, like this:

```
%s/original/replacement/gc
```

The preceding command tells Vim to search for the *original* text and replace it with *replacement* text if found, but to ask for confirmation first. The / character is a separator. The *g* in the command tells Vim that it is a global search and replace, and you want to replace all instances of the first term with the second term. The *c* in the command tells Vim that you want to confirm before replacing the first text for the second.

Editing Multiple Files Simultaneously

As discussed in Chapter 4, "Preparing a Book with DocBook," you will often be working with multiple files that will eventually be collated into one whole document for printing, posting, or whatever. Often, it would be a good thing to be able to edit two or more files at the same time. Luckily, Vim makes this fairly easy. If you're in Vim editing book.sgml and you want to simultaneously edit the index.sgml file located in the same directory, enter last line mode and type

split index.sgml.

Vim then splits the current window and opens the index.sgml file in the other half of the window. To switch between files, press Ctrl+w and then press the arrow key in the direction of the appropriate file. You can write and quit files normally. Whichever file is currently active can be written to or closed without changing the other file(s) that may be open. For instance, if you quit index.sgml without saving, it does not close the book.sgml file or change it in any way. It simply returns to a single pane window with one file open.

Inserting Another File

Often when using DocBook, you will want to start a new document with a pre-existing template. By starting Vim with the new filename and then reading in the contents of another file, you can save a little time.

To insert the contents of another file into the current buffer at the current cursor position, follow these steps:

1. Enter vi's command mode by pressing Esc.
2. Enter the last line mode by typing the colon (:).
3. Use the following syntax to tell vi the name of the file to open:

   `:r filename`

   or for a file not in the current directory:

   `:r/directory/filename`

This procedure inserts the contents of the named file into the current buffer. You can use this feature for cutting and pasting between files, or for inserting system files into another file for editing or modifying.

> Unless you really know what you're doing, it's much smarter to always edit a copy of a system configuration file rather than the original file. Actually, even if you do know what you're doing, it's still safer. If you don't, editing an original file is nearly suicidal.

Summary

If you're interested in learning about the more advanced features available, try using either the Vim man pages or some of the Web sites dedicated to Vim or vi clones. You can find a listing of those sites and other great resource sites in Appendix D, "More DocBook Resources." I think that you will find yourself addicted to Vim if you give it a try!

Customizing the DocBook DTD

n this chapter, I talk about customizing DocBook to do your nefarious bidding. As discussed in earlier chapters, DocBook is technically just the DTD, but we're using it as a reference to all the tools necessary to produce a document and render it with DocBook—namely, the DSSSL or XML processor, the DocBook DTD, and stylesheets of some kind. (I'll talk about that in a bit.)

This chapter covers customizing both the DocBook DTD (or Schema) and the default stylesheets to produce custom output from a DocBook document. It also covers the Document Style Semantics and Specification Language (DSSSL) and XSL Transformations (XSLT), although not in great depth.

It's possible to do useful work with DocBook without customizing the default stylesheets. For many purposes, the default stylesheets are sufficient. Although not gorgeous, the output is clean and easy to read. It looks professional, if a little generic. (No insult intended to the folks who put it together!)

On the other hand, maybe you want to add a little spice to your finished product. That's where the customization comes in, and I'll talk about that a little later in the chapter.

Customizing the DocBook DTD

It's also possible, even recommended, to work with the DocBook DTD without making any changes.

Because DocBook is the DTD, or the DTD is DocBook, customizing the DTD essentially makes it cease to be DocBook. That is, when you create a document using a different DTD, you're no longer working with something that is fully compatible with the DocBook DTD.

Ramifications of Customizing the DocBook DTD

Whether this is a big problem depends mostly on your plans for your DocBook document. Are you creating documentation only for use in-house, with no plans to distribute it to the outside world?

> Be sure to think this through. If you think that there's a slight chance you might want to share documents with another source in the future, keep the DocBook DTD. If it's a personal project, such as your Web page or a college paper that you know full well will be forever lost to the sands of time the instant you graduate, it's probably no big deal. If you're writing technical documents for a company or a research paper that will someday pave the way to a cancer cure, you can assume that the portability of DocBook will be important someday soon.

If you have no plans to distribute this documentation, it's not a big deal because compatibility isn't important to you. You won't have to worry about the logistics of distributing your customized DTD with the document to everyone with whom you share your document.

On the other hand, if you're going to be working with a document that you plan to share with others, in its DocBook form, you must think very hard before you customize the DTD. If you customize the DTD, you will have to make sure that everyone receives a copy of the DTD. If you make changes to that DTD later on, you will have to update everyone's copy yet again.

Also, although this is a small point, after you change the DTD, you can't call it DocBook anymore. The DocBook Technical Committee asks that no one distribute a changed DTD under the name Oasis DocBook. If you do, a large, scary man might show up at your door. Okay, not really, but it could cause some serious compatibility issues.

> Although the DocBook Technical Committee isn't likely to send any thugs to enforce it, the DocBook license does restrict distributing a modified DTD under the same name as the regular DocBook DTDs. You're free to make any modification you want, as long as you don't distribute it as official DocBook.

If you do customize the DocBook DTD, it should be labeled Variant, Subset, or Extension, depending on the modifications you've made to the DTD.

Modifications that reduce the number of elements should be labeled Subset. This is logical because you're distributing a DTD that makes use of a subset of the DocBook elements. Any change that adds elements to the DocBook

DTD should be labeled Extension, and any other changes to the DTD should be labeled Variant.

To give an example, the declaration for a DocBook book normally looks like this.

```
<!DOCTYPE book PUBLIC "-//OASIS//DTD DocBook V4.1//EN">
```

However, if you add five elements to the DocBook DTD and want to distribute the DTD, it should look something like this.

```
<!DOCTYPE book PUBLIC "-//ZONKER'S//DTD DocBook V4.1-Extension//EN">
```

Basically, all that needs to be done is to change the name of the DTD's owner from Oasis to whatever name is appropriate and to label the version number. This will tell anyone who's interested that your DTD is based on the Oasis DTD, not the official DTD. They will also know not to try to use the regular DTD.

Reasons to Customize the DTD

There are valid reasons to customize the DocBook DTD. As a matter of fact, Norman Walsh himself publishes a modified DocBook DTD.

Simplified DocBook

The modified DTD is called Simplified DocBook and has a small subset of the elements contained in the regular DocBook DTD. How small? The regular DocBook DTD comprises more than 300 elements, whereas the Simplified DocBook DTD comprises 105 elements.

Unlike the full DTD, the Simplified DocBook DTD has only one top-level element, the Article element.

If you're interested in trying out the Simplified DTD, you can find the latest version at Norman Walsh's Web site at **http://www.nwalsh.com/docbook/ simple/index.html**. Please note that the Simplified DTD is an XML DTD. Elements that are part of the subset appear in Appendix B, "DocBook Element Reference."

Reasons Not to Customize

Aside from laziness, there are several reasons not to customize the DocBook DTD. The most important reason is portability. After you customize the DTD, it becomes difficult to share with others and to keep current with the latest versions of DocBook.

Releases of DocBook don't happen every day, but regularly enough to make staying current a pain if you have to recustomize a DTD every time one is released. If you fail to keep current, your documents become less and less portable.

> Having said all that, if you are interested in learning a lot about SGML or XML and getting your hands dirty, so to speak, the DocBook DTD is a great sandbox to play in. The DTD is freely available for you to work with, and you can gain a lot of knowledge by playing with the DocBook DTD and customizing it to learn how it works. I wouldn't recommend doing it with important projects, but as a learning tool, this a great place to start. You will know that you truly understand SGML when you can easily read and modify the DocBook DTD.

Of course, I suppose that the portability and maintenance issues do come down to laziness at some point. DocBook enables you to avoid all the hassle of mucking about with the DTD by providing a ready-made, mature DTD that's been banged on for almost a decade.

A Guide to the DocBook DTD Structure

Because this book is about using DocBook, and not about the nitty-gritty internals, I won't spend long on this topic. This is some serious geekiness that should be approached with caution, and if SGML and XML theory and syntax aren't your bag, with a whole lot of caffeine.

If you've looked at the DocBook DTD included with this book, checked it out online, or found it nestled away in the bowels of your Linux distribution, you've noticed that DocBook's DTD is not just one file. The DocBook DTD, version 4.1.x, is distributed as nine files that form the DTD.

> Actually, the DocBook DTD is distributed as 14 files when you include the change logs that explain changes from earlier versions of DocBook, a README file, and a file explaining expected changes from 4.1.x DocBook to 5.0 DocBook. The DTD proper is nine files, though. The XML DTD is much the same but is also distributed with XML versions of the ISO's entity sets, which are not maintained by the DocBook Technical Committee.

The DocBook Driver

The first version of DocBook, 1.0, was just one lone DTD. It contained everything you needed to know about DocBook and was easy to read on its own.

The current version of DocBook is split into separate files to make it easier to maintain. The main file is the docbook.dtd that calls the rest of the files that make up the DocBook DTD when processed.

The rest of the files are modules that contain bits of DocBook, as well as the SGML ISO entity sets. The entity sets aren't part of DocBook, but they are required and are called from the DocBook DTD.

The Exception to the Rule

One file distributed with the DocBook DTD is kosher to modify without making a change in the DocBook Formal Public Identifier (FPI). That's the general entities module, dbgenent.mod.

Say that you want to add an entity like your company name or program to the entities because you're fed up typing Global Mega Corporation Central Division Office or something equally RSI-inducing (Repetitive Strain Injury).

The file you'd modify is the dbgenent.mod file. It is designed to have extra entities added to it. To add an entity, open the file and add a line like the following:

```
<!ENTITY companyname "Global Mega Corporation Central Division Office">
```

Then, any time you type **&companyname;**, it will automatically be expanded to Global Mega Corporation Central Division Office, and you will save yourself some RSI.

The Table DTD

The CALS Table model is one of the files also distributed with DocBook as cals-tbl.dtd. This is the DTD that describes table markup that DocBook uses. It is not a product of the DocBook Technical Committee. The CALS Table model was created by the United States Department of Defense as a standard for the exchange of electronic data between commercial suppliers.

DocBook Elements

The majority of DocBook elements are declared in the DocBook Information Pool module, dbpool.mod. This file contains most of the objects and elements used in DocBook. As mentioned previously, the table elements are declared

Buzzword

The *Formal Public Identifier* is found in the document declaration. It is the part of the declaration that identifies the owner of the DTD, and a description of it, and what language it's in. For example `-//OASIS// DTD DocBook V4.1//EN` is a Formal Public Identifier. This is not a DocBook-specific contrivance; the FPI is part of the ISO SGML standard.

elsewhere. The DocBook structural elements are also contained in a separate file, which you will get to in the next section.

Although I don't recommend making any modifications to the file, it is instructive to take a look at it. Take the Trademark element—not one of the most complicated elements but not the simplest, either. It has a few nonstandard attributes, so have a look at it to see what a typical element declaration looks like:

```
<!ENTITY % trademark.module "INCLUDE">
<![ %trademark.module; [
<!ENTITY % local.trademark.attrib "">
<!ENTITY % trademark.role.attrib "%role.attrib;">


<!ENTITY % trademark.element "INCLUDE">
<![ %trademark.element; [
<!ELEMENT Trademark - - ((#PCDATA
                 | %link.char.class;
                 | %tech.char.class;
                 | %base.char.class;
                 | %other.char.class;
                 | InlineGraphic
                 | InlineMediaObject
                 | Emphasis)+)>
<!--end of trademark.element-->]]>


<!ENTITY % trademark.attlist "INCLUDE">
<![ %trademark.attlist; [
<!ATTLIST Trademark
                 —
                 Class: More precisely identifies the item the element
names
                 —
                 Class           (Service
                                 |Trade
                                 |Registered
                                 |Copyright)      Trade
           %common.attrib;
           %trademark.role.attrib;
           %local.trademark.attrib;
```

```
>
<!—end of trademark.attlist—>]]>
<!—end of trademark.module—>]]>
```

That probably looks confusing, but it's just verbose. I will break it down so that it makes more sense.

```
<!ENTITY % trademark.module "INCLUDE">
<![ %trademark.module; [
<!ENTITY % local.trademark.attrib "">
<!ENTITY % trademark.role.attrib "%role.attrib;">
```

This is the Entity declaration, which tells a parser that there is an entity named Trademark and that it should be included. The third and fourth lines are declaring an attribute for the Trademark element named Role.

The next 11 lines let the parser know which elements can occur as child elements of the Trademark element. Some elements are declared as groups, such as the tech group of elements. Other elements, such as the InlineGraphic, are explicitly declared.

The final section of the Trademark declaration defines the attributes for Trademark, including acceptable values for the Class attribute.

The practical upshot of all this information is that Jade, or whatever parsing tool you're using, can give you an error message like the one in Figure 10.1, should you use an invalid attribute.

As you can see in Figure 10.1, the DocBook DTD is intricate. It's not that this stuff is complicated, certainly no more difficult than speaking English. However, as we all know, the English language is made up of many rules you have to understand before you can speak, at least intelligently. When you write a DTD, it's very similar to creating a language, so if you attempt to alter the language, you have to be very careful.

The DocBook Hierarchy

Although most elements in DocBook are contained in the Information Pool module, dbpool.mod, all the hierarchical elements in DocBook are contained in the DocBook hierarchy module, dbhier.mod. If you want to get information on any hierarchical elements in DocBook, such as the Sect1 element or the Book element, look in this file. The structure and syntax of the file are the same as the others, but for organizational purposes, the DocBook Technical Committee has segregated hierarchical content into this file.

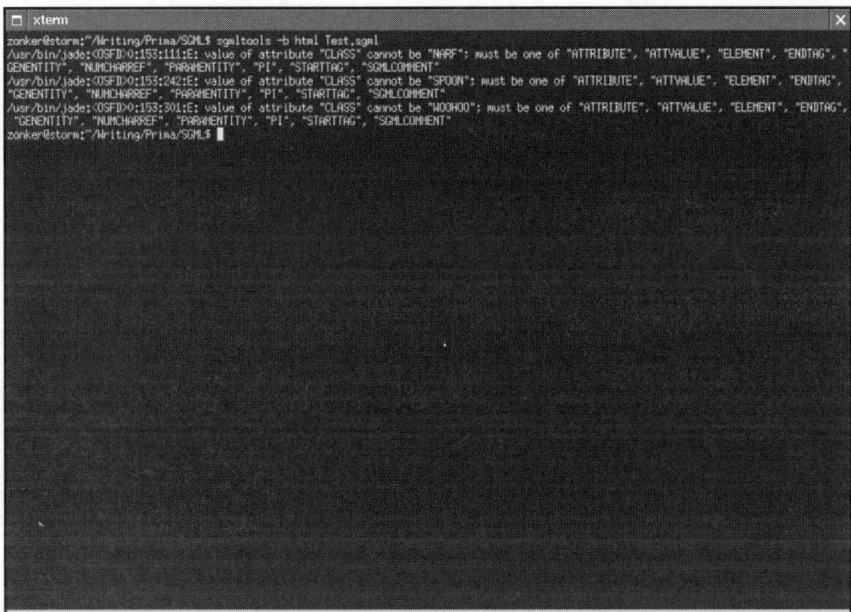

Figure 10.1 *Jade's error message for an invalid attribute*

The DocBook Character Entities

The DocBook Character Entities file is dbcent.mod. This file doesn't contain much information directly; rather, it calls the various files that have the ISO character entities' information. If you don't have the ISO entities on your system when you parse a DocBook document, you will get a whole bunch of errors.

The DocBook Catalog

All the DocBook Catalog information is contained in the docbook.cat for use in building your own catalog system files. The information here can be useful in debugging if you have Jade/OpenJade errors related to catalog files.

DocBook SGML Declarations

The docbook.dcl file contains all of DocBook's SGML declarations. When you see errors like the one in Figure 10.2, which complain about a missing tag but its declaration does not permit this, this is where the declaration not to omit tags is located.

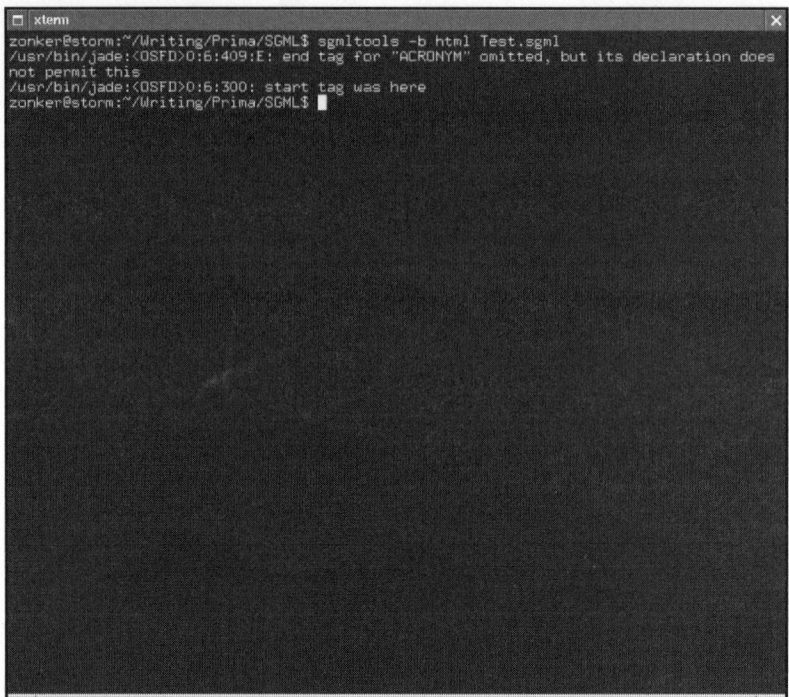

```
xterm                                                                    ✕
zonker@storm:~/Writing/Prima/SGML$ sgmltools -b html Test.sgml
/usr/bin/jade:<OSFD>0:6:409:E: end tag for "ACRONYM" omitted, but its declaration does
not permit this
/usr/bin/jade:<OSFD>0:6:300: start tag was here
zonker@storm:~/Writing/Prima/SGML$ █
```

Figure 10.2 *A Jade error*

DocBook Notations

The dbnotn.mod file contains the notations for DocBook. This includes references to most types of binary graphics files.

Customizing Stylesheets

If you want to get a different look and feel out of DocBook, it isn't necessary to change the DTD in any way. The look and feel of a document's output is determined by the stylesheet, not the DTD, as mentioned earlier.

The nice thing about DocBook is that it allows separation of structure and content from display. In fact, DocBook makes it easier to display the same information in different ways without reformatting any of the document itself. Simply by switching the stylesheets, you can completely change the look or medium of the output. This is one area where DocBook has an advantage over GUI tools such as Microsoft Word. Although Word does have a multitude of nifty features, it isn't possible to write a document in Word and have it completely reformat your document by the type of information contained in it. For instance, with DocBook, you can create a stylesheet that displays information contained only in the `Author` and `Editor` elements. Word would be stymied by this request because it doesn't distinguish the content in a document that way.

> It's my pet theory that after all these years, Microsoft Word contains at least one feature no one has ever used and several features about which the majority of folks working on Word have no idea.

Understanding DSSSL

Okay, you're probably looking at the acronym and thinking that it has to be really hard to rate an FLA (Five-Letter Acronym) instead of the standard TLA (Three-Letter Acronym). Don't worry, the Document Style Semantics and Specification Language isn't any worse than other technologies you've looked at. It just has a verbose title.

DSSSL is a style language. It's a derivative of the Scheme and Lisp programming languages, which is why it has so many parentheses.

> An older programmer I used to know once told me that Lisp should actually stand for Lots of InsidiouS Parentheses. If you program in Lisp, you will find yourself touch-typing the parenthesis keys, if nothing else.

A full overview of DSSSL is well beyond the scope of this book. DSSSL is a very full-featured language. However, I will provide a few examples of customizing a stylesheet to get you started.

Making Changes to Existing Stylesheets

Usually, it's better to make changes to existing stylesheets than to try to write them from scratch. Remember, DocBook has more than 300 elements, and you don't want to be writing a stylesheet from scratch to support more than 300 elements and their attributes.

Other Stylesheets

In addition to the stylesheets distributed with DocBook, several other versions of DocBook stylesheets are freely available. KDE, GNOME, Debian, FreeBSD, and a few other projects on the Web have made customized DocBook stylesheets available. Although you might still need to customize them further, especially if you're not writing about one of those projects, you might find that one of those organizations has a closer look and feel than the default DocBook stylesheets. Looking over the code to their stylesheets also will make the concepts clearer than if you just look at the DocBook stylesheets.

Writing a Local Stylesheet

To customize the DocBook stylesheets, you can either modify the stylesheets as they are or write a localized driver file that makes your modifications and then relies on the unmodified DocBook default stylesheets for the rest.

Writing a local stylesheet is much more sensible because it is more easily managed. Rather than wade through the stylesheets that are included, you simply write an add-on that works with the stylesheets and is a much smaller and more manageable file.

To start with, you want to have a document declaration, just like a regular DocBook document. It should look something like this.

```
<DOCTYPE style-sheet PUBLIC "-//Zonker's Stylish Sheet//EN" [
    <ENTITY dbstyle PUBLIC "-//Norman Walsh//DOCUMENT DocBook Print
Stylesheet//EN" CDATA DSSSL]>
```

Nothing you haven't seen before, at least to some extent. Instead of a DocBook element, you use stylesheet for the declaration, and you fill in your information for the Formal Public Identifier.

Then you fill in the document a little with a modification to the DocBook stylesheets:

```
<DOCTYPE style-sheet PUBLIC "-//Zonker's Stylish Sheet//EN" [
      <ENTITY dbstyle PUBLIC "-//Norman Walsh//DOCUMENT DocBook Print
Stylesheet//EN" CDATA DSSSL]>

      <style-sheet>
      <style-specification use="docbook">
      <style-specification-body>
```

```
(define %output-dir% "index.html")


</style-specification-body>
</style-specification>
<external-specification id="docbook" document="dbstyle">
</style-sheet>
```

This is a simple change. In fact, in all those lines of text, you're making only one change:

```
(define %output-dir% "index.html")
```

If you've ever processed a DocBook document into HTML, you've probably noticed that it writes files into a directory with the same name as the SGML or XML file you're processing. For instance, book.sgml becomes book/, and the resulting document files have weird names like book.html and x231.html. The purpose of this modification is to have the HTML written out to the standard index.html.

XML and Stylesheets

XML has its own stylesheet language, so if DSSSL isn't your bag, you will be happy to know that you have an alternative.

For online documents, XML can use Extensible Stylesheet Language (XSL) or Cascading Style Sheets (CSS). In a nutshell, stylesheets work by defining the formatting for an element separately from the element itself. For instance, one stylesheet might declare that all text in the HTML paragraph element should be 14 point text in a typeface with no serifs. A stylesheet for a Web site for senior citizens might want to bump that up to 22-point text. The first stylesheet would look something like this.

```
<style type="text/css">
                body {font-size: 14pt; font-family: sans-serif }
</style>
```

If you've done any kind of Web development, you probably have a good understanding of CSS already.

XSL actually makes use of CSS, but it's more than that. I'll talk about XSL for the remainder of the chapter. If you want to find out more about CSS, you might want to visit the W3C's CSS home page at **http://www.w3.org/ Style/XSL/**.

Understanding XSL

XSL consists of three technologies rolled into one:

- **XSL Formatting Objects (XSL-FO).** A language for transforming XML documents and the vocabulary for specifying formatting
- **XSL Transformations (XSLT).** A language for transforming an XML document into another XML document
- **XPath.** A language for addressing parts of an XML document

The XSLT and XPath technologies are still "candidate recommendations" with the W3C, so they're not fully mature yet. However, with things moving at Internet speed, many developers are already building solutions with the specifications given in the candidate recommendation. Most applications for XSLT and XPath are still more or less theoretical. The information in the recommendations as it relates to this book is probably stable. However, there is the possibility that specifics will change when the final drafts are released.

For the most part, I will ignore the XPath language because we're mostly concerned with the formatting aspects. For that, I'll be talking almost exclusively about XSL.

Customizing Stylesheets on the Web

Is all this too complicated or time consuming to mess with? Well, now there's a better way. Norman Walsh, genius that he is, has come up with a Web-based form for building a custom stylesheet with XSL online. That's right, it's mostly point and click, and you can develop your own stylesheet using a form.

You can find Norman's Stylesheet Customization Form online at **http://www. nwalsh.com/docbook/xsl/custom-html.html**. The site does warn that it's a beta release, but it seems to work fine. It might be official by the time this book is in your hands.

Norman Walsh comes up with so much great stuff that I have to wonder whether he really exists, or is "Norman Walsh" a collective or something. It would explain a lot. Great work, though.

Is It Possible to Transform DocBook XML into Other XML Formats?

At some point you might want to transform your DocBook XML document into XML data for another application. Because XML was designed with data interchange in mind, the W3C has created a technology called XSL Transformations. With XSL Transformations, also known as XSLT, it's also possible to take a DocBook XML document and convert it into another XML format.

What is XSLT?

XSLT is used to convert a document that conforms to a particular XML DTD into a document that conforms to another XML DTD. XSLT can work with XSL or separately. You can find the W3C's XSLT Recommendation here: **http://www.w3.org/TR/xslt.html**.

It's important to note that XSLT is a language, not an application. That means that you need a parser that supports XSLT to transform documents, in addition to XSLT stylesheets. There aren't a huge number of these yet, but you can find an Open Source tool to do the job if you're using Perl. The XML::XSLT Perl module is a possible solution. You can find the XML::XSLT project on SourceForge at **http://xmlxslt.sourceforge.net/**.

The XSLT technology is still in developmental stages, so we won't spend a lot of time on it in this book. However, if you have a need to transform DocBook into another XML format, be sure to check out XSLT. The XSLT 2.0 specification is being worked on now, so you might want to follow the development, and possibly get involved.

Summary

In this chapter, I covered the ways in which DocBook can be customized. Both the DocBook DTD and stylesheets can be customized, depending on your needs. In most cases, though, you should avoid the customization of DocBook unless absolutely necessary.

With DocBook taking two divergent paths at this time, SGML and XML, it's possible to use either DSSSL or XSL to customize DocBook output.

Although XSL is primarily targeted at Web output, you can produce printed documents using XSL as well. DocBook 5.0 primarily focuses on XML, although there will continue to be an SGML DTD, and DSSSL isn't going away any time soon. Which solution you choose depends entirely on what you need to use DocBook for. If you're primarily focused on printed documents and using DocBook for creating content for traditional publishing, you might want to go with SGML. SGML still has the edge in terms of compliant tools and documentation. However, if you're looking to the future, XML and the related technologies are probably the way to go. The final decision, of course, is up to you.

Chapter 11: XML Schema and DocBook XML

In this chapter you will look at XML Schema. An XML Schema takes the place of the Document Type Definition, or DTD. Although they are similar, XML Schemas and SGML DTDs have a few important differences you should understand.

Please note that both the XML Schema Recommendation and DocBook XML Schema are not final, so some specifications might change. However, I wanted to include the most up-to-date information in this book—not an easy task when writing about technologies that change so quickly. I also considered it important to include a chapter on Schema because, finished or not, it is already in use. Be sure to visit the World Wide Web Consortium's Web site for updates and the latest version of the XML Schema Candidate Recommendation. As XML Schema matures, more and more information will become available, and probably a book or two.

It's possible to write an entire book on XML Schema, but this chapter gives a brief overview so that you will be armed with enough information to utilize the DocBook XML Schema when it is finalized. XML Schema is a complex specification, but because you're dealing with a very limited scope, this chapter shouldn't be intimidating.

Remember that XML was designed with the intention of sharing information over the Web. Although SGML and the SGML DTDs can be adapted somewhat for that sort of task, they aren't well suited to exchanging data over the Web. In particular, DTDs do not provide a rich set of data types requisite for exchanging information. Although DTDs are ideal for publishing and contain the necessary data types for that use, SGML was never designed for the type of transactions of which XML is capable. Hence, XML Schema is being developed to take the place of the DTD for XML.

What Is an XML Schema?

The simplest definition of the XML Schema specification is to say that the Schema defines a document. The XML Schema, like a DTD, provides the rules and structure (or grammar) for a document. It defines the elements and attributes that may be used in a document. The document Schema also specifies the data types of elements and attributes with great specificity, something a DTD does not do.

How Does a Schema Differ from a DTD?

As you might remember from earlier chapters, the DTD defines the markup language used in a document and is also used by a parser to validate the document. The DTD is, essentially, the grammar or rules that define the structure of documents. The DocBook DTD, for example, determines which elements and attributes are valid in DocBook and how they may be used.

For instance, the Book element may be contained within a Set element but not within a Sect1 element. That's defined within the DocBook DTD.

However, not defined within the DocBook DTD are the number of characters that may be used for the Title element and whether the type of data used for the Title element has to be a string, an integer, or other possible data types. These limit your ability to use XML with programming languages or databases.

Another thing not specified in a DTD, but of great use to programmers, is the number of occurrences an element may have. For instance, there is no limit on the number of occurrences of the InvPartNumber element within the ObjectInfo element in the DocBook DTD. There's no way to specify a certain number of minimum or maximum times for that element to appear, so you could have a document that has an ObjectInfo element but no InvPartNumber. If you wanted, you could also have 20 of them without being in error.

Obviously, there's a very good reason for someone who is importing XML data with part numbers to want one part number for every object, and no more than one part number for every object. Therefore, XML Schema allows that kind of fine-grained control.

XML Schema Data Types

A plethora of data types are available when you use XML Schema. The XML Schema specification has a rich set of built-in data types that are predefined, as well as capable of combining data types to make custom data types out of the built-in data types.

You will look at some built-in data types and an example so that you can familiarize yourself with them. Note that because the DocBook XML Schema is already developed for you, you yourself don't have to give DocBook elements or attributes data types. However, it's useful to understand the data types so that if you create an application that makes use of the DocBook XML Schema, you can make use of these data types.

I'm not going to go into great detail about each data type or its specifications. This is just an overview so that you can get a feel for the types of information with which XML Schema is designed to work. Also, remember that this is not a final specification; some data types might change between the time this is written and the time XML Schema is finalized. For the latest information, visit the W3C's XML Schema home page (shown in Figure 11.1).

Text

The most familiar use of XML (and DocBook) is to create documentation, so, of course, there has to be a set of data types that handle text.

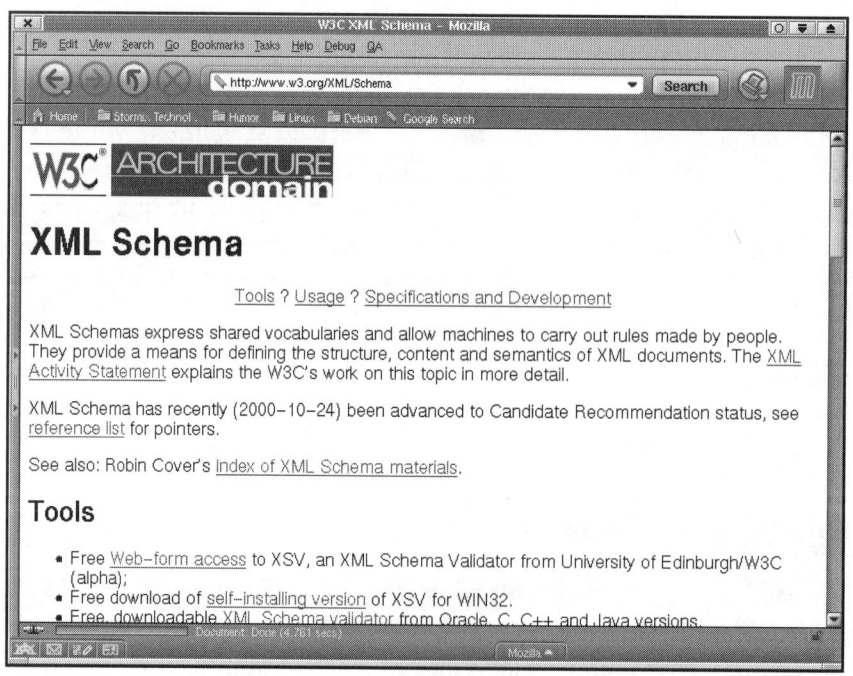

Figure 11.1 *The XML Schema home page*

Three main data types for holding text are built in to XML Schema:

- string
- CDATA
- token

If you're familiar with programming, you know that a string is a group of alphanumeric characters. The CDATA data type is already familiar because even the DTD supports that data type. Finally, the token data type handles character data but is more restrictive than the string and CDATA data types. A token cannot hold two or more spaces in a row, or carriage feeds or tab characters.

> Without getting bogged down in details, it might be of interest to note that the token data type is derived from the CDATA data type, but it is defined by its restrictions. In other words, the token data type is a subset of the CDATA data type. Many of the built-in Schema data types are derived from other data types but are more restrictive about what they may contain. The original data type is known as a *primitive* data type.

NOTE

Numeric Data Types

The Schema specification allows for a number of numeric data types:

- decimal
- float
- double
- binary
- integer
- nonPositiveInteger
- negativeInteger
- long
- int
- short
- byte
- unsignedbyte
- unsignedInt
- unsignedLong
- unsignedShort

As you can see, that's a rich array of numeric data types. If you're familiar with programming languages, data types such as double, float, and int look familiar to you, no doubt. The need for these data types in DocBook is not great, but the need for them in XML Schema is. Many programmers want to be able to exchange data over the Web that can then be imported into programs that have to know exactly what type of data they are working with.

Time

The XML Schema specification also contains a rich variety of data types for working with time. Again, this might be overkill for writing a technical paper with DocBook but can prove to be beneficial to programmers. This can also be valuable if your company or organization decides to standardize on DocBook for data exchange. It may be possible to extend the DocBook specification to use it for exchange of data beyond just papers and books. See Chapter 12, "Using DocBook for Inventory Control," for an example of using DocBook in an ordering system.

Here's a list of the time data types:

- time
- timePeriod
- timeInstant
- date
- month
- year
- century
- recurringDay
- recurringDate

The time data types allow anything as nonspecific as expressing the year or even the century to the ultra-specific, as in the case of the time data type that is down to the second.

Language

The XML Schema data types also include the language data type, which allows for the language data types as defined by RFC 1766. (See Appendix C, "More DocBook Resources," for more information on looking up RFCs.)

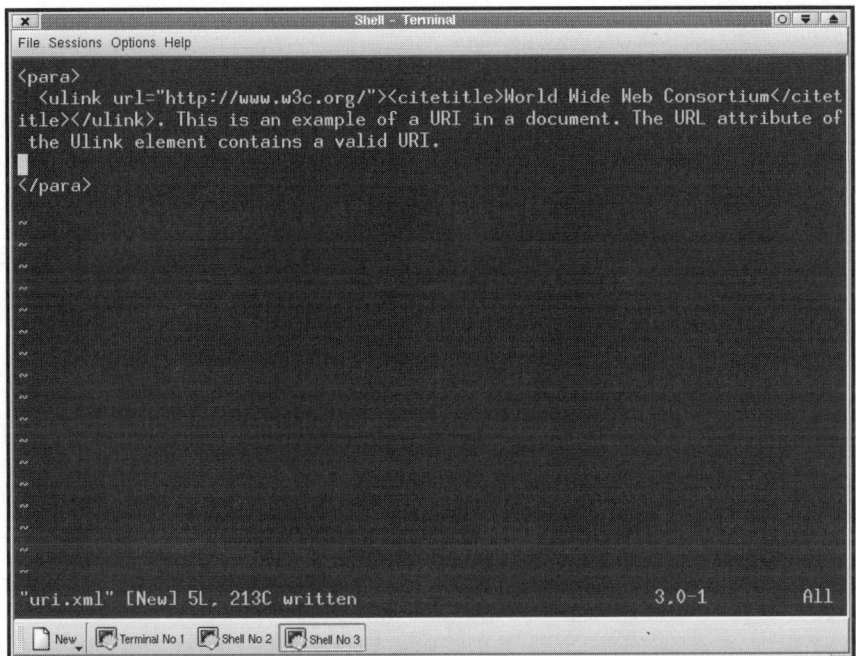

```
<para>
    <ulink url="http://www.w3c.org/"><citetitle>World Wide Web Consortium</citet
itle></ulink>. This is an example of a URI in a document. The URL attribute of
 the Ulink element contains a valid URI.

</para>
```

Figure 11.2 *An example of a URI in a document*

Reference

Another important data type that doesn't quite fit in the string or CDATA data types is the URI. If you recall, URIs are the Uniform Resource Identifiers. These are very important to DocBook and XML. The XML Schema specification allows for a uriReference data type, which can contain a URI or URL. Figure 11.2 shows a URI in a document.

There are a number of other data types, too numerous to discuss here. However, you must understand that data typing is very important to XML Schema. When the XML DocBook Schema becomes more commonly used, it will be necessary to understand which data types you can use with each element.

Elements and Attributes

Elements and attributes behave mostly as they do with a DTD. You use elements to define the data contained within them and attributes to further define the element.

However, in XML Schema some elements are not allowed to contain attributes. Elements that have a simple data type (such as the decimal data type) are, by definition, not supposed to contain attributes.

This is different from the DTD and from what you might be used to already with DocBook. All elements in DocBook may contain attributes.

Defining an Element

How do you know which data an element can contain? It's within the Schema specification for the element. Take a quick look at reading the element definition from an imaginary Schema that defines a simple element.

You will specify a simple element first, and then you will specify a few more complex elements to get the full picture. The first element is the Para element. It is simply an element containing any data that can be in a paragraph.

```
<xsd:schema xmlns:xsd="http://www.w3.org/2000/08/XMLSchema">
<xsd:annotation>
<xsd:documentation>
This is a sample Schema.
</xsd:documentation>
</xsd:annotation>
<xsd:element name="para" type="CDATA"/>
</xsd:schema>
```

The first thing you might have noticed is the format—each part of the Schema declaration begins with <xsd:, which stands for *Schema declaration*.

Another thing you might have noticed is the annotation and documentation elements. XML Schema allows for documentation of itself as it goes along. This means that when writing a Schema, the author of the Schema can add documentation explaining the elements that are being defined as they are included. This is exciting because it allows for self-generating documentation. Simply run the Schema through a parser with the proper stylesheet, and it can generate its own documentation. Nifty, isn't it?

Finally, the element declaration itself is simple. The <xsd:element markup lets you know that you're declaring an element. The Name attribute tells you the name the element will have, and the Type attribute defines the type of data the element can have. Because you want to allow just about anything in the Paragraph element, you specify the CDATA data type, covered earlier in the book.

Now for a slightly more complex set of elements. This example defines an element containing two other elements. Note that the top-level element itself contains only other elements, not other data.

```
<xsd:schema xmlns:xsd="http://www.w3.org/2000/08/XMLSchema">
<xsd:annotation>
<xsd:documentation>
This is a sample Schema for more complex elements.
</xsd:documentation>
</xsd:annotation>
<xsd:complexType name="ComplexElement">
<xsd:sequence>
<xsd:element name="SimpleElement1" type="xsd:string"/>
<xsd:element name="SimpleElement2" type="xsd:decimal"/>
</xsd:sequence>
</xsd:complexType>
<!- This is a comment ->
</xsd:schema>
```

As you look at this example, you will notice that the format is basically the same. However, the ComplexType element contains an xsd:sequence that defines the sequence of elements contained within the Complex element. If you see a MinOccurs or MaxOccurs attribute, you know that the elements must occur within the Complex element a specific number of times or the document will not be valid within the Schema.

Note that even within the XML Schema documents, HTML-style comments are valid.

The purpose of this section is not to get you started on writing your own Schema. Norman Walsh and the DocBook Technical Committee will be doing that. However, you might have to read an XML Schema to make use of the DocBook XML Schema as it enters widespread usage.

The DocBook XML Schema

The DocBook XML Schema is not yet final and isn't ready for production use at the time of this writing. Furthermore, none of the tools that you've used to process DocBook are geared to utilize the Schema for DocBook.

The first (alpha) release of the DocBook XML Schema was announced on November 8, 2000, to the DocBook mailing list. Not much documentation exists yet for the DocBook Schema, nor are there any tools for working with the Schema. However, it's valuable to follow the development and be ready for using Schema when it arrives.

You can find the latest versions of the DocBook Schema on the Sun Web site, at least for now. The URL is **http://www.sun.com/software/xml/developers/docbook/** (see Figure 11.3).

Validating the XML Schema

If you're trying your hand at creating DocBook documents that conform to the XML Schema, not many tools are available at this time to validate the Schema or your efforts at making a valid document. However, there is an online resource for checking your documents, provided that your Schema is available online. The World Wide Web Consortium offers this resource at **http://www.w3.org/2000/06/webdata/xsv** (see Figure 11.4).

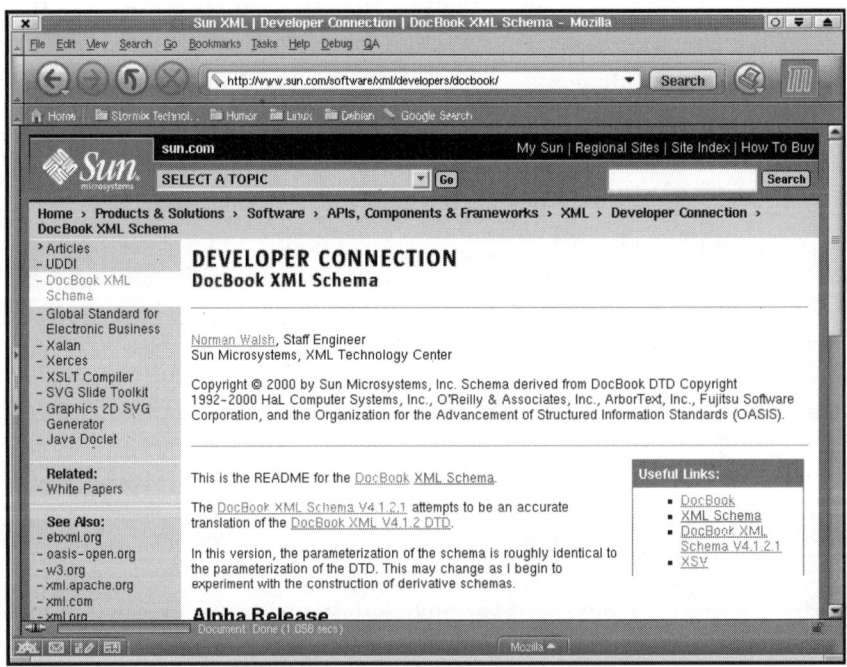

Figure 11.3 *The DocBook XML Schema home page*

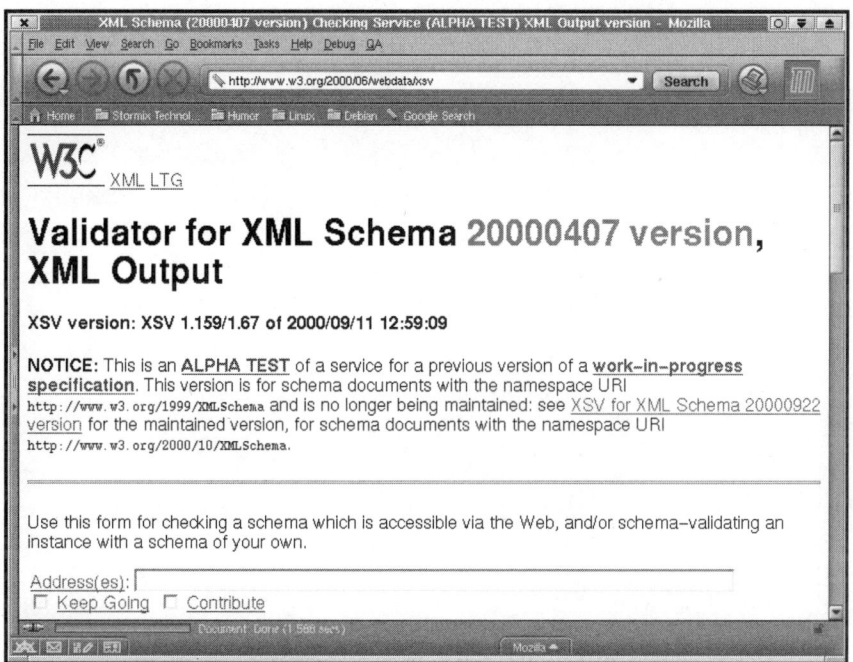

Figure 11.4 *The XSV validator*

Summary

In this chapter you've looked at the XML Schema specification and how it relates to DocBook XML. Although Schema is still in its developmental stage, the larval stage of a specification, it is likely going to become a very important technology as XML picks up steam and is used in more and more applications.

If you're deploying DocBook XML solutions, or any XML solution for that matter, you will want to develop an understanding of Schema so that you can utilize the technology in the near future.

The DocBook XML Schema, in particular, is not currently in practical use. There are no parsers or tools that work with the DocBook XML Schema, so for now you must stick with the DocBook XML DTD if you're using XML. In the near future, however, it may be possible to switch to the XML Schema for DocBook.

lthough DocBook is excellent for a lot of writing projects, it truly excels at technical documentation projects. This makes sense because that's where DocBook got its start. DocBook started as a markup language just for documentation of UNIX-type operating systems. It has changed considerably and gotten much more flexible since then.

DocBook now has elements to describe hardware, databases, elements of a GUI, command syntax, and much more. This chapter demonstrates some of the DocBook elements that are particularly useful for marking up technical documents. Using the right elements will make your documents much easier to read, especially when you need to include code samples.

This chapter will also briefly cover some elements that describe meta-information you might run into when working on a technical document for your employer or when writing a document for presentation at a conference. You're on your own when it comes to actually delivering the presentation. Speaking still gives me the jitters, and, despite the well-intentioned advice, picturing an audience of geeks naked is *not* a good idea.

Corporate Documents

Many technical documents written for large companies are credited with corporate authorship instead of being attributed to a single author.

To include corporate authorship information in a document, you use the CorpAuthor element in the meta-information for the document. For example, if you were preparing an article with DocBook, the markup would look like this.

```
<!DOCTYPE article PUBLIC "-//OASIS//DTD DocBook V4.1//EN">
<article>
<articleinfo>
<title>A Technical Manual</title>
<corpauthor>Mega-big Corporation</corpauthor>
</articleinfo>
...
</article>
```

Note that the ArticleInfo element is new with DocBook 4.0. If you're still maintaining documents from DocBook 3.0, you'll find the same information in the ArtHeader element, which is now deprecated.

If you have a corporate author but you still wish to list authors or contributors to the information, you can add them using the `Collab` and `CollabName` elements, as shown in this next example.

```
<!DOCTYPE article PUBLIC "-//OASIS//DTD DocBook V4.1//EN">
<article>
<articleinfo>
<title>A Technical Manual</title>
<corpauthor>Mega-big Corporation</corpauthor>
<collab><collabname>John Q. Public</collabname></collab>
<collab><collabname>Jane Doe</collabname></collab>
</articleinfo>
...
</article>
```

Some stylesheets supress the collaborator information when rendering output, so you might need to modify the stylesheets if you wish to display collaborators as well as the corporate author information. On the other hand, you might wish to supress it and simply use the information internally so that the people working on a project know who authored it and to whom they should go for further information. If you have a document with 100 co-authors, it could be just a little cumbersome to include them all on a title page.

With larger corporations you might need to assign a publication number to a document, or it might have been contracted by a client as part of a project. If the document has a specific contract number or publication number you can use the `ContractNum` and `PubsNumber` elements, respectively. The `ContractSponsor` element is used to indicate the client for whom the document is being produced. The next code example shows a document with the `ContractNum`, `ContractSponsor` and `PubsNumber` elements. As you can see they're not difficult to use.

```
<!DOCTYPE article PUBLIC "-//OASIS//DTD DocBook V4.1//EN">
<article>
<articleinfo>
<title>A Technical Manual</title>
<corpauthor>Mega-big Corporation</corpauthor>
<contractnum>2001-01-10</contractnum>
<contractsponsor>Bob's Bagel Bonanza</contractsponsor>
<pubsnumber>TM-01</pubsnumber>
</articleinfo>
...
</article>
```

Again, it depends on the stylesheets that you use whether the `ContractNum`, `ContractSponsor`, or `PubsNumber` are displayed when the document is actually rendered. Note that these elements are only to be nested within the `ArticleInfo` or other `Info` elements. If you refer to the publication number in the body of the document itself, you would not use the `PubsNumber` element.

Documents Written for Technical Conferences

If you're writing or marking up a paper for a technical conference, there are several elements used to include information about the conference in the meta-information of the document.

The elements are the `ConfDate`, `ConfGroup`, `ConfNum`, `ConfSponsor`, and `ConfTitle`. The `ConfDate` element is used to designate the dates of the conference, the `ConfTitle` indicates the name of the conference, and the `ConfSponsor` is used for the sponsor of the conference the document is being presented at. The `ConfNum` element is used to indicate the number or other designation of a conference. For instance, if you were presenting a paper at ComputerCon *X*, then the markup would look like this, as long as *X* is the indicator of a particular conference and not part of the permanent name of the conference:

```
<conftitle>ComputerCon</conftitle>
<confnum>X</confnum>
```

The `ConfGroup` element is used to enclose the other conference informational elements. If you were writing a paper for the NiftyCon 500, sponsored by Bob's Software Slaughterhouse and taking place from April 1, 2001 to April 2, 2001, it would look like this.

```
<!DOCTYPE article PUBLIC "-//OASIS//DTD DocBook V4.1//EN">
<article>
<articleinfo>
<title>Writing Code Makes Me Happy</title>
<author>
<firstname>John</firstname>
<surname>Doe</surname>
</author>
<confgroup>
<confname>NiftyCon</confname>
<confnum>500</confnum>
<confdates>April 1, 2001 - April 2, 2001</confdates>
```

```
<confsponsor>Bob's Software Slaughterhouse</confsponsor>
</confgroup>
</articleinfo>
...
</article>
```

Remember, the `Conf` elements are meta-information. The default stylesheets that come with SGMLTools will suppress the `Conf` elements so that the information does not show up when the document is rendered.

Making a man-Style Reference Page

If you've used Linux, one of the BSD variants or any UNIX-style operating system, you've no doubt used the **man** command to read up on a system utility or other program. In this section you'll walk through creating a reference page like the manual pages you all know and love.

Look at the markup for a simple reference entry. Then, it will be broken down so that it is easier to understand.

```
<!DOCTYPE reference PUBLIC "-//OASIS//DTD DocBook V4.1//EN">
<reference> <title>Reference Example</title>
<refentry>
<refmeta>
<refentrytitle>Example</refentrytitle>
</refmeta>
<refnamediv>
<refname>Example</refname>
<refpurpose>Provides an example of the Reference and RefEntry
elements</refpurpose>
</refnamediv>
<refsect1><title>Example Text</title>
<para>This is where you would find descriptive text about the subject of
the RefEntry element</para>
</refsect1>
</refentry>
</reference>
```

The `Reference` element might seem like it is misnamed at first. Although you might expect to use the `Reference` element to create a `Reference` term, the `Reference` element isn't used for a specific reference term. Instead it is used to create a reference section that holds a number of RefEntry elements. Each RefEntry element is an individual reference entry, similar to a man page. It could be used to hold just one RefEntry element, as showed in this example, but usually it would be used for a collection of RefEntry elements.

The RefEntry element is not restricted to use with the Reference element. It can be used nearly anywhere in a document.

The RefMeta element holds the meta-information about the RefEntry element, particularly the title of the RefEntry, which is included within the RefEntryTitle element.

The RefSect1 element is similar to the Sect1 element, which has already been covered, except that it is specific to the RefEntry element. There are three levels of RefSect element, RefSect1 through RefSect3. As with the Sect elements, the RefSect elements don't hold content directly. The Para element is used below the RefSect elements to hold content. Figure 12.1 shows the RefEntry element rendered in an HTML browser.

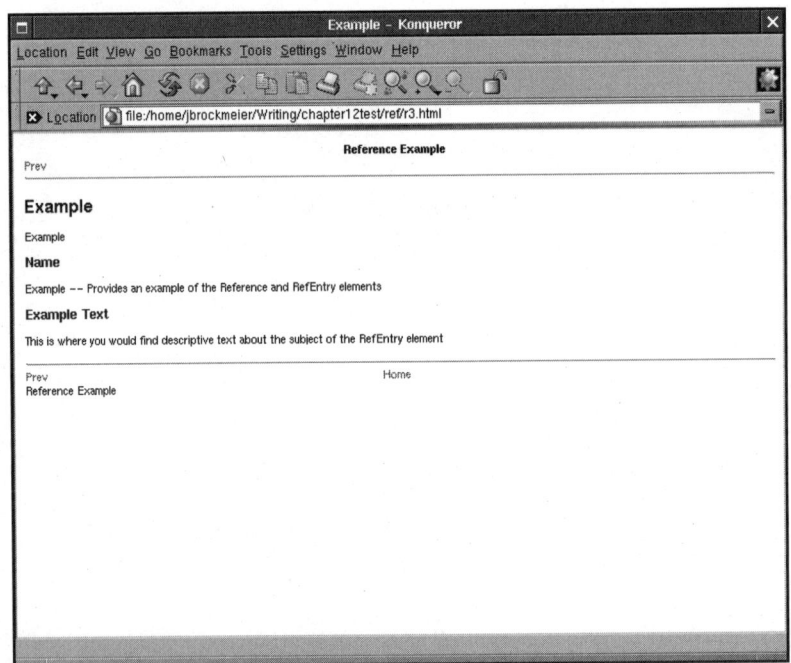

Figure 12.1 *A RefEntry rendered in HTML*

Including Code Samples

When writing a technical document, you might want to include some code samples so the reader can follow along with what you're doing with the code.

Listing Code

When listing code, you want to preserve the whitespace so that indentation is maintained. If you recall, most whitespace in DocBook is ignored when a document is rendered. For instance, if you picked up the habit of hitting the spacebar twice after a sentence, only one space will show up when the document is actually rendered.

However, the ProgramListing element in DocBook is designed to include code with indentations that should be preserved. If you need to include a ProgramListing in your document, it should look something like this example:

```
<para>
<programlisting>
&lt;?php echo "The Current Date and Time is: &lt;br&gt;";
        echo date("g:i A l, F j Y.");

// g = the hour, in 12-hour format
 // i = minutes
 // A = print AM or PM, depending...
 // l = print the day of the week
 // F = print the month
 // j = print the day of the month
 // Y = print the year - all four digits

?&gt;
&lt;br&gt;
&lt;?php echo "Hello, World!";?&gt;
</programlisting>
</para>
```

The ProgramListing element can appear almost anywhere in a document. In this example, it's under the Para element. You might notice that in the PHP code sample above I've had to replace the < and > characters with the entity codes < and &gt. This can be a royal pain if you have to do that with a large code sample.

Luckily, there's a solution. When you have a code sample that you want the DocBook parser to ignore any markup or anything that looks like markup, you can create a CData section under the ProgramListing element. The CData section is declared like this.

```
<!DOCTYPE article PUBLIC "-//OASIS//DTD DocBook V4.1//EN">
<article>
<title>Programlisting</title>
<programlisting>
<![CDATA[
<?php echo "The Current Date and Time is: <br>";
          echo date("g:i A l, F j Y.");

// g = the hour, in 12-hour format
 // i = minutes
 // A = print AM or PM, depending...
 // l = print the day of the week
 // F = print the month
 // j = print the day of the month
 // Y = print the year - all four digits

?>
<br>
<?php echo "Hello, World!";?>
]]>
</programlisting>
</article>
```

It looks almost exactly the same, but you get to avoid hassling with the < and > to produce the < and > characters. Using a CData section is especially useful when you're writing documents about DocBook, HTML, XML or other markup languages that use tags similar to DocBook.

> You might have guessed by now that when you render a document from DocBook into HTML that the < and > characters are automatically converted into < and >, or their numeric equivalent, < and > so that they'll display properly in a browser.

The CData section begins with `<![CDATA[` and ends with `]]>`, which signals the parser that regular markup is once again in effect. Any processing instructions between the `<![CDATA[` and `]]>` characters will be ignored. The white space in the CData section will be honored and reproduced exactly as is.

Formal Examples

If you have a larger code sample that you want to appear as a formal example set off from the text with a title, you can combine the ProgramListing element with the Example element. By the way, the Example element is not limited to code or program listings, it can be used for any type of example that should be set off from the main text with a title. The next code sample demonstrates how to use the Example element with a ProgramListing. Figure 12.2 shows the output from the ProgramListing code example, and Figure 12.3 shows the output from the ProgramListing nested within the Example element.

```
<!DOCTYPE article PUBLIC "-//OASIS//DTD DocBook V4.1//EN">
<article><title>Example</title>
<example>
<title>A Sample PHP Script</title>
<programlisting>
<![CDATA[
<?php echo "The Current Date and Time is: <br>";
        echo date("g:i A l, F j Y.");

// g = the hour, in 12-hour format
 // i = minutes
 // A = print AM or PM, depending...
 // l = print the day of the week
 // F = print the month
 // j = print the day of the month
 // Y = print the year - all four digits

?>
<br>
<?php echo "Hello, World!";?>
]]>
</programlisting>
</example>
</article>
```

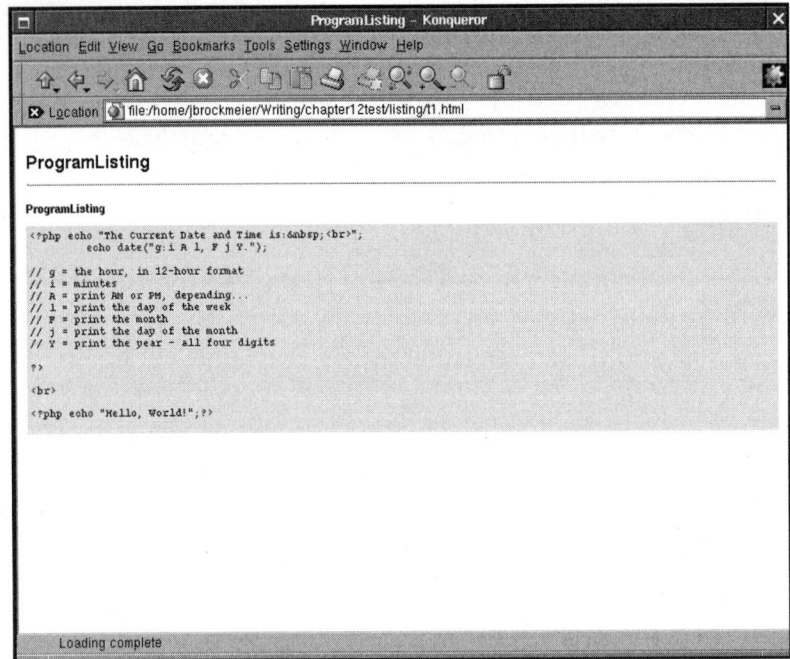

Figure 12.2 *The ProgramListing element output to HTML*

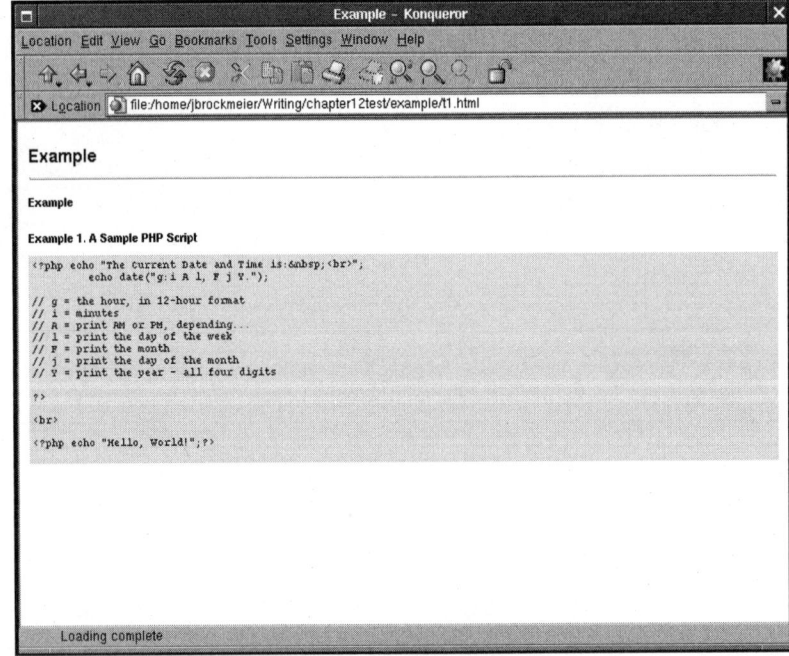

Figure 12.3 *The Example element output to HTML*

There is also an `InformalExample` element, if you want to have an example without a title. For general output, there's not much of a reason to use the `InformalExample` element in combination with the `ProgramListing` element.

Notes, Cautions, Tips, and Warnings

If you read a lot of computer books like I do, you've probably noticed that there is an abundance of tips, notes, and warnings. These are set off from the text with an icon to alert you to particularly evil things that can happen if you do the wrong thing, or clue you in to special commands or tricks that you can use.

DocBook has five elements that can be used to highlight sections of the documentation—`Caution`, `Important`, `Note`, `Tip` or `Warning`. The element names are pretty descriptive of their function, and they're all used in the same fashion. The next code sample shows the `Tip` element in use, but the general syntax is the same for any of these elements.

```
<!DOCTYPE article PUBLIC "-//OASIS//DTD DocBook V4.1//EN">
<article><title>Tip Example</title>
<para>This is a regular paragraph.</para>
<tip><title>A Helpful Tip</title>
<para>This paragraph contains the text of the Tip element.</para>
<para>The Tip element may contain several paragraphs and even
screenshots, figures, lists and other types of content.</para>
</tip>
</article>
```

Each of the five elements may have a `Title` element, but it isn't required. When rendered in HTML, PostScript, or several other formats, these elements will also have an icon or graphic that draws the reader's attention to the item. Figure 12.4 shows the tip from the code sample output as HTML.

When you render a document into plain text with SGMLTools using the default DocBook stylesheets, obviously you won't be able to include a great deal of special formatting. However, the text will be set off slightly from regular text to separate the tip from the rest of the content, as shown in Figure 12.5.

Often visual clues like these stick in our minds more clearly than the majority of the text, so it might be helpful to your readers if you try to make a point of using these elements when appropriate. Sometimes one really good tip or a warning that keeps you from sending your data to the big bit bucket in the sky is worth reading an entire article for. Using these elements appropriately, but sparingly, can be a big help to your readers.

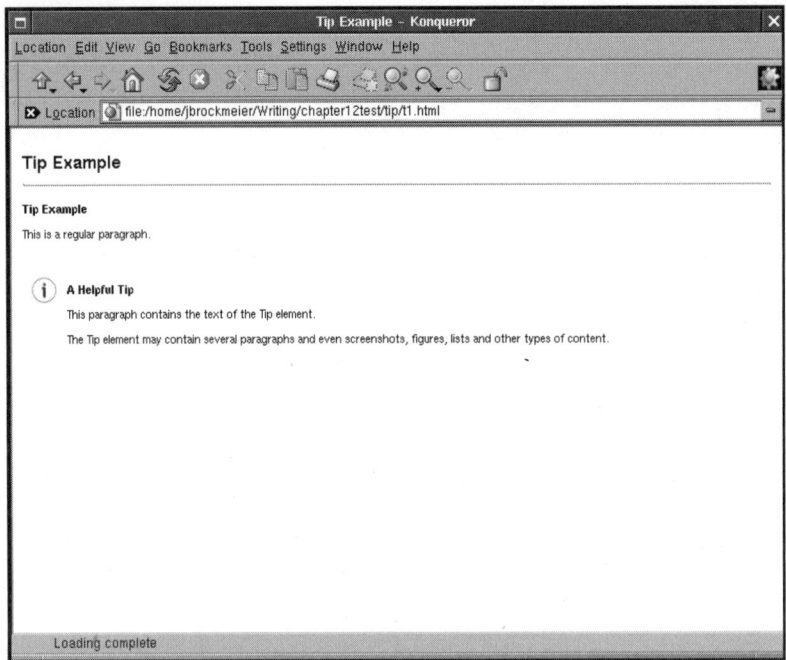

Figure 12.4 *The Tip element output to HTML*

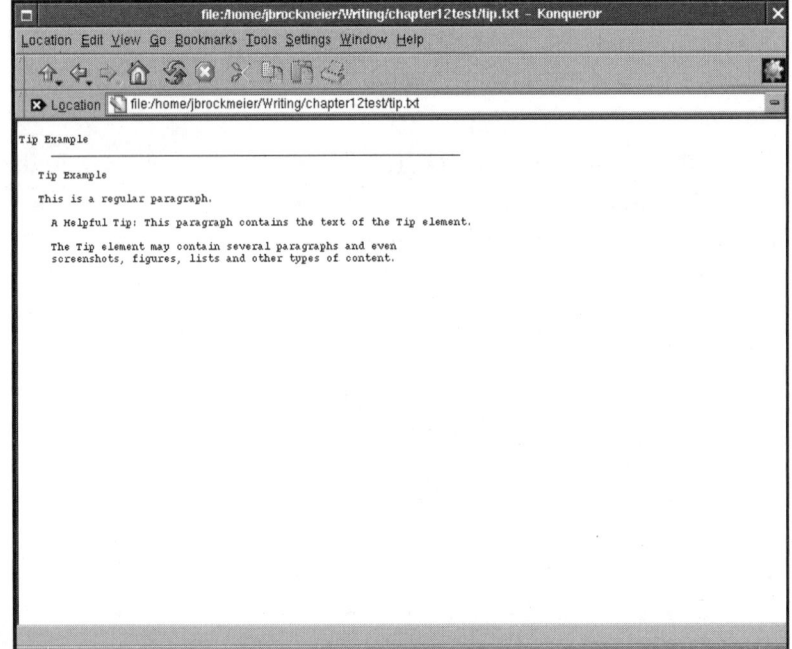

Figure 12.5 *The Tip element output to plain text*

Fun with Errors

Okay, computer errors usually aren't fun. Sometimes it's amusing when they happen to someone else, but they're never fun when they happen to us. It's a fact of life, though, occasionally when you're working with computers you're going to get some type of error message. Life is a little better if the documentation that comes with software actually covers the possible errors and explains what they mean, instead of a cryptic and undocumented error code that just makes the users scratch their head and wonder why they didn't buy your competitor's software.

DocBook has a few elements that are concerned with errors, namely the ErrorCode, ErrorName and ErrorType elements. The ErrorCode element is used to hold the error code, usually a numeric code. The ErrorName element is kind of misleading; it's not necessarily the name of the error, but the message that the user sees. The ErrorType element can be used to indicate the kind of error, whether it is critical or it can be ignored or somewhere in-between. Here's an example of using DocBook markup to describe an error.

```
<para>If you try to use <command>apt-get</command> when logged in as a
regular user you will get the following error message:</para>
<para><computeroutput><errorname>E: Could not open lock file
/var/lib/dpkg/lock - open (13 Permission denied)</errorname>
</computeroutput></para>
<para><computeroutput><errorname>E: Unable to lock the administration
directory, are you root?</errorname></computeroutput></para>
<para>The <errorcode>13 Permission denied</errorcode>  is
<errortype>recoverable</errortype>. You can avoid the  error by using the
<command>su</command> to log in as root before trying to use
<command>apt-get</command>. </para>
```

When documenting an error for a reference manual, you may want to use the RefEntry element to create a reference page for each classified error.

Writing about GUIs

DocBook has several elements for dealing with parts of the Graphical User Interface. The following example shows a combination of several DocBook elements used to describe the user interface.

```
<!DOCTYPE article PUBLIC "-//OASIS//DTD DocBook V4.1//EN">
<article>
```

```
<title>GUI Elements</title>
<sect1>
  <title>Saving a New File</title>
<para>Using the
<menuchoice><guimenu>File</guimenu><guisubmenu>Save</guisubmenu>
<guimenuitem>Save As</guimenuitem></menuchoice> option you can save the
current file. When the dialog box pops up, enter the name you'd like to
give the file and click <guibutton>Ok</guibutton>.</para>
</sect1>
</article>
```

The MenuChoice element is used to indicate a sequence of selections from a menu. The GuiMenu element holds the name of the top-level menu choice; the GuiSubMenu element holds any lower-level menus; and the GuiMenuItem holds the name of the selection from the menu. When output is generated from the DocBook document the sequence from the top-level menu to the menu choice will be indicated as shown in Figure 12.6 (HTML output) and Figure 12.7 (text output).

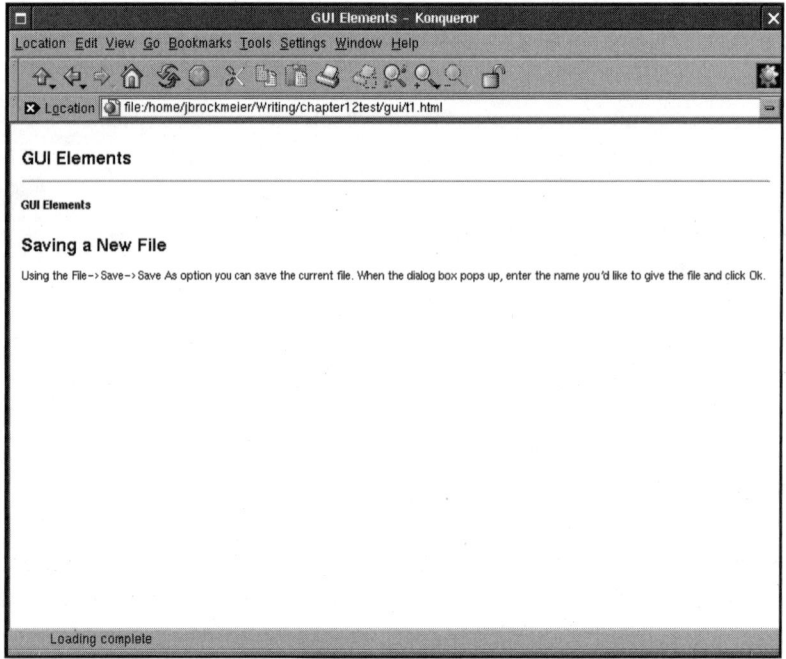

Figure 12.6 *Menu instructions output in HTML*

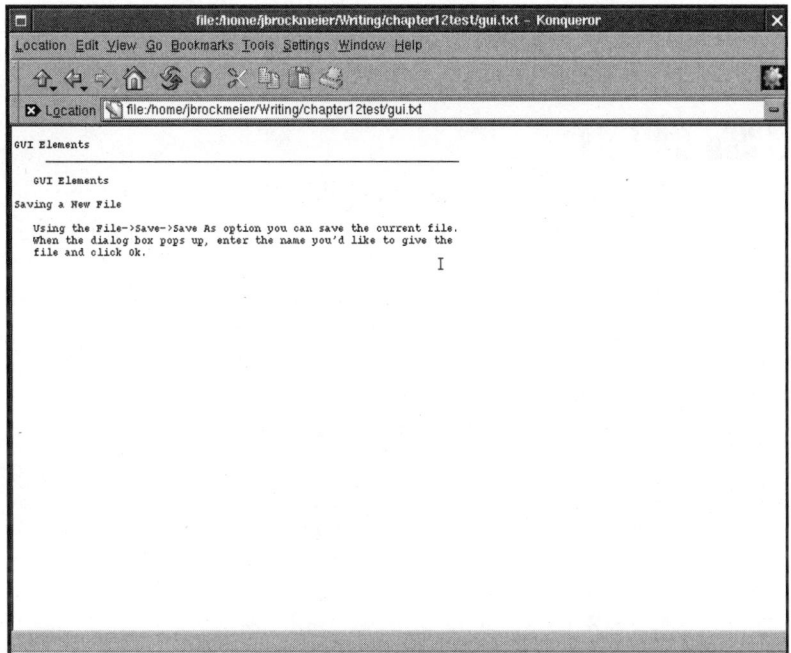

Figure 12.7 *Menu instructions output in text format*

As you can see, the output looks pretty similar whether it's in HTML or even plain text. This means that your document should be easily followed no matter what medium it's rendered in.

The GuiButton element, as its name implies, indicates text displayed to the user on a button. Whether the GuiButton text is rendered any differently from the regular text in your document depends on the stylesheets you use.

You might also want to include screenshots of the GUI with your document. That's covered in Chapter 3, "Using Images."

Marking Up Command Syntax

Because I spend most of my time using Linux, I think a lot about command-line tools. In addition to the GUI descriptive elements we just covered, DocBook provides a healthy set of elements to describe commands and their options, filenames, environmental variables, and other parts of the text-based interface.

This section will cover using DocBook markup to describe actions performed at the command line.

Commands and Options

The next example will probably look fairly familiar. It's a short paragraph describing how to use SGMLTools to create HTML output from a file called filename.sgml.

```
<!DOCTYPE article PUBLIC "-//OASIS//DTD DocBook V4.1//EN">
<article>
<title>Using SGMLtools</title>
<para>To render HTML from a DocBook file, use the following
syntax.</para>
<para><prompt>user@host:~$</prompt><command>sgmltools</command> <option>-b
html</option> <filename>filename.sgml</filename></para>
</article>
```

The Prompt element is used to indicate a command prompt, in this case a standard Linux prompt, but it can be used to indicate a DOS prompt or any other type of prompt as well. The Command element is used to indicate any program or executable name that you would type at the command line.

The Filename attribute is used to indicate any filename, including the name of a directory. Figure 12.8 shows the output from the example in HTML. Note the command name and options.

If you want to demonstrate the use of a command with optional arguments, you use the Optional element. For instance, if you want to demonstrate the use of the UNIX ls command with an optional argument like the color argument, then you would use a syntax like the next example. Figure 12.9 shows what this example looks like rendered in HTML.

```
<!DOCTYPE article PUBLIC "-//OASIS//DTD DocBook V4.1//EN">
<article>
<title>Using ls to list directories in Color</title>
<article>
<title>Using ls to list directories in Color</title>
<para>To display the contents of a directory use the <command>ls
</command> command>. To see the display in color, you can use the color
argument.</para>
<para><prompt>user@host:~$</prompt> <command>ls</command> <optional>
—color</optional></para>
</article>
```

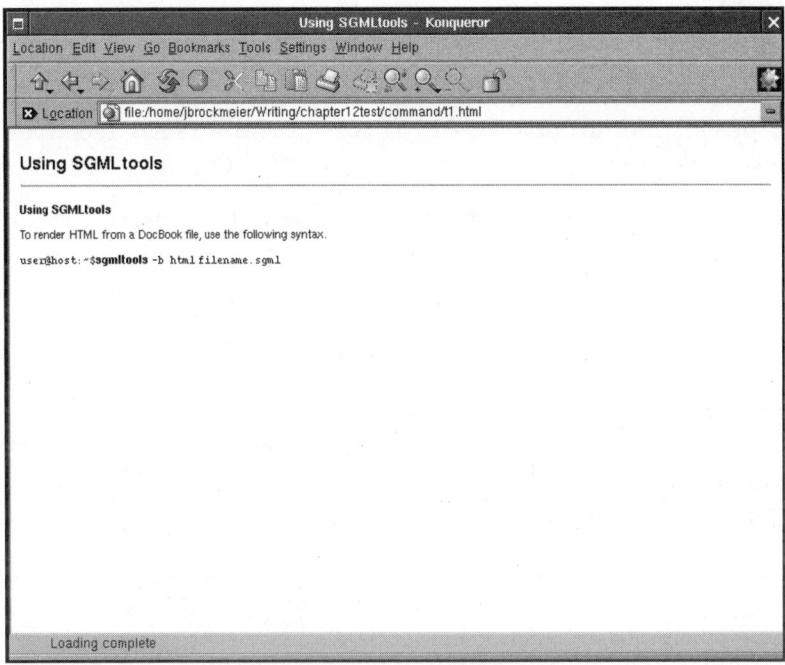

Figure 12.8 *Command example output in HTML*

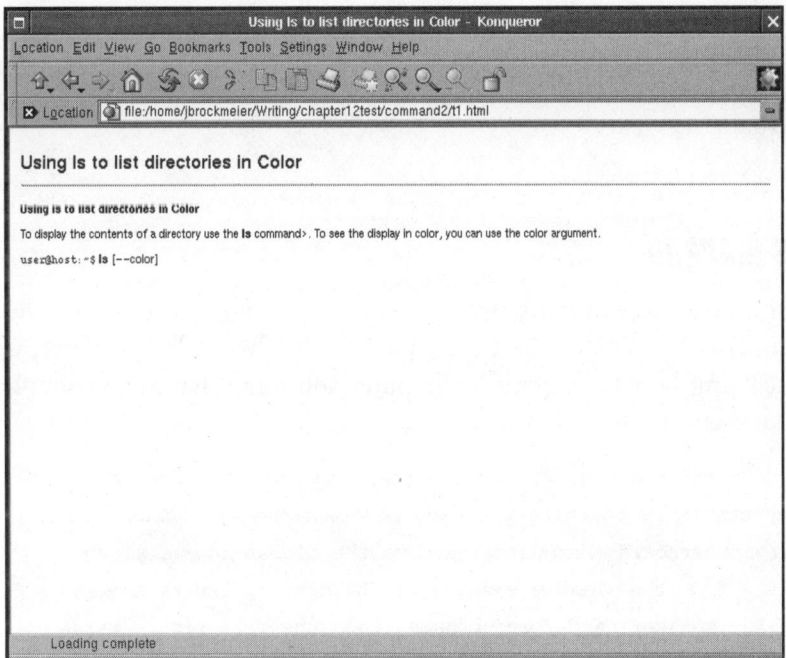

Figure 12.9 *Command example output in HTML*

Database Markup

If you're writing a manual on working with a database, such as MySQL, PostgreSQL, Oracle, Informix or any other database, there are a few DocBook elements that might be of use.

When naming your database in the text, you would want to use the `Database` element. The `Database` element is used to identify the name of an existing database or part of a database. For instance, if you are working with a MySQL database that you've created called bigdaddy then you'd use the `Database` element with it. However, you wouldn't use the `Database` element with the name MySQL, because it is the name of an application, not the name of a particular database. DocBook does have an `Application` element, however, that you do use to indicate the name of a particular application such as MySQL, PostgreSQL, or any other application.

Here is an example of the `Database` and `Application` elements; see Figure 12.10 for output.

```
<!DOCTYPE article PUBLIC "-//OASIS//DTD DocBook V4.1//EN">
<article>
<title>Using MySQL</title>
<para>If you want to work with a <application>MySQL</application>
database, type in the following command at the shell prompt:</para>
<para><command>mysql -u username -p</command></para>
<para><prompt>mysql&gt;</prompt> <userinput>use  <database>bigdaddy</
database></userinput></para>
</article>
```

Hardware Markup

When referring to a piece of hardware in a technical manual, you can use the `Hardware` element to indicate a particular piece of hardware. For instance, if you were discussing how to upgrade a computer you might have a paragraph that looks like this.

```
<para>Power down the computer and remove the case. Be sure that you
discharge any static by touching the case before coming in contact with
the <hardware>motherboard</hardware>. Remove the old <hardware>video
card</hardware> from the <hardware>AGP slot</hardware>. Insert the
<productname>AGP Monster Card</productname> into the free slot.</para>
```

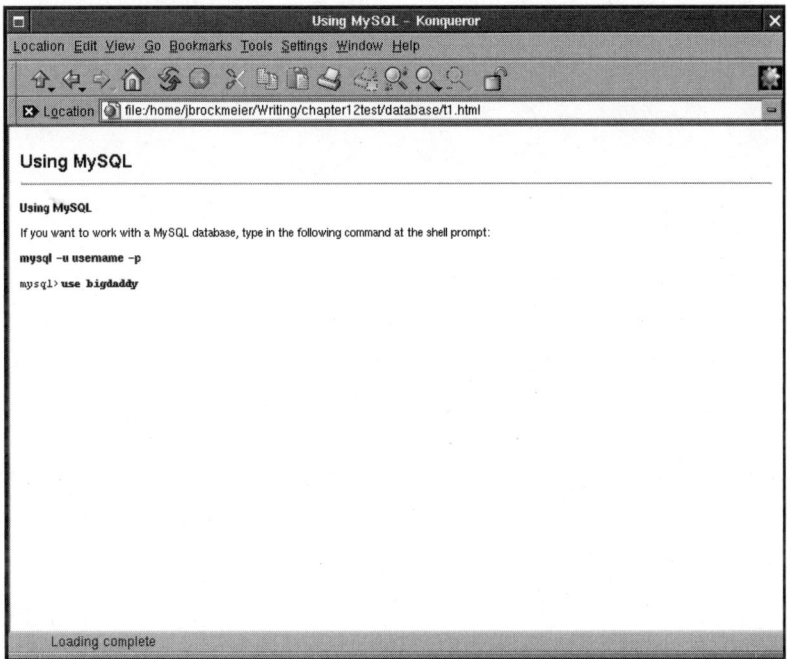

Figure 12.10 *Output of the Database and Application elements*

The Hardware element is fairly generic. There aren't elements for specific types of hardware like SCSI cards or hard drives. As shown in the previous example, you might wish to use the ProductName element when referencing a specific name brand of hardware.

Summary

In this chapter you've looked at some of DocBook's more common elements for writing technical documents. There are other elements that you might use in a technical document, but these are some of the elements that you'll probably use over and over again.

As you can see, the markup isn't that difficult. Don't try to memorize all of the elements when you start working with DocBook. In time you'll memorize the ones you need frequently, and the ones that aren't that important you can look up when you need them. It might seem like an overwhelming amount of material now, but after working with DocBook for a little while it will become second nature, just like riding a bike or driving a car. By using the elements that DocBook provides for technical documentation you'll find that you can produce very professional-looking documents that are easier to follow.

Appendix A: DocBook Glossary

ost professions and technologies have a small vocabulary of their own, usually called *jargon*. This is useful when you're familiar with a technology, or when discussing your profession with another person in the same line of work. It allows a person to communicate a complex idea in a concise manner but only if the receiver is versed in the jargon as well. If not, then the reader or listener starts to go slack-jawed and get a glazed look before they lose interest entirely. This is bad when trying to communicate to a new audience, but it is a great way to get rid of boring people at parties or other functions. Extra bonus points if you're a coroner, or know some coroner jargon. You could cut a swath in the crowd to the food and drinks faster than a hot knife through butter. This probably doesn't work at coroner conventions, though.

Because DocBook deals with a number of technologies, any discussion of DocBook invariably requires a smattering of jargon that can't be avoided. I've tried to be sure to explain new terms as I introduce them in the book, but from time to time it might be inconvenient to do so, or you might not read the particular chapter in which the term is introduced. To make things a bit less confusing, I've included this glossary to help nail down the really important, or really obscure, terms used in *DocBook Publishing*.

When you see terms in **bold** in this glossary, that means they're also defined here, so you can refer to those terms as well if you're unclear as to their meaning.

ANSI. *The American National Standards Institute.* The **American National Standards Institute** is a private, nonprofit membership organization supported by private and public sector organizations that works with members to develop standards for industries.

ASCII. *The American Standard Code of Information Interchange.* The acronym is usually pronounced *ASK-ee*. The ASCII standard has been around since 1968. It is a 7-bit code character set that is becoming lengthy but is still widely used.

Attribute. Used to further define the content of an **element**. Attributes are usually optional but may be required with some elements.

Cascading Style Sheets (CSS). Used to define the "look and feel" (style) of **XML** and **HTML** documents. The cascading stylesheet specification is developed by the World Wide Web Consortium (**W3C**). Currently, there are W3C recommendations for CSS levels 1 and 2, and the W3C is working on a level 3 draft. You can find out more about CSS on the W3C site at **http://www.w3.org/Style/CSS/**.

Catalog File. Used to resolve **public identifiers** to local files. The catalog file contains information about where the DocBook **DTD** and other associated files can be found.

CDATA. *Character data*, which can have several different meanings. When used in a marked section of a document it is a type of data in **SGML** and **XML** that includes characters normally recognized as **markup**, but the data is not processed. A CDATA section is indicated like this:

```
<![CDATA[
character data goes here
]]>
```

Any content is allowed in a CDATA section, with the exception of the string]]>, which tells a parser that the CDATA section has ended.

CDATA is also a data type for elements, meaning that an element may contain character data, or it can be the type of data accepted by an attribute within an element.

Child Element (or Children). **Elements** that occur within other elements are sometimes referred to as their *children* because they are dependent on the placement of the **parent element**. Element children are **nested** within other elements and may cause **parse** errors if they occur outside their parent element.

CLI. *Command-line interface.* Examples of a CLI are the Linux Bash shell and an MS-DOS command prompt. It is possible to access the command-line interface in a **GUI** through the use of an xterm or DOS window.

Comment. Specially marked text in DocBook **markup** or programming code that is ignored by a parser or compiler and is for the benefit of the author or programmer.

CSS. *See* **Cascading Style Sheets**.

DSSSL. *See* the **Document Style Semantics and Specification Language**.

DOCTYPE. Specifies the **root element** of a document. The DOCTYPE is indicated in the document declaration at the beginning of a document. All **SGML** documents and most **XML** documents begin with a document declaration.

Document Style Semantics and Specification Language (DSSSL). Used to specify formatting of an **SGML** or **XML** document. **ISO** standard 10179:1996 defines DSSSL.

Document Type Definition (DTD). Defines the structure and data **elements** for documents. DTDs are used with **SGML, HTML,** and **XML.** There are DocBook DTDs for SGML and XML.

DTD. *See* **Document Type Definition**.

Electronic Data Interchange (EDI). An **ANSI** standard for exchanging business data.

Element. Part of **SGML** and **XML** markup that defines document content. The meaning of an SGML or XML element is defined by the **DTD** of the document. DocBook documents are **parsed** by programs such as **Jade** or **OpenJade**, which interpret the **elements** and their **attributes** against the DTD and **stylesheets** to produce output in **HTML,** PostScript, PDF, and other formats.

Emacs. A text editor with a huge number of features, including content-sensitive editing modes, e-mail and newsgroup support, a Web browser, and even its own Lisp interpreter. Emacs is short for *Editor Macros*. Richard M. Stallman (*RMS*, for short) began work on the first version of Emacs in 1976 at M.I.T. Emacs is part of the **GNU** project and is a popular editor for working with DocBook.

End Tag. **Markup** indicating the end of an **element**.

Entity. A name or reference to a bit or type of data. In the body of a document containing DocBook markup, entities begin with the ampersand (&) and end with a semicolon (;). Entities can be classified as internal or external. They are declared in the **DTD** or document declaration, with the following **markup** for internal entities:

```
<!ENTITY entity_name "Entity text">
External entities are declared like this:
<!ENTITY entity_name SYSTEM "entity.sgml">
```

Escape Character. A substitute character for a reserved character in **SGML** or **XML**. For instance, the < and > characters are reserved for indicating **markup**. The escape characters (sometimes called *escape codes*) for these characters are < and >, which produce the < and > characters when the document is processed to create output.

FAQ. *Frequently Asked Questions*, pronounced *Fak*. A FAQ is a document that attempts to answer frequently asked questions. Usually posted or included with a download in the hopes that it will save the author time answering redundant or irritating questions.

GNU. A recursive acronym for *GNU's Not UNIX.* The GNU project is a project of the Free Software Foundation, designed to produce a free replacement for **UNIX**. The GNU project provides many tools included with the Linux and the FreeBSD, NetBSD, and OpenBSD operating systems. GNU software is provided under the **GPL**.

GPL. *General Public License.* The license used and promoted by the Free Software Foundation. The GPL is frequently referred to as *Copyleft* because it is similar to a regular copyright but gives the rights to software to all people rather than restrict them. (This is not the same as placing software in the public domain, because it does place some restrictions on use of the software. Namely, software licensed under the GPL cannot be placed under another license that restricts use of the software or code by anyone else.) You can find more information on the GPL at **http://www.fsf.org/**.

Grep. The program grep searches a file for a line or lines in the file that match a pattern specified on the command line. The program grep, and its variants, are available on most **UNIX**-type operating systems. In hacker-speak, *grep* is also a generic term for searching for something, as in "I grepped the entire house but still couldn't find my car keys. Turns out, I left them in my car."

GUI. *Graphical user interface*, pronounced *gooey*. Once considered exotic, GUIs are now the norm. *See also* **CLI**.

HTML. *Hypertext Markup Language.* HTML is actually an **SGML DTD** produced by the **W3C**. HTML **markup** looks very similar to DocBook markup, although the actual **elements** are different. DocBook documents can be used to produce HTML.

IETF. *The Internet Engineering Task Force.* The IETF publishes a number of **RFCs**, some of which affect work done on **XML** by the **W3C**, particularly the RFCs on **URLs** and **URIs**.

ISO. *International Organization for Standardization.* Contrary to popular belief, *ISO* is not an acronym for the name of the organization. Rather, *ISO* is taken from the Greek word *isos*, which means *equal.* The ISO produces a wide variety of standards, including the **SGML** standard.

ISO 8879:1986. The ISO document that provides the specifications for **SGML**.

Jade. The James' DSSSL Engine, an implementation of the **DSSSL**-style language. Jade is used in conjunction with DocBook to produce output. Jade is available on the CD-ROM that comes with this book, or you can find newer versions at **http://www.jclark.com/jade/**.

Keyword. A word or parameter that is a **reserved name**.

Linux. An operating system. Technically, Linux is just the kernel of the operating system, but a typical Linux distribution includes the Linux kernel, **GNU** tools, and various other programs that make up a usable system.

Lisp. A programming language used extensively with **Emacs**.

Markup. The instructions inserted in a text file to indicate how a document should be displayed. Markup gives information about a document's structure and content.

MathML. *The Mathematical Markup Language.* Based on **XML**, a language to describe mathematical expressions.

Metadata. The description of data.

Metalanguage. The description of language. **SGML** and **XML** are metalanguages because they are languages used to describe other language.

Minimization. The use of shortened **tags** when doing **SGML** markup. SGML allows minimization of markup, but **XML** does not.

Nested. Elements that reside within other elements are also referred to as *nested elements.* **Child elements** are nested within **parent elements**. If an element is supposed to be nested within another element and is mistakenly placed outside that element, it will produce **validation** errors.

Normative. Parts of a reference that provide guidelines and specifications. The **W3C** recommendation for **XML** is considered a normative document.

Non-normative. Non-normative documents are those that do not provide specifications but rather provide examples and expansion of the specifications laid down by normative documents. (This book would be considered a non-normative document.)

Nsgmls. A validating parser that **parses** an **SGML** document and checks for errors. Nsgmls is a command-line program included with James Clark's **SP**.

OASIS. *The Organization for the Advancement of Structured Information Standards.* OASIS is a multinational concern that creates specifications based on open standards such as SGML and XML. The most recent versions of DocBook were created by an OASIS Technical Committee. You can find OASIS on the Web at **http://www.oasis-open.org/**.

OpenJade. A project based on James Clark's Jade. OpenJade is essentially an extension of Jade.

Open Source. Software that is placed under a license that allows free redistribution, requires the accessibility of source code, allows derived works, and does not discriminate against persons or groups or against specific uses. You can find the full Open Source definition at **http://www. opensource.org/osd.html**.

Note that Open Source is not the same as Free Software as defined by the Free Software Foundation.

Parent Element. An element in DocBook markup that has one or more **children**. An element can be both a parent and child element.

Parse. To parse a markup language is to divide the elements and such into parts that can then be processed into output. A program that parses DocBook documents may or may not perform **validation** on them. Validation is not a necessary step of parsing a document.

Parser. A program that parses DocBook.

Perl. *The Practical Extraction and Reporting Language*, created by Larry Wall. A scripting language used on nearly all operating systems. Perl is often referred to as the *duct tape of the Internet* because of its popularity with system administrators and Webmasters.

Public Identifiers. A unique name for a document that resolves to a particular document on any given system with the proper **catalog file**.

PCDATA. *Parseable character data.* Content contained in an element is considered PCDATA.

RCDATA. *Replaceable character data.* References within an RCDATA section are recognized, but markup is not processed.

Reserved Name. A syntactic literal that is a **keyword** defined in the DTD and that cannot be used for other purposes in the document.

RFC. *Request for Comment.* RFCs are published by the **IETF** and define various technologies used on the Internet. The specifications for URIs and URLs are defined by RFCs.

Root Element. Also known as the *document element*, the top-level **tag** in a document.

Screenshot. A capture of the information or display output from a computer. Often used in technical manuals or books like this one.

SGML. *Standard Generalized Markup Language.* A **metalanguage** used to define a markup language such as HTML, XML, or DocBook. SGML is defined by **ISO 8879**.

SGMLtools. Now called *SGMLtools-lite*, an **Open Source** project that provides a front end for creating output from DocBook documents with **Jade** or **OpenJade**.

SP. *SGML Parser*, written by James Clark. Contains the nsgmls program and is freely distributed in source code and binary format.

Start Tag. **Markup** indicating the beginning of an **element**.

Stylesheet. A document or file that defines the layout for a type of document. **CSS**, **DSSSL**, and **XSL** are stylesheet formats. Stylesheets are used in conjunction with other tools to produce output from DocBook documents. The use of multiple stylesheets enables an author to create multiple output formats from one DocBook document.

Syntax. The rules that define the construction of a language. An **SGML** or **XML DTD** defines the syntax of a document. Syntax rules are similar to a grammar for a markup language.

System Identifiers. Specify a file or resource located on a computer.

Tag. Markup indicating an **element** in an **SGML** or **XML** document.

Text Editor. A program that works with plain-text files and does not perform extensive formatting on a text file. The most popular text editors are **Emacs** and **vi** and its clones.

Tidy. A small program that "cleans up" **HTML** and makes it more readable, as well as checks and fixes errors in syntax. Tidy also replaces deprecated HTML formatting **tags** with **cascading stylesheets**. Tidy is often used to clean HTML code produced by **SGMLtools**.

Unicode. The Unicode Worldwide Character Standard is a system for handling written texts of many diverse languages. Unicode includes support for the majority of written languages in the world, unlike **ASCII**, which is limited.

UNIX. An operating system originally developed in Bell Labs, UNIX was first released in 1969. It was designed to be a portable operating system, rather than lock into one particular hardware design, as many operating systems did originally. Many operating systems available today are UNIX variants or are designed to be like UNIX, including Linux, FreeBSD, NetBSD, OpenBSD, Solaris, AIX, HP-UX, and others.

URI. *Uniform resource indicator*, defined by **RFC** 1630. A URI specifies the protocol to access a resource, the machine that it is located on, and the specific name of the file on the computer within the directory structure.

URL. *Uniform resource locator*, defined by **RFC** 1738. URLs are a subset of URIs and are usually referred to as *addresses* on the Internet.

Validation. Comparison of a document to its DTD. A document is validated when it is checked against its DTD to check for proper use of **elements** and syntax.

Variable. A value that can change and is often used as a placeholder for future data.

Vi. A text editor originally developed by Bill Joy, vi is what is known as a *modal text editor* because it can operate in one of two modes: insert mode or command mode. The regular alphabetic keys are used for commands, and the mode is toggled with the Esc key. The original vi is somewhat outdated, but many vi clones are popular on **UNIX**-type operating systems, such as Linux.

Vim. The most popular of **vi** clones, Vim maintains compatibility with most of the features of the original vi by default but also has many features that the original vi lacks, including syntax highlighting and multiple editing buffers.

W3C. *The World Wide Web Consortium.* The W3C promotes many Web standards, including **HTML, XML, XHTML, CSS,** and **MathML.** The W3C is vendor neutral, and the standards it maintains are made freely available, unlike **ISO** standards.

Whitespace. The blank space in text documents, including blank lines, tab stops, and spaces between words.

Word Processor. A program that produces formatted output and typically operates on a **WYSIWYG** principle. Word processors usually save their files in proprietary document formats that cannot be parsed by tools used with DocBook. Microsoft Word, Corel WordPerfect, and AbiWord are examples of word processors.

WYSIWYG. *What You See Is What You Get.* WYSIWYG programs try to allow the user to define exactly what a document looks like while creating it, displaying the document as it will appear when printed.

XML. *The Extensible Markup Language.* (Yes, it should probably be *EML*, but computer geeks really like the letter *X*.) XML is a recommendation of the **W3C.** XML is a subset of **SGML** and is designed for sharing data over the Internet and to overcome the shortcomings of **HTML.**

XSL. *Extensible Stylesheet Language.* XSL stylesheets provide the definition for a document's presentation and appearance, or the look and feel of a document.

Appendix B: DocBook Element Reference

When learning DocBook, we had a terrible time trying to figure out the best element for a specific purpose. We found that, although the existing documentation was very thorough and accurate, it wasn't exactly organized in a user-friendly fashion. It was almost as if you already had to have a good working knowledge of DocBook to make use of the documentation—the sort of chicken and the egg conundrum that drives newbies insane, or at least frustrates them quite a bit.

When we started to write a book about DocBook, we decided that we wanted to do things differently. Take, for example, this appendix. We could have simply dropped all the elements available in DocBook into the appendix, provided some information about each, and called it a *reference*, and that would have been somewhat useful.

However, we felt that it would be much more helpful to the user to organize the elements by function rather than in alphabetical order. The reason for this is simple: If you know what an element does already, you're less likely to need to look it up. The most common need is to find an element that fulfills a specific purpose. Never fear, though. You can look up the elements by name using the index in the back of this appendix if you just need a little more information on an element with which you are already familiar.

These are not official categories, simply a logical ordering of elements for reference purposes. Some elements in DocBook don't fit into these categories, so we've included a miscellaneous category. Also, some elements can fit into one or more categories.

DocBook Elements 101

There are a ton of elements, more than 300 of them. Unless your document is particularly complicated, it's quite possible that you will never use more than a small fraction of the entire set.

If the idea of more than 300 elements is intimidating to you, you can always simplify a bit and try out Norman Walsh's simplified DocBook DTD instead. The simplified DTD is available on the CD-ROM included with this book or from Norman Walsh's site at **http://www.nwalsh.com/**. Elements that are part of the simplified DocBook set appear at the end of the chapter.

How to Read the Element Reference

The element reference is a guide to using the DocBook elements. Each element topic has an element description, the element attributes, the valid values for each attribute, and a usage example.

Attribute Types

Each DocBook attribute accepts a value that is one of several types. Each of these types is a particular form of data that the parser will accept as valid information. These are basically data types, similar to data types that are used in computer programming languages.

The DocBook SGML and XML DTD accept a limited number of data types. If you require a wider range of data types for your application or document, you can look into the DocBook XML Schema that is under development. The XML Schema specification by the W3C allows for a wide variety of data types, far more than the XML or SGML DTDs. The XML Schema proposal contains too many data types to explore here, particularly because the DocBook XML Schema is still in the development stages and not widely used.

CDATA

The CDATA data type is a string of characters that can include spaces, punctuation, and assorted characters that are not valid in other data types.

ENTITY

An ENTITY is the name of a declared SGML or XML entity. The ENTITY may be declared in the DTD or in the document itself.

ID

The ID data type is a unique name within the document. It declares the unique name called by IDREF and IDREFS.

IDREF

The IDREF data type refers to an ID declared elsewhere in a document. The ID must be unique, but it is acceptable for several IDREFs to refer to an ID value.

IDREFS

The IDREFS data type refers to more than one ID separated by a space.

NAME

The NAME data type holds a name that begins with an alphabetic character but might contain numbers or punctuation.

NAMES

The NAMES data type holds a list of NAMES in a space-separated list.

NUMBER

The NUMBER data type holds a number and may begin with a hyphen character for negative numbers. The NUMBER type may include a decimal point.

NMTOKEN

The NMTOKEN data type is similar to the CDATA data type, but it may not hold punctuation or spaces. It may contain only name characters.

NMTOKENS

The NMTOKENS data type holds a group of one or more NMTOKENs.

NUTOKEN

The NUTOKEN data type may contain numbers, hyphens, or decimal points. It should not be confused with the NMTOKEN data type.

Common Attributes

Certain attributes are common to every DocBook element. Rather than repeat them with each element, we list them here for convenience. You should note these are not required attributes, but simply are applicable to all DocBook elements. Note that each element in this element reference lists *Common Attributes* in the attribute list. Please refer to this list of attributes for each listing.

Arch

The Arch attribute indicates the computer hardware to which the element is referring. This attribute is germane not to all DocBook elements but to many elements that deal with programming.

The Arch attribute accepts a CDATA string as a value, has no default value, and is not required.

Condition

The Condition attribute is new to DocBook 4.0. Condition is a general-purpose attribute without any predefined values. The Condition attribute accepts CDATA values, has no default value, and is not required.

Conformance

The Conformance attribute refers to any standard to which the target of the element is conformant. This refers to any standard, such as the ISO standards or other named standards. The Conformance attribute accepts a NMTOKENS string as a value, has no default value, and is not required.

ID

The ID attribute provides a unique string of text as an identifier for an element. It accepts any unique string of text that begins with an alphabetic character. Each ID attribute within a document must be unique. Some elements do require the ID attribute.

Lang

The Lang attribute holds a language code that indicates an element's language type. This attribute tells the parser which character set to use. It accepts a CDATA string as a value and is not required.

OS

The OS attribute indicates the operating system to which the contents of an element are referring. This attribute is not applicable to all elements but is useful for many elements dealing with describing program elements or programming. The OS attribute accepts a CDATA string as a value, has no default value, and is not required.

Remap

The Remap attribute indicates the name of an element's content in earlier versions of DocBook or other markup languages. This attribute accepts a CDATA string as a value, has no default value, and is not required. The Remap attribute can be used with any element that needs to be mapped to an element in another markup specification.

Role

The Role attribute classifies an element. It accepts a CDATA string as a value and has no default value. The Role attribute is not required.

Revision

The Revision attribute indicates the revision number of the document containing the element. The Revision attribute is not used to refer to the element's contents but to the document of which the element is part. The Revision attribute accepts a CDATA string as a value and has no default value. It is not relevant to all elements.

RevisionFlag

The RevisionFlag attribute designates the revision status of a document. The RevisionFlag is not fine-grained and is not recommended as a substitute for a revision management system. This attribute has four possible values:

- Added
- Changed
- Delete
- Off

The default value is Off. The RevisionFlag attribute is never required.

Security

The Security attribute was added to the DocBook 4.0 specification. This attribute allows an element to be marked *Secret* or any other user-defined security scheme. The Security attribute accepts a CDATA value and has no default value.

UserLevel

The UserLevel attribute designates the level of expertise for which the contents of the element are targeted. For instance, a stylesheet could be written that produces one set of output for any Para element designated *beginner* and ignores any Para element designated *advanced*, or vice versa. The UserLevel attribute is not predefined. It accepts a CDATA value, has no default value, and is not required.

Vendor

The Vendor attribute refers to the vendor of the product to which the element's content refers. For instance, an element that contains the name of a software package or piece of hardware could have an attribute that refers to the vendor of the software or hardware. The Vendor attribute accepts a CDATA string as a value, has no default value, and is not required. It is probably not of much use outside technical documentation or the use of DocBook for print publishing.

XRefLabel

The XRefLabel attribute provides a target for the XRef element. When the XRef element is used to link to another element in a DocBook document, the XRefLabel should be used as a target to which the element can link. The XRefLabel is particularly useful for documents that are going to be rendered in an electronic medium such as HTML or PDF. This attribute accepts a CDATA string as a value, and each XRefLabel should be unique within a document. The XRefLabel is not required for any elements, but the XRef tag must have a target to which it can link.

Element Reference

As we have mentioned before, there are more than 300 DocBook elements. For easier consumption we have organized the elements for this section into twelve catagories. These categories include document types, document structures, attribution and citation, Web, media, meta-information, program and operating systems, literal layout, indexing, table, reference, and obsolete. You will find that some elements belong to multiple categories and have been referenced to in other sections.

Document Type Elements

The DocBook document elements are top-level elements that are often used to separate a document into segments, such as chapters, articles, and so forth.

Appendix

The Appendix element declares an appendix, a supplemental addition to the document (such as this supplemental element reference in *DocBook Publishing*). The Appendix element can be used as a sub-element of the Article or Book element.

The Appendix element accepts the following attributes in addition to the common attributes:

- Label
- Status

Example:

```
<!DOCTYPE appendix PUBLIC "-//OASIS//DTD DocBook V4.1//EN">
<appendix label="B" status="draft">
        <appendixinfo>
        <title>Appendix B</title>
        </appendixinfo>
        <para>...</para>
</appendix>
```

Article

The Article element declares an Article document type. Usually, Article is the document type chosen for stand-alone documents such as articles or academic papers that are not going to be related to other DocBook documents.

The Article element accepts the following attributes in addition to the common attributes:

- **Class.** Has no default value and is not required. May contain the following five possible CDATA values:
  - FAQ
  - JournalArticle
  - ProductSheet
  - TechReport
  - WhitePaper
- **ParentBook.** May contain an IDREF value that refers to a parent book, has no default value, and is not required.

Example:

```
<!DOCTYPE article PUBLIC "-//OASIS//DTD DocBook V4.1//EN">
<article>
        <articleinfo> ...</articleinfo>
        <para>...</para>
</article>
```

Bibliography

The Bibliography element starts a bibliography, a detailed listing of books and other published materials typically used as a reference for the document.

The Bibliography element accepts the following attribute in addition to the common attributes:

- **Status.** Accepts a CDATA value, has no default value, and is not required.

Example:

```
<!DOCTYPE bibliography PUBLIC "//OASIS//DTD DocBook V4.1//EN">
<bibliography>
      <title>Bibliography Sample</title>
      <biblioentry>
      <author>
            <firstname>Joe</firstname>
            <surname>Brockmeier</surname>
      </author>
      <title>DocBook Publishing</title>
      <publisher><publishername>Prima Tech</publishername></publisher>
</bibliography>
```

Book

The Book element begins a DocBook book.

The Book element accepts the following attributes in addition to the common attributes:

- **FPI (*Formal Public Identifier*).** Takes a CDATA value, has no default value, and is not required.
- **Label.** Accepts a CDATA value, has no default value, and is not required.
- **Status.** Accepts a CDATA value, has no default value, and is not required.

Example:

```
<!DOCTYPE book PUBLIC "//OASIS//DTD DocBook V4.1//EN">
<book>
<bookinfo>
            <title>...</title>
</bookinfo>
<chapter>...</chapter>
<index>...</index>
</book>
```

Chapter

The Chapter element begins a DocBook chapter.

The Chapter element accepts the following attributes in addition to the common attributes:

- **Label.** Accepts a CDATA value, has no default value, and is not required.
- **Status.** Accepts a CDATA value, has no default value, and is not required.

Example:

```
<chapter label="Chapter 2" status="editing">...</chapter>
```

Colophon

A *colophon* is the section that explains the steps used to produce a book. The Colophon element begins a DocBook colophon.

The Colophon element accepts the following attribute in addition to the common attributes:

- **Status.** Accepts a CDATA value, has no default value, and is not required.

Example:

```
<!DOCTYPE colophon PUBLIC "//OASIS//DTD DocBook V4.1//EN">
<colophon>
<para>...</para>
</colophon>
```

Dedication

The Dedication element starts a dedication section of a book. The Dedication element is similar to a Chapter element in that it holds the Para and other child elements that make up the text of a dedication. It is not a wrapper for the text of the dedication itself.

The Dedication element accepts the following attribute in addition to the common attributes:

- **Status.** Accepts a CDATA value, has no default value, and is not required.

Example:

```
<!DOCTYPE book PUBLIC "//OASIS//DTD DocBook V4.1//EN">
<book>
<title>,,.</title>
<dedication>
<para>This book is dedicated to my cat, Doogie.</para>
</dedication>
</book>
```

Glossary

The Glossary element starts a glossary section of a Book, an Article, a Section, or a Chapter in DocBook.

The `Glossary` element accepts the following attribute in addition to the common attributes:

- **Status.** Accepts a `CDATA` value, has no default value, and is not required.

Example:

```
<!DOCTYPE glossary PUBLIC "//OASIS//DTD DocBook V4.1//EN">
<glossary><title>My Glossary</title>
<glossentry id="foo"<glossterm>foo</glossterm>
<glossdef>
<para>A generic sample name or term</para>
</glossdef>
</glossentry>
</glossary>
```

Part

The `Part` element starts a part of a book. A part is typically a collection of several chapters. If you have introductory text to include, see the `PartIntro` element.

The `Part` element accepts the following attributes in addition to the common attributes:

- **Label.** Accepts a CDATA value, has no default, and is not required.
- **Status.** Accepts a CDATA value, has no default value, and is not required.

Example:

```
<!DOCTYPE part PUBLIC "-//OASIS//DTD DocBook V4.1//EN"[
<!ENTITY chapter4 SYSTEM "chapter4.sgml">
<!ENTITY chapter5 SYSTEM "chapter5.sqml"
]>
<part status="draft" label="Neat Stuff">
<partintro>
<para>This is an introduction to a DocBook Part</para>
</partintro>
&chapter4;
&chapter5;
</part>
```

PartIntro

The `PartIntro` element holds introductory text for a book part. The `Part` element may not contain a `Para` element directly, so if the part is to contain any introductory text, it must be nested within the `PartIntro` element. (See *Part*.)

The `PartIntro` element accepts the following attribute in addition to the common attributes:

- **Label.** Accepts a `CDATA` value, has no default, and is not required.

Example:

See `Part` Example.

Preface

The `Preface` element holds the preface of a book or part. Note that the `Preface` element can occur more than once for different types of introductory matter in a book.

The `Preface` element accepts the following attribute in addition to the common attributes:

- **Status.** Accepts a `CDATA` value, has no default value, and is not required.

Example:

```
<!DOCTYPE book PUBLIC "//OASIS//DTD DocBook V4.1//EN">
<book>
<title>My Book</title>
<preface>
          <title>My Preface</title>
          <para>...</para>
</preface>
...
</book>
```

Set

The `Set` element can hold one or more book elements. The `Set` element allows DocBook to be used for large-scope projects such as an encyclopedia or a multi-volume set.

The `Set` element accepts the following attributes in addition to the common attributes:

- **FPI (*Formal Public Identifier*).** Takes a `CDATA` value, has no default value, and is not required.
- **Status.** Accepts a `CDATA` value, has no default value, and is not required.

Example:

```
<!DOCBOOK set PUBLIC "//OASIS//DTD DocBook V4.1//EN">
<set><title>My Works</title>
```

```
<book><title>RHCE Exam Cram</title></book>
<book><title>DocBook Publishing</title></book>
</set>
```

Document Structure Elements

The elements listed in the document structure category deal with the hierarchal structure of a DocBook document.

FormalPara

The FormalPara element is used for paragraphs that are to have a title. (The Para element does not allow a Title child element.)

The FomalPara element uses common attributes.

Example:

```
<!DOCTYPE formalpara PUBLIC "//OASIS//DTD DocBook V4.1//EN">
<formalpara><title>My First Paragraph</title>
<para>...</para>
</formalpara>
```

Para

The Para element is used for standard paragraphs. Note that if you want a title for your paragraph, you must use the FormalPara element.

The Para element uses common attributes.

Example:

```
<!DOCTYPE para PUBLIC "//OASIS//DTD DocBook V4.1//EN">
<para>
The Para element is used for standard paragraphs. Note that if you want a
title for your paragraph, you must use the FormalPara element.
</para>
```

Sect1

The Sect1 element begins a level 1 section in a document. The Sect1 element may contain a Sect2 element directly but not a Sect3 or lower.

The Sect1 element accepts the following attributes in addition to the common attributes:

- **Label.** Accepts a CDATA value, has no default value, and is not required.

- **RenderAs.** Accepts one of the following values:
  - Sect2
  - Sect3
  - Sect4
  - Sect5

  The Renderas attribute is used by the processing system, has no default value, and is not required.
- **Status.** Accepts a CDATA value, has no default value, and is not required.

Example:

```
<!DOCTYPE chapter PUBLIC "//OASIS//DTD DocBook V4.1//EN">
<chapter>
        <title>Chapter 1</title>
<para>...</para>
<sect1><title>Introduction</title>
<para>,,,</para>
</sect1>
</chapter>
```

Sect2

The Sect2 element begins a level 2 section in a document. The Sect2 element may contain a Sect3 element directly but not a Sect4 element—you cannot skip Sect elements.

The Sect2 element accepts the following attributes in addition to the common attributes:

- **Label.** Accepts a CDATA value, has no default value, and is not required.
- **RenderAs.** Accepts one of the following values:
  - Sect1
  - Sect3
  - Sect4
  - Sect5

  The RenderAs attribute is used by the processing system, has no default value, and is not required.
- **Status.** Accepts a CDATA value, has no default value, and is not required.

Example:

```
<!DOCTYPE sect1 PUBLIC "//OASIS//DTD DocBook V4.1//EN">
<sect1><title>Introduction</title>
<para>...</para>
```

```
<sect2 id=subintro><title id=subintro.title>Subintroduction</title>
<para>...</para>
</sect2>
</sect1>
```

Sect3

The Sect3 element begins a level 3 section in a document. The Sect3 element may contain a Sect4 element directly but not a Sect5 or any higher Sect* elements.

The Sect3 element accepts the following attributes in addition to the common attributes:

- **Label.** Accepts a CDATA value, has no default value, and is not required.
- **RenderAs.** Accepts one of the following values:
  - Sect1
  - Sect2
  - Sect4
  - Sect5

  The RenderAs attribute is used by the processing system, has no default value, and is not required.
- **Status.** Accepts a CDATA value, has no default value, and is not required.

Examples:

The Sect3 element is used within a Sect2 element, as the example for Sect2 is shown as within Sect1. See Sect2 example.

Sect4

The Sect4 element begins a level 4 section in a document. The Sect4 element may contain a Sect5 element directly.

The Sect4 element accepts the following attributes in addition to the common attributes:

- **Label.** Accepts a CDATA value, has no default value, and is not required.
- **RenderAs.** Accepts one of the following values:
  - Sect1
  - Sect2
  - Sect3
  - Sect5

  The RenderAs attribute is used by the processing system, has no default value, and is not required.

- **Status.** Accepts a CDATA value, has no default value, and is not required.

Examples:

The Sect4 element is used within a Sect3 element, as the example for Sect2 is shown as within Sect1. See Sect2 example.

Sect5

The Sect5 element begins a level 5 section in a document. Sect5 is the lowest-level section in the DocBook hierarchy—DocBook has no provisions for any lower-level sections.

The Sect1 element accepts the following attributes in addition to the common attributes:

- **Label.** Accepts a CDATA value, has no default value, and is not required.
- **RenderAs.** Accepts one of the following values:
  - Sect1
  - Sect2
  - Sect3
  - Sect4

  The Renderas attribute is used by the processing system, has no default value, and is not required.
- **Status.** Accepts a CDATA value, has no default value, and is not required.

Examples:

The Sect5 element is used within a Sect4 element, as the example for Sect2 is shown as within Sect1. See Sect2 example.

Section

The Section element is an unnamed sectioning element used in DocBook when numbered sections are undesirable. The Section element may be nested more than five levels deep, unlike the Sect1–Sect5 elements.

The Section element accepts the following attributes in addition to the common attributes:

- **Label.** Accepts a CDATA value, has default value, and is not required.
- **Status.** Accepts a CDATA value, has no default value, and is not required.

Example:

```
<section>
<para>This is a section</para>
      <section>
      <para>And this is a section within a section</para>
      </section>
</section>
```

SimPara

The SimPara element is similar to the Para element but is more restrictive about the types of elements that may be nested within.

The SimPara element uses common attributes.

Example:

```
<!DOCTYPE simpara PUBLIC "//OASIS//DTD DocBook V4.1//EN">
<simpara>This is simple, huh?</simpara>
```

SimpleSect

The SimpleSect element is a section of a DocBook document that has no subsection.

The SimpleSect element uses common attributes.

Example:

```
<!DOCTYPE sect1 PUBLIC "//OASIS//DTD DocBook V4.1//EN">
<sect1><title>Our Elements</title>
<para>There are lots and lots of DocBook elements.</para>
<simplesect><title>Structure Elements</title>
<para>FormalPara is a Structure Element.</para>
</simplesect>
</sect1>
```

ToC

The ToC element begins a table of contents in a DocBook document.

The ToC element accepts the following attribute in addition to the common attributes:

- **PageNum.** Accepts a CDATA value, has no default, and is not required.

Example:

```
<!DOCTYPE toc PUBLIC "//OASIS//DTD DocBook V4.1//EN">
<toc>
<tocfront>Introduction</tocfront>
<tocpart>
        <tocchap>
                <tocentry>Getting Started with DocBook</tocentry>
                <toclevel1>
                        <tocentry>Creating DocBook Documents</tocentry>
                        <toclevel2>
                                <tocentry>SGML or XML</tocentry>
                        </toclevel2>
                <toclevel1>
        </tocchap>
</tocpart>
<tocback>Appendix</tocback>
</toc>
```

ToCBack

The ToCBack element contains a table of contents entry for back matter in a document, such as a glossary or appendix.

The ToCBack element accepts the following attributes in addition to the common attributes:

- **Label.** Accepts a CDATA value, has no default value, and is not required.
- **Linkend.** Accepts an IDREF value, has no default value, and is not required.
- **Pagenum.** Accepts a CDATA value, has no default, and is not required.

Example:

See ToC element example.

ToCChap

The ToCChap element contains a chapter entry in a table of contents.

The ToCChap element accepts the following attribute in addition to the common attributes:

- **Label.** Accepts a CDATA value, has no default value, and is not required.

Example:

See ToC element example.

ToCentry

The ToCentry element is used for any entry in a table of contents.

The ToCentry element accepts the following attributes in addition to the common attributes:

- **Linkend.** Accepts an IDREF value, has no default value, and is not required.
- **Pagenum.** Accepts a CDATA value, has no default, and is not required.

Example:

See ToC element example.

ToCfront

The ToCfront element contains any reference in a table of contents to front matter, such as a preface or introduction.

The ToCfront element accepts the following attributes in addition to the common attributes:

- **Label.** Accepts a CDATA value, has no default value, and is not required.
- **Linkend.** Accepts an IDREF value, has no default value, and is not required.
- **Pagenum.** Accepts a CDATA value, has no default, and is not required.

Example:

See ToC element example.

ToClevel1

The ToClevel1 element contains a reference to a level 1 section in a table of contents.

The ToClevel1 element uses common attributes.

Example:

See ToC element example.

ToClevel2

The ToClevel2 element contains a reference to a level 2 section in a table of contents.

The ToClevel2 element uses common attributes.

Example:

See ToC element example.

ToClevel3

The `ToClevel3` element contains a reference to a level 3 section in a table of contents.

The `ToClevel3` uses common attributes.

Example:

ToClevel3 is used within ToClevel2, as ToClevel2 is used with ToClevel1. See ToC example.

ToClevel4

The `ToClevel4` element contains a reference to a level 4 section in a table of contents.

The `ToClevel4` element uses common attributes.

Example:

ToClevel4 is used within ToClevel3, as ToClevel2 is used with ToClevel1. See ToC example.

ToClevel5

The `ToClevel5` element contains a reference to a level 5 section in a table of contents.

The `ToClevel5` element uses common attributes.

Example:

ToClevel5 is used within ToClevel4, as ToClevel2 is used with ToClevel1. See ToC example.

ToCpart

The `ToCpart` element contains a reference to a part-level entry in a table of contents.

The `ToCpart` element uses common attributes.

Example:

See ToC example.

Attribution and Citation Elements

Ackno

The Ackno element holds an acknowledgment for an article. It takes the place of a preface or an introduction in an article.

The Ackno element uses common attributes.

Example:

```
<!DOCTYPE article PUBLIC "//OASIS//DTD DocBook V4.1//EN">
<article>
<para>...</para>
<ackno>Thank-you Zonker for giving us all these examples</ackno>
</article>
```

Acronym

The Acronym element holds an acronym, such as GNOME or KDE.

The Acronym element uses common attributes.

Example:

```
<para>I wish I worked for the <acronym>CIA</acronym>.</para>
```

Address

The Address element holds an address, usually a container for the elements that make up someone's entire postal address.

The Address element accepts the following attribute in addition to the common attributes:

- **Format.** Accepts one default value, LineSpecific, which indicates that the processing system should keep white space intact when rendering the address.

Example:

```
<para>Here's my address:
            <address>
               Steven and Kara Pritchard
             <street>42 Wishing Lane</street>
               <city>Notgunna Tellya</city>, <state>CA</state>
<postcode>12345-4242</postcode>
               <country>USA</country>
               </address>
</para>
```

Affiliation

The Affiliation element holds the organization information for an individual, a group, or an institution to which an author might be connected, for instance.

The Affiliation element uses common attributes.

Example:

```
<author>
<firstname>Tony</firstname>
<surname>Soprano</surname>
<affiliation>New Jersey Mob</affiliation>
</author>
```

ArtPageNums

The ArtPageNums element holds the page numbers of an article that is being referenced. It can also be used in an article that is being published, but knowing which page numbers it is going to be is more difficult when writing the document.

The ArtPageNums element uses common attributes.

Example:

```
<!DOCTYPE article PUBLIC "//OASIS//DTD DocBook V4.1//EN">
<article>
<artheader>
                <artpagenums>1-25</artpagenums>
                ...
</artheader>
</article>
```

Attribution

The Attribution element holds the attribution information for a quote.

The Attribution element uses common attributes.

Example:

```
<!DOCTYPE blockquote PUBLIC "//OASIS//DTD DocBook V4.1//EN">
<blockquote>
<attribution>Eric S. Raymond</attribution>
<literallayout>May the Source be With You</literallayout>
</blockquote>
```

Author

The `Author` element holds information about an author. Note that the `Author` element does not hold the information directly, but it is broken down into elements such as `FirstName`, `Surname`, and `OtherName`.

The `Author` element uses common attributes.

Example:

```
<author>
        <firsthame>Joe</firstname>
        <othername>"Zonker"</othername>
        <surname>Brockmeier</surname>
</author>
```

AuthorBlurb

The `AuthorBlurb` element contains a biography for an author or other information relating to an author.

The `AuthorBlurb` element uses common attributes.

Example:

```
<author>
        <firstname>Joe</firstname>
        <othername>"Zonker"</othername>
        <surname>Brockmeier</surname>
        <authorblurb>
                <para>Joe "Zonker" Brockmeier is a big fan of Linux and Mob
Movies. We're not quite sure how they're related...</para>
        </authorblurb>
</author>
```

AuthorGroup

The `AuthorGroup` element holds information about multiple authors.

The `AuthorGroup` element uses common attributes.

Example:

```
<!DOCTYPE authorgroup PUBLIC "//OASIS//DTD DocBook V4.1//EN">
<authorgroup>
                <author>...</author>
                <editor>...</editor>
</authorgroup>
```

AuthorInitials

Self-explanatory, the `AuthorInitials` element holds an author's initials or other brief reference to an author.

The `AuthorInitials` element uses common attributes.

Example:

```
<author>
        <firstname>Kara</firstname>
        <surname>Pritchard</surname>
        <authorinitials>KP</authorinitials>
</author>
```

BlockQuote

The `BlockQuote` element holds a longer quote or citation that is set off from the text.

The `BlockQuote` element uses common attributes.

Example:

```
<blockquote>
        <attribution>Lloyd Dobler</attribution>
        <para>I don't want to sell anything, buy anything, or process
anything as a career. I don't want to sell anything bought or processed,
or buy anything sold or processed, or process anything sold, bought, or
processed, or repair anything sold, bought, or processed. You know, as a
career, I don't want to do that.</para>
</blockquote>
```

Citation

The `Citation` element makes a reference to a book or publication in the text of the document. The `Citation` element is used with citations in the body of the document. If you want to cite a work in a bibliography, see the `BiblioEntry` element.

The `Citation` element uses common attributes.

Example:

```
<!DOCTYPE para PUBLIC "//OASIS//DTD DocBook V4.1//EN">
<para>
See <citation>DocBook Publishing</citation> for more help on DocBook.
</para>
```

CiteRefEntry

The `CiteRefEntry` element cites a reference page, as opposed to the `Citation` element, which cites a book or publication.

The `CiteRefEntry` uses common attributes.

Example:

```
<para>If you want to learn more about the <command>ls</command> you might
want to refer to the
<citerefentry><refentrytitle>ls</refentrytitle></citerefentry> man page or
GNU Info entry.</para>
```

CiteTitle

The `CiteTitle` element holds the title of a cited work and is used in conjunction with many other elements, including the `Citation` and `ULink` elements.

The `CiteTitle` element accepts the following attribute in addition to the common attributes:

- **URL.** Accepts a `CDATA` value of any valid URL.

Example:

```
<ulink url="http://www.yahoo.com/"><citetitle>Yahoo!</citetitle></ulink>
```

Collab

The `Collab` element holds information about a collaborator on a document.

The `Collab` element uses common attributes.

Example:

```
<book>
<bookinfo>
            <title>DocBook Publishing</title>
              <authorgroup>
                        <collab><collabname>Joe Brockmeier
</collabname></collab>
                        <collab><collabname>Kara Pritchard
</collabname></collab>
              </authorgroup>
</bookinfo>
...
</book>
```

CollabName

The `CollabName` element holds the name of a collaborator.

The `CollabName` element uses common attributes.

Example:

See `Collab` element example.

ConfDates

The `ConfDates` element holds the dates of a conference and is often used for holding information about a conference at which a document was presented. For instance, if a DocBook article was written for a conference held from August 1 to August 3, 2000, that information could be listed using this element. This element can also be used for discussing a conference in the text of a document.

The `ConfDates` element uses common attributes.

Example:

See `ConfGroup` example below.

ConfGroup

The `ConfGroup` element holds other elements that provide information about a conference.

The `ConfGroup` element uses common attributes.

```
<!DOCTYPE confgroup PUBLIC "//OASIS//DTD DocBook V4.1//EN">
<confgroup>
<confdates>March 29, 2001</confdates>
<conftitle>CLIQ 2001</conftitle>
<confnum>2</confnum>
<address>Denver, Colorado USA</address>
<confsponsor>Linux Weekly News</confsponsor>
</confgroup>
```

ConfNum

The `ConfNum` element holds the conference number and is useful when a conference is held regularly.

The `ConfNum` element uses common attributes.

Example:

See `ConfGroup` element example.

ConfSponsor

The ConfSponsor element holds the information about a conference sponsor.

The ConfSponsor element uses common attributes.

Example:

See ConfGroup element example.

ConfTitle

The ConfTitle element holds the title of a conference.

The ConfTitle element uses common attributes.

Example:

See ConfGroup element example.

ContractNum

The ContractNum element holds the document's contract number.

The ContractNum element uses common attributes.

Example:

See ContractSponsor element example.

ContractSponsor

The ContractSponsor element holds the name of the company or organization that has contracted for the document.

The ContractSponsor element uses common attributes.

Example:

```
<!DOCTYPE article PUBLIC "//OASIS//DTD DocBook V4.1//EN">
<article>
<artheader>
            <title>Kara's Todo Document</title>
            <contractsponsor>The Kara Group, Inc.</contractsponsor>
            <contractnum>2001-03-17a</contractnum>
            <pubsnumber>...</pubsnumber>
            <corpauthor>Some Writing Group, Inc.</corpauthor>
</artheader>
</article>
```

Contrib

The `Contrib` element holds the contribution information for a contributor to a document. The `Contrib` element lists the contributions made to the document, not the name of the contributor.

The `Contrib` element uses common attributes.

Example:

```
<editor>
        <firstname>Kara</firstname>
        <surname>Pritchard</surname>
        <contrib>Technical editing and co-author</contrib>
</editor>
```

Copyright

The `Copyright` element holds the elements that make up the copyright information for the document.

The `Copyright` element uses common attributes.

Example:

```
<copyright>
        <holder>
        <author>...</author>
        <corpname>Prima Publishing</corpname>
        </holder>
        <year>2001</year>
</copyright>
```

CorpAuthor

The `CorpAuthor` is used when a corporation, not an individual, is given credit for a document.

The `CorpAuthor` element uses common attributes.

Example:

```
<synopsis>
<corpauthor>Sun Microsystems</corpauthor>
...
</synopsis>
```

CorpName

The CorpName element holds the name of a corporation, used in meta-information only. The CorpName element is not used in inline markup to designate corporations, only in meta-informational elements, such as the *Info elements.

The CorpName element uses common attributes.

Example:

See Copyright element example.

Country

The Country element holds the name of a country as a child to the Address element.

The Country element uses common attributes.

Example:

```
<country>USA</country>
```

Date

The Date element holds date information. Note that the Date element is not used to mark up all dates that appear in a document, only those that appear in meta-information or reference elements.

The Date element uses common attributes.

Example:

```
<date>February 23, 1970</date>
```

Edition

The Edition element holds edition information about a document.

The Edition element uses common attributes.

Example:

```
<!DOCTYPE bookinfo PUBLIC "//OASIS//DTD DocBook V4.1//EN">
<bookinfo>
            <title>...</title>
            <authorgroup>...</authorgroup>
            <edition>DocBook Publishing V1.0</edition>
             <copyright>...</copyright>
</bookinfo>
```

Editor

The Editor element holds information about the editor of a DocBook document or cited work.

The Editor element uses common attributes.

Examples:

See Contrib *element sample.*

Epigraph

The Epigraph element holds an epigraph for a chapter, a section, or another DocBook element.

The Epigraph element uses common attributes.

Example:

```
<!DOCTYPE chapter PUBLIC "//OASIS//DTD DocBook V4.1//EN">
<chapter>
<title>...</title>
<epigraph>
        <attribution>Einstein</attribution>
        <para>Mathematics deals exclusively with the relations of concepts
to each other without consideration of their relation to experience.
</para>
</epigraph>
</chapter>
```

FirstName

The FirstName element holds the first name of an author, an editor, or other meta-information element. The FirstName element isn't used to designate every first name mentioned in the text of a document.

The FirstName element uses common attributes.

Example:

```
<firstname>Joe</firstname>
```

Footnote

The Footnote element creates a footnote. The Footnote element is very convenient for authors because it requires no special formatting or worries about placement of the footnote in layout. Simply use the Footnote element in-line after text you want to footnote, and the processing system will handle setting it off from the text.

The `Footnote` element accepts the following attribute in addition to the common attributes:

- **Label.** Accepts a CDATA value, has no default value, and is not required.

Example:

```
<para>If you need a foot note, simply declare the footnote in the text
where you want it to appear like this:<footnote><para>This is a footnote
and it will appear in the text when rendered.</para></footnote></para>
```

FootnoteRef

The `FootnoteRef` element is used for creating a link or reference to a footnote.

The `FootnoteRef` element accepts the following attributes in addition to the common attributes:

- **Label.** Accepts a CDATA value, has no default value, and is not required.
- **Linkend.** Accepts an IDREF value, has no default value, and is not required.

Example:

```
<!DOCTYPE informaltable PUBLIC "//OASIS//DTD DocBook V4.1//EN">
<informaltable>
<tgroup cols=3>
<tbody>
<row>
<entry>First entry<footnote id=entry1><para>This is the first
entry</para></footnote></entry>
</row>
</tbody>
</tgroup>
</informaltable>
```

ForeignPhrase

The `ForeignPhrase` element designates a foreign phrase in the text. This allows the processing system to format foreign phrases differently than the rest of the text, making them stand out.

The `ForeignPhrase` element uses common attributes.

Example:

```
<foreignphrase>E Pluribus Unum</foreignphrase>
```

Highlights

The `Highlights` element presents the highlights or summary of an element.

The `Highlights` element uses common attributes.

Example:

```
<!DOCTYPE chapter PUBLIC "//OASIS//DTD DocBook V4.1//EN">
<chapter><title>My First Chapter</title>
<highlights>
<para>
This chapter is going to talk about all the years of my life, including
<itemizedlist>
<listitem><para>Year 1</para></listitem>
<listitem><para>Year 2</para></listitem>
</itemizedlist>
</para>
</highlights>
</chapter>
```

Holder

The `Holder` element contains information about a copyright holder.

The `Holder` element uses common attributes.

Example:

```
<holder>
        <corpname>Prima</corpname>
</holder>
```

Honorific

The `Honorific` element contains a title such as *Dr.* or *Professor* or any title that should be attached to someone's name. This is used only with meta-information elements, not with in-line text. For instance, if you are using the `Author` element and writing about someone with a Ph.D., you use the `Honorific` element. However, it's not necessary to use this element when writing *Dr.* in the document itself.

The `Honorific` element uses common attributes.

Example:

```
<author>
        <firstname>Kara</firstname>
        <surname>Pritchard</surname>
        <honorific>Mrs.</honorific>
```

IssueNum

The IssueNum element refers to the issue number of a cited work or the document itself, depending on the context in which it is used.

The IssueNum element uses common attributes.

Example:

```
<!DOCTYPE article PUBLIC "//OASIS//DTD DocBook V4.1//EN">
<article>
<artheader>
            <author>...</author>
            <volumenum>1</volumenum>
            <issuenum>1</issuenum>
            <pubdate>2001</pubdate>
            <title>...</title>
</artheader>
<para>...</para>
</article>
```

LegalNotice

The LegalNotice element contains a legal notice of some type.

The LegalNotice element uses common attributes.

Example:

```
<legalnotice>
<para>Don't reproduce this in any medium or you'll be gnawed to death by
angry lawyers.</para>
</legalnotice>
```

Lineage

The Lineage element name is misleading. It designates titles such as *Sr.* or *Jr.*

The Lineage element uses common attributes.

Example:

```
<author>
            <firstname>Theodore</firstname>
            <surname>Graddy</surname>
            <lineage>Jr.</lineage>
             <othername>Dad</othername>
</author>
```

OrgDiv

The OrgDiv element holds the division name of a company or organization. It is used only in conjunction with the Affiliation element.

The OrgDiv element uses common attributes.

Example:

```
<affiliation>
                <jobtitle>Director or Exam Development</jobtitle>
                <orgname>Linux Professional Institute</orgname>
                <orgdiv>Exam Development</orgdiv>
</affiliation>
```

OrgName

The OrgName element contains the name of an organization.

The OrgName element uses common attributes.

Example:

```
<orgname>Red Cross</orgname>
```

OtherAddr

The OtherAddr element holds address information for which there are no other appropriate elements.

The OtherAddr element uses common attributes.

Example:

```
<address>
Kara Pritchard
<street>42 Yourstreet</street>
<otheraddr>Unit C</otheraddr>
<city>...</city>, <state>...</state> <postcode>...</postcode>
</address>
```

OtherCredit

The OtherCredit element holds information about other contributors to a document.

The OtherCredit element uses common attributes.

Example:

```
<!DOCTYPE artheader PUBLIC "//OASIS//DTD DocBook V4.1//EN">
<artheader>
```

```
                <title>DocBook Publishing</title>
                <author>
                        <firstname>Joe</firstname>
                        <surname>Brockmeier</surname>
                </author>
                <othercredit>
                        <firstname>Kara</firstname>
                        <surname>Pritchard</surname>
                        <contrib>Tech Editor turned Co-author</contrib>
                </othercredit>
</artheader>
```

OtherName

The OtherName element is a handy catchall for use when listing author names for people who have nicknames or middle names that should be included. Note that if it is a nickname and you want to have the nickname appear in quotes, you must write it as such.

The OtherName element uses common attributes.

Example:

```
<author>
                <firstname>Kara</firstname>
                <surname>Pritchard</surname>
                <othername>Ol' Lady</othername>
</author>
```

PageNums

The PageNums element contains page number information for a cited work.

The PageNums element uses common attributes.

Example:

```
<pagenums>55-102</pagenums>
```

Phone

The Phone element holds, surprisingly, a phone number.

The Phone element uses common attributes.

Example:

```
<phone>555-555-FAKE</phone>
```

POB

The POB element holds post office box information.

The POB element uses common attributes.

Example:

```
<address>
Kara Pritchard
<pob>PO Box 42</pob>
<city>...</city>, <state>CA</state> <postcode>...</postcode>
</address>
```

PostCode

The PostCode element holds a Zip code or other postal code information, depending on the country. It is used with the Address element.

The PostCode element uses common attributes.

Example:

```
<postcode>80015</postcode>
```

PubDate

The PubDate element holds information about the publication date of a document or cited work.

The PubDate element uses common attributes.

Example:

See IssueNum example.

Publisher

The Publisher element holds information about a publisher of a cited work or the current DocBook document.

The Publisher element uses common attributes.

Example:

```
<publisher>
          <publishername>Prima Publishing</publishername>
          <address>...</address>
</publisher>
```

PublisherName

The `PublisherName` element holds the name of the publisher.

The `PublisherName` element uses common attributes.

Example:

See `Publisher` element example.

Quote

The `Quote` element holds a quotation used in-line. The `Quote` element is used for shorter quotations that appear in the text, not longer quotations that are broken out from the text, such as a `BlockQuote`.

The `Quote` element uses common attributes.

Example:

```
<quote>Clothes make the man. Naked people have little or no influence in
society.</quote>
```

SeriesInfo

The `SeriesInfo` element holds information about the series containing a book.

The `SeriesInfo` element uses common attributes.

Example:

```
<seriesinfo>
            <title>DocBook Publishing</title>
            <seriesvolnums>1</seriesvolnums>
            <editor>
            <firstname>Melody</firstname>
            <surname>Layne</surname>
            </editor>
            <publisher>...</publisher>
</seriesinfo>
```

SeriesVolNums

The `SeriesVolNums` element holds information about volume numbers for a series.

The `SeriesVolNums` element uses common attributes.

Example:

See `SeriesInfo` element example.

ShortAffil

The `ShortAffil` element is used for abbreviated affiliation information about an author or contributor in meta-information.

The `ShortAffil` element uses common attributes.

Example:

```
<affiliation>
            <shortaffil>LPI</shortaffil>
            <jobtitle>Director of Exam Development</jobtitle>
            <orgname>Linux Professional Institute</orgname>
</affiliation>
```

State

The `State` element holds the state name in an address. The `State` element can also be used to hold the name of a province.

The `State` element uses common attributes.

Example:

See `Address` *element example.*

Street

The `Street` element holds street information in an address.

The `Street` element uses common attributes.

Example:

See the `Address` *element example.*

Trademark

The `Trademark` element holds trademark information cited in the text of a document itself.

The `Trademark` element accepts the following attribute in addition to the common attributes:

- **Class.** Accepts one of the following values:
  - Copyright
  - Registered
  - Service
  - Trade

Example:

```
<para>When writing, I really love to drink <trademark
class="registered">Coke</trademark> and eat gummi bears.</para>
```

Year

The Year element holds a year.

The Year element uses common attributes.

Example:

```
<year>2001</year>
```

Web/Linking Elements

Alt

The Alt element provides alternative text for a graphic element.

The Alt element uses common attributes.

Example:

```
<alt>You'd see an image here if your browser displayed them</alt>
```

Email

The Email element holds an e-mail address.

The Email element uses common attributes.

Example:

```
<email>kara@luci.org</email>
```

Graphic

The Graphic element calls a graphical element that is displayed outside the text flow. Note that the Graphic element is essentially an empty element.

The Graphic element accepts the following attributes:

- Align
- Depth
- EntityRef
- FileRef
- Format
- Scale
- SrcCredit
- ScaleFit

Example:

```
<graphic fileref="image.tiff"></graphic>
```

Link

The Link element holds information for a link that will be created by the processing system. For URLs, use ULink.

The Link element accepts the following attributes:

- **Endterm.** Accepts a CDATA value with no default and is not required. The Endterm value, if given, is the element displayed as the link.
- **Linkend.** Accepts an IDREF value, has no default value, but is required.
- **Type.** Accepts an IDREF value, has no default value, and is not required.

Example:

```
<sect1>
<para>This <link linkend=sent2>link</link> is linked to the title "Here"
in the next section.</para>
<sect2 id=sent2><title id=sent2.title>Here</title.
<para>...</para>
</sect2>
</sect1>
```

OLink

The OLink element holds information that accesses a link through a third-party element.

The OLink element accepts the following attributes in addition to the common attributes:

- **LinkMode.** Accepts an IDREF value, has no default, and is not required.
- **LocalInfo.** Accepts a CDATA value, has no default, and is not required.
- **TargetDocEnt.** Gives the name of an ENTITY and has no default value.
- **Type.** Accepts an IDREF value, has no default value, and is not required.

Example: Due to the unusual nature of the OLink element and its possible exclusion in future versions of DocBook, we cannot provide an example.

ULink

The ULink element holds information for a URL.

The ULink element accepts the following attributes in addition to the common attributes:

- **Type.** Accepts a CDATA value, has no default, and is not required.
- **URL.** Accepts a CDATA value, has no default, but is required.

Use this syntax if you want the URL to reproduce in plain text or similar formats:

```
<ulink url="http://www.slashdot.org/>http://www.slashdot.org</ulink>
```

XRef

The XRef element holds a reference to another portion of a document.

The XRef element accepts the following attributes:

- **Endterm.** Accepts a CDATA value with no default and is not required. The Endterm value, if given, is the element displayed as the link.
- **Linkend.** Accepts an IDREF value, has no default value, but is required.

Example:

```
<sect1>
<para>Review the following sections</para>
<itemized list>
<listitem><para>Section 1<xref linkend="sec1"></para></listitem>
<listitem><para>Section 2<xref linkend="sec2"></para></listitem>
</itemized list>
<sect2 id="sec1">
            <title>Section 1</title>
            <para>This is text for Section 1</para>
</sect2>
<sect2 id="sec2">
            <title>Section 2</title>
            <para> This is text for Section 2</para>
</sect2>
</sect1>
```

Media Elements

DocBook deals with a number of media formats, as well as plain text. If your document is going to make use of sound or video, you will want to check these out.

AudioObject

The AudioObject element holds information and meta-information about audio referenced in a DocBook document.

The AudioObject element uses common attributes.

Example:

```
<!DOCTYPE mediaobject PUBLIC "//OASIS//DTD DocBook V4.1//EN">
<mediaobject>
<audioobject>
            <objectinfo>Pronouncing Linux</objectinfo>
            <audiodata fileref="english.au">
</audioobject>
</mediaobject>
```

Caption

The Caption element provides a caption for a figure or other graphical element in DocBook.

The Caption element uses common attributes.

Example:

```
<caption>This is a caption. Groovy, huh?</caption>
```

Figure

The Figure element is used for a figure displayed with a title.

The Figure element accepts the following attributes in addition to the common attributes:

- **Float.** Accepts a NUMBER value with a default of 0 and is not required.
- **Label.** Accepts a CDATA value, has no default, and is not required.
- **PgWide.** Accepts a NUMBER value, has no default, and is not required.

Example:

```
<figure>
<title>Jade's Error Message for Invalid Attribute</title>
<screenshot>
<graphic fileref="ch10/10-01"></graphic>
</screenshot>
</figure>
```

GraphicCO

The GraphicCO element references a graphic that has callout areas. GraphicCO is going to be phased out and replaced by MediaObjectCO in version 5.0 of DocBook.

The GraphicCO element accepts common attributes.

See the MediaObjectCO example for usage.

ImageData

The `ImageData` element holds information about an image, such as the filename or type of image.

The `ImageData` element accepts the following attributes:

- Align
- Depth
- EntityRef
- FileRef
- Format
- Scale
- SrcCredit
- ScaleFit

Example:

```
<!DOCTYPE mediaobject PUBLIC "//OASIS//DTD DocBook V4.1//EN">
<mediaobject>
<imageobject>
<imagedata fileref="images/tux.gif" format "gif">
</imageobject>
</mediaobject>
```

ImageObject

The `ImageObject` element holds information about an image, including meta-information.

The `ImageObject` element uses common attributes.

Example:

See `ImageData` element example.

ImageObjectCO

The `ImageObjectCO` element holds image information for an image with callouts. The `ImageObjectCO` element is depricated and is to be replaced in DocBook 5.0 by the `MediaObjectCO` element.

The `ImageObjectCO` element uses common attributes.

See the `MediaObjectCO` example for usage.

InlineMediaObject

The `InlineMediaObject` element holds information about any in-line media—images, audio, or video.

The `InlineMediaObject` element uses common attributes.

Example:

```
<para>Tux is the cute little penguin
<inlinemediaobject>
<imageobject>
<imagedata fileref="tux.gif">
</imageobject>
</inlinemediaobject>
that we have all grown to love.</para>
```

MediaObject

The `MediaObject` element holds information about any type of media object—audio, graphics, or video.

The `MediaObject` element uses common attributes.

Example:

See the `ImageData` *element example.*

MediaObjectCO

The `MediaObjectCO` element holds information about any type of media object that also has callouts.

The `MediaObjectCO` element uses common attributes.

Example:

```
<mediaobjectco>
<imageobjectco>
<areaspec units="calspair">
        <areaset id="example" coords="">
        <area id="example-a" coords="1 10">
        <area id="example-b" coords="2 20">
</areaspec>
</imageobject>
</mediaobjecco>
```

ObjectInfo

The `ObjectInfo` element contains any meta-information about an object in DocBook.

The `ObjectInfo` element uses common attributes.

Example:

See `AudioObject` *element example.*

VideoData

The `VideoData` element refers to a video file or source.

The `VideoData` element accepts the following attributes:

- Align
- Depth
- EntityRef
- FileRef
- Format
- Scale
- SrcCredit
- ScaleFit

Example:

```
<videodata format="mpeg" fileref="video.mpg"></videodata>
```

VideoObject

The `VideoObject` element holds information and meta-information about any video object used in DocBook.

The `VideoObject` element uses common attributes.

Example:

```
<!DOCTYPE mediaobject PUBLIC "//OASIS//DTD DocBook V4.1//EN">
<mediaobject>
<videoobject>
<videodata fileref="sample.avi">
</videoobject>
<para>...</para>
</mediaobject>
```

Meta-Information Elements

DocBook allows for a great deal of meta-information to be included with a document. Some of these elements are also relevant to other categories. The usage for all of the `*Info` elements is similar.

AppendixInfo

The `AppendixInfo` element contains meta-information about an appendix.

The `AppendixInfo` element uses common attributes.

See the `BookInfo` element for an example.

BibliographyInfo

The `BibliographyInfo` element contains meta-information about a bibliography.

The `BibliographyInfo` element uses common attributes.

See the `BookInfo` *element for an example.*

BookInfo

The `BookInfo` element contains the meta-information about a DocBook book.

The `BookInfo` element uses common attributes.

Example:

```
<!DOCTYPE book PUBLIC "-//OASIS//DTD DocBook V4.1//EN">
<bookinfo>
<title>A Nifty Book</title>
<author>
        <firstname>Joe</firstname>
        <surname>Brockmeier</surname>
</author>
<publisher>
        <publishername>Prima Tech</publishername>
</publisher>
<pubdate>2001</pubdate>
</bookinfo>
...
</book>
```

ChapterInfo

The `ChapterInfo` element contains meta-information about a chapter.

The `ChapterInfo` element uses common attributes.

See the `BookInfo` *element for an example.*

GlossaryInfo

The `GlossaryInfo` element contains meta-information about a glossary.

The `GlossaryInfo` element uses common attributes.

See the `BookInfo` *element for an example.*

IndexInfo

The `IndexInfo` element contains meta-information about an index.

The `IndexInfo` element uses common attributes.

See the `BookInfo` *element for an example.*

PartInfo

The PartInfo element contains meta-information about a part.

The PartInfo element uses common attributes.

See the BookInfo element for an example.

PrefaceInfo

The PrefaceInfo element contains meta-information about a preface.

The PrefaceInfo element uses common attributes.

See the BookInfo element for an example.

RefentryInfo

The RefentryInfo element contains meta-information about a reference entry.

The RefentryInfo element uses common attributes.

See the BookInfo element for an example.

ReferenceInfo

The ReferenceInfo element contains meta-information about a reference.

The ReferenceInfo element uses common attributes.

See the BookInfo element for an example.

Sect1Info

The Sect1Info element contains meta-information about a Sect1 in a DocBook document.

The Sect1Info element uses common attributes.

Example:

```
<!DOCTYPE sect1 PUBLIC "//OASIS//DTD DocBook V4.1//EN">
<sect1>
        <sect1info>
                <title>My First Section</title>
                <subtitle>...</subtitle>
        </sect1info>
</sect1>
```

Sect2Info

The Sect2Info element contains meta-information about a Sect2 in a DocBook document.

The Sect2Info element uses common attributes.

Example:

Sect2Info is used within a Sect2 element, similar to the use of Sect1Info within the Sect1 element. See Sect1Info element example.

Sect3Info

The Sect3Info element contains meta-information about a Sect3 in a DocBook document.

The Sect3Info element uses common attributes.

Example:

Sect3Info is used within a Sect3 element, similar to the use of Sect1Info within the Sect1 element. See Sect1Info element example.

Sect4Info

The Sect4Info element contains meta-information about a Sect4 in a DocBook document.

The Sect4Info element uses common attributes.

Example:

Sect4Info is used within a Sect4 element, similar to the use of Sect1Info within the Sect1 element. See Sect1Info element example.

Sect5Info

The Sect5Info element contains meta-information about a Sect5 in a DocBook document.

The Sect5Info element uses common attributes.

Example:

Sect5Info is used within a Sect5 element, similar to the use of Sect1Info within the Sect1 element. See Sect1Info element example.

SectionInfo

The SectionInfo element contains meta-information about a particular section.

The SectionInfo element uses common attributes.

Example:

```
<section>
<sectioninfo>
<abstract><para>...</para></abstract>
</sectioninfo>
</section>
```

SetIndexInfo

The `SetIndexInfo` element contains meta-information about a `SetIndex`.

The `SetIndexInfo` element uses common attributes.

See the `BookInfo` element for an example.

SidebarInfo

The `SidebarInfo` element contains information about a `SideBar` element.

The `SidebarInfo` element uses common attributes.

See the `BookInfo` element for an example.

Program and Operating System Elements

This section contains elements that are used when writing about computers, programming, and user interfaces—any elements used to document computer use. As you might expect, this section contains a rich selection of elements because of DocBook's heritage as a markup language for technical writing.

Accel

The `Accel` element indicates a hot key.

The `Accel` element uses common attributes.

Example:

```
<guimenu><accel>F</accel>ile</guimenu>
```

Action

The `Action` element indicates some type of output in response to a user's input.

The `Action` element uses common attributes.

Example:

```
<para>Pressing Cntrl + Alt + Del on a Linux system will
<action>reboot</action> the system.</para>
```

Application

The Application element indicates the name of an application in a document.

The Application element uses common attributes.

Example:

```
<para><application>Jade</application>is a popular application for using
DocBook.</para>
```

Arg

The Arg element is used to mark up an argument to a command.

The Arg element accepts the following attributes in addition to the common attributes:

- Choice
- Rep

Example:

```
<command>ls</command>
                <arg>-l</arg>
                <arg>-a</arg>
```

ClassSynopsis

The ClassSynopsis element indicates information about a class in a programming language.

The ClassSynopsis element accepts the following attributes in addition to the common attributes:

- CmdLength
- Label
- SepChar

Example:

```
<classsynopsis language="perl">
                <classname>...</classname>

                <classsynopsisinfo>...</classsynopsisinfo>
</classsynopsis>
```

CmdSynopsis

The CmdSynopsis element provides information about the use of a command, including the command's arguments and syntax.

The CmdSynopsis element accepts the following attributes in addition to the common attributes:

- CmdLength
- Label
- SepChar

Example:

```
<cmdsynopsis>
        <command>ls</command>
        <arg>-l</arg>
        <arg>-a</arg>
</cmdsynopsis>
```

Command

The Command element indicates a command when referred to in-line.

The Command element accepts the following attribute in addition to the common attributes:

- MoreInfo

Example:

```
<cmdsynopsis>
<command>mysqladmin create <database>MYDATABASE</database></command>
    <sbr>
<command>cd <filename class="directory">/path/to/database</filename>
</command>
</cmdsynopsis>
```

ComputerOutput

The ComputerOutput element indicates some type of computer output, usually output from a command.

The Command element accepts the following attribute in addition to the common attributes:

- MoreInfo

Example:

```
<para>
<computeroutput>Command failed: Abort, Retry, Fail?</computeroutput>
</para>
```

ConstructorSynopsis

The `ConstructorSynopsis` element indicates information about a constructor used in a programming language.

The `ConstructorSynopsis` element uses common attributes.

Example:

```
<constructorsynopsis>
      <methodname>...</methodname>
      <methodparam choice="req"><parameter>...</parameter></methodparam>
</constructorsynopsis>
```

Database

The `Database` element indicates the name of a database when referred to in in-line text. Note that it is not used to refer to the name of a database application, such as *MySQL* or *Oracle*, but to the name of a database with which the reader may interact.

The `Database` element accepts the following attributes in addition to the common attributes:

- Class
- MoreInfo

Example:

```
<command>mysqladmin create <database>MYDATABASE</database></command>
```

DestructorSynopsis

The `DestructorSynopsis` element is used with information about a destructor used in a programming language.

The `DestructorSynopsis` uses common attributes.

Example:

```
<destructorsynopsis>
      <methodname>...</methodname>
      <void>
</destructorsynopsis>
```

EnVar

The `EnVar` element indicates an environmental variable.

The `EnVar` element uses common attributes.

Example:

```
<para>To check your <envar>CVSROOT</envar> environment variable,
<command>echo $CVSROOT</command></para>
```

ErrorCode

The `ErrorCode` element indicates a returned error code from a command or program.

The `ErrorCode` element uses common attributes.

Example:

```
<para><errorcode>EIO</errorcode> is returned when a <errorname>I/O
Error</errorname> has occurred. <errorcode>EIO</errorcode> is a
<errortype>FATAL</errortype> error.</para>
```

ErrorName

The `ErrorName` element refers to the actual name of an error returned by a command or program.

The `ErrorName` element uses common attributes.

Example:

See `ErrorCode` element example.

ErrorType

The `ErrorType` element refers to the kind of error being referred to and is used in conjunction with the `ErrorCode` element.

The `ErrorType` element uses common attributes.

Example:

See `ErrorCode` element example.

ExceptionName

The `ExceptionName` element indicates an exception in a programming language.

The `ExceptionName` element uses common attributes.

Example:

```
<para>When writing the program, the toughest part was dealing with the
<exceptionname>ERR_OUT_OF_MEMORY</exceptionname> exception.</para>
```

FieldSynopsis

The `FieldSynopsis` element is used when providing summary information about a field.

The `FieldSynopsis` element uses common attributes.

Example:

```
<fieldsynopsis>
        <modifier>...</modifier>
        <type>...</type>
        <varname>...</varname>
</fieldsynopsis>
```

Filename

The `Filename` element indicates the name of a file referenced inline.

The `Filename` element accepts the following attribute in addition to the common attributes:

- Class

Example:

```
<filename class="directory">/etc/apt/</filename>
```

FuncDef

The `FuncDef` element holds the name of a function in a programming language.

The `FuncDef` element uses common attributes.

Example:

```
<para>Many programming languages use different syntax to define a
function. In pseudocode, defining a function might look like this:</para>
<funcsynopsis>
<funcprototype>
<funcdef>function</funcdef> <function>apply</function></funcdef>
<paramdef>foo <parameter>par1</parameter></paramdef>
<paramdef>bar <parameter>par2</parameter></paramdef>
</funcprototype>
</funcsynopsis>
```

FuncPrototype

The `FuncPrototype` element indicates a prototype of a function.

The `FuncPrototype` element uses common attributes.

See the FuncDef *element for an example.*

FuncSynopsis

The FuncSynopsis element is used when describing the syntax of a function.

The FuncSynopsis element uses common attributes.

See the FuncDef *element for an example.*

FuncSynopsisInfo

The FuncSynopsisInfo element includes information about a FuncSynopsis. The FuncSynopsisInfo element is not a meta-information element.

The FuncSynopsisInfo element uses common attributes.

See the FuncDef *element for an example.*

Function

The Function element holds the name of a function in a programming language.

The Function element uses common attributes.

Example:

```
<para>When working with XML you might want to use the
<function>foo_xml</function> function.</para>
```

GUIButton

The GUIButton element indicates the text of a button.

The GUIButton element uses common attributes.

Example:

```
<para>Press the <guibutton>OK</guibutton> to continue or the
<guibutton>Cancel</guibutton> to bail.</para>
```

GUIIcon

The GUIIcon element indicates an icon referenced in the text of a document. GUIIcon can be used with other elements to display a graphic of the icon.

The GUIIcon element accepts the following attribute in addition to the common attributes:

- **MoreInfo.** Accepts a value of either None or RefEntry, has the default value None, and is not required.

Example:

```
<para>
For more information, click the <guiicon><inlinegraphic
fileref="icons/fmi.gif"></inlinegraphic></guiicon> icon below.
</para>
```

GUILabel

The GUILabel element contains text or a label used in a GUI.

The GUILabel element accepts the following attribute in addition to the common attributes:

- **MoreInfo.** Accepts a value of either None or RefEntry, has the default value None, and is not required.

Example:

```
<para>
The <guilabel>Help</guilabel> screen displays an <guimenu>About</guimenu>
menu  containing options such as <guimenuitem>Author</guimenuitem>,
<guimenuitem>Application</guimenuitem>, and <guimenuitem>Quit
</guimenuitem>.
</para>
```

GUIMenu

The GUIMenu element holds the name of an entire GUI menu. Note that GUIMenu is not used to indicate a single menu choice but the top-level menu name, such as File, Edit, or Help.

The GUIMenu element accepts the following attribute in addition to the common attributes:

- **MoreInfo.** Accepts a value of either None or RefEntry, has the default value None, and is not required.

Example:

See GUILabel element example.

GUIMenuItem

The GUIMenuItem element holds the name of a selection in a GUI menu.

The GUIMenuItem element accepts the following attribute in addition to the common attributes:

- **MoreInfo.** Accepts a value of either None or RefEntry, has the default value None, and is not required.

Example:

See GUILabel element example.

GUISubmenu

The GUISubMenu contains the name of a submenu in a GUI menu.

The GUISubMenu element accepts the following attribute in addition to the common attributes:

- **MoreInfo.** Accepts a value of either None or RefEntry, has the default value None, and is not required.

Example:

```
<para>
In <application>StarOffice</application> you can open a new document by
selecting the <guimenuitem>Text Document</guimenuitem> option under the
<guisubmenu>New</quisubmenu> submenu under the <guimenu>File</guimenu>
menu.
</para>
```

Hardware

The Hardware element indicates a reference to computer hardware in in-line text.

The Hardware element accepts the following attribute in addition to the common attributes:

- **MoreInfo.** Accepts a value of either None or RefEntry, has the default value None, and is not required.

Example:

```
<para>Insert the <hardware>video card</hardware> into the <hardware>
motherboard</hardware>.</para>
```

Initializer

The Initializer element is used with the ClassSynopsis element.

The Initializer element uses common attributes.

Example:

```
<fieldsynopsis>
<modifier>public</modifier>
<initializer>Initializer</initializer>
</fieldsynopsis>
```

InterfaceName

The `InterfaceName` element indicates the name of a programming language interface element.

The `InterfaceName` element uses common attributes.

Example:

```
<para>In Perl <interfacename>GnuPG::Interface</interfacename> allows you
to work with GnuPG.</para>
```

KeyCap

The `KeyCap` element indicates the text of a key on the keyboard, such as Ctrl or F1.

The `KeyCap` element uses common attributes.

Example:

```
<para>Pressing the <keycap>Enter</keycap> key will insert a line break or
carriage return in your document.</para>
```

KeyCode

The `KeyCode` element indicates the code sent to the OS when a key is pressed.

The `KeyCode` element uses common attributes.

Example:

```
<para>Pressing the <keycap>[</keycap> key may generate
<keycode>42foo</keycode> and have the symbolic name
<keysym>LBRACKETT</keysym>.</para>
```

KeyCombo

The `KeyCombo` element indicates a combination of keys and mouse input used to execute a command or perform an action.

The `KeyCombo` element uses common attributes.

Example:

```
<para>To reboot your Linux machine, press
<keycombo>
        <keycap>Control</keycap>
        <keycap>Alt</keycap>
        <keycap>Delete</keycap>
</keycombo>
```

```
</para>
```

KeySym

The `KeySym` element indicates the true name of a key on the keyboard.

The `KeySym` element uses common attributes.

Example:

See `KeyCode` element example.

Markup

The `Markup` element indicates text that is to be displayed as-is in-line as markup of one form or another. This is not necessarily DocBook markup. It can be HTML, XML, XSL, or any other markup language.

The `Markup` element uses common attributes.

Example:

```
<para>
To force spaces in a line of your <acronym>HTML</acronym> document, use
<marckup role="html"> </markup> as multiple spaces between words are
otherwise ignored.
</para>
```

MediaLabel

The `MediaLabel` element indicates the medium on which a media object is stored.

The `MediaLabel` element uses common attributes.

Example:

```
<para>To install Linux on your system, place the Red Hat
<mediallabel>Disk 1</mediallabel> into your CD-ROM.</para>
```

MenuChoice

The `MenuChoice` element indicates a choice or choices on a GUI menu that the user should follow.

The `MenuChoice` element accepts the following attribute in addition to the common attributes:

- **MoreInfo.** Accepts a value of either None or RefEntry, has the default value None, and is not required.

Example:

```
<para>
You can exit from <application>StarOffice</application> by selecting
<menuchoice>
        <guimenu>File</guimenu>
        <guimenuitem>Exit</guimenuitem>
</menuchoice>
<para>
```

MethodName

The `MethodName` element indicates the name of a method in a programming language.

The `MethodName` element uses common attributes.

Example:

```
<para>In the Perl Digest::MD5 module, the <methodname>reset</methodname>
method is an alias for <methodname>new</methodname>.
```

MethodParam

The `MethodParam` element indicates parameters for a method.

The `MethodParam` element uses common attributes.

MethodSynopsis

The `MethodSynopsis` element is used when describing the use of a method.

The `MethodSynopsis` element uses common attributes.

MouseButton

The `MouseButton` element indicates the name of a mouse button—usually left, right, and middle for UNIX folks. For Mac folks, there shouldn't be much confusion about which button is being discussed.

The `MouseButton` element accepts the following attribute in addition to the common attributes:

- **MoreInfo.** Accepts a value of either None or RefEntry, has the default value None, and is not required.

Example:

```
<para>Press the <mousebutton>Left</mousebutton> button to get a context
menu.</para>
```

MsgAud

The `MsgAud` element indicates the audience for a message.

The `MsgAud` element uses common attributes.

Example:

See `MsgSet` *element example.*

MsgEntry

The `MsgEntry` element is a sub-element of a `MsgSet` that contains a `Msg`, a `MsgText`, and other child elements.

The `MsgEntry` element uses common attributes.

Example:

See `MsgSet` *element example.*

MsgExplan

The `MsgExlplan` element is short for *message explain*, which explains what a computer message means. Usually, the messages themselves are cryptic and not much use to the uninitiated.

The `MsgExplan` element uses common attributes.

Example:

See `MsgSet` *element example.*

MsgInfo

The `MsgInfo` element contains information about a message. The `MsgInfo` element is not a meta-information element.

The `MsgInfo` element uses common attributes.

Example:

See `MsgSet` *element example.*

MsgLevel

The `MsgLevel` element indicates the severity of the message because messages are typically errors of some type.

The `MsgLevel` element uses common attributes.

Example:

See `MsgSet` *element example.*

MsgMain

The `MsgMain` element contains the `MsgText` element that indicates the actual text of the message being described.

The `MsgMain` element uses common attributes.

Example:

See `MsgSet` element example.

MsgOrig

The `MsgOrig` element indicates the origin of a message and where or how it is produced.

The `MsgOrig` element uses common attributes.

Example:

See `MsgSet` element example.

MsgRel

The `MsgRel` element contains messages that are related to, and possibly occur with, the main message being issued (`MsgMain`).

The `MsgRel` element uses common attributes.

Example:

See `MsgSet` element example.

MsgSet

The `MsgSet` element contains all the markup used to indicate a message in Doc-Book.

The `MsgSet` element uses common attributes.

Example:

```
<!DOCTYPE msgset PUBLIC "//OASIS//DTD DocBook V4.1//EN">
<msgset>
        <msgentry>
            <MSGINFO>
                    <MSGAUD>System Users</MSGAUD>
                    <MSGORIG>Red Hat Linux 7.1</MSGORIG>
                    <MSGLEVEL>Warning</MSGLEVEL>
            </MSGINFO>
            <msg>
```

```
            <msgmain>
                    <msgtext><para>Warning</para></msgtext>
            </msgmain>
            <msgsub>
                    <msgtext><para>Protected</para></msgtext>
            </msgsub>
            <msgrel>
                    <msgtext>Group Protected</msgtext>
            <msgrel>
     </msg>
            <msgexplan><para>Indicates you've entered a bad
            password</para></msgexplan>
     </msgentry>
</msgset>
```

MsgSub

The MsgSub element contains parts of a message.

The MsgSub element uses common attributes.

Example:

See MsgSet element example.

MsgText

The MsgText element contains the actual text of a message.

The MsgText element uses common attributes.

Example:

See MsgSet element example.

Option

The Option element indicates an option to a command.

The Option element uses common attributes.

Example:

```
<para>
<command>ls <option>-l</option></command>
</para>
```

Parameter

The Parameter element indicates a value passed to a command or function or as an option.

The Parameter element uses these attributes in addition to common attributes:

- **Class.** Type of parameter.
- **MoreInfo.** Accepts a value of either None or RefEntry, has the default value None, and is not required.

Example:

```
<para>Use the <parameter>-l</parameter> parameter with the
<command>ls</command> command to retrieve a listing of directory files
with full details in Unix.</para>
```

Procedure

The Procedure element holds a list of steps to be performed.

The Procedure element uses common attributes.

Example:

```
<procedure><title>Making Scrambled Eggs</title>
<step><para>Break two eggs in a bowl</para></step>
<step><para>Whip eggs with a whisk or fork</para></step>
        <substeps><para>Whip in small amount of milk</para></substeps>
<step><para>Add beaten eggs to a hot skillet with oil</para></step>
<step><para>Using spatula, stir eggs until desired
consistancy</para></step>
</procedure>
```

ProgramListing

The ProgramListing element contains a listing from a program. It contains part or all of a program verbatim and indicates that the contents of the element should be reproduced as-is.

The ProgramListing element uses common attributes.

Example:

```
<programlisting>
<![CDATA[
<?php echo "The Current Date and Time is: <br>";
        echo date("g:i A l, F j Y.");?>
]]>
</programlisting>
```

Prompt

The Prompt element indicates the character or characters that make up a command-line prompt.

The Prompt element accepts the following attribute in addition to the common attributes:

- **MoreInfo.** Accepts one of two CDATA values:
  - None
  - RefEntry

Example:

```
<para>You can select what kernel, usermode, or operating system to run
when your Linux system boots to the <prompt>LILO:</prompt> prompt.</para>
```

Property

The Property element indicates a system property, such as the color of the background, the width of a scrollbar, or any other property of the system.

The Property element uses common attributes.

Example:

```
<para>The default <property>background</property> of my xterm is
black.</para>
```

Replaceable

The Replaceable element indicates that text inside the markup is replaceable. This element is good for describing the syntax of a command or any other operation where there are variable elements the user can replace.

The Replaceable element uses common attributes.

Example:

```
<para>To change your password, enter <command>passwd</command>
<replaceable>username</replaceable> at the command prompt.</para>
```

ReturnValue

The ReturnValue element indicates a value returned by a user action, function, or command.

The ReturnValue element uses common attributes.

Example:

```
<para>To see what version of <application>RPM</application> you have
installed, run <command>rpm</command> <option>—version</option> and you'll
get output like <returnvalue>RPM version 3.0.5</returnvalue>.</para>
```

SBR

The SBR element indicates a line break in a CmdSynopsis or an Arg.

The SBR element accepts the following attributes in addition to the common attributes.

Example:

```
<cmdsynopsis>
<command>foo</command>
<arg>—bar</arg>
<sbr>
<arg>—none</arg>
</cmdsynopsis>
```

Screen

The Screen element indicates output to a computer screen.

The Screen element uses these attributes in addition to the common attributes.

- Format
- Width

Example:

```
<screen>
[kara@varstation kara]$ df
Filesystem              1k-blocks       Used Available   Use% Mounted on
/dev/sda2               4054571      3387789    456974    88% /
/dev/hdc                  33154        33154         0   100% /mnt/cdrom
</screen>
```

ScreenInfo

The ScreenInfo element provides information about a screenshot. The ScreenInfo element is not a meta-information element.

The ScreenInfo element uses common attributes.

Example:

See ScreenShot *element example.*

ScreenShot

The ScreenShot element indicates a computer screenshot.

The ScreenShot element uses common attributes.

Example:

```
<screenshot>
<screeninfo>640x480</screeninfo>
<graphic fileref="screen.jpg"></graphic>
</screenshot>
```

SGMLTag

The SGMLTag element indicates SGML markup or an SGML attribute. This comes in quite handy when writing about DocBook, XML, SGML, or HTML.

The SGMLTag element accepts the Class attribute in addition to the other common attributes.

Example:

```
<para>This is how you would mark an <sgmltag
class="element">element</sgmltag> using the <sgmltag
class="element">SGMLTag</sgmltag>element.</para>
```

Step

The Step element indicates a step in a procedure.

The Step element uses common attributes.

Example:

See the Procedure *element example.*

Symbol

The Symbol element indicates a name that will be replaced with a value.

The Symbol element accepts the Class attribute in addition to the common attributes.

Example:

```
<para>The <symbol>$</symbol> symbol is used to represent a dollar
amount.</para>
```

SynopFragment

The SynopFragment element indicates a fragment of a CmdSynopsis.

The SynopFragment element uses common attributes.

Example:

```
<cmdsynopsis>
<command>foo</command>
<arg>–bar</arg>
<group choice=""opt">
<arg>–help</arg>
<arg>–verbose</arg>
</group>
<synopfragment id="markup">
<group choice="opt">
<arg>–xml</arg>
<arg>–none</arg>
<arg>–sgml</arg>
</group>
</synopfragment>
</cmdsynopsis>
```

SynopFragmentRef

The SynopFragmentRef element provides a reference for a SynopFragment.

The SynopFragmentRef uses common attributes.

Example:

See SynopFragment element example.

SystemItem

The SystemItem element indicates an item or a term from the computer system.

The SystemItem element uses these attributes in addition to the common attributes.

- Class
- MoreInfo

Example:

```
<para>The primary name server for Prima Publishing is
<systemitem>ns1.primapub.com</systemitem></para>
```

Token

The Token element indicates a bit of information from the computer system.

The Token element uses common attributes.

Type

The Type element indicates the data type of a value.

The Type element uses common attributes.

Example:

```
<para> The <function>ctime()</function>, <function>gmtime()</function> and
<function>localtime()</function> functions all take an argument of data
type <type>time_t</type> which represents calendar time.
```

UserInput

The UserInput element indicates input that should be entered by the user who is reading the document.

The UserInput element uses common attributes.

Example:

```
<para>Now type in <userinput>username</userinput>.</para>
```

VarArgs

The VarArgs element indicates possible arguments. When run through many processing systems, this element produces something like (. . .). The VarArgs element is an empty element.

The VarArgs element uses common attributes.

VariableList

The VariableList element contains a list of terms. The VariableList element contains one or more of the VarListEntry elements.

The VariableList uses common attributes.

Example:

```
<variablelist>
<varlistentry><term>HTML</term>
<listitem><para>Hyper Text Transport Protocol</para></listitem>
</varlistentry>
```

VarListEntry

The `VarListEntry` is a child element to the `VariableList` element. It contains a possible variable.

The `VarListEntry` element uses common attributes.

Example:

See `VariableList` element example.

VarName

The `VarName` element indicates the name of a variable.

The `VarName` element uses common attributes.

Example:

```
<para>The <varname>$_</varname> variable in Perl is the default input and
patern-searching space.</para>
```

Void

The `Void` element is an empty element used to indicate a void, meaning the function has no arguments.

The `Void` element uses common attributes.

Example:

```
<funcdef>int <function>pause</function></funcdef><
void>
```

Literal Layout Elements

Although DocBook is primarily structural markup, some elements are used for literal layout. Sometimes you do have to indicate a page break, for instance.

BeginPage

The `BeginPage` element indicates where a page should begin.

The `BeginPage` element accepts the Pagenum attribute in addition to the common attributes.

Example:

```
<beginpage pagenum="300">
```

BlockQuote

The `BlockQuote` element indicates a quote that should be set off from the rest of the text. Usually, any quote that is three or more lines should be enclosed in a `BlockQuote`.

The `BlockQuote` element uses common attributes.

Example:

```
<para>A quote from "Mythical Man Month": </para>
<blockquote><attribution>Frederick Brooks Jr.</attribution>
<para>As the system comes up, the component builders will from time to
time appear, bearing hot new versions of their pieces -- faster, smaller,
more complete,or putatively less buggy.  The replacement of a working
component by a new version requires the same systematic testing procedure
that adding a new component does, although it should require less time,
for more complete and efficient test cases will usually be
available.</para>
</blockquote>
```

BridgeHead

The `BridgeHead` element creates a heading that has no text associated with it.

The `BridgeHead` element uses this attribute in addition to common attributes.

- **RenderAs.** Identifies how to render the BrideHead.

Example:

```
<chapter>
...
<bridgehead rederas="sect1">Our Header</bridgehead>
<para>...</para>
</chapter>
```

Callout

The `Callout` element indicates a callout of some sort.

The `Callout` element uses this required attribute in addition to common attributes.

- **AreaRefs**

Example:

```
<Calloutlist>
<title>My Comments</TITLE>
<callout arearefs="opinion1">
<para>This guy is a doofus</para>
</callout>>
</CALLOUTLIST>
```

CalloutList

The `CalloutList` element contains a list of the `Callout` element.

The `CalloutList` element uses common attributes.

Example:

See `Callout` element example.

Caution

The `Caution` element indicates a block of text that should be set off from the rest of the text to draw attention to its contents. With most formatting systems, the `Caution` element also causes a caution graphic of some sort to be displayed with the `Caution` element.

The `Caution` element uses common attributes.

Example:

```
<caution>
<para>Don't run with scissors</para>
</caution>
```

CO

The `CO` element indicates the position of a callout inline.

The `CO` element uses common attributes.

See the `MediaObjectCO` element for examples.

Emphasis

The `Emphasis` element indicates text that should be emphasized in some way. This is better than markup such as HTML, which allows for italic or bold text to be called directly. Both italic and boldface are lost when the text is read through a text-to-speech device or is rendered in plain text.

The `Emphasis` element uses common attributes.

Example:

```
<para>I am <emphasis>really</emphasis> tired.</para>
```

Equation

The `Equation` element indicates an equation.

The `Equation` element accepts the following attribute in addition to the common attributes:

- **Label.** Accepts a `CDATA` value, has no default value, and is not required

Example:

```
<equation><title>Pythagorean Theorem</title>
        <alt>a^2 + b^2 = c^2</alt>
        <graphic fileref="equations/pythagorean.gif"></graphic>
</equation>
```

Important

Like the `Caution` element, the `Important` element indicates text that should be set off from the main body as important.

The `Important` element uses common attributes.

Example:

```
<important>
<para>Never judge a book by its cover.</para>
</important>
```

InlineEquation

The `InlineEquation` element indicates an element that should be displayed in the main body of text.

The `InlineEquation` element uses common attributes.

Example:

```
<para>The Pythagorean Theorum is:
<inlineequation>
      <alt>"a^2 + b^2 = c^2</alt>
      <graphic fileref="equations/pythagorean.gif"></graphic>
</inlineequation>
</para>
```

ItemizedList

The ItemizedList element contains a list of items marked with a bullet or other designated marker. This is somewhat different from the OrderedList element, which contains a list that is sequentially labeled.

The ItemizedList element uses these attributes in addition to the common attributes.

- **Spacing.** Accepts either Compact or Normal as a value, has no default value, and is not required.
- **Mark.** Accepts bullet, dash, or other symbol, and is not required.

Example:

```
<itemizedlist mark=dash>
<listitem><para>HTML</para></listitem>
<listitem><para>SGML</para></listitem>
<listitem>para>XML</para></listitem>
</itemizedlist>
```

LiteralLayout

The LiteralLayout element indicates text that should be displayed as-is. White space and line breaks should be rendered exactly as they are between the LiteralLayout markup tags.

The LiteralLayout element uses common attributes.

Example:

```
<literallayout>
   If you wanted to have a section
            with spacing and linebreaks wherever you want
 you could use literallayout.
</literallayout>
```

Note

The Note element indicates text that should be set off from the main body as a note.

The Note element uses common attributes.

Example:

```
<note>
<para>This is a note.</para>
</note>
```

OrderedList

The OrderedList element contains a list of items that are sequentially enumerated. This is different from the ItemizedList element, which separates the items in the list with a bullet or another designated symbol other than a sequential designator.

The OrderedList element accepts the following attributes in addition to the common attributes:

- **Continuation.** Accepts one of two values:
  - Continues
  - Restarts

  The default is Restarts. The Continuation attribute is not required.
- **InheritNum.** Accepts either Ignore or Inherit as a value, has the default value Inherit, and is not required.
- **Numeration.** Accepts one of the following values, has no default value, and is not required.
  - Arabic
  - LowerAlpha
  - LowerRoman
  - UpperAlpha
  - UpperRoman
- **Spacing.** Accepts either Compact or Normal as a value, has no default value, and is not required.

Example:

```
<orderedlist numberation="Upperroman"
<listitem><para>Chapter 1</para></listitem>
<listitem><para>Chapter2</para></listitem>
</orderedlist>
```

Sidebar

The `Sidebar` element indicates that the information contained inside the `Sidebar` markup should be displayed as a sidebar set off from the main text, if the processing system allows that.

The `Sidebar` element uses common attributes.

Example:

```
<para>...</para>
<sidebar><title>My Sidebar</title>
<para>This is a sidebar.</para>
</sidebar>
<para>...</para>
```

SimpleList

The `SimpleList` element contains a list that contains a simple list.

The `SimpleList` element uses these attributes in addition to common attributes.

- **Columns**. Accepts number of columns to display list. Default is 1.
- **Type**. Sets column type, vertical, horizontal, in-line. The default is Vertical.

Example:

```
<para>My phone keypad looks like this:
<simplelist type=horiz columns=3>
<member>1</member>
<member>2</member>
<member>3</member>
<member>4</member>
...
</simplelist>
</para>
```

Tip

The `Tip` element indicates information that should be set off from the main body of text as a tip.

The `Tip` element uses common attributes.

Example:

```
<tip>
<para>If I had any useful tips for you, I'd put them here.</para>
</tip>
```

Warning

The Warning element indicates text that should be set off from the main body of text as a warning to readers.

The Warning element uses common attributes.

Example:

```
<warning>Using <command>:q!</command> in <application>vi</application>
will not save changes to your text file and exit!</warning>
```

Indexing Elements

DocBook contains a rich set of indexing elements for anyone who wants to create his or her own index using DocBook markup or, if used correctly and the processing system supports it, to have the processing system generate the index automatically.

Index

The Index element holds the markup for a DocBook index.

The Index element uses common attributes.

Example:

```
<index><title>Index</title>
<indexdiv><title>C</title>
<indexentry>
        <primaryie>Class networks, 65</primaryie>
        <secondaryie>A, 65, 80</secondaryie>
        <secondaryie>D, 65, 66, 80</secondaryie>
</indexentry>
</indexdiv>
</index>
```

IndexDiv

The IndexDiv element indicates a division in the index.

The IndexDiv element uses common attributes.

Example:

See Index element example.

IndexEntry

The `IndexEntry` indicates an entry in the index that can contain `PrimaryIE`, `SecondaryIE`, and other child elements.

The `IndexEntry` element uses common attributes.

Example:

See `Index` element example.

IndexTerm

The `IndexTerm` element indicates terms that should be indexed. The `IndexTerm` element is not included in the index markup but is in-line in the regular text.

The `IndexTerm` uses common attributes.

Example:

```
<para>I only use Linux <indexterm><primary>Operating System</primary>
<secondary>Open Source</secondary></indexterm> on my computers.</para>
```

ItermSet

The `ItermSet` is used in the meta-information of a document to indicate a group of `IndexTerms`.

The `ItermSet` element uses common attributes.

Example:

```
<chapter>
<docinfo>
<itermset>
<indexterm><primary>DocBook</primary></indexterm>
<indexterm><primary>SGML</primary></indexterm>
</itermset>
</docinfo>
</chapter>
```

Subject

The `Subject` element indicates a term that describes a document.

The `Subject` element accepts the following attribute in addition to the common attribute:

- **Weight.** Accepts a NUMBER value, has no default, and is not required.

Example:

```
<subjectset>
<subject><subjectterm>DocBook</subjectterm></subject>
<subject><subjectterm>XML</subjectterm></subject>
</subjectset>
```

SubjectSet

The SubjectSet element contains one or more of the Subject elements.

The SubjectSet element accepts the following attribute in addition to the common attributes:

- **Scheme.** Accepts a NAME value, has no default value, and is not required.

Example:

See Subject element example.

SubjectTerm

The SubjectTerm element holds a term that describes a document. The SubjectTerm is a child element of the Subject element.

The SubjectTerm element uses common attributes.

Example:

See Subject element example.

Table Elements

The Table elements used in DocBook correspond with the CALS table model.

Colspec

The Colspec element gives the specifications for a column in a table.

The Colspec element accepts the following attributes:

- **Align.** Accepts one of the following values:
  - Center
  - Char
  - Left
  - Justify
  - Right

  There is no default value, and the Align attribute is not required.

- **Char.** Accepts a CDATA value, has no default, and is not required.
- **Charoff.** Accepts a NUTOKEN value, has no default, and is not required.
- **Colnum.** Accepts a NUMBER value, has no default, and is not required.
- **Colname.** Accepts a NMTOKEN value, has no default, and is not required.
- **Colwidth.** Accepts a CDATA value, has no default value, and is not required.
- **Rowsep.** Accepts a NUMBER value, has no default value, and is not required.

Example:

See Table *element example.*

Entry

The Entry element holds the information for an entry in a DocBook table.

The Entry element accepts the following values:

- **Align.** Accepts one of the following values:
  - Center
  - Char
  - Left
  - Justify
  - Right

  The Align attribute has no default value and is not required.
- **Char.** Accepts a CDATA value, has no default, and is not required.
- **Charoff.** Accepts a NUTOKEN value and has no default. It is not required.
- **Colname.** Accepts a NMTOKEN value, has no default, and is not required.
- **Colsep.** Accepts a NUMBER value, has no default value, and is not required.
- **Namest.** Accepts a NMTOKEN value, has no default, and is not required.
- **Rotate.** Accepts a NUMBER value, has no default value, and is not required.
- **Rowsep.** Accepts a NUMBER value, has no default value, and is not required.
- **Valign.** Accepts one of the following values:
  - Bottom
  - Middle
  - Top

  The Valign attribute has no default value and is not required.

Example:

See Table *element example.*

Entrytbl

The `Entrytbl` element can be used in place of the `Entry` element.

The `Entrytbl` element accepts the following values:

- **Align.** Accepts one of the following values:
  - Center
  - Char
  - Left
  - Justify
  - Right

The Align attribute has no default value and is not required.

- **Char.** Accepts a CDATA value, has no default, and is not required.
- **Charoff.** Accepts a NUTOKEN value, has no default, and is not required.
- **Colname.** Accepts a NMTOKEN value, has no default, and is not required.
- **Colsep.** Accepts a NUMBER value, has no default value, and is not required.
- **Namest.** Accepts a NMTOKEN value, has no default, and is not required.
- **Rotate.** Accepts a NUMBER value, has no default value, and is not required.
- **Rowsep.** Accepts a NUMBER value, has no default value, and is not required.

Example:

```
<tbody>
<row>
<entrytbl cols=1>
<colspec align="left" colnum="1" colname="col1">
<thead>
<row>
<ENTRY>FIRST</ENTRY>
<ENTRY>LAST</ENTRY>
<ENTRY>M.I.</ENTRY>
</row>
</thead>
```

InformalTable

The `InformalTable` element indicates a table in casual dress. Just kidding. Actually, it's a table without a title.

The `InformalTable` element accepts the following attributes:

- Colsep
- Label
- Frame
- Orient
- Pgwide
- Rowsep
- Shortentry
- ToCentry

Example:

```
<informaltable>
<tgroup cols="3">
<colspec align="left" colnum="1">
<thead>
<row>
<entry>First Name</entry>
<entry>Last Name</entry>
<entry>Middle Initial</entry>
</row>
</thead>
</tgroup>
</informaltable>
```

Row

The Row element indicates a row in a DocBook table.

The Row element accepts the following attributes.

- **Rowsep.** Accepts a NUMBER value, has no default value, and is not required.
- **Valign.** Accepts one of the following values:
  - Bottom
  - Middle
  - Top

  The Valign attribute is not required and has no default value.

Example:

See InformalTable element example.

Spanspec

The Spanspec element provides information for columns in a table that span more than one column. This allows a cell to take up more than one column.

The Spanspec element accepts the following attributes:

- Align
- Char
- Charoff
- Colsep
- Nameend
- Namest
- Rowsep
- Spanname

Example:

```
<spanspec spanname=header namest=col1 nameend=col2 align="left">
...
```

Table

The `Table` element indicates a DocBook table with a title.

The `Table` element accepts the following attributes:

- Colsep
- Label
- Frame

- Orient
- Pgwide
- Rowsep

- Shortentry
- ToCentry

Example:

```
<table frame="all"><title>My First Table</title>
<tgroup cols="5" align="left colsep=1 rowsep=1>
<colspec colname=col1>
<colspec colname=col2>
<thead>
<row>
        <entry>FIRST</entry>
        <entry>LAST</entry>
        <entry>M.I></entry>
        <entry>D.O.B.</entry>
        <entry>SSN</entry>
</row>
<thead>
<tfoot>
<row>
        <entry>n1</entry>
        <entry>n2</entry>
        <entry>n3</entry>
        <entry>d1</entry>
        <entry>s1</entry>
</row>
</tfoot>
<tbody>
<row>
        <entry>Kara</entry>
        <entry>Pritchard</entry>
        <entry>J</entry>
        <entry>8-23-00</entry>
        <entry>123-45-6789</entry>
</row>
</tbody>
</tgroup>
</table>
```

TBody

The TBody element holds the rows of a table or an informal table in a DocBook document.

The TBody element accepts the following attribute:

- **Valign.** Accepts one of the following values:
  - Bottom
  - Middle
  - Top

  The Valign attribute has no default value and is not required.

Example:

See Table *element example.*

TFoot

The TFoot element holds any footer information about a table.

The TFoot element accepts the following attribute:

- **Valign.** Accepts one of the following values:
  - Bottom
  - Middle
  - Top

  The Valign attribute has no default value and is not required.

Example:

See Table *element example.*

TGroup

The TGroup element holds the information for all or part of a table.

The TGroup element accepts the following values:

- **Align.** Accepts one of the following values:
  - Center
  - Char
  - Left
  - Justify
  - Right

  The Align attribute has no default value and is not required.
- **Char.** Accepts a CDATA value, has no default, and is not required.
- **Charoff.** Accepts a NUTOKEN value, has no default, and is not required.

- **Colname.** Accepts a NMTOKEN value, has no default, and is not required.
- **Colsep.** Accepts a NUMBER value, has no default value, and is not required.
- **Rowsep.** Accepts a NUMBER value, has no default value, and is not required.

Example:

See Table *element example.*

THead

The THead element holds the header information, if any, for a table.

The THead element accepts the following attribute:

- **Valign.** Accepts one of the following values:
  - Bottom
  - Middle
  - Top

  The Valign attribute has no default value and is not required.

Example:

See Table *element example.*

Reference Page Elements

The reference page elements in DocBook were originally created for marking up UNIX-style manpages. However, the markup for reference pages is very useful for other references as well.

RefClass

The RefClass element indicates the usability of the reference page.

Example:

See RefEntry *element example.*

RefDescriptor

The RefDescriptor element holds the description of a reference page.

Example:

```
<refdescriptor>string</refdescriptor>
```

RefEntry

The RefEntry element indicates an entry in a reference.

Example:

```
<refentry id="shutdown">
<refmeta>
<refentrytitle>shutdown</refentrytitle>
<manfolnum>1</manvolnum>
</refmeta>
<refnameddiv>
<refname>shutdown</refname>
<refpurpose>Used to properly shutdown a Linux system</refpurpose>
</refnamediv>
<refsynopsisdiv>
<cmdsynopsis>
<command>/usr/bin/shutdown</comand>
</cmdsynopsis>
</refentry>
```

RefEntryTitle

The RefEntryTitle indicates the title of a RefEntry.

Example:

See RefEntry element example.

Reference

The Reference element holds a number of the RefEntry elements. A Reference is usually a section, or sometimes even a stand-alone document.

Example:

```
<reference><title>My References</title>
<referentry>...</refentry>
...
</reference>
```

RefMeta

The RefMeta element holds meta-information for a DocBook reference.

Example:

See RefEntry element example.

RefMiscInfo

The RefMiscInfo element holds meta-information for a reference other than the information contained in the RefMeta element.

Example:

```
<refmiscinfo class="pubdate">Published 2001</refmiscinfo>
```

RefName

The RefName element holds the subject name of a reference.

Example:

See RefEntry element example.

RefNameDiv

The RefNameDiv element contains the name and classification for a reference page.

Example:

See RefEntry element example.

RefPurpose

The RefPurpose element holds the description of a reference's purpose.

Example:

See RefEntry element example.

RefSect1

The RefSect1 element is a level 1 section of a reference.

Example:

```
<refsect1 ID="rsec1">
<title>This section</title>
<para>Some more text here</para>
<para>...</para>
</refsect1>
```

RefSect1Info

The RefSect1Info element contains meta-information about a RefSect1 section.

Example:

```
<refesect1info><date>March 21, 2001</date></refesect1info>
```

RefSect2

The RefSect2 is a level 2 section of a reference.

Example:

See RefSect1 *element example.*

RefSect2Info

The RefSect2Info element contains meta-information about a RefSect2 section.

Example:

See RefSect1Info *element example.*

RefSect3

The RefSect3 element is a level 3 section of a reference.

Example:

See RefSect1 *element example.*

RefSect3Info

The RefSect3Info element holds meta-information about a RefSect3 section.

Example:

See RefSect1Info *element example.*

RefSynopsisDiv

The RefSynopsisDiv element holds the synopsis information for a reference.

Example:

See RefEntry *element example.*

RefSynopsisDivInfo

The RefSynopsisDivInfo element contains meta-information about a RefSynopsisDiv section.

Example:

See RefEntry *element example.*

Obsolete Elements from Previous Versions

Some elements from DocBook version 3.0 are no longer valid DocBook elements. If you need to maintain a document that was written in DocBook 3 or earlier, you must remove these elements and replace them with elements that are used in DocBook 4.

Don't panic, though. Only a few elements from version 3 are obsolete, so it shouldn't be difficult to upgrade to version 4.

ArtHeader

The `ArtHeader` element has been replaced in DocBook version 4 with the `ArticleInfo` element.

BookBiblio

The `BookBiblio` element has been removed. There is no replacement.

Comment

The `Comment` element has been replaced by the `Remark` element in DocBook version 4.

DocInfo

The `DocInfo` element has been split into a number of more specific elements: `AppendixInfo`, `BibliographyInfo`, `ChapterInfo`, `GlossaryInfo`, `IndexInfo`, `PartInfo`, `PrefaceInfo`, `RefentryInfo`, `ReferenceInfo`, `SetIndexInfo`, and `SidebarInfo`.

InterfaceDefinition

The `InterfaceDefinition` element has been removed. There is no replacement.

SeriesInfo

The `SeriesInfo` element has been removed. There is no replacement.

Future Versions of DocBook

The DocBook Technical Committee has a rough road map for DocBook version 5.0 at this time, but it might be some time before that specification is presented to OASIS, and even longer before it is the official version of DocBook.

There was some talk of moving completely to XML for version 5.0, but it looks as though there has been enough interest in SGML that there will be a DocBook 5.0 SGML version as well. However, the emphasis in the future will probably be XML. As mentioned earlier in the book, all things being equal, it's probably best to start any new DocBook projects with XML, barring a compelling reason to use SGML instead.

The Simplified DocBook DTD

Norman Walsh has created a simplified DocBook DTD that you can use if the entire set of elements is overwhelming. This is advisable if you're trying to maintain compatibility with other DocBook systems but don't want to deal with all the elements yourself. This is a list of all the elements available under the simplified DTD. For those who are interested, the simplified DTD contains nearly the same number of elements as the HTML DTD.

- Abbrev
- Abstract
- Acronym
- Affiliation
- Appendix
- Article
- ArticleInfo
- Attribution
- AudioData
- AudioObject
- Author
- AuthorBlurb
- AuthorGroup
- AuthorInitials
- Bibliography
- BiblioMisc
- BiblioMixed
- Biblioset
- BlockQuote
- CiteTitle
- Colspec
- Command
- ComputerOutput
- Copyright
- CorpAuthor
- Date
- Edition
- Editor
- Email
- Emphasis
- Entry
- Epigraph
- Example
- Figure
- Filename

- FirstName
- Footnote
- Holder
- Honorific
- ImageData
- ImageObject
- InformalTable
- InlineMediaObject
- IssueNum
- ItemizedList
- JobTitle
- Keyword
- KeywordSet
- LegalNotice
- Lineage
- LineAnnotation
- Link
- ListItem
- Literal
- LiteralLayout
- MediaObject
- Note
- ObjectInfo
- Option
- OrderedList
- OrgName
- OtherCredit
- OtherName
- Para
- Phrase
- ProgramListing
- PubDate
- PublisherName
- Quote
- ReleaseInfo

- Replaceable
- RevDescription
- RevHistory
- Revision
- RevNumber
- RevRemark
- Row
- Section
- SectionInfo
- Sidebar
- Subject
- SubjectSet
- SubjectTerm
- Subtitle
- Surname
- SystemItem
- Table
- TBody
- Term
- TextObject
- TGroup
- THead
- Title
- Trademark
- ULink
- UserInput
- VariableList
- VarListEntry
- VideoData
- VideoObject
- VolumeNum
- XRef
- Year

Appendix C: More DocBook Resources

Finding Out More about DocBook

Open Source Publishing Resources

ocBook Publishing explains as thoroughly as possible how to work with DocBook. However, many topics are associated with DocBook (and publishing)—such as SGML, XML, Open Source, and editors—but there just isn't room to cover everything relating to DocBook. In this appendix, I provide several resources for you, in case you'd like to strike out on your own and learn more about these topics.

Finding Out More about DocBook

Plenty of information about DocBook is out there on the Web. Many organizations are using DocBook, especially Open Source projects such as the Linux Documentation Project, the GNOME and KDE projects, and many others. If you need to find sample documents and stylesheets, these are great places to start.

XML is taking off as well, and you can find a wealth of information about XML on the Web to help you get up and running using XML for all sorts of fun and exciting projects.

DocBook Resources

The best place to get up-to-date information about DocBook is the *OASIS* official DocBook page (see Figure C.1) at **http://oasis.oasis-open.org/docbook/**.

The DocBook Technical Committee oversees the DocBook updates and revisions, so its site, OASIS, is the best place to check for a new version of DocBook or news about DocBook. The site also posts minutes from the technical committee's meetings, so if DocBook is important to your business or organization, you might want to follow what's going on.

The OASIS page also provides a list of tools, commercial and otherwise, that are available for use with DocBook. Finally, if you're looking for a place to ask questions (or answer them), you can sign up for DocBook mailing lists. The mailing lists are low-traffic but do occasionally contain good insights into using DocBook.

The official documentation for DocBook is *DocBook: The Definitive Guide*, published by O'Reilly and Associates. *DocBook: The Definitive Guide* is also

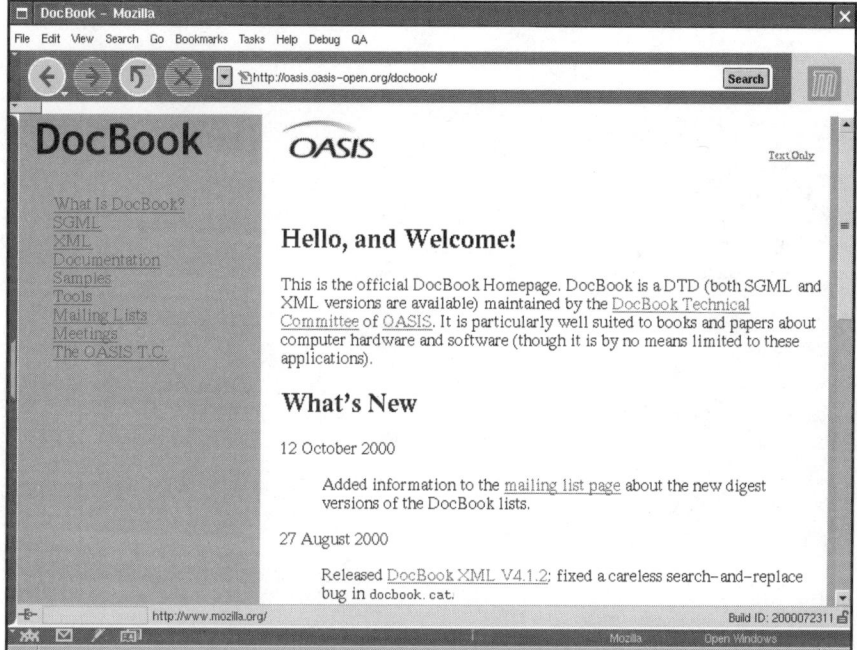

Figure C.1 *The OASIS DocBook page*

published on the Web and is available for free download for personal use (see Figure C.2). At the time of this writing, the printed book is slightly out of date, focusing on DocBook version 3.1. However, it is in the process of revision, and drafts can also be found on the Web site: **http://www.docbook.org/**.

O'Reilly deserves kudos for its role in creating and supporting the DocBook DTD and for making the book freely available on the Web. *DocBook: The Definitive Guide* is an excellent technical reference, and I encourage anyone who finds the online version useful to purchase the book as well.

SGML Resources

SGML has been around for years, so entirely too many sites have information about SGML to list them all. I've picked a handful of sites to get you started.

My favorite SGML resource on the Web is Robin Cover's SGML page (see Figure C.3). This is one of the most comprehensive SGML resources on the Web, so be sure to check it out at **http://www.oasis-open.org/cover/general.html**.

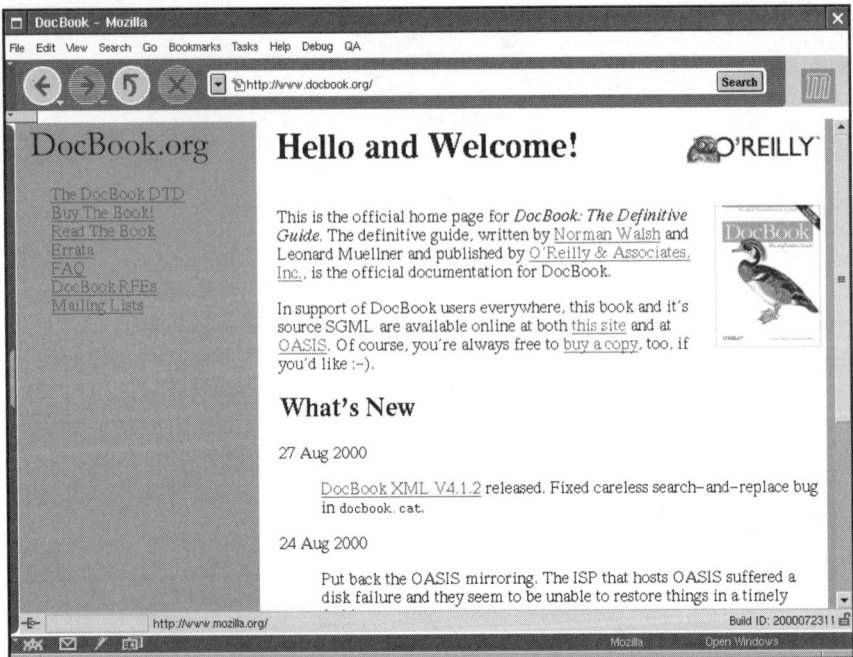

Figure C.2 *DocBook: The Definitive Guide Web site*

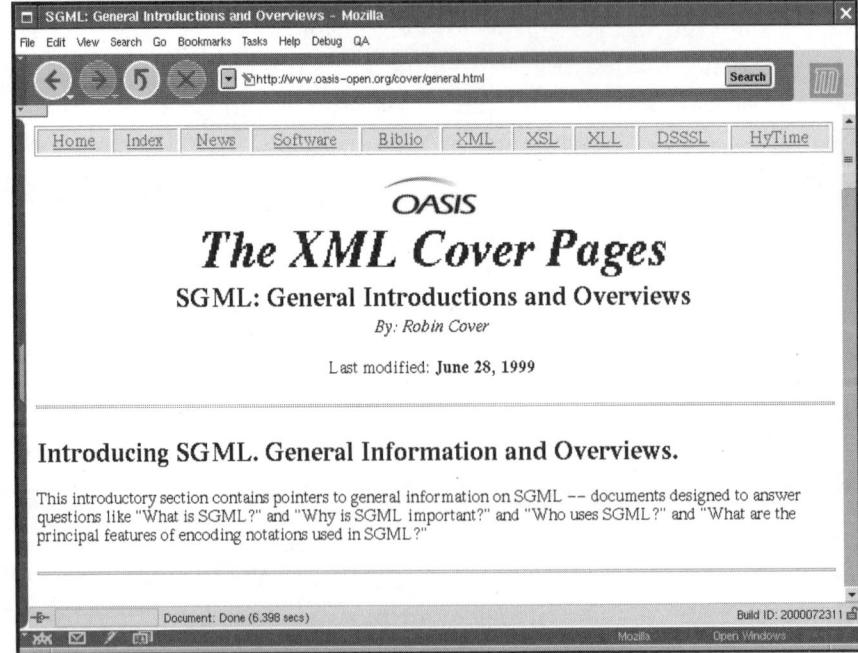

Figure C.3 *Robin Cover's SGML page*

The *SGML Source Home Page* by Charles F. Goldfarb is a simple page (see Figure C.4), but it includes some valuable information on the history of SGML from the perspective of someone who was there from the beginning. Charles also includes interesting papers and other resources for the SGML enthusiast. You can visit his SGML source page at **http://www.sgmlsource.com/**.

Arbortext provides an excellent SGML resource page (see Figure C.5), including a paper titled "SGML: Getting Started" that not only explains SGML in easy-to-understand language but also makes the business case for SGML. If you need to convince your boss to convert to SGML or XML, this is the place to get ammunition: **http://www.arbortext.com/ Think_Tank/SGML_Resources/Getting_Started_with_SGML/getting_ started_with_sgml.html**.

Finally, there's a good directory of SGML-related links on the *Open Directory Project site* (see Figure C.6). The Open Directory site is a Web directory and search engine compiled by volunteers, and they do a great job of sifting through the junk and finding good Web sites. Unlike search sites and directories compiled by Web spiders, the Open Directory Project is compiled solely by humans. Each link is subjected to perusal by a volunteer who signed

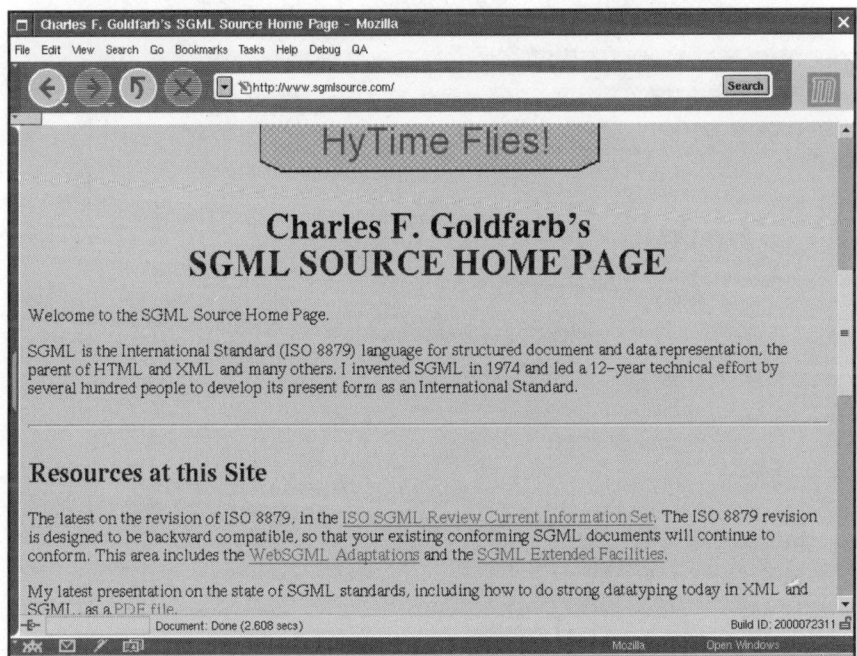

Figure C.4 *Charles Goldfarb's SGML Source Web page*

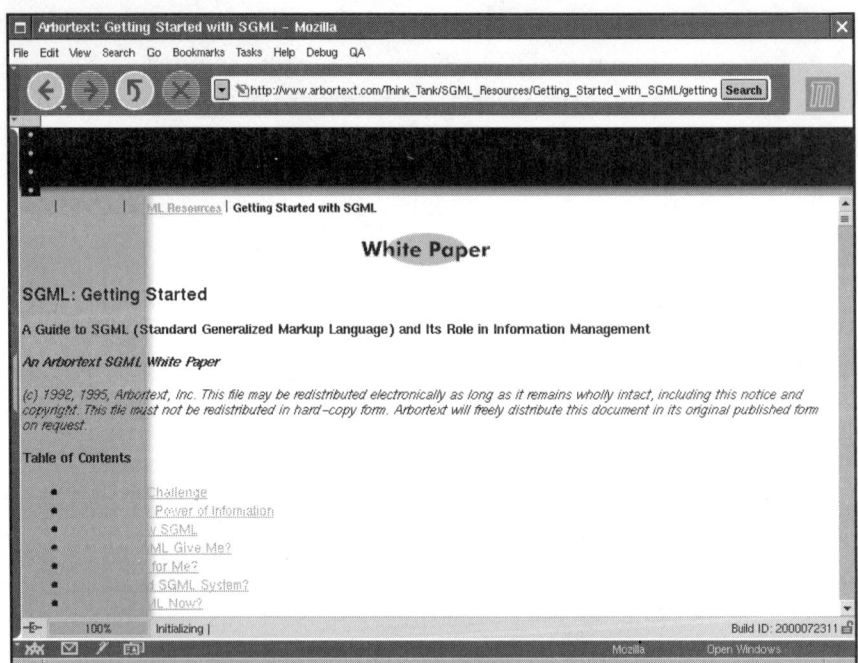

Figure C.5 *The Arbortext SGML resource page*

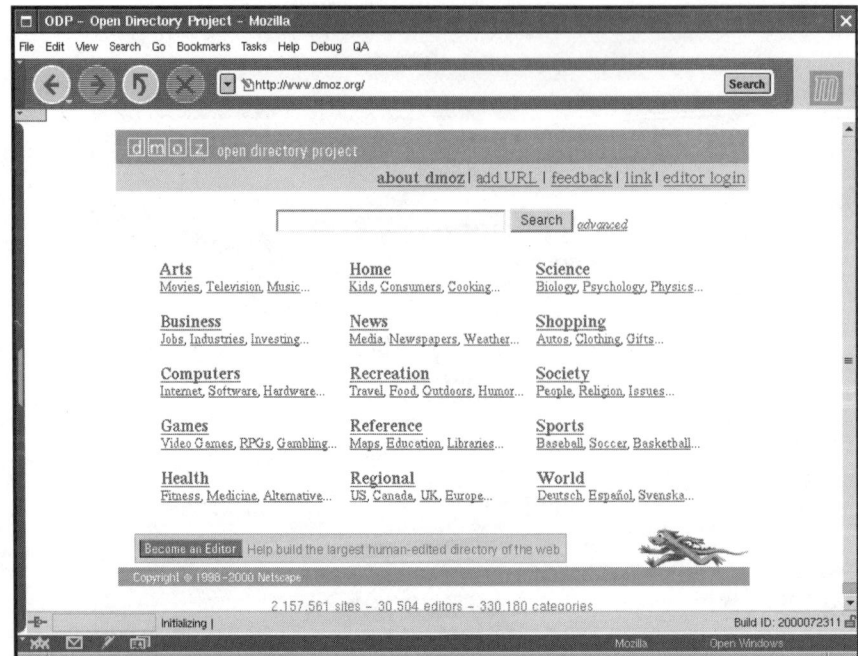

Figure C.6 *The Open Directory Project*

up specifically to handle one or more subjects of interest to him or her. If you've never visited the site, it's worth a look: **http://www.dmoz.org/**. The SGML page is located at **http://dmoz.org/Computers/Data_Formats/ Markup_Languages/SGML/**.

XML Resources

XML is really, really taking off. I've mentioned this before, but it bears repeating. The resources I've listed here are the best ones as of the writing of this book. I fully expect that more wonderful resources will become available, so be sure to do a little hunting on your own for sites that might pop up in the future.

The best place to go for information is usually straight to the source. In this case, the source for information on XML is the *World Wide Web Consortium (W3C)*. They're the folks who have come up with the standard. Okay, technically, it's a recommendation, not a standard, but let's not get picky here. You can find information on XML, XSL, CSS, MathML, and other related technologies on the W3C's Web site (see Figure C.7) at **http://www.w3.org/**.

Figure C.7 *The World Wide Web Consortium home page*

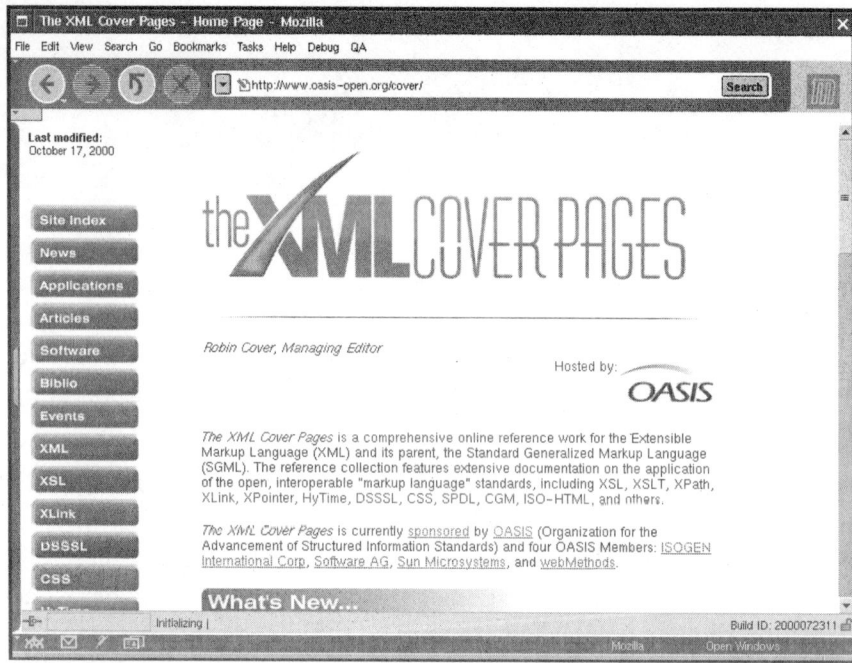

Figure C.8 *The XML Cover Pages*

Robin Cover provides not only great SGML resources but also an awesome XML resource page (see Figure C.8). *The XML Cover Pages*, as it is called, includes resources for XML, XSL, CSS, and XLink, recent news and developments, and probably the most extensive SGML/XML bibliography you will ever see. The Cover Pages are part of the OASIS Web site at **http://www.oasis-open.org/cover/**.

Finally, *XML.com* is a site with plenty of XML resources and feature articles about XML and its uses (see Figure C.9). This is a must-read for XML users. The featured articles alone are worth a visit, and if you're just now finding out about this XML stuff, you can browse through the article archive and get up to speed. XML.com is located at **http://www.xml.com/**.

Other Open Source Software and Stuff

You've probably noticed that I've mentioned Linux, FreeBSD, NetBSD, OpenBSD, and other Open Source and Free Software projects in this book. Even though you can use DocBook on Windows, the MacOS, and other operating systems, its strongest user base is in the Open Source world.

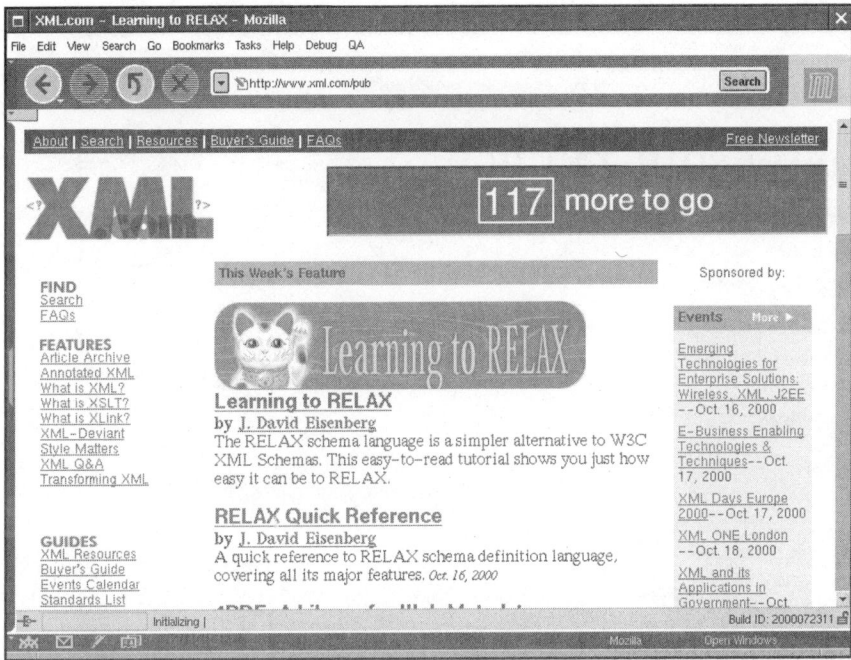

Figure C.9 *The XML.com home page*

Why is that? Well, probably because the DocBook DTD itself is freely available and a great number of Open Source tools are available for working with DocBook. DocBook also lends itself quite well to the collaborative environment in which Open Source software is developed. In addition, it was easy to work with DocBook with the tools available early on with Linux and other Open Source OSes before there were office suites and such. By the time StarOffice, Applix, and AbiWord came on the scene, people had been using SGML to produce documentation under Linux for some time.

Numerous Open Source projects are using DocBook for their documentation. A few of them have created some great references, and here I've listed the best I've found.

The *Debian Project* makes an SGML/XML HOWTO (see Figure C.10) available for anyone who'd like to produce documentation for the Debian Project. This HOWTO is interesting because it includes information on working with the LinuxDoc and DebianDoc DTDs, as well as DocBook's DTD. You can find the latest version at **http://www.debian.org/~bortz/SGML-HOWTO/potato/howto.html**.

Figure C.10 *The Debian SGML/XML HOWTO*

Debian is the most popular noncommercial distribution of GNU/Linux. (Debian likes to call it *GNU/Linux*, instead of plain *Linux*. Check out its Web site at **http://www.debian.org/** to find out why.) Debian is known for its stability and the extremely useful *apt-get* utility, which allows you to update packages or your entire system from the command line. Install Debian once, and you may never need to do a reinstall, ever.

Another useful site for those learning DocBook SGML is the *Linux Documentation Project*, or LDP (see Figure C.11). Not only does it have a HOWTO with information on getting started with DocBook, but it also has a multitude of documents marked up with DocBook so that you can download and examine to see how it's done. Oh, and there are lots of HOWTOs and guides on Linux, too. The Linux Documentation main site can be found at **http://www.linuxdoc.org/**.

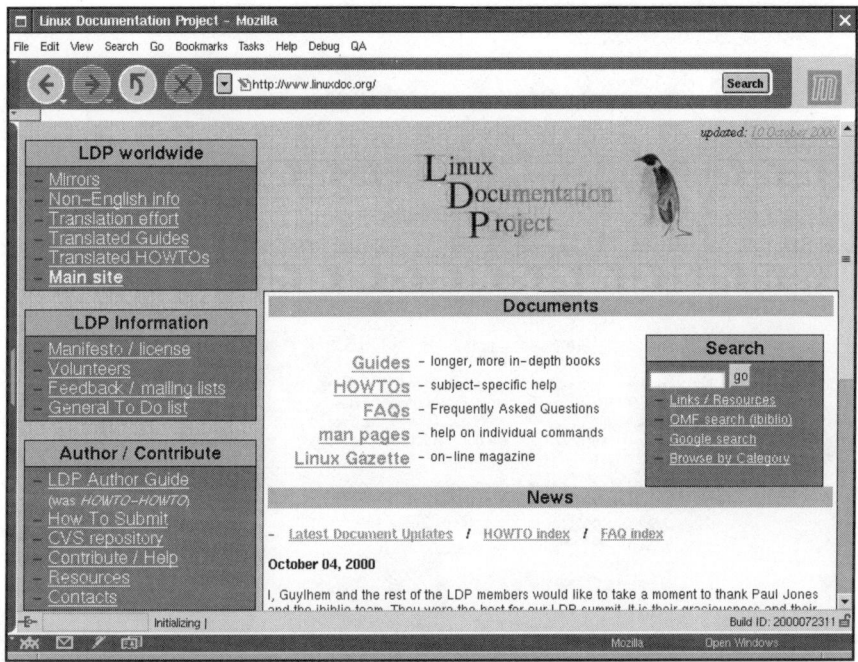

Figure C.11 *The Linux Documentation Project (LDP) home page*

Yes, *HOWTO* is the proper capitalization.

However, if you're going to use the site much, be sure to look for a mirror near you to save stress on the main server. You can find a list of mirrors at **http://www.linuxdoc.org/mirrors.html**.

Most of the guides, HOWTOs, and FAQs have DocBook source available. If you want to sharpen your DocBook skills but don't have a project that needs doing right away, you might consider volunteering to do DocBook markup for the LDP. A number of authors who don't know DocBook yet could use a hand.

The FreeBSD project also uses DocBook for its documentation, and Nik Clayton has written a nice guide for producing documentation for the FreeBSD project. A large portion of the document is on using DocBook and

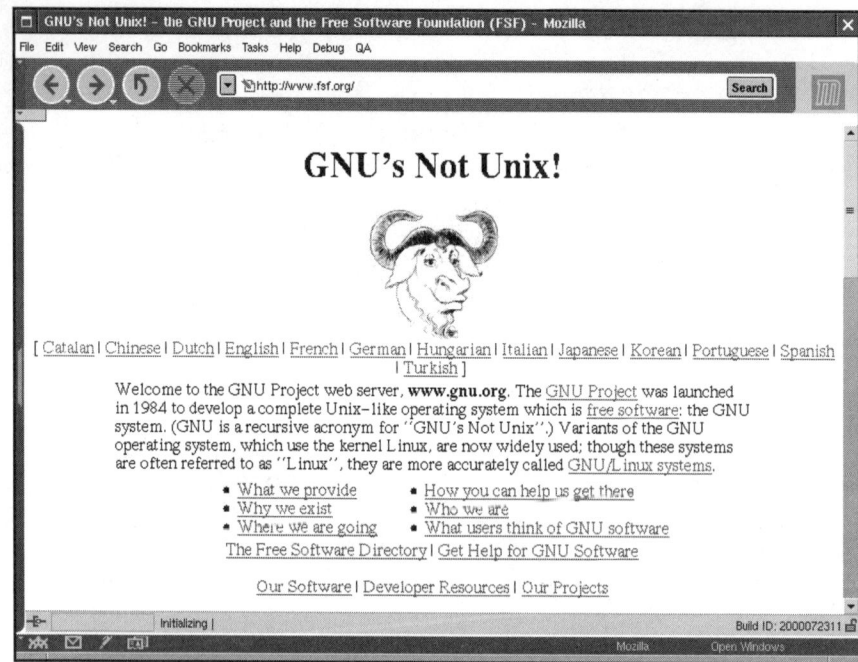

Figure C.12 *The Free Software Foundation Web site*

related tools, and it's worth a look. You can find the FreeBSD project at **http://www.freebsd.org/**. The *FreeBSD Project Primer* can be found at **http://www.freebsd.org/tutorials/docproj-primer/book.html**.

If you want to find out more about free software, the best place to start is the *Free Software Foundation*'s (FSF) GNU Project Web site (see Figure C.12): **http://www.fsf.org/**.

There isn't any DocBook-specific information on the FSF Web site, but you can find the Free Software Directory, information on the GNU Project, and the philosophy behind Free (as in speech, not beer) Software.

To learn more about Linux, the best place to start is *Linux Online* (see Figure C.13). Linux Online has a comprehensive list of distribution, links to other sites with information about Linux, and lists of Linux User Groups. Linux Online can be found at **http://www.linux.org/**.

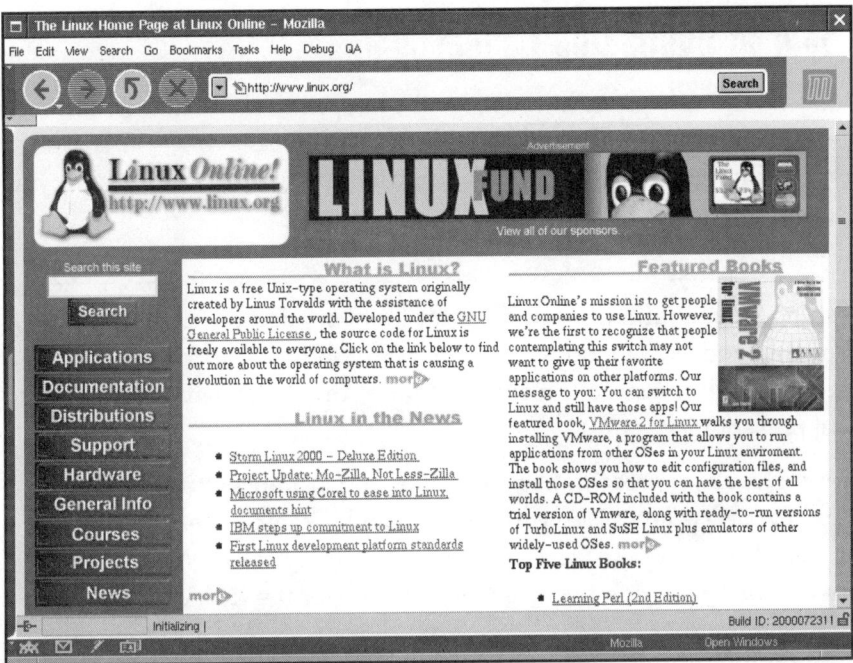

Figure C.13 *The Linux Online Web site*

If you're not already using Linux or one of the *BSDs, I hope that you will check them out and see what they have to offer. I've been using Linux for almost five years now, and I wish that I had started sooner!

There isn't a huge amount of difference between Linux and FreeBSD, NetBSD, or OpenBSD, especially compared to the difference between them and Windows or the MacOS. They're all free, UNIX-like OSes that run on a variety of hardware, including Intel-based PCs. Linux is the most popular, but they all have great features to offer. They are also very powerful, make great use of hardware, and are extremely stable. Not only that, a huge amount of free software is available for these OSes that would cost thousands (yes, I said thousands) of dollars for other OSes. Give one of 'em a whirl. You will be glad you did. Even if you decide that they're not for you, you will know more about them than you did before, and you will know that you made a conscious decision to use whatever OS you're using.

Open Source Publishing Resources

DocBook isn't the only game in town. Now I happen to think that it's the *best* game in town, but it's not the only one. In the Open Source world is a variety of typesetting languages and other tools for typesetting that I think you should know about.

NOTE

Typesetting languages are much different in theory and practice from a markup language like DocBook. As mentioned before, DocBook markup is concerned with the structure and content of the document, not the physical presentation.

However, if you're a presentation maniac or you just absolutely have to have control over every pixel, you will want to look into typesetting languages like TeX or LaTeX. They're not easy, and they're not WYSIWYG, but they certainly provide fine-grained control over the look and feel of your document.

I would like to point out that I'm not going to provide resources for commercial programs like Adobe Illustrator or QuarkXPress. They do enough marketing that I'm sure that you've heard of them often if you've looked for typesetting solutions for the MacOS or Windows. However, most of the Open Source projects aren't backed by big companies with a lot of capital to publicize them. It doesn't mean that the software isn't great, but it does mean that you won't be seeing dual-page ad spreads in *MacUser* magazine or anything like that.

I'm not necessarily recommending any of these programs or languages, mind you, but it never hurts to know what the alternatives are.

Typesetting Languages

If you're interested in trying your hand at a typesetting language, TeX and LaTeX are the best two available. Luckily, a fair amount of free software is also available to work with TeX and LaTeX, so the value proposition is good.

Beware, TeX and LaTeX are not for the faint of heart. If you looked at DocBook markup and thought, "Hmmm, this might be tricky," you will probably look at a TeX file and think, "I'm in real trouble now." TeX is powerful, but it's not what I would call user-friendly.

The best place to start is with the man himself, *Donald E. Knuth*. He's the man who invented TeX, and he is also one of the most respected people in computer science. His books are considered classics in computer science. Knuth's home page is hosted on Stanford University's Web server at **http://www-cs-faculty.Stanford.EDU/~knuth/** (see Figure C.14).

The *Comprehensive TeX Archive Network (CTAN)* includes a comprehensive listing of all available TeX software (see Figure C.15). Not much documentation here, but all the software you can eat. You can find the CTAN Web Interface at **http://www.ctan.org/**.

The *LaTeX Project* home page provides quite a few resources for the LaTeX beginner (see Figure C.16). If you're looking for a foundation to build on with LaTeX, this is where to go: **http://www.latex-project.org/**.

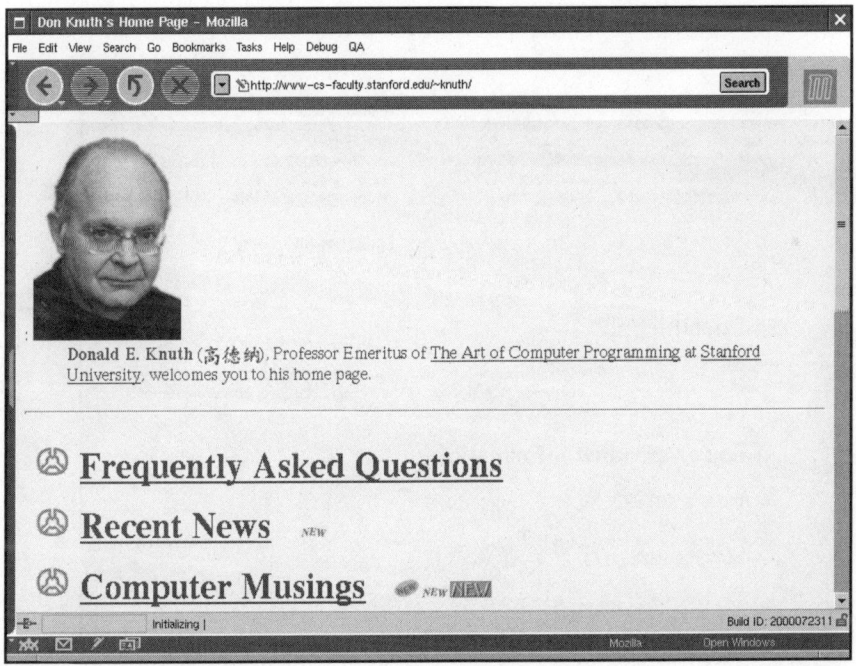

Figure C.14 *Donald Knuth's home page*

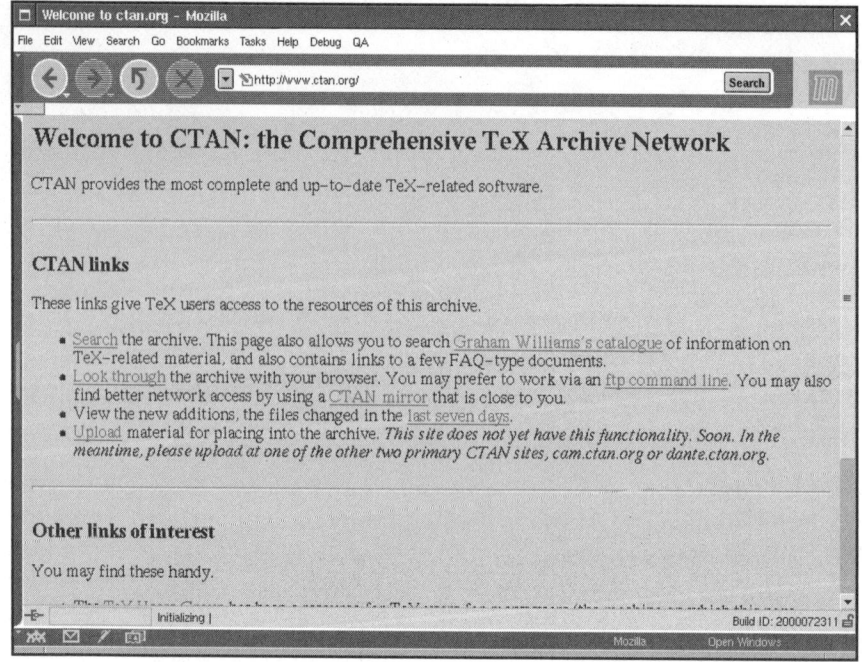

Figure C.15 *The CTAN Web Interface*

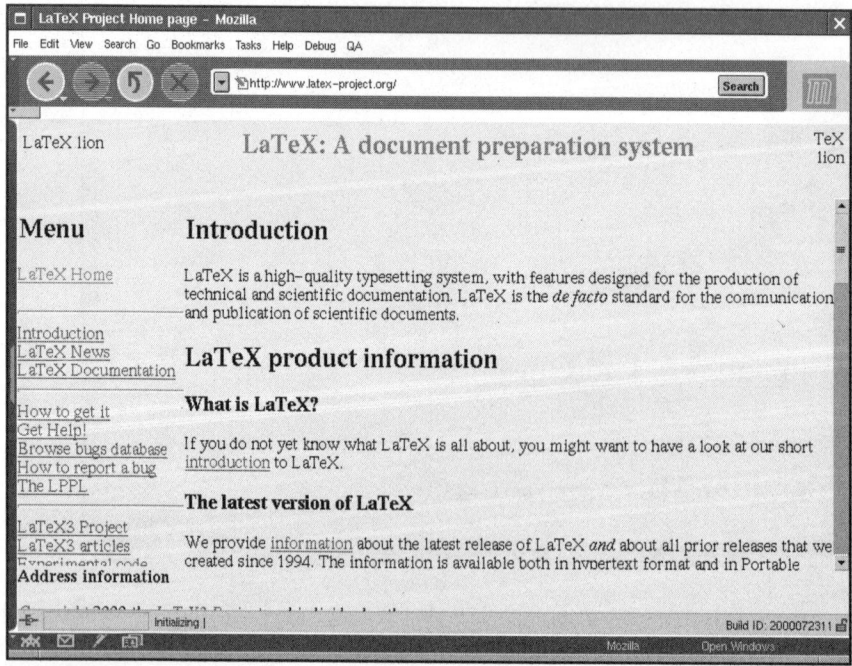

Figure C.16 *The LaTeX Project home page*

Typesetting Programs

The two Open Source programs for typesetting that I would recommend taking a look at are ImPress and LyX. ImPress is an Illustrator-like program for Linux that produces output in PostScript. LyX is a semi-WYSIWYG program that produces LaTeX output, from a friendly front end.

ImPress is a vector-based program written in Tcl/Tk and licensed under the GPL. It is in a late beta stage but seems usable and stable to me. I haven't used ImPress for serious production, but when testing it, I didn't have any crashes or issues. ImPress could be used to produce typeset documents or to produce PostScript figures for inclusion with DocBook documents. It should run on any system that has a Tcl/Tk interpreter. You can find ImPress at **http://www.ntlug.org/~ccox/impress/** (see Figure C.17).

LyX is a program that tries to simplify the interface between the user and LaTeX. It is a decent program that can be used to produce LaTeX output for publishing or just to create LaTeX figures for use with DocBook documents. There are versions of LyX for Linux and UNIX variants, Windows, and OS/2. For a good look at LyX, visit the LyX home page at **http://www.lyx.org/** (see Figure C.18).

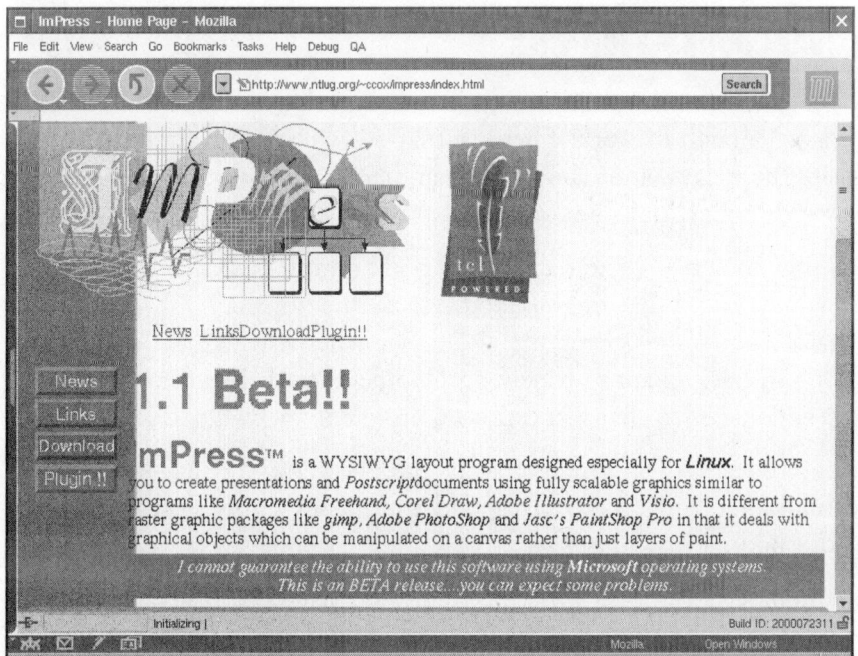

Figure C.17 *The ImPress typesetting program*

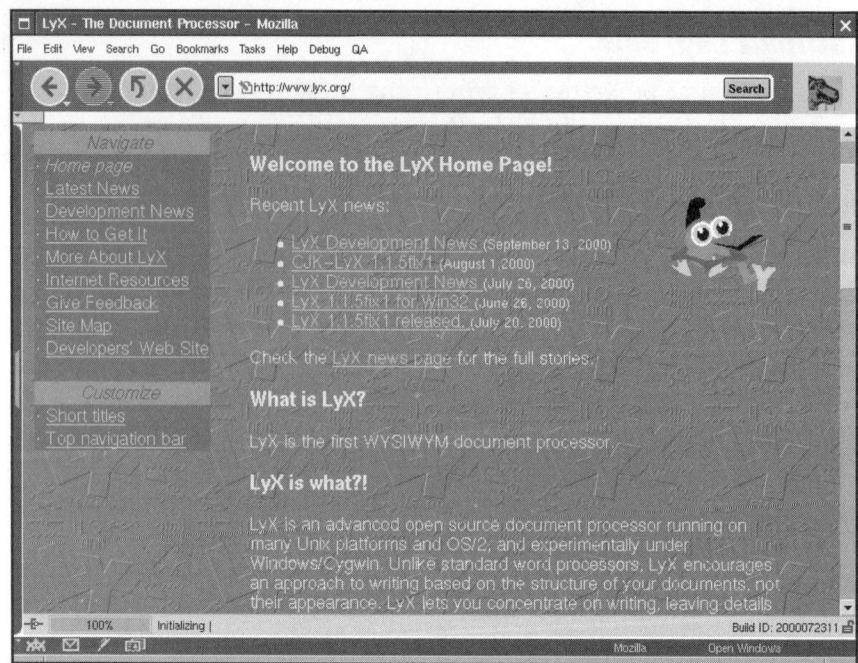

Figure C.18 *The LyX home page*

The ZonkerBooks Web Site

Oddly enough, I do this writing thing for a living. Yes, it's crazy, but I'm hoping it's crazy enough to work! They say that every commercial venture needs a Web site these days, and who am I to argue? You can find my Web site at **http://www.ZonkerBooks.net/**.

You can find an entire section about this book on my Web site, including an errata page for errors that might creep into the text of the book. I hope that this doesn't happen, but check the site to see whether there are any corrections. I'll also post updates on new developments with DocBook and other related technologies so that you can keep up to date with DocBook easily.

If you have questions or corrections for me, please send them to Zonker@ ZonkerBooks.net, and I'll try to respond and fix any errors for the next edition of this book.

There's also a section for my other book, also published by Prima Publishing, *Install, Configure, and Customize Slackware Linux*. If you're new to the whole Linux thing, it is well worth picking up.

License Agreement/Notice of Limited Warranty